Longitudinal Studies of Adult Psychological Development

Adult Development and Aging
K. Warner Schaie, Editor

Longitudinal Studies of Adult Psychological Development

Edited by
K. WARNER SCHAIE
The Pennsylvania State University

THE GUILFORD PRESS
New York   London

© 1983 The Guilford Press
A Division of Guilford Publications, Inc.
200 Park Avenue South, New York, N.Y. 10003

Printed in the United States of America

LIBRARY OF CONGRESS CATALOGING IN PUBLICATION DATA

Main entry under title:
Longitudinal studies of adult psychological development.

  (Adult development and aging)
  Includes indexes.
    1. Adulthood—Longitudinal studies—Addresses, essays,
lectures.   I. Schaie, K. Warner (Klaus Warner), 1928-
II. Series. [DNLM. 1. Adult—Psychology.   2. Human
development—In adulthood.   3. Longitudinal studies.
BF 724.5 L855]
BF724.5.L66 1983   155.6   82-18368
ISBN 0-89862-131-3

Contributors

David Arenberg, PhD
Section on Learning and Problem Solving, Laboratory of Behavioral Sciences, Gerontology Research Center, National Institute on Aging, National Institutes of Health, Baltimore, Maryland

Lew Bank, PhD
Brentwood Veterans Administration Medical Center and Department of Psychology, University of California at Los Angeles, Los Angeles, California

Douglas W. Bray, PhD
American Telephone and Telegraph Company, Basking Ridge, New Jersey

Paul T. Costa, Jr., PhD
Section on Stress and Coping, Laboratory of Behavioral Sciences, Gerontology Research Center, National Institute on Aging, National Institutes of Health, Baltimore, Maryland

Walter R. Cunningham, PhD
Department of Psychology and the Center for Gerontological Studies, University of Florida, Gainesville, Florida

Ann Howard, PhD
American Telephone and Telegraph Company, Basking Ridge, New Jersey

Lissy F. Jarvik, MD, PhD
Brentwood Veterans Administration Medical Center and Department of Psychiatry and Biobehavioral Sciences, University of California at Los Angeles, Los Angeles, California

Robert R. McCrae, PhD
Section on Stress and Coping, Laboratory of Behavioral Sciences, Gerontology Research Center, National Institute on Aging, National Institutes of Health, Baltimore, Maryland

William A. Owens, Jr., PhD
Department of Psychology, University of Georgia, Athens, Georgia

K. Warner Schaie, PhD
Department of Individual and Family Studies and Department of Psychology, The Pennsylvania State University, University Park, Pennsylvania

Reinhard Schmitz-Scherzer, Prof. Dr.
Department of Social Work, Gesamthochschule und Universität Kassel, Kassel, Federal Republic of Germany

Ilene C. Siegler, PhD
Department of Psychiatry and Center for the Study of Aging and Human Development, Duke University Medical Center, Durham, North Carolina

Hans Thomae, Prof. Dr.
Department of Psychology, Universität Bonn, Bonn, Federal Republic of Germany

Preface

The literature on adult development and aging is filled with information on age differences based on the comparison of young and old persons observed at the same specific time. None of this material can tell us whether the old have changed from the time they were young. We therefore hear the repeated and urgent call for longitudinal studies that follow the same persons as they age. Such studies are expensive and consequently few in number. Most of the better known longitudinal studies (e.g., the Berkeley Growth and Guidance Studies or the Terman Study of Genius) were originally designed as studies of children and their families. Only as both investigators and study participants aged were these studies extended into adulthood. Longitudinal studies, however, are necessarily limited by design decisions made at a study's origin. Studies originating in childhood are therefore most valuable in exploring the effect of early influences and behaviors on adult functioning; they are less useful for the analysis of behavioral change from early to late adulthood.

Longitudinal data that are most likely to shed light on the complex issues of adult development therefore will come from studies of psychological phenomena judged to be important in adulthood, using measurement instruments explicitly constructed for or validated on adult populations. This volume is the first collection of integrative reports of psychological change in adulthood from such studies. The seven studies described here were specifically designed to investigate problems of adulthood; none were afterthought follow-ups of children. Included are investigations of intelligence, personality, and motivation, as well as of aging in twins and in managers. The American studies are supplemented by a comprehensive report from the major German longitudinal study of adult psychological development.

Each of the studies has had a major impact upon our knowledge of adult development and has generated voluminous contributions to the journal literature. Although the integrative reports written for this volume can and do stand by themselves as major contributions, it was my thought that much could be learned by juxtaposing these studies. I consequently decided to add an introductory chapter, which serves two functions. First, it provides a discussion of the advantages and problems of the longitudinal method in order to alert the reader to the questions that can be answered by the studies reported here. Second, I preview the substantive chapters in order to provide the reader with a time frame, which may help in reconciling otherwise inconsistent findings, and, once again, to alert the reader to what seem to me to be the outstanding features of each of these comprehensive reports.

Edited volumes often seem to lack focus in terms of their intended audiences. This is not the case here. The studies reported in this volume are among those most frequently cited in the literature on adult psychological development, even though the source literature is scattered across many different journals. The volume therefore provides an attractive supplement for courses in adult development and aging. It provides an authoritative account of most of the major longitudinal studies of adult psychological aging and includes descriptions of the historical development of each study. The latter feature also provides an important resource for researchers planning longitudinal inquiries. Extensive bibliographies, moreover, make the book a useful reference source for researchers interested in psychological and social aging, adult education, the older worker, and other aspects of gerontology.

I would like to acknowledge the patient secretarial assistance of Pat Hollender and the love and support of my wife, Sherry Willis, in completing this project. Because I am fully committed to the need to emphasize the longitudinal approach to the study of adult development, conceptualizing and completing this book has indeed been a labor of love. I hope our readers will learn as much from it as I have during the lengthy editorial process.

K. Warner Schaie
University Park, Pennsylvania

Contents

Longitudinal Studies of Adult Psychological Development

1   What Can We Learn from the Longitudinal Study of Adult Psychological Development?

K. WARNER SCHAIE

Introduction

Developmental psychologists have long felt that the understanding of lawful relationships pertaining to the developmental processes must sooner or later require that the same organisms be observed over that period of time during which the developmental phenomena of interest are thought to occur. But since developmental phenomena in humans occur relatively slowly, except during some critical periods in early infancy and shortly before death, it has often been found impractical to follow the same subjects over the entire developmental period. In fact, some researchers who simply cannot see the enormous investment of time and effort required for longitudinal studies have been willing to make strong assumptions to support arguments that developmental phenomena can be adequately modeled by cross-sectional designs.

Good longitudinal studies develop because they occur in a collaborative network that develops its own social system. And often a major study may have been instrumental in providing the training for young scientists, who will then carry on the study and in turn use it as a training vehicle for a further generation. Indeed, the existence of this volume is testimony to the possibility of carrying on longitudinal studies across long periods of time and to the fact that much can be learned from these studies. Nevertheless, it seems appropriate to orient the reader by specifying as succinctly as possible those aspects of developmental research that can only be gleaned from longitudinal inquiry. It seems appropriate also to alert the reader to some of the methodological pitfalls in the data from the older

K. WARNER SCHAIE. Department of Individual and Family Studies and Department of Psychology, The Pennsylvania State University, University Park, Pennsylvania.

studies. This is not done to criticize these endeavors; all of the studies in the volume represent the best of the state of the art available at their inception. But the reader should know the limitations of the data bases, which are summarized in this chapter. These issues have recently appeared elsewhere; the reader is referred to Nesselroade and Baltes (1979) and Schaie and Hertzog (1982) for greater technical detail. In addition, the purposes of this introductory chapter are to attempt to chart, at least briefly, the manner in which the various studies reported here reach common ground or diverge from one another; to provide a chronology that may be useful for relating them to one another; and to indicate those themes and findings that to the editor seem to weave a common thread.

Advantages of Longitudinal Studies

The principal advantage of the longitudinal approach to the study of human development is, of course, the possibility of gaining information about intraindividual change (IAC). By contrast, cross-sectional studies can provide data and make inferences only about interindividual variability (IEV). Even in the case where successive independent samples are longitudinally drawn from the same cohort, the emphasis is on change within the population examined rather than on the typical cross-sectional comparison of samples possibly coming from different populations. In spite of this emphasis on IAC, most longitudinal studies do, of course, also permit analyses of IEV.

It is possible to identify five distinct rationales for the longitudinal study of behavioral development. Three of these involve developmental descriptions, while the remaining two are explanatory in nature (cf. Baltes & Nesselroade, 1979).

Direct Identification of Intraindividual Change

Intraindividual change can be quantitative and continuous, or it can involve qualitative change, such as the transformation of one behavior into another. Alternatively, changes may occur in the pattern of observed variables as they relate to or assess theoretical constructs. For a determination of any of these changes, observations based on a single occasion are simply inappropriate. To be even more explicit, if cross-sectional data were to be used to estimate IAC, the necessary assumptions to be met would include that (1) different-aged subjects come from the same parent population at birth, (2) subjects be matched across age levels, and (3) different-aged subjects have experienced identical life histories. It is clear that such assumptions cannot be met in human studies.

Identification of Interindividual Variability in Intraindividual Change

Longitudinal studies permit assessment of the degree of variability displayed by different individuals in their behavioral course over time. Determination of typologies of growth curves requires the examination of similarities and differences in developmental patterns, data that require the availability of measures of longitudinal change within *individuals*. Barring such data, it would not be possible to answer the question whether or not group parameters are descriptive of the development of any particular individual. In addition, the valuable hypothesis-generating source of single-subject research must depend on longitudinal analyses (cf. Shontz, 1976).

Interrelationships among Intraindividual Changes

Modern developmental psychology has recognized that it must operate within a multivariate domain of variables. When individual behaviors are followed over time, it is then possible to discover constancies and change for the entire organism, especially when the theoretical model followed is of a holistic or structural persuasion (e.g., Riegel & Rosenwald, 1975). Longitudinal studies alone, by virtue of multiple observations over time, permit the discovery of structural relationships among behavior changes. The multivariate longitudinal approach is essential for the identification of progressive differentiation processes and for any type of systems analysis (cf. Lund, 1978; Urban, 1978).

Analysis of Determinants of Intraindividual Change

In the inferential realm, longitudinal studies are required to permit the identification of time-ordered antecedents and consequents as necessary, albeit not sufficient, conditions for causal interpretations. Specifically, it is the longitudinal approach alone that can provide requisite data to show that a causal process involves discontinuities, such as the so-called sleeper effects, or where causal chains are multidirectional or contain multivariate patterns of influence (see also Baltes, Reese, & Nesselroade, 1977; Heise, 1975).

Analysis of Interindividual Variability in the Determinants of Intraindividual Change

Finally, longitudinal data permit inferences concerned with the fact that many individuals can show similar patterns in IAC that may be determined by different change processes. Such individual differences are found for persons at different levels in the range of talent or other behavioral attributes. Alternatively, interindividual differences in patterns of change may be attributable to the operation of alternative combinations of causal sequences.

Longitudinal Studies as Quasi-Experiments

Although the longitudinal approach has many advantages over studies based on one-time observations, it is also beset with many methodological problems, some of which have led to a variety of design refinements which may be noted as the reader follows the accounts in this volume from the earlier to the later studies. In this section, I attempt to alert the reader to some of these issues by discussing internal and external validity, the traditional single-cohort design, sequential strategies in general, and the longitudinal sequence in particular; finally, I suggest some possible solutions to the remaining difficulties, which were applied to one or another of these studies.

Internal and External Validity

Longitudinal studies do not conform to the rules for true experiments since age is a subject attribute that cannot be experimentally assigned. Consequently, they are subject to all the problems inherent in what Campbell and Stanley (1967) term "quasi-experiments." These problems may be threats to the internal validity of a study; that is, factors analyzed in a given design that are thought to be measures of the hypothesized construct may be confounded by other factors not explicitly included in the design. Alternatively, the problems are threats to the external validity of a study, which limits the extent to which valid generalizations from the sample can be applied to other populations (see also Cook & Campbell, 1975).

Internal Validity

Eight different threats to the internal validity of quasi-experiments such as longitudinal studies have been enumerated (Campbell & Stanley, 1967): maturation, effects of history, testing, instrumentation, statistical regression, mortality, selection, and the selection–maturation interaction. The first two of these, history and maturation, have, for the developmental psychologist, special meaning beyond their threat to the internal validity of any pretest–posttest design. *Maturation*, quite obviously, is not a threat to the validity of developmental studies, but rather is the specific effect of interest to the investigator. Nevertheless, its measurement is not always unambiguous, since, given a specific developmental model, it may be necessary to go beyond a test of the null hypothesis negating maturational effects in order to test instead some explicit alternative hypothesis that specifies direction and magnitude of the expected maturational effect.

On the other hand, *historical effects* are the primary concern regarding internal validity problems for the developmental scientist. History is directly involved in both cohort and time-of-measurement (period) effects. "Cohort" is here defined as a group of individuals born in the same historical period, who consequently share similar environmental circumstances at equivalent points in their maturational sequence. "Time-of-measurement effects," by contrast, represent those events that affect all members of a population, regardless of cohort membership, living through a given period of history. The specific threat to longitudinal studies is that historical effect may threaten the internal validity of designs attempting to measure the effects of maturation.

The traditional longitudinal design is a special case of the pretest–posttest design in that it repeatedly measures the same individuals over time; as a result it is affected also by the other six threats to internal validity proposed by Campbell and Stanley. There are actually two different effects of *testing*: practice and reactivity. Reactivity involves the possible effect upon subsequent behavior of being exposed to a certain procedure. Longitudinal study subjects might respond to a second test in a very different manner than if they had not been previously tested, a behavior change that could be confused with the effects of maturation. Practice effects, on the other hand, may simply mean that, upon subsequent tests, subjects have to spend less time in figuring out items previously solved and thus can improve their overall performance.

The internal validity threat of *instrumentation* refers to differences in measurement techniques that covary with measurement occasions. In long-term longitudinal studies, such differences may occur when study personnel changes, or when records regarding study protocol on previous occasions are lost, and slight variations are introduced inadvertently. Again, such changes may lead to the wrong inference of having found maturational trends or may tend to obscure reliable, but small, developmental changes actually occurring.

Statistical regression involves the tendency of variables containing measurement error to regress toward their mean from one occasion to the next. This problem is of particular importance in two-occasion longitudinal studies. As has recently been shown, regression effects do not necessarily cumulate over extended series (Nesselroade, Stigler, & Baltes, 1980).

Since human panels cannot be forced to continue participation in long-term studies, another serious threat is that of *experimental mortality*. This term describes the attrition of subjects from a sample between measurement occasions, whether such attrition be due to biological mortality, morbidity, other psychological and sociocultural factors, or sheer experimenter ineptness. Most empirical studies of experimental mortality suggest that attrition is nonrandom at least between the first and second measurement occasion (cf. Gribbin & Schaie, 1979; Schaie, Labouvie, & Barrett, 1973).

Selection refers to the process of obtaining a sample from the population such that the effect obtained is a function of the sample characteristics rather than of the maturational effect to be estimated. The *selection-maturation interaction*, of course, refers to the case where maturational effects may be found in some samples but not in others.

External Validity

As quasi-experiments, longitudinal studies also share certain limitations with respect to the generalizability of their findings. Four major issues can be identified here. The first concerns *experimental units*, that is, the extent to which longitudinal data collected on one sample can permit inference to other populations. The second involves *experimental settings*, or the extent to which findings have cross-situational validity (cf. Scheidt & Schaie, 1978). The third is concerned with *treatment variables*, that is, the limitations imposed by specific settings or measurement-implicit reinforcement schedules (cf. Birkhill & Schaie, 1975; Schaie & Goulet, 1977). Finally, external validity may be threatened by certain aspects of the *measurement variables*, with regard to the extent to which task characteristics remain appropriate at different developmental stages as a longitudinal study progresses (cf. Schaie, 1977/1978; Sinnott, 1975).

Traditional Single-Cohort Designs

The purpose of the classical longitudinal design is to estimate development of IAC within the same individuals. As such, the design explicitly represents a time series, with an initial pretest, a subsequent intervention (the maturational events occurring over time), and a posttest, all on the same individual organisms. If there is more than one time interval, then there is a succession of alternating treatments (further maturational events) and posttests. Traditionally, the longitudinal design was applied to only one group of individuals of relatively homogeneous chronological age at first testing and thus to a single birth cohort. In principle, the first two studies reported in this volume are of this kind; two of the latter also began in this manner.

In reviewing the single-cohort studies, the reader needs to keep in mind that several of the threats to internal validity just enumerated may be plausible alternative explanations for the observed behavioral change (or lack thereof) reported as a function of age for these studies. To be explicit, in a single-cohort longitudinal study, time-of-measurement (period) and aging effects must be confounded, and the presence of period effects related to the dependent variable of interest will render estimates of age effects internally invalid. These period effects may either mimic or suppress maturational changes occurring over a particular age span, depending on whether age and time-of-measurement effects covary positively or negatively.

It must also be noted that the single-cohort longitudinal design does not directly control for the other internal validity threats. The reader should be alert to the fact that some of the latter threats can be and have been controlled by careful researchers such as those represented in this volume. That is, great pains were generally taken to eliminate the confound of instrumentation by taking steps to ensure that the measurement procedures remained as consistent as possible throughout the course of the studies. Statistical regression effects were minimized in all these studies by including at least two, and often more, retest occasions. But clearly, except in those cases where collateral control samples were studied for this very purpose, there is no way for single-cohort longitudinal studies to circumvent the confounds of testing and experimental mortality.

Although I have generally argued that it would be unwise to start new single-cohort longitudinal studies (e.g., Schaie, 1972), I do believe that such studies were necessary and appropriate in the early stages of the developmental sciences. Moreover, there continue to be instances when a single-cohort longitudinal design may be the best approach to providing preliminary evidence for developmental functions, which can later be replicated for additional cohort and measurement occasions. Single-cohort studies may also prove useful in particular applications such as defining typologies of developmental patterns in a specifically targeted single-cohort population.

The reader will see in this volume that early longitudinal studies served the preceding purposes well, but also that those investigations started more recently were soon found to require buttressing by conversion to a multiple-cohort approach (e.g., the Baltimore, Bonn, Duke, and Seattle longitudinal studies).

Sequential Strategies

To reduce the limitations inherent in the single-cohort longitudinal design, several alternative sequential strategies have been suggested (Baltes, 1968; Schaie, 1965, 1973, 1977). The term "sequential" merely implies that the required sampling frame involves a sequence of samples taken across several measurement occasions. Sequential strategies can best be understood by first differentiating between sampling design and analysis design (Schaie & Baltes, 1975), although both are closely interrelated. Sampling design refers to the particular cells of a cohort-by-age (time) matrix that are sampled in a developmental study. Analysis design refers to the manner in which the cells that have been sampled may be organized in order to analyze for the effects of age (A), cohort (C), and time of measurement. (T). Figure 1.1 gives a typical cohort-by-age matrix showing sequential designs. This figure also illustrates the confounding of the three parameters of interest. A and C appear as the rows and columns of the matrix, while T is the parameter contained within the matrix cells. The reader interested in the debate on whether and how these effects should be unconfounded is referred to papers by Adam (1978); Horn and McArdle (1980); Mason, Mason, Winsborough, and Poole (1973); and Schaie and Hertzog (1982). The issues involved are quite complex, highly technical, and beyond the scope of this introductory chapter.

Sampling Designs

Two types of sequential sampling designs may be distinguished: those using the same panel of individuals repeatedly to fill the cells of the

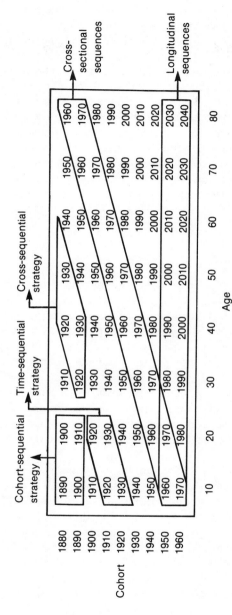

FIGURE 1.1. Schematic showing cross-sectional and longitudinal sequences and the modes of analysis deduced from the general developmental model. Table entries represent times of measurement (period).

matrix, and those using independent samples of individuals (each observed only once) from the same cohorts to do so. The matrix shown in Figure 1.1 could have been produced by either approach. In this volume, the Bonn study uses the former approach, and the Baltimore, Duke, and Seattle studies employ both. Using Baltes's (1968) terminology, we can call the two designs longitudinal and cross-sectional sequences, respectively. Typically, a cross-sectional sequence involves the replication of a cross-sectional study such that the same age range of interest is assessed at least for two different time periods, obtaining the estimate for each age level across multiple cohorts, where each sample is measured only once. By contrast, the longitudinal sequence represents the measurement of at least two cohorts over the same age range. Again, estimates from each cohort are obtained at two or more points in time. The critical difference, however, is that the longitudinal sequence provides data that permit the evaluation of IAC and of IEV in IAC (see preceding discussion in this chapter).

Analysis Designs

Matrices like Figure 1.1 contain data permitting a variety of alternate strategies of analysis (Schaie, 1965, 1977). To be specific, each row of this matrix can be treated as a single-cohort longitudinal study, each diagonal as a cross-sectional study, and each column as a time-lag study (comparison of behavior at a specific age across successive cohorts). Sequential sampling designs do not permit complete disentanglement of all components of the $B = f(A, C, T)$ function because of the obvious linear dependence of the three factors. Nevertheless, I have suggested that, given this model, there exist three distinct analysis designs, which are created by considering the separate effect of two of the components while assuming the constancy or irrelevance of the third on theoretical or empirical grounds.

As exemplified by the minimum designs shown in Figure 1.1, I have suggested that the *cohort-sequential* strategy will permit separation of age changes (IAC) from cohort differences (IEV), under the assumption of trivial time-of-measurement effects. Further, the *time-sequential* strategy will permit the separation of age differences from period differences (both IEV), assuming only trivial cohort effects. And finally, the *cross-sequential* strategy will permit separation of cohort differences (IEV) from period differences (IAC). The time-sequential strategy, of course, is not a truly longitudinal approach (i.e., the same individual cannot be the same age at two different points in time), but it does have merit for the estimation of age differences for social policy purposes, for those dependent variables for which cohort effects are likely to be minimal. It is also an appropriate strategy to use in estimating time-of-measurement (period) effects for studies including a wide range of age/cohort levels.

Longitudinal Sequences

When data are collected in the form of longitudinal sequences in order to examine IAC, it is possible to apply both the cohort-sequential and cross-sequential strategies for data analysis. Developmental psychologists find the cohort-sequential design of greatest interest because it explicitly differentiates IAC within cohorts from IEV between cohorts (cf. Baltes & Nesselroade, 1979; Schaie & Baltes, 1975). This design, in addition, permits a check of the consistency of age functions over successive cohorts, thereby offering greater external validity than would be provided by a single-cohort longitudinal design.

As was noted earlier, a critical assumption of the cohort-sequential design is that there are no time-of-measurement effects contained in the data. Although this assumption may be parsimonious for many psychological variables, others may still be affected by "true" period effects or because of the confounds presented by occasion-specific internal validity threats such as differences in instrumentation or experimenter behavior across test occasions. The question arises, then, how violations of the assumptions of no time-of-measurement (T) effects would be reflected in the cohort-sequential analysis. Logical analysis suggests that all estimated effect will be perturbed, albeit the most direct evidence would be shown by a significant C (cohort)-by-A (age) interaction (cf. Schaie, 1973). However, absence of such an interaction does not guarantee the absence of T effects; such effects might localize in a small subset of occasions in extensive studies, in which case all our effect estimates would be biased.

It is well recognized by now that the essential consequence of the interpretational determinancy in sequential analysis is that, if the assumptions that justify the specific design are violated, then all effect estimates will be inaccurate to some degree. The interpretational problem may be reduced, however, to estimating the relative likelihood of confounded T effects, given a strong theory about the nature and direction of estimated and confounded effects. Indeed, a practical application of strong theory to sequential designs involves specification of confounds in an invalid design in order to obtain estimates of the confounded effects.

An important example of planned violation of assumptions is the use of the cross-sequential design under the assumption of no A effects, an assumption most developmental psychologists might find quite unreasonable. Such a design may be useful when longitudinal data are available for only a limited number of measurement occasions but for a wide range of cohort groups. The cross-sequential design can be implemented after only two measurement occasions, whereas a cohort-sequential design requires at least three. Moreover, the number of measurement occasions required to estimate cohort-sequential designs that span a wide age and/or cohort range would be prohibitive if we insist that no data analyses be performed until the cohort-sequential design appropriate for the research question had been accomplished. Given a strong developmental theory about the nature of the confounded A effects, a misspecified cross-sequential design can provide useful information about the significance of the A effects represented in both the T and the C-by-T design. My early work on the sequential analysis of intelligence began with such misspecification in cross-sequential design in order to permit drawing preliminary inferences concerning the relative importance of C and A effects prior to the availability of data that could have permitted direct simultaneous assessment of these effects (cf. Schaie, Labouvie, & Buech, 1973; Schaie & Strother, 1968).

Although it is always preferable to estimate the "true" parameter effects from the appropriate design—one that makes the correct limiting assumptions—the developmental psychologist must often settle for something less than the optimal design, whether this be a temporary expedient or dictated by the nature of the phenomenon being studied. The studies represented in this volume individually and collectively provide good illustrations of the evolution of a field that has seen much methodological turmoil and change, the end of which is not yet in sight.

Empirical Studies of Adult Psychological Development

This volume consists of fairly detailed descriptions of the design, methodology, and results of seven longitudinal studies, which probably represent the bulk of work on what is securely known about age changes in psychological variables from young adulthood into old age. The first two of these studies represent single-cohort designs, but their interpretability was enhanced by later collateral work with other comparison groups.[1]

---

[1]There are several other important longitudinal studies that could have been included but were not, because of either space limitations or study personnel changes, which made it difficult to commission adequate reviews for this volume. The most noteworthy omissions are probably the Berkeley Growth and Guidance Studies (Eichorn, Clausen, Haan, Honzik, & Mussen, 1981), the Terman Study of Genius (Sears, 1977; Terman & Oden, 1959), and the Boston Normative Aging Study (Bell, Rose, & Damon, 1972).

The remaining five studies either were conceptualized as multicohort studies or were designed in such a way that conversion to a multicohort format was possible, once the desirability of more extended data collections became obvious.

In this section, I will introduce the substantive accounts by calling attention to some of the highlights and reflect briefly on some unique aspects of each study.

Chronology of the Studies

Table 1.1 summarizes the basic chronology of the studies reported here. With the exception of the American Telephone and Telegraph (AT&T) study, the oldest cohort includes persons born before or around the turn of the century. And with the exception of the Iowa State Study, data collections began after World War II. Although the Iowa State Study has precedence in order of first data collection, it did not really begin as a longitudinal study; its first longitudinal data point occurred in 1953.

The Aging Twins Study began in the mid-1940s as a special population study. All of the remaining studies began in the decade from the mid-1950s to the mid-1960s. Time frames covered a range from 20 to over 40 years, and age ranges investigated are from the early 20s to over 100 years. Except for the AT&T study, whose oldest subjects were born in the 1930s, studies examine wide cohort ranges: members of the oldest cohort were born in the last quarter of the 19th century, and those of the youngest cohort during the 1950s.

Specific Study Characteristics

The Iowa State Study

This was the first carefully reported, long-term longitudinal follow-up of a group of people whose intellectual functioning had been studied first in young adulthood. It is a good model for illustrating how a sound longitudinal study can develop from an existing data base collected long ago, provided that subject identifications are carefully maintained and prospective subjects belong to a population whose whereabouts will likely be followed for other reasons (in this case, as university alumni). Indeed, although it is important for ethical reasons to protect the confidentiality of subjects' records, it is scientifically unsound to destroy subject name rosters. Without such records, the important data yielded by the Iowa study would not have been obtained. Substantively, the initial reports from the Iowa study (Owens, 1953) were important in stimulating

TABLE 1.1. Chronology and Age Ranges of Studies

Name of study	Year study began	Reported data collections	Last reported data point	Age range covered	Birth year of oldest cohort
1. Iowa State Study	1919	3	1961	19–61	1900
2. Aging Twins Study	1946	5	1973	60–87	1886
3. Seattle Longitudinal Study	1956	4	1977	25–88	1889
4. Duke Longitudinal Studies					
I	1955	11	1976	59–102	1874
II	1968	4	1976	46–77	1899
5. Bonn Longitudinal Study on Aging	1965	7	1976/1977	60–86	1890
6. Baltimore Longitudinal Study of Aging	1958	3	1978	17–97	1881
7. AT&T Longitudinal Studies of Managers	1956	3	1977	25–45	1931

a critical reexamination of the inevitability of intellectual decline in adulthood. But other methodological advances introduced by Cunningham (see Chapter 2) are also of interest. The reader will find a good example of how a retrospective study can be strengthened by collecting a variety of additional data in matched samples, which permit more fine-grained exploration of possibly inconsistent findings. Substantively, Cunningham concludes that the Iowa data argue for peaks in performance in intellectual ability (at least in college men) to occur during the 40s and 50s, with decline thereafter not reaching practical significance until the 60s.

The Aging Twins Study

In 1946 Franz Kallmann and Gerhard Sander became interested in the study of the hereditary aspects of aging and longevity. Both monozygotic and dizygotic twin pairs who had reached age 60 were included in this study, survivors of which were last examined in 1973. This study is of particular interest because it permitted at least limited assessment of the interaction between genetic and environmental factors. Although heavily emphasizing biochemical data, the study also included carefully collected psychometric data, which are featured here.

In the highly selected sample of survivors, cognitive functioning was maintained, at least on a nonspeeded test, until age 75. Psychological test scores and survival were positively associated, and women outscored men on most tests. Of particular interest are findings suggesting that hereditary factors are important in some of the Wechsler Adult Intelligence Scale (WAIS) tests and intriguingly, that, in women, chromosome loss in old age appears to be related to poorer psychological test performance.

The Seattle Longitudinal Study

This study, begun in 1956, with the latest data collected in 1977, was limited primarily to tracking five of Thurstone's Primary Mental Abilities (PMAs) as well as some personality characteristics across the adult life span. It was during the course of this study that some of the formal relations between cross-sectional and longitudinal data became clear and were formalized in what has come to be known as "sequential methodology" (cf. Schaie, 1965, 1977). The study includes four cross-sectional waves and several longitudinal studies extending from 7 to 21 years.

Substantively, it was found that several of the abilities increase into midlife; show statistically reliable, but small-magnitude, age changes in the late 50s; and increasingly decline once the 60s are reached, although the decline does not reach substantial magnitude until the late 70s and early 80s. Patterns of substantial decrement differ across the abilities, with so-called fluid abilities beginning to decline earlier, but crystallized abilities declining more precipitously in advanced old age. Intriguing relationships are also reported among health, life-style, and personality factors in midlife, predicting maintenance or decline of intellectual ability in advanced age.

The Duke Longitudinal Studies

Two broadly multidisciplinary studies of normal aging were begun in 1955 and 1968, respectively, and were continued until 1976. Many aspects of the Duke studies have been reported elsewhere (e.g., Palmore, 1970, 1974). The chapter in this volume focuses on the psychological aspects. In the first study, these included measures of intelligence, memory, reaction time (RT), and sensory functioning; in the second study, measures of psychological well-being and complex psychomotor tasks were added. Of particular interest is that, at least in the first study, there were as many as 11 data collections, and consequently much was learned about interindividual patterns of change. Because of the multidisciplinary nature of the study, attention could also be focused upon the relationship between psychological variables and health factors. As in the Seattle Longitudinal Study, the findings suggest a complex pattern of interaction between cardiovascular disease (CVD) and the maintenance of intellectual competence.

As compared with other findings reported in this volume, substantive findings from the Duke study indicate somewhat later encounter with substantial intellectual decrement. In healthy individuals, performance-scale decrements do not occur until the 70s, and for the verbal scales not until the late 70s. Remarkable stability of personality patterns was seen, and the conclusion was reached that, for many psychological variables, sex is a much more important individual difference than is age.

The Bonn Longitudinal Study on Aging

In contrast to most American studies, the Bonn study, conducted from 1965 to 1977, emphasized from the very beginning the phenomenological aspects of aging. That is, it was greatly concerned about chronicling the individual's perception of his or her own aging. Nevertheless, the study also included substantial objective measurements from intelligence and personality tests, as well as a broad sweep of motivational, biological, and biographical indexes. The particular focus of the Bonn study was on defining differential patterns of constancy and change beyond age 60. Some of this material has been previously reported in segmented form (Thomae, 1976). The chapter in this volume provides an integrative overview of the entire study and its implications.

Perhaps the most important contribution of this study is its thorough coverage of topics often conspicuously absent in longitudinal inquiry. Personality data were collected by questionnaire as well as by observational techniques; other topics discussed include social participation, leisure-time activities, perceived life space, perceptions of self, and reactions to life stress, health problems, and family stress. Substantive results are too complex to summarize here. They strongly point, however, to the wide variety of adaptive patterns and to the dangers of premature identification of presumed normative models of aging.

The Baltimore Longitudinal Study of Aging

This study is the longitudinal study on normative aging conducted over the past two decades by the intramural research program associated with the National Institute on Aging. The study originally focused on biological aspects of aging, with a variety of psychological variables successively being added. The chapter in this volume focuses more narrowly on the personality-change data acquired during that study, but seeks to set that material within the context of a broad discussion of the research issues involved in the study of personality change and aging.

The chapter presents an application of both traditional and sequential methodology to personality data. Substantively, persuasive evidence is provided supporting stability of adult personality as expressed by mean levels of dispositions, age-invariant personality structure, and consistency, over time, of individual differences. This evidence is bolstered further by a detailed analysis of the effects of response bias as a possible source of spurious stability across time. In addition, the chapter includes important discussion on the effects of mood states, predicting across periods of the life span, and identifying cause and effect in psychosomatic research.

The AT&T Longitudinal Studies of Managers

The final chapter in this volume has a more applied bent. It is concerned with the longitudinal follow-up of industrial managers who were carefully studied in young adulthood as part of the selection process for entry managerial positions. A 20-year study follows the young managers into midlife and is supplemented by comparisons with the initial assessments of a new cohort of managers recruited 20 years after the initial cohort.

Longitudinal findings are presented on changes in abilities, attitudes, life interests, motivation, and personality as well as the relationships of these variables to career and personal success and happiness.

Of substantive interest in this chapter are the findings suggesting that intial emotional adjustment was an important predictor of career success. Although most members of the study tended to lower their expectations and become less positive about their careers, the emotionally healthy men changed less in that direction, as well as increasing their motivation to lead and direct others. Data on generational differences are also of considerable importance, suggesting much greater heterogeneity in the new generation of managers.

References

Adam, J. Sequential strategies and the separation of age, cohort, and time-of-measurement contributions to developmental data. *Psychological Bulletin*, 1978, *85*, 1309–1316.

Baltes, P. B. Longitudinal and cross-sectional sequences in the study of age and generation effects. *Human Development*, 1968, *11*, 145–171.

Baltes, P. B., & Nesselroade, J. R. History and rationale of longitudinal research. In J. R. Nesselroade & P. B. Baltes (Eds.), *Longitudinal research in the study of behavior and development*. New York: Academic Press, 1979.

Baltes, P. B., Reese, H. W., & Nesselroade, J. R. *Life-span developmental psychology: Introduction to research methods*. Monterey, Calif.: Brooks/Cole, 1977.

Bell, B., Rose, C. L., & Damon, A. The normative aging study: An interdisciplinary and longitudinal study of health and aging. *Aging and Human Development*, 1972, *3*, 5–17.

Birkhill, W. R., & Schaie, K. W. The effect of differential reinforcement of cautiousness in the intellectual performance of the elderly. *Journal of Gerontology*, 1975, *30*, 578–583.

Campbell, D. T., & Stanley, J. C. *Experimental and quasi-experimental designs for research*. Chicago: Rand McNally, 1967.

Cook, T. C., & Campbell, D. T. The design and conduct of quasi-experiments and true experiments in field settings. In M. D. Dunette (Ed.), *Handbook of industrial and organizational research*. Chicago: Rand McNally, 1975.

Eichorn, D. H., Clausen, J. A., Haan, N., Honzik, M. P., & Mussen, P. H. (Eds.). *Present and past in middle life*. New York: Academic Press, 1981.

Gribbin, K., & Schaie, K. W. Selective attrition in longitudinal studies: A cohort-sequential approach. In H. Orino, K. Shimada, M. Iriki, & D. Maeda (Eds.), *Recent advances in gerontology*. Amsterdam: Excerpta Medica, 1979.

Heise, D. R. *Causal analysis*. New York: Wiley, 1975.

Horn, J. L., & McArdle, J. J. Perspectives on mathematical/statistical model building (MASMOB) in research on aging. In L. F. Poon (Ed.), *Aging in the 1980s: Selected contemporary issues in the psychology of aging*. Washington, D.C.: American Psychological Association, 1980.

Lund, R. D. *Development and plasticity of the brain*. New York: Oxford University Press, 1978.

Mason, W. M., Mason, K. O., Winsborough, H. H., & Poole, W. K. Some methodological issues in cohort analysis of archival data. *American Sociological Review*, 1973, *38*, 242–258.

Nesselroade, J. R., & Baltes, P. B. (Eds.). *Longitudinal research in the study of behavior and development*. New York: Academic Press, 1979.

Nesselroade, J. R., Stigler, S. M., & Baltes, P. B. Regression towards the mean and the study of change. *Psychological Bulletin*, 1980, *88*, 622–637.

Owens, W. A., Jr. Age and mental abilities: A longitudinal study. *Genetic Psychology Monographs*, 1953, *48*, 3–54.

Palmore, E. (Ed.). *Normal aging*. Durham, N.C.: Duke University Press, 1970.

Palmore, E. (Ed.). *Normal aging II*. Durham, N.C.: Duke University Press, 1974.

Riegel, K. F., & Rosenwald, G. C. *Structure and functions: Developmental and historical aspects*. New York: Wiley, 1975.

Schaie, K. W. A general model for the study of developmental problems. *Psychological Bulletin*, 1965, *64*, 92–107.

Schaie, K. W. Can the longitudinal method be applied to psychological studies of human development? In F. Z. Moenks, W. W. Hartup, & J. DeWitt (Eds.), *Determinants of human behavior*. New York: Academic Press, 1972.

Schaie, K. W. Methodological problems in descriptive developmental research on adulthood and aging. In J. R. Nesselroade & H. W. Reese (Eds.), *Life-span developmental psychology: Methodological issues*. New York: Academic Press, 1973.

Schaie, K. W. Quasi-experimental research designs in the psychology of aging. In J. E. Birren & K. W. Schaie (Eds.), *Handbook of the psychology of aging*. New York: Van Nostrand Reinhold, 1977.

Schaie, K. W. Toward a stage theory of adult cognitive development. *Journal of Aging and Human Development*, 1977/1978, *8*, 129–138.

Schaie, K. W., & Baltes, P. B. On sequential strategies in developmental research: Description or explanation. *Human Development*, 1975, *18*, 384–390.

Schaie, K. W., & Goulet, L. R. Trait theory and verbal learning processes. In R. B. Cattell & R. M. Dreger (Eds.), *Handbook of modern personality theory*. New York: Hemisphere/Halsted Press, 1977.

Schaie, K. W., & Hertzog, C. Longitudinal methods. In B. B. Wolman (Ed.), *Handbook of developmental psychology*. Englewood Cliffs, N.J.: Prentice-Hall, 1982.

Schaie, K. W., Labouvie, G., & Barrett, T. J. Selective attrition effects in a fourteen-year study of adult intelligence. *Journal of Gerontology*, 1973, *28*, 328–334.

Schaie, K. W., Labouvie, G., & Buech, B. U. Generational and cohort-specific differences in adult cognitive behavior: A fourteen-year study of independent samples. *Developmental Psychology*, 1973, *9*, 151–166.

Schaie, K. W., & Strother, C. R. A cross-sequential study of age changes in cognitive behavior. *Psychological Bulletin*, 1968, *70*, 672–680.

Scheidt, R. J., & Schaie, K. W. A situational taxonomy for the elderly: Generating situational criteria. *Journal of Gerontology*, 1978, *33*, 848–857.

Sears, R. Sources of life satisfactions of the Terman gifted men. *American Psychologist*, 1977, *32*, 119–128.

Shontz, F. C. Single-organism designs. In P. M. Bentler, D. J. Lettieri & G. A. Austin (Eds.), *Data analysis, strategies and designs for substance abuse research*. Washington, D.C.: U.S. Government Printing Office, 1976.

Sinnott, J. D. Everday thinking and Piagetian operativity in adults. *Human Development*, 1975, *28*, 430–443.

Terman, L. M., & Oden, M. H. *Genetic studies of genius, V. The gifted group at mid-life*. Palo Alto, Calif.: Stanford University Press, 1959.

Thomae, H. *Patterns of aging*. Basel, Switzerland: S. Karger, 1976.

Urban, H. B. The concept of development from a systems perspective. In P. B. Baltes (Ed.), *Life-span development and behavior* (Vol. 1). New York: Academic Press, 1978.

2 The Iowa State Study of the Adult Development of Intellectual Abilities

WALTER R. CUNNINGHAM AND
WILLIAM A. OWENS, JR.

Introduction

The Iowa State Study of intellectual development in adulthood has considerable historical significance. It was the first-reported long-term longitudinal follow-up study of intelligence in adulthood. Male college freshmen originally tested with the Army Alpha Test in 1919 were retested in 1950 (Owens, 1953), at about 50 years of age. They were retested again in 1961 (Owens, 1966). A similar follow-up was reported by Cunningham and Birren (1976). Longitudinal differences in factor structure were also reported (McHugh & Owens, 1954) for the first two occasions of measurement. A factor analysis of the data for three occasions of measurement has also been reported recently (Cunningham & Birren, 1980). Many other substantive and methodological papers, directly or indirectly, grew out of this work. Although the study constituted an important substantive contribution, its greatest merit was in terms of its strong heuristic value, in stimulating new thinking and further empirical research, particularly studies of a longitudinal nature.

The publication of the first report of the Iowa State longitudinal follow-up (Owens, 1953) ushered in an era of new ideas in research on adult development and intelligence. It is from this time that the beginning of a much fuller and more complex understanding of intelligence and methods of studying development can be dated. This study began a period of important progress in the understanding of intelligence in adulthood.

WALTER R. CUNNINGHAM. Department of Psychology and the Center for Gerontological Studies, University of Florida, Gainesville, Florida.

WILLIAM A. OWENS, JR. Department of Psychology, University of Georgia, Athens, Georgia.

At the time at which the first follow-up was completed, the substantive view of intellectual development in adulthood was that it involved inevitable declines. The Iowa State Study represented the first major crack in this conceptual iceberg. True, there had previously been murmurs of discontent. Kuhlen (1940) had expressed skepticism regarding the plausibility of the assumptions intrinsic to making ontogenetic interpretations of cross-sectional differences in performance. Also, there had been suggestions that some variables were more sensitive to age than others (Foulds & Raven, 1948; Lorge, 1936). But the overriding impression in the professional psychological community was that peak intellectual performance occurred early (i.e., about age 20) and declines were expected thereafter.

The first report of the Iowa State Study marked the beginning of a new perspective on these issues, a sharpening of ideas as to *how* intelligence should be studied and also how developmental phenomena generally should be considered. This work provided fuel for the fires of skepticism regarding the validity of cross-sectional comparisons, because at a very concrete, factual level, it was clear that the individual intellectual performances of this group of subjects were not undergoing universal declines in middle adulthood. The discrepancies between these longitudinal findings and unusually well replicated previous results were striking.

Various explanations were advanced to explain these discordant outcomes. It was noted that the sample consisted of men who were college students in 1919. They were in many ways an elite group. Some critics suggested that perhaps the gains or stability observed were atypical of more heterogeneous, representative populations. Along these lines, there was substantial attrition from the first occasion of measurement to the second. Perhaps these gains and stability were not even representative of the original parent population of college students.

Another issue was college experience in a narrow sense. Perhaps because of their college training, their peak performance was not apparent as college freshmen. This was a plausible argument, and academics generally were not reluctant to consider the possibility that advanced education might have a favorable impact on intellectual performance. In this regard, it was observed that two occasions of observation were not fully adequate to reliably extrapolate age functions, even mathematically simple ones (see Figures 2.1 and 2.2). Could the results be an artifact of a failure to make observations at intermediate points, particularly at the end of the period of college training?

Another alternative explanation concerned repeated measures. Could the results be biased to some extent by the fact that the participants took the test a second time? Were there effects over this long a time period? And, if so, of what magnitude were such effects?

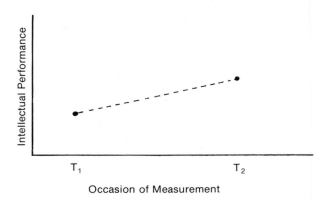

FIGURE 2.1. Hypothetical gain curve.

These issues were to become increasingly critical to the interpretations of longitudinal research on intellectual functioning in adulthood. The 1953 report was followed up quickly by Bayley and Oden's report (1954), yielding similar results. This sharpened the debate further. To a large extent, the next three decades of research on intelligence in adulthood could be understood as a working through and an amplification of questions and controversies brought into clearer awareness by the first report of the Iowa State Study.

FIGURE 2.2. Hypothetical decline curve.

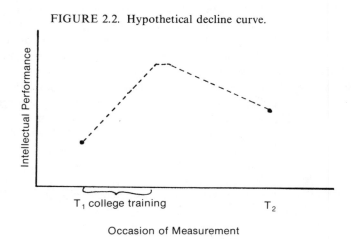

Although Owens was sensitive to these issues and considered them probably as well as was possible with the data available, many of these problems were not resolved and are still with us today (e.g., Nesselroade & Reese, 1973). Findings such as Owens's undoubtedly contributed to Schaie's formulation (1965) of the general developmental model and his subsequent recommendations for sequential studies (e.g., Schaie, 1970). Thus Owens's study produced ideas and questions that have been with us for many years and that still, in some cases, are controversial (Adam, 1978; Baltes & Schaie, 1976; Botwinick, 1977; Botwinick & Siegler, 1980; Horn & Donaldson, 1976).

Study Characteristics

Sample Characteristics

In January 1919, a total of 363 freshmen were tested with the Army Alpha being used as an entrance exam at Iowa State College. Of these, 162 had no ascertainable address or were deceased in 1950. In addition, 63 were noncooperating. Of these 63, 29 refused, and 34 did not reply. One hundred thirty-eight cooperated, but 10 were not tested, and for 1 subject, the results were judged invalid. Thus the sample observed at the first retest in 1949–1950 consisted of 127 males. Ninety-six of these individuals were retested again in 1961, when the average age of the participants was about 61 years. Most of the subjects came from rural backgrounds. They were 19 years of age, on average, at initial testing, and the typical participant was either an engineering or an agriculture major. The average eventual education beyond high school was from 4 to 5 years. Most were married and had an average of two children at the time of the initial retest. Owens (1953) compared total Alpha scores for the 127 subjects tested in 1919 with data on more than 3000 college men and also with a second set of data on more than 15,000 officers from World War I. It was concluded that the sample at first retest was quite similar to these groups in terms of total Army Alpha score.

Recruitment Procedures

The subject recruitment was as follows. Current addresses were obtained for as many persons in the original test group as possible. These were secured from the Iowa State College Alumni Office. Each person was sent an initial contact letter describing the study and requesting that the self-addressed postcard be returned to indicate participation. For out-of-state subjects, psychological examiners were recruited, and the necessary instruments and information were mailed to the testers so that they could contact the participant in question and effect the data gathering. Although some of the retesting within Iowa was carried out individually by Iowa State personnel, one of the participants suggested that a class reunion banquet at Iowa State might attract a number of participants to the university and that this would be a convenient mechanism by which to elicit cooperation and an efficient way of gathering retest data. This procedure was successful in retesting an additional 26 subjects.

To convey a sense of seriousness about the study, subjects were offered a $5 honorarium for their services. Testers received a similar fee. A minimum of three appeals was made to each potential participant, which usually consisted of two form letters and a third attempt, which was a phone call, a wire, or a personal letter.

Instrument

The intelligence test employed in the investigation was Form 6 of the Army Alpha Test (Yerkes, 1921). Guilford (1954) reported a factor analysis of the eight subtests from a later revision. This analysis resulted in three factors, which Guilford characterized as Verbal, Numerical, and Relations. These factors are discussed in more detail later. A brief description of the eight subtests follows:

> *Subtest 1: Following Directions.* A series of instructions are given, and on command the subject carries out these instructions on the largely geometrical patterns for each item. The abilities tapped include comprehending orally presented instructions, retaining these instructions in memory, and executing them quickly. Between 5 and 15 sec are allowed for each of the 12 items. Clearly, this subtest has a strong implicit speed component.
>
> *Subtest 2: Arithmetical Problems.* This subtest consists of verbally presented problems that require the subject to translate them into arithmetic problems and solve them. The level of difficulty of the items is steeply graded, and few subjects progress past the halfway point before confronting items that they are unable to solve. Few subjects complete this subtest. Because of the steep item-difficulty gradient, the test appears to have a high power component.
>
> *Subtest 3: Practical Judgment.* This is a multiple-choice test of verbally stated questions. Reading comprehension is an important ability in this

subtest. (In the later Nebraska edition of the Army Alpha, this subtest is referred to as Common Sense.)

Subtest 4: Synonym–Antonym. This test consists of pairs of words that have either the same or the opposite meaning. The subject is to determine which. The task is essentially a vocabulary test.

Subtest 5: Disarranged Sentences. Each problem consists of a group of words, which, when put in the correct order, make up a sentence that is either true or false. The subject's task is to rearrange the words and evaluate whether the sentence is true or false.

Subtest 6: Number Series Completion. In this subtest, each item consists of a series of numbers with a distinct pattern. The subject's task is to identify the two numbers that would logically come next.

Subtest 7: Analogies. This subtest consists of fairly easy vocabulary, simple relationship verbal analogies. In each item, three words are presented in the form X is to Y as Z is to _____. The subject's task is to fill in the missing word from four choices. Since the level of difficulty of the items is fairly low throughout, but since most subjects fail to complete the subtest, it appears to have a high speed component.

Subtest 8: Information. The questions involve general knowledge, and the subject selects one of four choices. The vast majority of subjects complete this subtest, and it thus has power characteristics.

Guilford's (1954) factor analysis of the Nebraska revision of the instrument yielded three factors consisting of the subtests indicated in Table 2.1. Integral weights for computing factor scores, suggested by Guilford, are also given in the table.

In terms of the test's validity, Yerkes (1921) reports various correlations between .60 and .75 between total score and years of education and also correlations of approximately .50 with officers' ratings of the "general intelligence" of enlisted men. However, the samples employed were highly heterogeneous, so these correlations may be spurious.

Owens (1953) reports odd–even (internal consistency) and test–retest reliabilities (from his first follow-up data). These reliabilities are listed in Table 2.2. Since the subtests are timed, the odd–even reliabilities are undoubtedly spurious. (An exception to this is Subtest 1, Following Directions, which has a separate timing for each item, as previously noted.) Test–retest over a 30-year period, on the other hand, underestimates immediate test–retest reliability. Thus reliabilities for Owens's sample are probably between the two estimates given.

Comparisons were made between various groups to evaluate possible retest sample bias. Although these comparisons of original total test scores showed a statistically significant positive bias in favor of those

TABLE 2.1. Subtests and Integral Weights of Three Factors, after Guilford (1954)

Factors and subtests	Integral weight
Verbal factor	
Practical Judgment	1
Synonym–Antonym	2
Disarranged Sentences	2
Information	1
Numerical factor	
Arithmetical Problems	3
Number Series Completion	1
Relations factor	
Following Directions	1
Analogies	1

successfully retested as compared with the other groups, these differences were relatively small in absolute magnitude (roughly about a third of a standard deviation), and Owens concluded that these differences appeared too small to invalidate his conclusions. It should be noted, however, that no comparisons for bias in developmental trajectory were possible, since, clearly, such data were unavailable.

For the 1961 testing, 31 additional participants were lost: 13 were deceased, 5 were disabled, 5 were not located, and 8 other subjects now refused to participate. Thus a total of 96 subjects were retested in 1961. Again, comparisons of various groups seemed to suggest to Owens that retest sample bias was not large enough to call into question the conclusions drawn.

TABLE 2.2. Estimates of the Reliability of Subtest Scores for the Army Alpha Test (Owens, 1953)

Subtest	Odd–even	Test–retest (1919–1950)
1. Following Directions	.49	.30
2. Arithmetical Problems	.77	.69
3. Practical Judgment	.93	.56
4. Synonym–Antonym	.93	.64
5. Disarranged Sentences	.87	.48
6. Number Series Completion	.76	.62
7. Analogies	.96	.56
8. Information	.73	.63

Structural Properties

Preliminary Comments

A key issue in the assessment of age changes in intellectual functioning concerns the structure of measurement. When the same tests are given to individuals at different ages, are we measuring the same construct in the same way? For example, will a speeded verbal test be sensitive to a knowledge factor in the young and to a speed factor in the old? These issues of comparative construct validity are clearly fundamental to studies on aging since they represent a basic assumption of age-comparative research. Some studies of aging have neglected this issue and have assumed, in the absence of empirical evidence, that the construct validity of measures is equivalent. Fortunately, in the case of the Army Alpha, several studies bear on this question, and though reliable qualitative differences in construct validity appear to be present, they do not appear to be of sufficient magnitude to do conceptual violence to the usual kinds of interpretations that are made in developmental studies.

Construct validity is usually studied by applications of factor analysis. Several published studies of the age-comparative factor structure of the Army Alpha are reviewed in the remainder of this section.

Principal Component Analyses

McHugh and Owens (1954) carried out a principal component analysis for the 1919 and 1950 data sets from the Iowa State Study. Although some cross-sectional investigations of the factor structure of intelligence (e.g., Balinsky, 1941) had occurred previously, the McHugh and Owens report was the first longitudinal comparison that had been reported. It was to retain this status for more than 25 years.

McHugh and Owens were particularly concerned about the possible impact of qualitative differences in educational experience by different generations and raised the possibility that longitudinal comparisons might thus be more valid. However, it was also possible that this structure might change within generations over time. McHugh and Owens examined this possibility.

A general-intelligence-factor model was assumed. Separate analyses were carried out for the two occasions of measurement. Prior to analysis, the correlation matrices were corrected for attenuation. The Following Directions test was dropped because of low reliability. In each case, a general factor with large loadings on all seven of the tests analyzed occurred.

The results suggested were that the two structures were relatively similar; both contained a first component, or G factor. Also, in each analysis, the second component showed loadings in one direction for Number Series Completion and Arithmetical Problems and reversed loadings for the two highly verbal tests: Information and Synonym–Antonym tests. However, one important difference in the second analysis was that the proportion of variance accounted for by the G factor increased considerably from 54% at the first occasion of measurement to 63% at the second occasion. These findings generally were consistent with Balinsky's cross-sectional data in suggesting that the G factor becomes more prominent in later adulthood.

Multiple-Factor Studies of Factor Structure

Cunningham and Birren (1980) reanalyzed the Iowa State data for the 96 subjects tested at three occasions of measurement. A multiple-factor model, rather than a G model, was adopted, based on Guilford's (1954) hand-rotated analysis of the Army Alpha Test. Cunningham and Birren employed a maximum-likelihood approach (Jöreskog, 1971), which allowed various specific hypotheses concerning factor structure to be tested. In particular, the approach adopted involved specific sequential hypotheses: equivalence of the number of factors, equivalence of the factor-loading patterns, equivalence of the factor covariances, and, last, the equivalence of the specificity matrix.

It was found that a three-factor solution was satisfactory across the three occasions of measurement. A model specifying equivalent factor loadings across the first two occasions of measurement was found to be plausible. However, the hypothesis of equivalent factor covariances was rejected. The plausible model with equivalent factor loadings showed increases for all factor covariances from the first occasion to the second. Thus the three factors became more interdependent with age. Taking into account the different model (G vs. multiple-factor) underlying the two investigations, this is the outcome that one would expect from McHugh and Owens's results.

Further comparisons were made between the second and third occasions of measurement. While the number of factors was found to be the same, the model requiring equivalent factor loadings was rejected. Subsequent independent Promax rotations for the 1961 data indicated a similar pattern of factor loadings, but with further increased factor covariances.

Again, the general finding was that intellectual factors became more interdependent with age, although this occurred with slight changes in factor loadings. These findings extended the earlier McHugh and Owens report to the older age range and showed similar conceptual results.

One of the problems with longitudinal comparisons is that cultural changes may be confounded with ontogenetic changes (Schaie, 1965, 1970). This possibility led Cunningham and Birren (1980) to gather further data on college students of approximately the same age as the students in the Iowa State Study at the first occasion of measurement. This time-lag comparison in the factor structure of subjects of approximately the same age, but of widely different cohorts and occasions of measurement, allowed for the evaluation of possible cohort- or time-related cultural influences. An analytic approach was taken that was similar to that used in the previous longitudinal comparisons. The model specifying equivalent factor-loading patterns was found to be plausible. When the model was strengthened by specifying equivalent factor co-variances, the model was again found to be plausible. Finally, a model was considered in which factor loadings, factor intercorrelations, and the specificities were all identical, but this model was found to be inconsistent with the data. These results, however, showed that the time-lag comparison for young samples had a more similar structural result (indeed, an unusually similar structural result) compared with the other longitudinal comparisons previously discussed. Thus it appeared that cohort- and time-related cultural changes were playing a relatively negligible role in these factor-structure comparisons.

In general, the longitudinal reanalysis reported by Cunningham and Birren suggests that ability factors become more interdependent with age, while the results of the time-lag comparison raise the possibility that cohort and other time-related cultural influences on factor structure are relatively small. In drawing this conclusion, however, it would be desirable to carry out additional time-lag comparisons within samples of older adults. Unfortunately, any such comparisons for the Army Alpha are not currently reported in the literature.

Construct Validity in a Theoretical Context

To better interpret the results of the mean-level comparisons to be considered in the next section, it is of some interest to consider how the different Army Alpha subtests relate to theoretically developed factors of intelligence. In an adolescent sample, a study by Witt and Cunningham (1980) considered, among other issues, the relationships between Army

Alpha subtests and factors of Fluid Intelligence and Crystallized Intelligence (e.g., Horn, 1970, 1980). As one would expect, Information, Synonym–Antonym, and Common Sense showed high loadings on the Crystallized Intelligence factor. Disarranged Sentences and Analogies showed moderate loadings on this factor as well. Number Series Completion and Following Directions both showed moderate loadings on the Fluid Intelligence factor. Number Series Completion also showed a high loading on a Number Facility factor, with Arithmetical Problems showing a moderate loading.

Concluding Remarks

It is apparent from this review of various studies of structural relationships within the Army Alpha Test that there is a fairly clear understanding of the construct validity of the measures and that therefore the test has attractive properties for psychometric research on age changes. The information considered in this section provides a basis for the interpretation of changes in mean level for Army Alpha subtest scores.

Age Changes in Mean Levels

This section considers longitudinal changes in means for both factor scores and subtest scores for the Army Alpha. It is emphasized that these comparisons are appropriate only because earlier structural analyses showed considerable similarity (e.g., in factor-loading patterns) across occasions of measurement, even though some qualitative differences were present. The factor scores are considered first, and individual subtest scores later.

Changes in Factor Scores

Owens (1966) considered age changes in three factors—Verbal, Numerical, and Relations—for the 96 subjects who were tested at the three occasions of measurement based on Guilford's factor analysis (1954; see Table 2.3). The Verbal factor score showed an increment of about one standard deviation ($p < .01$) from the first to the second occasion of measurement. The Numerical factor showed a very small decrement, while the Relations factor showed a very slight increment. In terms of the factor scores from 1950 until 1961, the Verbal factor score showed a nonsignificant and

TABLE 2.3. Eight Subtests and Three Estimated Factor
Score Averages for 96 Subjects across Three Occasions
of Measurement

	Occasion		
	1919	1950	1961
Average factor scores			
Verbal	4.413	5.435	5.151
Numerical	5.121	5.052	4.827
Relations	4.584	4.737	5.679
Average subtest scores			
Following Directions	4.752	4.864	5.384
Arithmetical Problems	5.135	5.045	4.820
Practical Judgment	4.904	5.626	4.470
Synonym–Antonym	4.293	5.031	5.676
Disarranged Sentences	4.727	5.460	4.813
Number Series Completion	5.045	5.052	4.903
Analogies	4.587	4.734	5.679
Information	4.444	5.631	4.925

Note. Standard scores were derived by (1) pooling variances across
three occasions, (2) obtaining a grand mean across occasions, (3) sub-
tracting the grand mean from each occasion mean, (4) dividing each
entry by the square root of the pooled variance estimate, and (5) adding
a constant of five: $StSc = [(M_{occ} - M_{gr})/(\sqrt{Var_{pooled}})] + 5$. The factor scores are estimated using the weights from Guilford's analysis
(1954); see Table 2.1.

small decrement. The Relations factor score showed a nonsignificant
increment. In contrast, the Numerical factor showed a highly statistically
significant ($p < .01$) decrement. Although this decrement cannot be considered large in magnitude, it did show an accelerating decrease compared
with the earlier longitudinal comparison (1919 vs. 1950).

For the Verbal and Relations factors, this additional evidence was quite
useful in that it tended to contradict one previous interpretation of the
data. Thus opponents of intellectual stability in adulthood argued that
Owens's earlier work, involving only two points, could be described by a
straight-line function, or, alternatively, that it could have decelerated
rapidly from an early peak (Figure 2.2) and that actually the observed
1950 data might reflect declines from the earlier hypothetical peaks.
Contrary to this viewpoint, Owens argued that the results obtained were
not consistent with the model of accelerating declines within the 1950-to-
1961 comparisons. The fact that relative stability was observed for the
Verbal and Relations components was consistent with Owens's earlier
(1953) interpretation and seemed contrary to an early-peak, large-
decrement model of the data. Also, though the Numerical factor decline

was statistically significant, it would not seem to be sufficiently large to be consistent with an early-peak, large-decrement model. Thus the second follow-up provided important data with which to evaluate these two competing models.

Owens was also sensitive to the issue of cultural change. He noted that Kuhlen, as early as 1940, called attention to the possibility of cultural influences on cross-sectional data. Similarly, Owens was aware that his longitudinal comparisons might be influenced by time-related cultural change. He carried out an interesting analysis, which attempted to evaluate one model that took into account cultural change. He first carried out a time-lag comparison, in which he gave the same form of the Army Alpha to a random sample of 101 males who were freshmen and attending Iowa State University during 1961–1962. He compared factor scores as well as subtest scores for the two sets of data for undergraduates in 1919 and in 1961–1962. He used the data from the time-lag comparisons to estimate cultural change for the various factor scores. In terms of Schaie's (1965) general developmental model, Owens was assuming that cohort influences were negligible and that the time-lag comparison could be used to estimate the time-related cultural change. In some ways, this was an implausible assumption, but the results were quite interesting. He corrected the longitudinal-change scores for the cultural changes, which were mostly positive. The "true gain scores" across the period of 1919 to 1961 still showed gains for the Verbal factor, but now a slight loss was apparent for the Numerical factor, and a larger loss was apparent for the Relations factor.

Clearly, the relative stability of the Verbal factor is consistent with a large number of findings in the field. The large turnabout for the Relations factor, however, seemed to reflect primarily the very large gain due to cultural changes for the Analogies subtest, which is further discussed later. Owens interpreted these findings as being consistent with Cattell's (1963) concept of fluid and crystallized intelligence. However, the Witt and Cunningham factor analysis discussed in the section on structural properties suggests that the Relations factor is less related to Fluid Intelligence than some of the other measures of the Army Alpha.

Actually, given the results of the Witt and Cunningham analysis, the Numerical factor may be more related to Fluid Intelligence, and actually, the slight losses for this factor may be more consistent with recent findings, such as Schaie's sequential results (Schaie & Labouvie-Vief, 1974) for the Primary Mental Abilities Test's Inductive Reasoning and Spatial Ability, both of which are probably good markers of Fluid Intelligence (see Witt & Cunningham, 1980).

Owens suggested that the lack of decline for the Relations factor could have been reflecting some positive cultural changes. That the largest cultural change was found for the Analogies subtest led Owens to speculate that perhaps such a test was relatively unfamiliar even to college-educated subjects in 1919, but that it became more widely known within the culture over the several decades of the two retests, and that further such culture-related gains might in fact mask ontogenetic decline for this variable.

Cunningham and Birren (1976) explored this possibility with the follow-up study of 32 individuals who were tested originally with the Army Alpha as undergraduates at the University of Southern California in 1944. These former students were retested 28 years later, in 1972. It was found that the Relations factor showed a decrement of one standard deviation over the period of retest. These findings were interpreted as supporting Owens's earlier speculations regarding the Relations factor. Similarly to Owens's findings, statistically significant increments were found by Cunningham and Birren for the Verbal factor, and no significant declines were found for the Numerical factor.

Variable Subtest Scores

The individual subtest patterns are now considered for the two retests. First, for the 1950 retest, it should be noted that seven of the eight subtests showed at least positive trends in 1950 from the level found in 1919. Only Arithmetical Problems showed a negative trend, and this was not statistically significant (see Table 2.3). Practical Judgment, Synonym–Antonym, Disarranged Sentences, and Information (all four subtests making up the verbal component) showed statistically significant increases at the .01 level. The Analogies subtest showed a significant increment at the .05 level of significance. The other gains were nonsignificant.

The gains in the subtests making up the Verbal factor were consistent with a wide variety of the findings of the previous (e.g., Foulds & Raven, 1948) and later literature (e.g., Cunningham & Birren, 1976; Schaie & Strother, 1968). The increments in the Verbal tests that the Witt and Cunningham (1980) article showed to be highly related to Crystallized Intelligence were consistent with the general Horn–Cattell theoretical predictions for Crystalized Intelligence. As previously discussed, the gain in the Analogies test probably reflects cultural changes.

It is interesting theoretically that the subtest that showed the earliest decrement (Arithmetical Problems) is a task involving considerable mental effort and active thinking, since it involves transposing a verbally stated problem into an arithmetical problem and then solving it. For example, Number Series Completion is a relatively good marker of Fluid Intelligence, but shows a later pattern of smaller decrement. This raises the possibility that, although the Fluid Intelligence construct's declines may be most consequent theoretically, some specific abilities may be much more sensitive to age. The Arithmetical Problems task is one example of such an ability. Perceptual Speed and Psychomotor Speed tasks may be of this character also (Birren, Woods, & Williams, 1980).

Changes in level for subtest scores for the period 1950–1961 are now considered. Whereas in the previous comparison only one test showed a nonsignificant trend toward decrement, in this decade, five of the eight subtests showed decremental trends. However, none of these trends was statistically significant by itself. The largest and third-largest decrements (Arithmetical Problems and Number Series Completion) seemed to result in the highly statistically significant decrement for the composite Numerical factor score. Following Directions, Analogies, and Information all showed slight and nonsignificant small gains, while the other five subtests showed losses that were not statistically significant.

It appears that the age decade of the 50s is the time in which some decline in intellectual functions becomes apparent for this cohort, and this is even reflected in the Verbal subtest scores. These declines are not large and are not statistically significant, but they do appear to reflect the beginning of decline even in a positively biased, well-educated, and healthy sample, and even with the repeated-measures bias intrinsic to conventional, longitudinal comparisons.

General Conclusions

What was learned from the Iowa State Study? The general conceptual conclusion favors stability of intellectual functioning through middle age. Clearly, the results contradict the kinds of early declines indicated by the early, well-replicated cross-sectional studies. The results suggest peak performance and the beginning of declines of overall intellectual functioning roughly in the age decade of the 50s for this elite sample. The losses appear to be small and probably are not of much practical significance until at least age 60.

What specific substantive conclusions can be drawn from the study? Before entertaining this question, it is necessary to consider what can be learned in general from a repeated-measures longitudinal study in terms of stability and decrement of psychological functioning. Clearly, there are a number of biasing influences on such studies. An important bias had to do with volunteering behavior. Questions arise as to the generalizability to parent populations of results taken from volunteer samples. Often the initial test sample is biased by being constituted of volunteers. That particular problem was not present in the current study because the original participants were required to take the test as an entrance exam. However, almost inevitably in longitudinal studies, the number of persons retested is a subgroup of those originally tested. Although comparisons can be made on original test scores for those retested and those not, there is no possibility of making comparisons for gains or losses in the interim period. It seems only reasonable that those individuals showing large intellectual declines will be differentially less likely to volunteer for retest. Thus the issue of generalizability must be approached very cautiously. And though this issue is difficult to evaluate empirically, the idea persists that declines for the "average person" may begin earlier than are indicated by the retesting of volunteers.

Taking into account these general observations, what limitations are specific to this study? College students in 1919 would clearly constitute an elite group, and so the question arises as to how a more average group might fare in a similar study. Thus the current study may be positively biased by elite status, and such status might be present by way of volunteering behavior in other longitudinal studies as well.

This issue was addressed directly by Tuddenham, Blumenkrantz, and Wilkin (1968), who carried out a study of retiring military personnel (mostly in their 40s) in a constructed sample with a mean IQ of approximately 100 and a standard deviation of 20. Of the four intelligence scores derived from the Army General Classification Test, significant declines were found only for a test of Perceptual Reasoning-Pattern Analyses. On the other hand, Vocabulary, Arithmetical Computation, and Arithmetical Reasoning showed trends toward declines, but were not statistically significant. Study of individual gains and losses suggested that gains in performance were almost as common as losses for the different variables. Thus the Tuddenham *et al.* study of Army personnel was consistent with relative stability, but did suggest declines occurring somewhat earlier than in the Iowa State Study.

Another limitation of the current study concerns the three occasions of measurement. It is certainly desirable to have more occasions of measurement, particularly in the range between the 20 and 50 years of age. Later studies (Schaie & Labouvie-Vief, 1974; Schaie & Strother, 1968) were more complete in this respect, and conclusions regarding peak performance were roughly the same as the conclusions drawn for the Iowa State Study—showing peak performance in the late 40s for most variables, except for Verbal Comprehension, which tended to peak in the 50s. Also, declines from these peaks tended to be modest, and Schaie has speculated that they are probably not of practical significance until much later, probably well into the 60s.

Another limitation of the study concerning the Analogies subtest may have been intrinsic to the cohort studied. Owens, in attempting to explain a lack of decline for the highly speeded Analogies subtest, suggested that cultural differences may be masking ontogenetic declines. Subsequent studies of another cohort (Cunningham & Birren, 1976) did find significant declines for the Relations factor, whose variance principally consists of the Analogies subtest. This result tended to support Owens's interpretation.

Another limitation of most longitudinal studies concerns repeated measures. It is plausible that sensitization or biasing effects may have been produced by administering the test repeatedly. Schaie (1973, 1977) has discussed the advantages of an independent-sample approach to longitudinal studies. The point of this observation regarding repeated measures is again a tendency toward a slight upward bias working against decrement hypotheses.

In this light, it is possible to consider conclusions specific to the Iowa State Study. For the cohorts studied, it appears that Verbal Comprehension peaks in the 50s. The Number factor appears to peak earlier than the 50s. The status of the Relations factor was unclear from the data from the Iowa State Study, though the Cunningham and Birren results suggested that this factor peaks before the 50s and perhaps much earlier. These conclusions appear to be fairly consistent with the results of Schaie's sequential study (Schaie & Labouvie-Vief, 1974; Schaie & Strother, 1968). It seems that what decrements are observed are relatively small and do not appear sufficiently large to have practical significance up until the decade of the 60s. However, from a theoretical point of view, in terms of human development, intellectual functioning as reflected on longitudinal comparisons appears to peak in the late 40s or the 50s for most functions studied. Bearing in mind the kinds of biases (discussed previously) inherent in methods of studying intellectual change, it seems likely that population peaks occur somewhat earlier, but in the absence of such data, it is not possible to know precisely when peaks do occur for optimal, unbiased data.

What kinds of further research are suggested by the Iowa State project as well as by other longitudinal studies considered? Methodologically, it seems clear that far more work needs to be done in attempting the very difficult problem of assessing the impact of volunteering behavior and selective dropout in longitudinal studies.

Taking a general perspective on the results of this and other longitudinal studies, it appears that, for most intellectual variables, the period of 20 to 40 years of age involves either growth or stability (except for highly speeded tasks; Schaie & Strother, 1968). After age 60, declines are common within individuals and across most variables, but individual differences are large and important. The interim period between 40 and 60 years is a period of heterogeneity in which different individuals show gains and losses, and there are clearly different patterns for different variables.

One of the challenges of the next decade will probably be to elucidate specific mechanisms that are precursors to variations of these patterns of change. There is a need to better understand why some variables peak later and some peak earlier for group data. In terms of individual functioning, there will undoubtedly be attempts to specify mechanisms that account not only for why some individuals show earlier decrements than others, but also for why other individuals continue to show increments in functioning even into fairly late life.

The Iowa State Study also had some pioneering properties in the sense that Owens attempted to use biographical items to assess different patterns of intellectual development. These particular analyses and results have not been considered in detail because many of the methods employed (e.g., correlations of difference scores) are no longer current. Also, the kinds of items employed were probably more pertinent to intellectual functioning in young adults. Items concerned with the measurement of health and life-style in middle age would probably have been more sensitive to differential patterns of intellectual development. This, of course, is easier to see at the beginning of the 1980s, when many investigators are becoming more interested in the way in which health status and life-style interact with intellectual development in later life, than was possible when Owens constructed his biographical questionnaire three decades ago. It seems likely that this early attempt to understand antecedents of intellectual development in adulthood will be continued with considerable vigor in the years ahead.

References

Adam, J. Sequential strategies and the separation of age, cohort, and time-of-measurement contributions to developmental data. *Psychological Bulletin*, 1978, *85*, 1309–1316.

Balinsky, B. An analysis of the mental factors of various age groups from nine to sixty. *Genetic Psychology Monographs*, 1941, *23*, 191–234.

Baltes, P. B., & Schaie, K. W. On the plasticity of intelligence in adulthood and old age: Where Horn and Donaldson fail. *American Psychologist*, 1976, *31*, 720–725.

Bayley, N., & Oden, M. The maintenance of intellectual ability in gifted adults. *Journal of Gerontology*, 1954, *10*, 91–107.

Birren, J. E., Woods, A. M., & Williams, M. V. Behavioral slowing with age: Causes, organization, and consequences. In L. W. Poon (Ed.), *Aging in the 1980s*. Washington, D.C.: American Psychological Association, 1980.

Botwinick, J. Intellectual abilities. In J. E. Birren & K. W. Schaie (Eds.), *Handbook of the psychology of aging*. New York: Van Nostrand Reinhold, 1977.

Botwinick, J., & Siegler, I. Intellectual ability among the elderly: Simultaneous cross-sectional and longitudinal comparisons. *Developmental Psychology*, 1980, *16*, 49–53.

Cattell, R. B. Theory of fluid and crystallized intelligence: A critical experiment. *Journal of Educational Psychology*, 1963, *54*, 122.

Cunningham, W. R., & Birren, J. E. Age changes in human abilities: A 28-year longitudinal study. *Developmental Psychology*, 1976, *12*, 81–82.

Cunningham, W. R., & Birren, J. E. Age changes in the factor structure of intellectual abilities in adulthood and old age. *Educational and Psychological Measurement*, 1980, *40*, 271–290.

Foulds, G. A., & Raven, J. C. Normal changes in the mental abilities of adults as age advances. *Journal of Mental Science*, 1948, *94*, 133–142.

Guilford, J. P. *Psychometric methods*. New York: McGraw-Hill, 1954.

Horn, J. L. Organization of data on life-span development of human abilities. In L. R. Goulet & P. B. Baltes (Eds.), *Life-span developmental psychology*. New York: Academic Press, 1970.

Horn, J. L. Concepts of intellect in relation to learning and adult development. *Intelligence*, 1980, *4*, 285–317.

Horn, J. L., & Donaldson, G. On the myth of intellectual decline in adulthood. *American Psychologist*, 1976, *31*, 701–719.

Jöreskog, K. G. Simultaneous factor analysis in several populations. *Psychometrika*, 1971, *36*, 409–426.

Kuhlen, R. G. Social change: A neglected factor in psychological studies of the life span. *Scholastics and Society*, 1940, *52*, 14–16.

Lorge, I. The influence of the test upon the nature of mental decline as a function of age. *Journal of Education Psychology*, 1936, *27*, 100–110.

McHugh, R. B., & Owens, W. A. Age changes in mental organization—A longitudinal study. *Journal of Gerontology*, 1954, *9*, 296–302.

Nesselroade, J. R., & Reese, H. W. (Eds.). *Life-span developmental psychology: Methodological issues*. New York: Academic Press, 1973.

Owens, W. A. Age and mental abilities: A longitudinal study. *Genetic Psychology Monographs*, 1953, *48*, 3–54.

Owens, W. A. Age and mental ability: A second adult follow-up. *Journal of Educational Psychology*, 1966, *57*, 311–325.

Schaie, K. W. A general model for the study of developmental problems. *Psychological Bulletin*, 1965, *64*, 92–107.

Schaie, K. W. A reinterpretation of age-related changes in cognitive structure and functioning. In L. R. Goulet & P. B. Baltes (Eds.), *Life-span developmental psychology*. New York: Academic Press, 1970.

Schaie, K. W. Methodological problems in descriptive developmental research on adulthood and aging. In J. R. Nesselroade & H. W. Reese (Eds.), *Life-span developmental psychology: Methodological issues*. New York: Academic Press, 1973.

Schaie, K. W. Quasi-experimental research designs in the psychology of aging. In J. E. Birren & K. W. Schaie (Eds.), *Handbook of the psychology of aging*. New York: Van Nostrand Reinhold, 1977.

Schaie, K. W., & Labouvie-Vief, G. Generational versus ontogenetic components of change in adult cognitive behavior: A fourteen-year cross-sequential study. *Developmental Psychology*, 1974, *10*, 305–320.

Schaie, K. W., & Strother, C. R. A cross-sequential study of age changes in cognitive behavior. *Psychological Bulletin*, 1968, *70*, 671–680.

Tuddenham, R. D., Blumenkrantz, J., & Wilkin, W. R. Age changes on the AGCT. A longitudinal study of average adults. *Journal of Consulting and Clinical Psychology*, 1968, *32*, 659–663.

Witt, S. J., & Cunningham, W. R. Family configuration and fluid-crystallized intelligence. *Adolescence*, 1980, *15*, 105–121.

Yerkes, R. M. (Ed.). Psychological examining in the United States Army. *Memoirs of the National Academy of Sciences*, 1921, *15*, 1–890.

3 Aging Twins: Longitudinal Psychometric Data

LISSY F. JARVIK AND LEW BANK

Introduction

Just about a century ago, Galton (1876) initiated the use of twins in human research, thus taking advantage of the regular natural occurrence of both monozygotic (one-egg, or identical) and dizygotic (two-egg, or fraternal) twins. Inasmuch as monozygotic (MZ) twins are genetically identical whereas dizygotic (DZ) twins are no more alike in terms of their genes than any other pair of siblings, and since twin partners generally share a similar environment from conception on, comparisons of differences between the two members of a twin pair provide cues to genetic and environmental influences on various traits. To say it another way, if within-pair differences are significantly smaller for one-egg than for two-egg pairs (i.e., if the one-egg pairs have the significantly higher concordance rates), then we have presumptive evidence for a significant influence of genetic factors on that trait.

Another method of gaining helpful information from the lives of twins is to observe a group of MZ twins with their cotwins in different life conditions or under different planned regimes. This method, called the "cotwin control method," is also useful when natural discordance takes place (e.g., one psychotic and one nonpsychotic twin, or one married and one unmarried twin). In such cases, "longitudinal comparisons of aging patterns, biochemical tests, or psychometric scores may prove illuminating as to etiology, diagnostic classification, treatment procedures or personality assessment, provided the given twins are monozygotic" (Kallmann & Jarvik, 1959).

LISSY F. JARVIK. Brentwood Veterans Administration Medical Center and Department of Psychiatry and Biobehavioral Sciences, University of California at Los Angeles, Los Angeles, California.

LEW BANK. Brentwood Veterans Adminstration Medical Center and Department of Psychology, University of California at Los Angeles, Los Angeles, California.

Literally hundreds of studies of twins investigating human attributes and behaviors have been performed since Galton's time. The majority of these studies, however, concentrate on children and young adults and do not provide information on the later stages of life. The study of elderly twins allows comparisons over virtually the entire human life span. Thus childhood and adulthood factors may relate to particular adult and senescent traits and behaviors; in addition, relationships between these life-history variables and survival may be studied.

The particular study on which this chapter focuses is the New York State Psychiatric Institute Study of Aging Twins, begun in 1946 by Franz Kallmann and Gerhard Sander, in the course of which data from more than 2000 twins were collected for a long-term investigation of hereditary aspects of aging and longevity (Kallmann & Sander, 1948, 1949). Data analyses were limited to 1603 "index cases" of twins who had reached the age of 60 and were residents of New York State or neighboring areas. A subset of intact pairs in this sample was selected for psychological testing based on further restrictions, including fluency in English—so that language difficulties would not obscure interpretations of psychological test results—and availability of both twins at the time of field visits (a period of several months). In addition, among the DZ twins, only same-sex partners were used so as not to confound zygosity differences with sex differences. Initially, 120 pairs fit all constraints (Feingold, 1950). In 1949, 14 more pairs were added, giving a total sample of 268 subjects. These 268 subjects either have been followed to the completion of their lives or are still alive; they were originally tested in 1947–1949 (Feingold, 1950; Kallmann & Sander, 1949), and survivors were retested in 1955, 1957, 1967, and 1973. As of 1973, there were 61 survivors, but less than a dozen of them were still alive at last contact.

A great deal of information has emerged from this longitudinal study of senescent twins, the only such study reported to date, and some of the psychometric data are reviewed in this chapter.

The 268 twins constituted 134 intact pairs, who were English-speaking, white, residing in or near New York State, and 60 years of age or older. They closely resembled the population of New York State with regard to both sex ratio (male : female ratio 1 : 1.26 in twins, 1 : 1.2 in New York whites 60 years and older) and education (29% of twins with high school degree or better, in comparison with 27% of New York State population). There were, however, proportionately more farmers in the sample than in the population of New York State, and correspondingly fewer residents of metropolitan areas; this difference was due to the large number of twins drawn from rural areas with stable populations.

Practically none of the twins had ever taken a psychological test before, and a major consideration in selecting the tests was to make the experience as interesting and nonthreatening to a group of elderly persons as was possible (Feingold, 1950). Further, since testing was done in the subject's homes, constraints of practicality dictated that the tests be easily transported and administered. The battery included five subtests from the Wechsler–Bellevue (Similarities, Digits Forward, Digits Backward, Digit Symbol Substitution [DSS], and Block Design; Wechsler, 1944); Vocabulary List 1 of the Stanford–Binet (Terman, 1916); and a simple paper-and-pencil Tapping test to evaluate hand–eye coordination. The formats of all tests except the Tapping test are commonly known. The Tapping test consisted of a 10×10 matrix of boxes. Subjects were instructed to put a dot into as many of the 100 boxes as they could within a 30-sec interval; single-dotted as well as multidotted boxes counted for 1 point, and stray dots were ignored (Feingold, 1950).

Psychometric Data from Initial Test Round

The initial test round (Feingold, 1950; Kallmann, Feingold, & Bondy, 1951; Kallmann & Sander, 1949) revealed no significant differences between scores achieved by the twins (ranging in age from 60 to 89 years) and those achieved by the oldest standardization groups (ages 50–54 and 55–59 years) then available (Wechsler, 1944). Since Wechsler sums Digits Forward and Digits Backward to obtain a single score (Digit Span), only four subtest scores could be compared. Since the twins were, on the average, 15 years older than Wechsler's subjects, and since they did not exceed the educational level achieved by the general population of New York State, their scores evidenced no significant decline in ability on these measures (Kallmann et al., 1951). In addition, their performance indicated that twins—at least twins over 60—appear to do every bit as well as singletons on these tests. (Wechsler's standardization group consisted of single-born individuals). This finding stands in contrast to results reported for school-aged twins, in which performance of twins averaged below that of singletons (e.g., Byrns & Healy, 1936; Mehrotra & Maxwell, 1949).

First-round psychometric test scores were also used to compare MZ and DZ twin pairs. The mean *intrapair* differences in test scores measuring abstract intellectual functioning were smaller for MZ than for DZ twins. For women, these MZ-DZ comparisons attained statistical significance on the Vocabulary, Digits Backward, DSS, Block Design, and Similarities tests. There was a similar trend for the male zygosity groups, but differences were not statistically significant. The failure to find significantly larger mean within-pair differences in DZ than in MZ male pairs may indicate that changes in intellectual abilities (at least the ones reported here) occur at an earlier age in men than in women (Feingold, 1950; Kallmann et al., 1951). Possibly the longer life span of women is paralleled by differences in the adult developmental patterns of the two sexes, with intellectual change occurring later in women than in men. A longitudinal study of men and women from around age 50 or 55 (rather than 60 and over) may be more likely to reveal such differences.

Longitudinal Psychometric Changes

Initial Retests

Half of the original group was retested about 1 year after the initial evaluation (Feingold, 1950), while others were retested over the next few years; in a third test round, 79 available surviving twins were tested again about 8 years after the initial test round (Jarvik, Kallmann, Falek, & Klaber, 1957). A fourth round, approximately 9 years after the first assessment, succeeded in obtaining data from only 17 surviving twins; this dearth of subjects resulted from a lack of funding, rather than from the demise of an extraordinarily large number of twins (Jarvik, Kallmann, & Falek, 1962).

The first retest data revealed no significant changes in any of the tests, whether the entire retested sample was considered together or separately for the four zygosity × sex subgroups (i.e., MZ male, MZ female, DZ male, DZ female). Test–retest intraclass correlations were above .9 for each subtest, with a high of .996 for Vocabulary. The magnitude of these correlations demonstrated adequate reliability of assessment and provided baseline data for subsequent retests.

Because of various health problems (e.g., visual and auditory impairments), not all subtests could be administered to the 79 twins tested at the second retest period (26 MZ and 10 DZ intact pairs plus 7 broken-pair survivors, with a mean age of 74.5 years). In fact, for one subject, no usable scores could be obtained. The number of subjects taking each test ranged from a low of 66 (Block Design) to a high of 78 (Similarities). Although the average performance on each test declined over the 8-year interval, the decrements in *nonspeeded* tasks were small, ranging from 3.0% to 6.5% and were statistically not significant. By contrast, decreases in performance on the speeded tasks (Block Design, DSS, and Tapping) ranged from 12.1% to 21.6% and were statistically significant. In general, over the years, there was considerable variability among test-score patterns, with some subjects consistently declining, others staying much the same, and still others improving in performance (Jarvik *et al.*, 1957).

The 48 subjects who completed all subtests at all three testings (Jarvik, Kallmann, & Falek, 1962) showed consistently higher scores than those exhibited by Wechsler's standardization group on the five Wechsler–Bellevue subtests. Digits Forward, Digits Backward, and Similarities test scores remained stable, while performance on the two speeded tasks—DSS and Block Design—showed some decline; the decrease in Block Design scores was not significant. Analyses on all seven subtests revealed significant decline in score only on the Tapping and DSS tests. Since the subgroup of 48 healthy subjects should be representative of the elderly who are functioning well in the community, comparisons of this subgroup with the Wechsler standardization group appear to be justified.

The 21-Year Follow-Up

After a 12-year testing hiatus, 81 surviving twins participated in the 1967 follow-up round. Of these twins, 46 had taken the psychological test battery three times (1947, 1955, and 1967); for statistical analysis, however, 11 cotwins were removed from the sample. Mean ages for the remaining 12 men and 23 women were 85.7 and 84.6 years, respectively. Analyses revealed that significant declines had occurred both for sexes on all subtests, with the single exception of Vocabulary, where women scored slightly lower, but not statistically significantly lower, than they had in 1947 (Blum, Jarvik, & Clark, 1970). These data suggest that, at least among subjects who are sufficiently healthy and cooperative to continue to participate in a study over a 20-year span, there is general stability of nonspeeded cognitive performance to age 75 and possibly even longer. During the ninth decade of life, however, many abilities declined.

It should be pointed out that the first retest showed a general *increase* in scores, an unexpected finding that was attributed to test familiarity acquired during the first test round. After all, most of the twins had been out of school at least 40 years at the time of the first test round and had no prior experience with the kinds of tests used in the study. Nonetheless, as noted earlier, some decline in performance—especially on speeded tasks—was seen at the second testing. In general, given an elderly non-test-wise group of subjects, one would expect artificially low initial scores and substantial practice effects on subsequent retests. Thus, to gain a clearer perspective on changing (or stable) scores in a longitudinal study, plans should be made to administer a test battery on at least three different occasions (Jarvik, Kallmann, & Falek, 1962).

The importance of the stability of scores on nonspeeded tasks (at least to age 75), as compared with a general decline on the speeded tasks, ought to be emphasized. These results indicate that aging processes affect diverse skills differently. In fact, a factor analysis showed almost every variable forming its own specific factor; only Vocabulary and Similarities shared a factor (*verbal* ability), and Digits Forward and Digits Backward also loaded on a single factor, but Digits Backward did not load nearly so high as Digits Forward (Jarvik, Kallmann, Lorge, & Falek, 1962). It may therefore be appropriate, as the authors pointed out, to revise our thinking so as not to concentrate on intelligence *per se* in the elderly, but rather on a number of readily distinguishable intellectual functions. Besides, the intelligence construct itself has proved valid only in predicting an individual's educational success; even if we possessed a reliable measure of intelligence for the aged, we would hardly be interested in predicting their success in school. Working with individual mental abilities would do away with such problems as dealing with the importance of speed in assessing the intelligence of an aging population. In recent years, the assessment of *competence* in the aged has been recognized as vital, and work in progress (e.g., Krauss, 1976; Marquette, 1976; Ohta, 1976; Schaie, 1978; Scheidt, 1978) is concentrating on the measurement of individual abilities.

Another way of looking at longitudinal change in the psychological tests is, of course, to compare MZ and DZ intact twin pairs. The obvious hypothesis is that MZ twins are more similar than DZ twins. As already noted, initial mean intrapair difference scores were smaller for MZ twins than DZ twins on all seven subtests. These differences were statistically significant on four of the seven.

By 1955, although the same trend was evident, the differences were no longer statistically significant, and the mean intrapair difference on Digit Span was smaller for the DZ than for the MZ group (Jarvik et al., 1957; Falek, Kallmann, Lorge, & Jarvik, 1960). The lack of statistical significance might have been due to the small numbers of intact twin pairs tested in 1955 (26 MZ and 10 DZ pairs) in comparison with 1947 (75 MZ and 45 DZ pairs) and to the increased intrapair variability observed among MZ twins.

Based on scores from the 1967 follow-up (Jarvik, Blum, & Varma, 1972), mean intrapair differences of 13 MZ and 6 DZ twin pairs were compared. By this time, the gradually increasing variability among the MZ twins and the now-evident decrease in variability among the DZ twins had resulted in highly similar intrapair differences between the zygosity groups; only on DSS did the MZ pairs still demonstrate substantially smaller mean intrapair differences than the DZ pairs. What these data suggest is unclear at present, but it is likely that a meaningful part of the variance can be explained by the selective nature of all longitudinal studies. As the twins grew older, those DZ pairs not endowed with a similar genetic propensity for survival were eliminated from analyses through the death of one partner, so that only the more similar DZ pairs remained intact. Although based on limited data, blood groups are consistent with this hypothesis, with 5 of the 6 DZ pairs participating in the 1967 test round showing very few within-pair differences (Jarvik et al., 1972). If one assumes that survival and cognitive functioning are related, then decreasing variability on test performance within DZ pairs seems reasonable.

By contrast, the genetically identical MZ twin partners tended to show increasing dissimilarities over the years. Possibly, the additional years (1947–1967) allowed environmental factors to play an increasing role in determining intellectual change. Thus, as the surviving intact pairs grew closer and closer to completing their lives (in 1967, the mean age for the 19 intact pairs was over 83), there was a tendency for intrapair differences between MZ and DZ twins to approach one another.

Psychometric Performance and Survival

In 1955, 168 of the original 268 twins were alive and 100 were dead. The retested survivors were found to have scored higher at initial testing on *each* of the seven subtests than had the nonsurviving twins. It was reasoned that these differences might reflect a positive relationship between ability and survival (Jarvik et al., 1957).

In an effort to investigate the relationship between psychometric test score and survival, each of the 78 subjects participating in the 1955 follow-up study was labeled as increased, decreased, or unchanged on each of the seven subtests (Jarvik & Falek, 1963). Operationally defined, an increased score indicated a higher score in 1955 (the second retest round) than at either of the earlier testing periods; conversely, a decreased score represented poorer performance at the third test round than at either of the first two. A subject with a score neither higher nor lower than either of the first two test-round scores was said to be unchanged for that particular inability. Percentages of the third-round sample labeled as increased, decreased, or unchanged are shown for each subtest in Table 3.1.

Note that the mean ages for each category in the table do not associate increasing age with decreasing score, as might be expected were intellectual

TABLE 3.1. Mean Ages at Last Testing for Subjects with Increased, Unchanged, or Decreased Retest Scores[a]

	Number of subjects	Mean age (years)		
		Increased scores[b]	Unchanged scores[b]	Decreased scores[b]
Vocabulary	75	75.8 (22.7%)	75.7 (45.3%)	75.6 (32.0%)
Digit Symbol	66	74.1 (13.6%)	77.7 (22.7%)	74.6 (63.6%)
Similarities	76	76.2 (17.1%)	75.4 (50.0%)	75.4 (32.9%)
Block Design	66	72.2 (16.7%)	74.7 (42.4%)	76.5 (40.9%)
Digits Forward	76	75.4 (23.7%)	76.0 (63.2%)	74.8 13.2%)
Digits Backward	75	75.4 (17.3%)	75.9 (56.0%)	75.5 (26.7%)
Tapping	64	76.4 (3.1%)	77.9 (17.2%)	75.0 (79.7%)

[a]From "Intellectual Stability and Survival in the Aged" by L. F. Jarvik and A. Falek, *Journal of Gerontology*, 1963, *18*, 174. Copyright 1963 by the Gerontological Society. Reprinted by permission.
[b]Figures in parentheses are percentage in each group.

decline to be a direct functioning of aging. Only Block Design shows subjects with decreased performance to have a higher mean age at the last testing than subjects with unchanged or increased scores. For the four nonspeeded tasks, from 67.1% to 86.9% of the twins either improved or remained unchanged. Even on the speeded tasks, 36.3%, 59.1%, and 20.3% of the sample either remained unchanged or improved on DSS, Block Design, and Tapping, respectively. A general lack of consistency on subtest change for individual profiles was found, with increased or unchanged scores on some tests and decreased scores on others seeming to be the rule.

At the time the association between test score and survival was first examined (Jarvik & Falek, 1963), 14 of the 78 subjects who had participated in three test rounds had died. The remaining subjects had survived their third test session by 2½ to more than 6 years. Using 5-year posttest survival as a criterion, subjects were classified as (1) survivors—that is, survived more than 5 years since last testing (this group included 1 person who died 9 years after his last testing)—34 persons; (2) nonsurvivors— that is, survived less than 5 years—13 persons; or (3) alive, but fewer than

5 years elapsed since the last testing—31 persons. Subjects in the third category could be classified neither as survivors nor as nonsurvivors, so analyses were performed on the first two groups only.

A statistically significant relationship resulted for Vocabulary such that survivors were more likely to have improved or remained stable and nonsurvivors to have declined in this ability. For no other subtest did a significant difference between the two groups result until an annual rate of decline (*ARD*) was computed:

$$ARD = \frac{T_H - T_L}{T_H \times Y} \times 100$$

In this computation, T_H is the highest score on either of the first two testings, T_L is the score on the last testing, and Y is the number of years intervening between T_H and T_L. This computation, based on the average test–retest period of 6 to 8 years, demonstrated a relationship between 5-year survival and an *ARD* greater than 10% on the Similarities test and greater than 2% on the DSS test.

Critical Loss

In accord with these findings, the concept of "critical loss" was developed and used to describe a change in score consisting of at least two of the following: (1) a yearly decrement of 10% or greater on Similarities, (2) a decrement of 2% or greater on DSS, and (3) any decline on Vocabulary. Returning (*post hoc* to the subsample of twins with complete data on each of the three critical tests for each of the three test rounds, 22 of the 26 twins without critical loss were survivors, while 7 of the 8 twins with critical loss were deceased. It is worth noting that the deceased twins with critical loss constituted the *youngest* subgroup. It is also interesting that (Birren, Riegel, & Robbin, 1962). Siegler (1975), however, in her thorough review of the "terminal drop" literature, notes that among Wechsler Adult Intelligence Scale (WAIS) subtests, DSS is the most highly correlated with RT, which presumably is a pure measure of speed. Siegler comments that a "confusing aspect of the NYS studies is the assertion that speeded measures are age-related (Tapping and Block Design) while DSS is a critical loss sub-test." Siegler's point is well taken, but since the Tapping subtest—which is a pure test of speed (with hand–eye coordination)—did not predict survival, whereas DSS did, it is possible that the sensitivity of DSS is due mostly to the associative processes operating. Consistent with this hypothesis are the results of factor analysis showing high loading on one of the factors (VI) for both the DSS and the Similarities test. In addition, another factor (V)—apparently a "speed" factor—had fairly low DSS loading (Jarvik, Kallmann, Lorge, & Falek, 1962).

By 1967, all the twins could be classified as either having survived the test round by 5 years or more (60 persons) or having died within 5 years of the third testing (18 persons). A total of 14 survivors and 2 decedents had not taken the three critical tests on all three occasions and consequently had to be omitted (Jarvik & Blum, 1971). Only 4 of the 46 remaining survivors, but 11 of the 16 decedents, had shown critical loss. Also examined were the data from 26 intact twin pairs who formed a subgroup of the 1955 sample of 78. In 16 of the pairs, both members were 5-year survivors; 1 twin was deceased in each of 9 pairs; and in 1 pair, neither twin had survived 5 years beyond the last testing. There was no evidence for greater concordance in survival for one-egg than for two-egg twins in this group; this result can be attributed, however, to the small number of DZ twin pairs still intact (5) and to the likelihood of the members of the intact DZ twin pairs being selected for survival. One-egg twins did show greater concordance for critical loss (actually, the absence of critical loss) than did two-egg twins (13 of 21 for MZ pairs as compared with 2 of 5 for DZ pairs), but once again, the small number of intact DZ twin pairs makes this comparison unreliable. In 10 of 11 pairs discordant for critical loss, the deceased twin was the one with the critical loss; in the 11th pair, both twins survived, but the twin who had shown a critical loss was suffering from severe organic brain syndrome (OBS), whereas his cotwin was judged to be in good health. Although these predictions were in a sense *post hoc*, 53 correct predictions out of 62 tend to support the validity of the critical loss construct and are in accord with Kleemeier's (1962) terminal drop hypothesis.

A case history of two MZ twin sisters, "A" and "L," demonstrates the relationship between intellectual decline on the critical subtests and earlier death. These two women lived their entire lives together, with the exception of a 6-year period in their early 20s during which they were separated, with work duties requiring their living in different cities. The twins were extraordinarily similar at their first testing, but at the third testing, "A" showed a critical loss, whereas "L" had maintained her performance on Vocabulary and Similarities and had, in fact, increased her score on DSS. Within 3 years of the third testing, "A" had died; many years after her sister's death, "L," when last seen at age 87, was still a vital, active person. Possibly the onset of myocarditis in "A's" late 50s was the crucial factor differentiating the life histories of the twins (Jarvik & Blum, 1971).

Another possible sign of the sisters' diverging survival potential was that "L" outweighed "A" by 15 to 20 pounds for much of their adult lives.

The weight difference brings to mind reports of "twin transfusion syndrome," in which one twin gains a greater share of placental nourishment than the other (e.g., Babson, Kangas, Young, & Bramhall, 1964; Churchill, 1965); a 500-g or greater discrepancy in weight of MZ twins at birth has been used as a criterion for twin transfusion syndrome (Munsinger, 1977), but "A" and "L" reported themselves as having weighed the same at birth.

Although the explanation for critical loss and earlier mortality in one twin and not the other remains unclear, in MZ twins, the observed discordance can be attributed neither to genetic variability nor to an age difference.

The twins "A" and "L" constituted one of the 8 MZ twin pairs discordant for critical loss; these 8 pairs failed to show statistically significant intrapair differences in mean scores at any time. At the time of the third test round, however, the twins with critical loss had declined significantly not only on the three tests of critical loss, but also on all four other subtests; their cotwins also showed general decline, but decrements reached statistical significance only on Tapping and Block Design, two *speeded* tasks. Once again, we see that declines in cognitive functioning portend impending death (and are probably pathognomonic of cerebral disease; Birren, 1968; Jarvik, 1967), whereas decreases in performance on speeded psychomotor tasks are probably "normal" (though not necessarily inevitable) concomitants of aging.

Considering the 8 cotwins who did not exhibit critical loss, 3 were still alive at the time of the 1967 test round (approximately 11 years after their last testing), and the other 5 had died, on the average, 5.6 years after their third testing. Of the 8 critical-loss twins, 7 died an average of 3.1 years after the third test round, while the lone survivor was a victim of severe OBS (compared with a very healthy cotwin as previously indicated). These data are sufficiently striking to suggest the use of the critical-loss subtests as periodic assessors of the elderly, perhaps at the time of health exams. Identification of at-risk cases, with possible intervention, could help many people to spend additional years of satisfying, more optimally functioning lives.

A case study that illustrates the potential of the at-risk diagnosis is that of the "W" twins. The MZ "W" twins were 70.5 years of age at the time of their third testing in 1955. Both were in good health and were vigorous and strong men; they refused to consult a physician until 2 years later, when "CW" suffered a sudden diabetic coma that proved to be fatal. Had the meaning of "CW's" psychological scores been understood at that time (critical loss was indicated), he might have been persuaded to see a physician and could possibly have survived an additional 8 years, as did his cotwin (Jarvik & Blum, 1971).

Although the predictive power of critical loss with regard to mortality appears impressive into the eighth decade of life, it has not been demonstrated for higher ages. Thus critical loss and 5-year mortality were examined in the group of 22 twins retested in 1973. As of 1978, 12 had died, but critical loss failed to distinguish them from the 10 who survived (Steuer, LaRue, Blum, & Jarvik, 1981). By contrast, in the ninth decade of life and beyond, the presence of OBS was associated with high mortality (Jarvik, Ruth, & Matsuyama, 1980). Moreover, retrospective examination of test scores (LaRue & Jarvik, 1980) revealed that, on the three critical loss subtests (Vocabulary, Similarities, and DSS), the twins diagnosed as suffering from OBS during the 1967 follow-up had scored significantly lower than their unaffected counterparts 20 years before the diagnosis of OBS was made (i.e., 1947–1949 test round).

It is possible that low scores of the initial test round identified a sociocultural or biological subgroup of individuals likely to receive a diagnosis of OBS as the result of the losses ordinarily accompanying advancing chronological age. In other words, it may be postulated that individuals at the lower end of the normal distribution curve for certain cognitive functions are more likely than others to receive the diagnosis of OBS. On the other hand, there is the distinct possibility that OBS is the result of a prolonged disease process lasting decades rather than years. The role of genetic factors in such a disease process remains to be adequately defined. Family history and other data do point toward genetic influences in the development of OBS (Larsson, Sjogren, & Jacobsen, 1963). Chromosomal changes are among these genetic influences.

Chromosomal Changes in Old Age

Human cells characteristically have 46 chromosomes. If enough cells are inspected, however, cells with fewer or more than 46 chromosomes can be found. Such cells have been termed "aneuploid" and were first reported to increase with age by Jacobs, Brunton, and Court-Brown (1964); Jacobs, Brunton, Court-Brown, Doll, and Goldstein (1963); and Jacobs, Court-Brown, and Doll (1961). It is possible that mitotic errors are propagated throughout the course of a lifetime, "with the eventual attainment of a level at which homeostatic mechanisms can no longer cope with primary and secondary metabolic dysfunctions" (Jarvik, 1965). At that level, the organism can no longer survive. Aneuploid changes in the brain (especially in the glial cells, which are known to reproduce) may then contribute to cognitive decline through the degeneration of neural support tissue, a possibility under investigation in our laboratory (Matsuyama & Jarvik, in preparation).

The relationship between aneuploidy and age has been the subject of numerous publications during the past two decades, but many of the reports have been contradictory (Bloom, Archer, & Awa, 1967; Cadotte & Fraser, 1970; Court-Brown, Buckton, Jacobs, Tough, Kuenssberg, & Knox, 1966; Demoise & Conrad, 1972; Fitzgerald, 1975; Galloway & Buckton, 1978; Goodman, Fechheimer, Miller, & Zartman, 1969; Hamerton, Taylor, Angell, & McGuire, 1965; Jarvik & Kato, 1970; Jarvik, Yen, & Moralishvili, 1974; Mattevi & Salzano, 1975; Neurath, DeRemer, Bell, Jarvik, & Kato, 1970; Nielsen, 1970; Sandberg, Cohen, Rimm & Levin, 1967). Upon careful reevaluation of all available published data, one may conclude that women over the age of 50 years have a higher frequency of aneuploidy than do younger women and that this increased frequency is due largely to the loss of a C-group chromosome, most likely the female sex, or X, chromosome. The data for men are contradictory and must be considered unclear at present (Matsuyama & Jarvik, in preparation).

To our knowledge, there is only one longitudinal study of chromosomal changes in old age, and that was carried out with the same group of New York State twins previously described (Jarvik, Yen, Fu, & Matsuyama, 1976). It showed an increase in aneuploidy and loss of a C-group chromosome in women, but not in men, during a 6-year follow-up period when their mean ages increased from 83 to 89 years. The group was too small (only 11 women) to examine the relationship between chromosome loss and mental function on a longitudinal basis, but such a relationship had been found for the larger group for whom both chromosome and psychometric data were available from the 1967 follow-up (Jarvik, Altschuler, Kato, & Blumner, 1971).

Psychological tests administered to the 61 twins for whom chromosome data were available included the Memory-for-Designs test of Graham and Kendall (1960) and the Stroop Color–Word Interference Test (Comalli, Wapner, & Werner, 1962), as well as the seven-subtest battery of intellectual functioning used throughout the longitudinal study. The subjects had also been psychiatrically evaluated for OBS according to the diagnostic criteria of Goldfarb (1964) and were classified as OBS present or absent; if present, OBS was further defined as mild, moderate, or severe. Complete data were not obtained for all 61 twins, so the numbers of subjects vary from one analysis to another. Detailed reports of the methodology and findings can be found in previous publications (Bettner, Jarvik, & Blum, 1971; Jarvik et al., 1971). Summaries of the results from work with these psychological data as they relate to chromosome loss have been reported elsewhere (Jarvik, 1973a, 1973b, 1973c); only the most salient findings are discussed here.

Because cerebral arteriosclerosis is itself known to cause OBS, a relationship between OBS and chromosome loss could be masked if subjects with arteriosclerosis were included. Hence, only persons judged to be free of cerebral arteriosclerosis were used for analysis; this restriction limited the sample to 13 men and 23 women. Organic brain syndrome was found to relate significantly to hypodiploidy in women; no similar relationship resulted for males. Figures 3.1 and 3.2 demonstrate the OBS–hypodiploidy relationship in women and its absence in men.

FIGURE 3.1. Frequency of chromosome loss (% hypodiploidy) in 23 aged women with and without OBS. Nine subjects with suspected cerebral arteriosclerosis were excluded. (From "Organic Brain Syndrome and Chromosome Loss in Aged Twins" by L. F. Jarvik, K. Z. Altschuler, T. Kato, and B. Blumner, *Diseases of the Nervous System*, 1971, *32*, 164. Copyright 1971 by the Physicians Postgraduate Press. Reprinted by permission.)

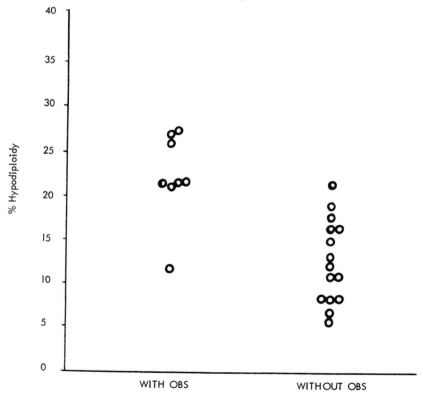

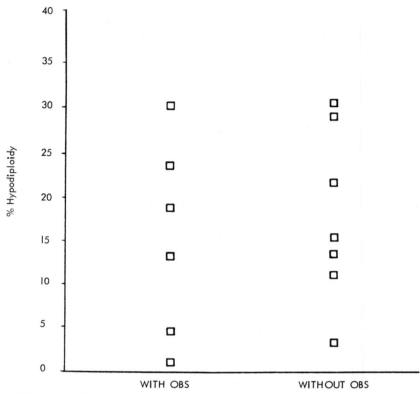

FIGURE 3.2. Frequency of chromosome loss (% hypodiploidy) in 13 aged men with and without OBS. Ten subjects with suspected cerebral arteriosclerosis were excluded. (From "Organic Brain Syndrome and Chromosome Loss in Aged Twins" by L. F. Jarvik, K. Z. Altschuler, T. Kato, and B. Blummer, *Diseases of the Nervous System*, 1971, *32*, 164. Copyright 1971 by the Physicians Postgraduate Press. Reprinted by permission.)

Analyses of the psychological test results indicated that, for women, on all of the seven subtests of intellectual functioning, poorer scores were associated with greater hypodiploidy. The Graham–Kendall test as an indicator of memory loss and the Stroop test, which has been used as a measure of cognitive decline and may measure at least some aspects of OBS, were both significantly related to chromosome loss in female twins: the more hypodiploidy, the poorer the performance. The absence in males of any relationships between test performance and hypodiploidy is intriguing and remains unexplained.

To date, three other investigators have looked at the relationship between hypodiploidy and OBS, and, in agreement with our findings, all reported an association between aneuploidy of chromosomes and presenile (Nordenson, Adolfsson, Beckman, Bucht, & Winblad, 1980; Ward, Cook, Robinson, & Austin, 1979) or senile (Nielsen, 1970) dementia. One of these studies included women only; the others reported abnormalities in both sexes. To our knowledge, there are no studies other than the ones reported here for the New York State twins relating psychometric data to chromosome data.

In these twins, greater mental impairment, as measured by psychiatric evaluation, correlated significantly with higher Graham–Kendall and Stroop scores among women; nonsignificant associations resulted for the men. The important Stroop factor for women was shown to be Color Difficulty, a task in which the name of a color (e.g., red) is printed in ink of a different color (e.g., green) and the subject must report the color of the ink rather than read the *name* of the color (e.g., green, not red). No particular Stroop factor emerged as salient for men.

That there is a relationship between hypodiploidy and general mental impairment seems likely, but this information still leaves us in a rather perplexed state regarding chromosome loss and intellectual decline, as well as the sex differences. Whether chromosome loss is actually related to long-term intellectual decline or is associated only with deficits in memory will remain unknown until the completion of longitudinal and prospective studies of chromosome loss covering at least the senescent years of the human life span.

Sex Differences and Other Variables

In the course of this 30-year longitudinal study of senescent twins, detailed descriptions of sex differences and mental functioning have been reported by Blum (1969); Blum, Fosshage, and Jarvik (1972); Blum et al. (1970); Feingold (1950); and Jarvik (1975).

At the time of the first testing, mean scores for women exceeded those for men on five of the seven psychometric subtests; men achieved higher scores only on Digits Forward and Digits Backward (Wechsler's Digit Span), and these differences were not significant. By contrast, sex differences on the Tapping, DSS, and Block Design tests were statistically significant in favor of women. Since women enjoy a longer life span than men, it is likely that the superior performance exhibited by the female twins is a reflection of differential rates of aging in the sexes, with earlier declines in men presaging earlier mortality. However, the facts that

(1) women excel on verbal tasks in comparison with men (Jarvik, 1975; Maccoby, 1966; Maccoby & Jacklin, 1974) and (2) some of the Wechsler–Bellevue subtests used load high on verbal ability (Wechsler, 1958), when added to the finding of minimal decline in intellectual functioning through the third test round for both sexes, strongly suggest that the observed differences favoring women reflect, at least in part, the stability into senescence of the greater verbal facility of women compared to men.

The 1967 follow-up revealed that, for the 54 subjects included for analyses (19 members of intact pairs were omitted), the *initial* 1947 mean score differences again showed higher scores for women on all tests except Digit Span, but significant differences were found only for Tapping and DSS. The 1967 test round again favored the women, but this time on all tests except Digits Backward; moreover, the differences on Vocabulary and Similarities, as well as Tapping and DSS, now reached statistical significance. In addition, men showed greater losses than women over the 20-year span on all but the Tapping and DSS tests. Thus, although lifelong sex differences (especially on Vocabulary, Similarities, and DSS) are probably exerting some influence, it appears that senescent men *do* decline more rapidly than their female contemporaries on tests of intellectual functioning. It is interesting to note that the three tests found useful for the prediction of critical loss and impending death are, in fact, Vocabulary, Similarities, and DSS, tests on which women of all ages tend to do better than their male counterparts.

Aside from sex differences, educational and other life-history variables are known to affect late-life mental functioning (Birren & Morrison, 1961). The data on twins permit assessment of the effects of some of these variables.

The 1967 follow-up found 81 senescent twins still living; of these, 73 twins were tested, including 19 intact pairs (Blum & Jarvik, 1974). To avoid any possible effects of "twinning," the 19 cotwins of the intact pairs were eliminated from the analytical procedures. (Members of each of the intact pairs were randomly labeled as "twin" or "cotwin.")

Initial ability was determined by each subject's first-round Vocabulary test score. The high correlation of vocabulary with general intelligence and the previously noted stability of vocabulary with advancing age (Jones, 1959; Thorndike & Gallup, 1944) justify its use as an indicator of ability. Remember, the subjects had attended school before the turn of the century, and therefore before the advent of intelligence testing. High and low ability were defined as scores one-half of a standard deviation or more above or below the mean, respectively. Classified in this way were 17 high- and 18 low-ability twins; the remaining 19 cases fell within one-half standard deviation of the mean and were omitted from analyses. Results indicated higher scores for the more able than the less able twins on all seven subtests, both at the first testing and at the 1967 follow-up testing. All differences were statistically significant except for Block Design (first test round) and DSS (1967 round). Regression to the mean, predicted by Baltes, Nesselroade, Schaie, and Labouvie (1972), failed to materialize. In fact, every one of the seven subtests evinced a greater percentage decline for the low- than for the high-ability group.

Entrance into high school operationally defined the high-education group (32 twins), whereas the low-education group (22 twins) did not attend school beyond the elementary grades. Subtest means for the high-education twins exceeded those for the low-education twins at both test periods for all tests. The first-round test differences were significant for four tests: Vocabulary, Similarities, DSS, and Tapping. By 1967, differences on all seven subtests were statistically significant. The percentage decline was greater for the less educated group on every test.

The difference between the more and less favored groups clearly emerged with both the ability and the education classifications. Presumably, a relationship between high ability and high education does exist, and therefore, not unexpectedly, the two high–low dichotomies were not independent of each other. The groups were *far* from identical, however, with 29% of the high-*ability* group classified as less *educated*, and 11% of the low-*ability* group classified as more *educated*. As pointed out earlier (Jarvik & Blum, 1971), the sample was most characteristic of the average. Neither a lack of the formally educated nor a glut of PhDs (or even college graduates) marked the education groups; analogously, evidence of extremely high or low intellectual accomplishment was infrequent in the ability groups. "It is remarkable, therefore, that even under such limiting circumstances, the 'low' categories consistently showed larger declines than the 'high' categories" (Blum & Jarvik, 1974).

Apparently, then, age is less deleterious to the initially more able. This finding extends beyond intellectual functioning to survival itself. Survivors as of the 1955 third-round testing had achieved higher mean scores initially than had the decedents; this finding has now been supported by numerous other longitudinal studies. (For reviews, see Jarvik & Blum, 1971; Jarvik, Eisdorfer, & Blum, 1973.)

It seems likely that a positive relationship between continued mental activity and successful aging exists; utilizing "activity" data (described by Jarvik, Bennett, & Blumner, 1973) from this same longitudinal study, DeCarlo (1971) found evidence supporting this hypothesis. Better educated persons are likely to engage in intellectual activities more frequently throughout their lives, including senescence, and this mental exercise probably protects against cognitive declines. If it is true that the better educated are more likely to continue intellectual endeavors throughout their lifetimes, then their enjoyment of mental activity, rather than their extended school years, may be the valuable attribute.

The education–test performance relationship has also been evaluated in another way (Feingold, 1950; Jarvik & Erlenmeyer-Kimling, 1967). From the original group of 120 senescent twin pairs, 23 were discordant for formal education; the criterion for discordance was 1 year or more discrepancy in education. Of these twin pairs, 15 differed by 1 to 3 years (Group I), and the remaining 8 (Group II) by 4 years or more. Figure 3.3 illustrates the intrapair differences for each of these 23 twin pairs on all seven subtests. One might expect the Group II DZ pairs to vary most on the psychometric subtests, with the better educated (and most likely more capable) twin consistently scoring higher than the cotwin. Though borne out by 1 of the 4 Group II DZ pairs, this hypothesis is not clearly affirmed in Figure 3.3. Other individual cases contradict this commonsense prediction as well. For example, Lester, of the "L" twins, concluded his

FIGURE 3.3. Intrapair differences in raw scores of 23 senescent twin pairs on seven tests. Group I: education of one twin exceeded cotwin's by 1 to 3 years; Group II: education of one twin exceeded cotwin's by 4 or more years. Positive difference indicates higher score made by more educated partner; negative difference indicates higher score made by less educated partner. (From "Survey of Familial Correlations in Measured Intellectual Functions" by L. F. Jarvik and L. Erlenmeyer-Kimling, in J. Zubin and G. Jervis, Eds., *Psychopathology of Mental Development,* Grune & Stratton, New York, 1967, p. 455. Copyright 1967 by Grune & Stratton. Reprinted by permission.)

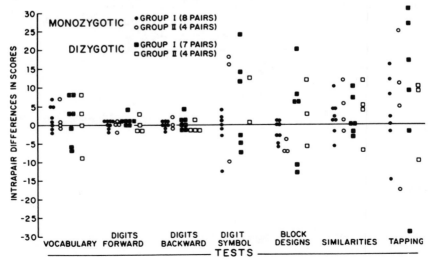

formal education in seventh grade, whereas his cotwin graduated from law school. Lester performed better on Similarities, Block Design, and Tapping (Jarvik & Erlenmeyer-Kimling, 1967).

Monozygotic pairs exhibit even less consistent trends. One pair, the "D" twins, had rather divergent education and work careers, with the professionally educated twin enjoying a successful and apparently stimulating position and the less educated cotwin drifting from one job to the next, including numerous ill-fated business ventures. Despite these disparate educational and work histories, their psychometric test scores were quite similar, except for DSS, on which the less educated twin outscored his cotwin, and Similarities, on which the better educated twin excelled.

There is a statistically nonsignificant trend toward higher scores for the better educated twin partner, but the most striking configurations of Figure 3.3 are (1) the low variability on Digits Forward, Digits Backward, Vocabulary, and Similarities (in that order), and the far greater variability on the three tasks with speed components (Block Design, Digit Symbol, and Tapping); and (2) the exhibition by the DZ groups of variability equal to or greater than that of the MZ groups on each subtest.

Intellectual decline in senescence could account for the inability to demonstrate the expected education–psychological test performance relationship in these 23 twin pairs, but this rationale seems unlikely in light of the findings of cognitive stability with the larger ("parent") sample.

Combining these results with the analyses of Blum and Jarvik (1974), it appears that formal education does in some way exert an influence on intellectual functioning, but whatever differences can be accounted for in this way are frequently not sufficiently powerful to overcome genetic endowment, as is exemplified by the lack of consistent intrapair differences in the data just reviewed (Jarvik & Erlenmeyer-Kimling, 1967).

Conclusions

The longitudinal psychometric data gathered over three decades indicate the following:

1. Nonspeeded cognitive functioning is maintained, at least to age 75 in relatively healthy survivors.
2. Psychological test scores and survival were positively associated.
3. For certain tests, heredity was found to relate to cognitive abilities.
4. Women outscored men on most of the psychological tests administered.
5. Data on chromosome change support the hypothesis that hypodiploidy (chromosome loss) is a frequent concomitant of aging in women, but not in men.

6. Again only among women, hypodiploidy related significantly both to OBS and to poorer psychological test performance.

Many questions have been raised in the course of this study. For instance, why is the relationship between chromosome loss and cognitive decline observed in women and not in men? What are the mechanisms underlying the observed association between chromosome loss and intellectual decline, and how can we intervene to prevent the latter?

Similarly, when we turn to cognitive decline and critical loss, the very same questions asked of chromosome loss and related variables are equally appropriate. Our knowledge of the critical loss phenomenon is sufficient at this point, however, to suggest that those persons found to be at risk on the basis of psychometric testing should be thoroughly examined. A standard list of medical tests to be performed on the at-risk aged (e.g., the list published by the National Institute on Aging [NIA] Task Force; 1980) should be compiled, made available to physicians, and brought to the attention of those working with the aged.

Acknowledgment

This chapter is a modified version of "A Longitudinal Study of Aging Human Twins" by L. Bank and L. F. Jarvik, in E. L. Schneider (Ed.), *The Genetics of Aging*, Plenum Press, New York, 1978. Copyright 1978 by Plenum Publishing Corp. Reprinted by permission.

References

Babson, S. G., Kangas, J., Young, N., & Bramhall, J. Growth and development of twins of dissimilar sizes at birth. *Pediatrics*, 1964, *33*, 327–333.

Baltes, P. B., Nesselroade, J. R., Schaie, K. W., & Labouvie, E. W. On the dilemma of regression effects in examining ability level-related differentials in ontogenetic patterns of intelligence. *Developmental Psychology*, 1972, *6*, 18–26.

Bettner, L. G., Jarvik, L. F., & Blum, J. E. Stroop color–word test, nonpsychotic organic brain syndrome and chromosome loss in aged twins. *Journal of Gerontology*, 1971, *26*, 458–469.

Birren, J. E. Psychological aspects of aging. *Gerontologist*, 1968, *1*, 16–20.

Birren, J. E., & Morrison, D. F. Analysis of the WAIS subtests in relation to age and education. *Journal of Gerontology*, 1961, *16*, 363–369.

Birren, J. E., Riegel, K. F., & Robbin, M. A. Age differences in continuous word associations measured by speech recordings. *Journal of Gerontology*, 1962, *17*, 95–96.

Bloom, A. D., Archer, P. G., & Awa, A. A. Variation in the human chromosome number. *Nature (London)*, 1967, *216*, 467–487.

Blum, J. E. Psychological changes between the seventh and ninth decades of life. Unpublished doctoral dissertation, St. John's University, Jamaica, N.Y., 1969.

Blum, J. E., Fosshage, J. L., & Jarvik, L. F. Intellectual changes and sex differences in octogenarians: A twenty-year longitudinal study of aging. *Developmental Psychology*, 1972, *7*, 178–187.

Blum, J. E., & Jarvik, L. F. Intellectual performance of octogenarians as a function of education and initial ability. *Human Development*, 1974, *17*, 364–375.

Blum, J. E., Jarvik, L. F., & Clark, E. T. Rate of change on selective tests of intelligence: A twenty-year longitudinal study of aging. *Journal of Gerontology*, 1970, *25*, 171–176.

Byrns, R., & Healy, J. The intelligence of twins. *Journal of Genetic Psychology*, 1936, *49*, 474–478.

Cadotte, M., & Fraser, D. Etude de l'aneuploidie observée dans les cultures de sang et de moelle en fonction du nombre et de la longueur des chromosomes de chaque groupe et de l'âge et du sexe des sujets. *Union Médicale du Canada*, 1970, *99*, 2003–2007.

Churchill, J. A. The relationship between intelligence and birthweight in twins. *Neurology*, 1965, *15*, 341–347.

Comalli, P. E., Wapner, S., & Werner, H. Interference effects of Stroop color–word test in childhood, adulthood and aging. *Journal of Genetic Psychology*, 1962, *100*, 47–53.

Court-Brown, W. M., Buckton, K. C., Jacobs, P. A., Tough, I. M., Kuenssberg, E. V., & Knox, J. D. E. *Chromosome studies in adults* (Monograph XLII). London: Cambridge University Press, 1966.

DeCarlo, T. *Recreation patterns and successful aging: A twin study.* Unpublished doctoral dissertation, Columbia University, 1971.

Demoise, C. F., & Conard, R. A. Effects of age and radiation exposure on chromosomes in a Marshall Island population. *Journal of Gerontology*, 1972, *27*, 197–201.

Falek, A., Kallmann, F. J., Lorge, I., & Jarvik, L. F. Longevity and intellectual variation in a senescent twin population. *Journal of Gerontology*, 1960, *15*, 305–309.

Feingold, L. A psychometric study of senescent twins. Unpublished doctoral dissertation, Columbia University, 1950.

Fitzgerald, P. H. A mechanism of X chromosome aneuploidy in lymphocytes of aging women. *Humangenetik*, 1975, *28*, 153–158.

Galloway, S. M., & Buckton, K. E. Aneuploidy and aging: Chromosome studies on a random sample of the population using G bonding. *Cytogenetic Cell Genetics*, 1978, *20*, 78–95.

Galton, F. The history of twins, as a criterion of the relative powers of nature and nurture. *Journal of the Royal Anthropological Institute of Great Britain and Ireland*, 1876, *6*, 391–406.

Goldfarb, A. I. The evaluation of geriatric patients following treatment. In P. H. Hoch & J. Zubin (Eds.), *The evaluation of psychiatric treatment.* New York: Grune & Stratton, 1964.

Goodman, R., Fechheimer, N., Miller, R., & Zartman, O. Chromosomal alterations in three age groups of human females. *American Journal of Medical Science*, 1969, *258*, 26–33.

Graham, F. K., & Kendall, B. S. Memory-for-designs tests: Revised general manual. *Perceptual and Motor Skills, Monograph Supplement*, 1960, *11* (2-VII), 147–188.

Hamerton, J. L., Taylor, A. I., Angell, R., & McGuire, V. M. Chromosome investigations of a small isolated human population: Chromosome abnormalities and distribution of chromosome counts according to age and sex among the population of Tristan da Cunha. *Nature (London)*, 1965, *206*, 1232–1234.

Jacobs, P. A., Brunton, M., & Court-Brown, W. M. Cytogenetic studies in leukocytes on the general population: Subjects of ages 65 years and more. *Annals of Human Genetics*, 1964, *27*, 353–365.

Jacobs, P. A., Brunton, M., Court-Brown, W. M., Doll, R., & Goldstein, H. Change of human chromosome count distributions with age: Evidence for sex difference. *Nature (London)*, 1963, *197*, 1080–1081.

Jacobs, P. A., Court-Brown, W. M., & Doll, R. Distribution of human chromosome counts in relation to age. *Nature (London)*, 1961, *191*, 1178–1180.

Jarvik, L. F. Chromosomal changes and aging. In R. Kastenbaum (Ed.), *Contributions to the psychology of aging.* New York: Springer, 1965.

Jarvik, L. F. Survival and psychological aspects of aging in man. *Symposia of the Society of Experimental Biology,* 1967, *21,* 463–482.

Jarvik, L. F. Memory loss and its possible relationship to chromosome changes. In C. Eisdorfer & W. E. Fann (Eds.), *Psychopharmacology and aging.* New York: Plenum, 1973. (a)

Jarvik, L. F. Genetic disorders late in life. *Medical World News, Geriatrics,* 1973, 13–16. (b)

Jarvik, L. F. Mental functioning related to chromosome findings in the aged. In *Proceedings of the Vth World Congress of Psychiatry* (Mexico, D. F., November 25–December 4, 1971). Amsterdam: Excerpta Medica, 1973. (c)

Jarvik, L. F. Human intelligence: Sex differences. *Acta Geneticae Medicae et Gemellologiae,* 1975, *4,* 189–211.

Jarvik, L. F., Altschuler, K. Z., Kato, T., & Blumner, B. Organic brain syndrome and chromosome loss in aged twins. *Diseases of the Nervous System,* 1971, *32,* 159–170.

Jarvik, L. F., Bennett, R., & Blumner, B. Design of comprehensive life history interview schedule. In L. F. Jarvik, C. Eisdorfer, & J. Blum (Eds.), *Intellectual functioning in adults.* New York: Springer, 1973.

Jarvik, L. F., Blum, J. E., & Varma, A. O. Genetic components and intellectual functioning during senescence: A 20-year study of aging twins. *Behavior Genetics,* 1972, *2,* 159–171.

Jarvik, L. F., & Blum, J. E. Cognitive declines as predictors of mortality in twin pairs: A twenty-year longitudinal study of aging. In E. Palmore & F. C. Jeffers (Eds.), *Prediction of life span.* Lexington, Mass.: D. C. Heath, 1971.

Jarvik, L. F., Eisdorfer, C., & Blum, J. *Intellectual functioning in adults.* New York: Springer, 1973.

Jarvik, L. F., & Erlenmeyer-Kimling, L. Survey of familial correlations in measured intellectual functions. In J. Zubin & G. Jervis (Eds.), *Psychopathology of mental development.* New York: Grune & Stratton, 1967.

Jarvik, L. F., & Falek, A. Intellectual stability and survival in the aged. *Journal of Gerontology,* 1963, *18,* 173–176.

Jarvik, L. F., Kallmann, F. J., & Falek, A. Intellectual changes in aged twins. *Journal of Gerontology,* 1962, *17,* 289–294.

Jarvik, L. F., Kallmann, F. J., Falek, A., & Klaber, M. M. Changing intellectual functions in senescent twins. *Acta Genetica et Statistica Medica,* 1957, *7,* 421–430.

Jarvik, L. F., Kallmann, F. J., Lorge, I., & Falek, A. Longitudinal study of intellectual changes in senescent twins. In C. Tibbits & W. Donahue (Eds.), *Social and psychological aspects of aging.* New York: Columbia University Press, 1962.

Jarvik, L. F., & Kato, T. Chromosome examination in aged twins. *American Journal of Human Genetics,* 1970, *22,* 562–573.

Jarvik, L. F., Ruth, V., & Matsuyama, S. Organic brain syndrome and aging: A six-year follow-up of surviving twins. *Archives of General Psychiatry,* 1980, *37,* 280–286.

Jarvik, L. F., Yen, F. S., Fu, T. K., & Matsuyama, S. S. Chromosomes in old age: A six-year longitudinal study. *Human Genetics,* 1976, *33,* 17–22.

Jarvik, L. F., Yen, F. S., & Moralishvili, E. Chromosome examinations in aging institutionalized women. *Journal of Gerontology,* 1974, *29,* 269–276.

Jones, H. E. Intelligence and problem solving. In J. E. Birren (Ed.), *Handbook of aging and the individual.* Chicago: University of Chicago Press, 1959.

Kallman, F. J., & Jarvik, L. F. Individual differences in constitution and genetic background. In J. E. Birren (Ed.), *Handbook of aging and the individual.* Chicago: University of Chicago Press, 1959.

Kallmann, F. J., & Sander, G. Twin studies on aging and longevity. *Journal of Heredity,* 1948, *39,* 349–357.

Kallmann, F. J., & Sander, G. Twin studies on senescence. *American Journal of Psychiatry,* 1949, *106,* 29–36.

Kallmann, F. J., Feingold, L., & Bondy, E. Comparative adaptational, social, and psychometric data on the life histories of senescent pairs. *American Journal of Human Genetics*, 1951, *3*, 65–73.

Kleemeier, R. W. Intellectual changes in the senium. *Proceedings of the Social Statistics Section of the American Statistics Association*, 1962, *1*, 290–295.

Krauss, I. *Predictors of adult competence.* Paper presented at the annual meeting of the Western Psychological Association, Los Angeles, 1976.

Larsson, T., Sjogren, T., & Jacobsen, G. Senile dementia: A clinical, sociomedical and genetic study. *Acta Psychiatrica Scandinavica*, 1963, *39*, 1–259.

LaRue, A., & Jarvik, L. F. Reflections of biological changes in the psychological performance of the aged. *Age*, 1980, *3*, 29–32.

Maccoby, E. E. Sex differences in intellectual functioning. In E. E. Maccoby (Ed.), *The development of sex differences.* Stanford, Calif.: Stanford University Press, 1966.

Maccoby, E. E., & Jacklin, C. N. *The psychology of sex differences.* Stanford, Calif.: Stanford University Press, 1974.

Marquette, B. W. *The trans-situational generalizability of adult competence.* Paper presented at the annual meeting of the Western Psychological Association, Los Angeles, 1976.

Matsuyama, S. S., & Jarvik, L. F. Manuscript in preparation.

Mattevi, M. S., & Salzano, F. M. Senescence and human chromosome changes. *Humangenetik*, 1975, *27*, 1–8.

Mehrotra, S. N., & Maxwell, J. The intelligence of twins: A comparative study of eleven-year-old twins. *Population Studies (London)*, 1949, *3*, 295–302.

Munsinger, H. *The identical twin transfusion syndrome.* Unpublished manuscript, 1977.

National Institute on Aging Task Force. Senility reconsidered: Treatment possibilities for mental impairment in the elderly. *Journal of the American Medical Association*, 1980, *244*, 259–263.

Neurath, P., DeRemer, K., Bell, B., Jarvik, L. F., & Kato, T. Chromosome loss compared with chromosome size, age and sex of subjects. *Nature (London)*, 1970, *225*, 281–282.

Nielsen, J. Chromosome in senile, presenile and arteriosclerotic dementia. *Journal of Gerontology*, 1970, *25*, 315–321.

Nordenson, I., Adolfsson, R., Beckman, G., Bucht, G., & Winblad, B. Chromosomal abnormality in dementia of Alzheimer type. *Lancet*, 1980, *1*, 481–482.

Ohta, R. J. *The role of cautiousness in research on adult competence.* Paper presented at the annual meeting of the Western Psychological Association, Los Angeles, 1976.

Sandberg, A. A., Cohen, W. M., Rimm, A. A., & Levin, M. L. Aneuploidy and age in a population survey. *American Journal of Human Genetics*, 1967, *19*, 633–643.

Schaie, K. W. External validity in the assessment of intellectual development in adulthood. *Journal of Gerontology*, 1978, *33*, 695–701.

Scheidt, R. J. A taxonomy of situations for the elderly population: Generating situational criteria. *Journal of Gerontology*, 1978, *33*, 872–883.

Siegler, I. C. The terminal drop hypothesis: Fact or artifact? *Experimental Aging Research*, 1975, *1*, 169–185.

Steuer, J., LaRue, A., Blum, J., & Jarvik, L. F. Critical loss in the eighth and ninth decades. *Journal of Gerontology*, 1981, *36*, 211–213.

Terman, L. M. *The measurement of intelligence.* Boston: Houghton Mifflin, 1916.

Thorndike, E. L., & Gallup, G. H. Verbal intelligence of the American adult. *Journal of Genetic Psychology*, 1944, *30*, 75–85.

Ward, B. E., Cook, R. H., Robinson, A., & Austin, J. H. Increased aneuploidy in Alzheimer disease. *American Journal of Medical Genetics*, 1979, *3*, 137–144.

Wechsler, D. *The measurement of adult intelligence.* Baltimore: Williams & Wilkins, 1944.

Wechsler, D. *The measurement and appraisal of adult intelligence* (4th ed.). Baltimore: Williams & Wilkins, 1958.

4 The Seattle Longitudinal Study: A 21-Year Exploration of Psychometric Intelligence in Adulthood

K. WARNER SCHAIE

Introduction

If scientists had all the resources they could wish for, they would probably study a problem area by collecting large amounts of data on a great many individuals selected in as representative a manner as possible. Barring such utopian conditions, some scientists collect large amounts of data on a few carefully selected individuals. They can then proceed to write case histories, which may or may not be generalizable. Alternatively, many of us restrict our ambitions to a few carefully selected variables and then try to collect data bases sufficiently large enough to permit relatively rigorous statistical analyses and attempt generalizations to larger populations. The resultant danger here, of course, lies in the possibility that one knows a lot about a restricted variable set, which may or may not have practical importance.

I have probably erred in the latter direction, by restricting my efforts to the exploration of one definition of intelligence (the psychometric one) by means of a very small number of variables, the five major dimensions emerging from L. L. Thurstone's (1938) factor-analytic mapping of the Primary Mental Abilities (PMAs). Taking this narrow approach, however, has had the advantage of permitting the systematic exploration of experimental artifacts and the mounting of collateral studies leading to some degree of causal analysis which might get us eventually beyond the stage of mere description.

K. WARNER SCHAIE. Department of Individual and Family Studies and Department of Psychology, The Pennsylvania State University, University Park, Pennsylvania.

In this chapter, I attempt to survey the results of efforts that have preoccupied me for the past quarter century. Many of the individual pieces of this work have been reported in the journal literature, and a concise account of the natural history of the Seattle Longitudinal Study and its findings through 1970 has previously been published (Schaie, 1979). This chapter refers to many of these materials and brings matters up to date by including the 21-year follow-up data from the fourth (1977) cycle. It also reviews a number of contextual studies of a methodological and substantive nature that have been previously reported as convention papers and that either are not easily accessible or make little sense out of context.

There has been much recent discussion regarding the validity and utility of the sequential methods that were developed in the process of trying to account for the findings of our empirical studies (Baltes, 1968; Schaie, 1965, 1970, 1973b, 1975a, 1977). Each of these discussions (cf. Adam, 1978; Botwinick & Arenberg, 1976; Buss, 1979/1980) raises legitimate questions regarding (1) the interpretation of sources of developmental change and differences and (2) the estimation of the relative or absolute importance to be assigned to the various components. None of these critiques, however, offers constructive alternatives or even seriously impugns our recommendations for developmental data collection. Given explicitly stated assumptions, we continue to believe that the sequential methods offer much (cf. Baltes & Nesselroade, 1979; Schaie & Hertzog, 1982). In this chapter, their application is shown as clearly as possible, duly heeding the legitimate admonitions of our critics.

Controversy has also arisen regarding the substance of the study (cf. Baltes & Schaie, 1976; Horn & Donaldson, 1976; Schaie & Baltes, 1977). Again, some legitimate criticisms have been raised, particularly regarding the magnitude of changes in age in the general population as estimated from longitudinal studies of highly selected panels. These criticisms are addressed in this chapter by appropriate comparisons with our control samples. I have no stake in fitting one particular theoretical model or another to the data, nor do I desperately seek to reconstrue the data of others to fit my preferred outcome. I can take that position because I have consistently believed that the final arbiter of scientific disputes must be the collection of *appropriate* empirical data, rather than opinions stated in the heat of acrimonious debate.

This chapter begins with an outline of some of the programmatic objectives of the Seattle study, those that seemed clear at the beginning and others that emerged as we went along. Next, I describe the variables and review the emergent design of the study. Findings reviewed are restricted to the material on the PMAs; the personality data from the study are of almost equal interest, but would detract from the clear focus of the topic covered here. I hope that the systematic application of our control data will serve as a response to many of the reservations raised regarding the internal and external validity of findings from long-term studies. I also hope that our conclusions will be relevant to the thoughtful discussion of a number of social policy questions.

As is the case in most longitudinal studies, colleagues and students made many contributions to the collection, analysis, and interpretation of data from the study. Much credit for the many aspects of the work that went well goes to these contributors; the responsibility for what went awry is, of course, mine.[1]

Why Should One Study Intelligence in Adulthood?

Applied psychology virtually began with the investigation of intellectual competence, whether its purpose was to determine the orderly removal of mentally retarded children from the public school classroom (Binet & Simon, 1905) or to study the distribution of individual differences in the interest of demonstrating their Darwinian characteristics (Galton, 1869). What kind of complex mental function did the early investigators seek, one that we are still pursuing today? Binet's definition remains a classic guide: "To judge well, to comprehend well, to reason well, these are the essentials of intelligence. A person may be a moron or an imbecile if he lacks judgment; but with judgment he could not be either" (Binet & Simon, 1905, p. 196).

Early empirical work on intelligence investigated how complex mental functions were acquired early in life (Brooks & Weintraub, 1976). But interest was awakened quickly by theoretical writers, such as G. Stanley Hall (1922), H. L. Hollingsworth (1927), and Sydney Pressey (Pressey, Janney, & Kuhlen, 1939), who were concerned in following the complexities of intellectual development beyond childhood. Questions raised concerned the age of attaining peak performance level, the maintenance or transformation of intellectual structures, and the decremental changes thought to occur from late midlife into old age.

[1]The following colleagues and students (in alphabetical order) participated in the various data collections and analyses and/or contributed to the resultant scholarly products: Margaret Baltes, Paul Baltes, Tom Barrett, Gisela Bertulis, Barbara Buech, Michael Gilewski, Kathy Gribbin, Christopher Hertzog, Judy Higgins, Eric Labouvie, Gisela Labouvie-Vief, Karen Laughlin, Ann Nardi, John Nesselroade, Iris Parham, Robert Peterson, Alan Posthumer, Margaret Quayhagen, Pat Sand, Coloma Harrison Schaie, Michael Singer, Vicki Stone, Charles Strother, Nathaniel Wagner, Sherry Willis, and Elizabeth Zelinski.

Empirical work relevant to these questions soon began to appear. For example, Terman (1916), in his original standardization of the Binet tests for American use, assumed that intellectual development reached a peak at age 16 and then remained level through adulthood. Large-scale studies with the Army Alpha Intelligence Test (Yerkes, 1921) suggested that the peak level of functioning for young adults might already be reached, on the average, by age 13. Other early empirical studies, however, questioned these inferences. Perhaps one of the most influential studies, that of Jones and Conrad (1933), obtained cross-sectional data on most of the inhabitants of a New England community who were between the ages of 10 and 60 years. Interestingly enough, age differences found in this study were substantial on some of the subtests of the Army Alpha, but not on others. Likewise, Wechsler's standardization studies, leading to the development of the Wechsler–Bellevue scales, found that growth of intelligence does not cease in adolescence. Of even greater interest was the finding that peak ages differed for various aspects of intellectual functioning and that decrements at older ages were not uniform across the different subtests used to define intelligence (Wechsler, 1939).

The interest in intelligence testing reached a peak after World War II with the widespread introduction into clinical practice of the Wechsler Adult Intelligence Scale (WAIS) and its derivatives (Matarazzo, 1972), the almost universal introduction of intelligence and/or aptitude testing in the public schools, and the development of widely accepted classification batteries such as the Differential Aptitude Test (DAT) and the General Aptitude Test Battery (GATB; cf. Cronbach, 1970). But soon disenchantment set in, with widespread criticism of the misapplication of intelligence tests in education (e.g., Kamin, 1974). Clinicians learned that profile analyses of intelligence tests were less useful than was previously thought and that the information gained on intellectual status seemed to contribute little to the programming of therapeutic intervention.

In spite of these criticisms, the fact remains that omnibus measures of intelligence have been rather useful in predicting a person's competence in dealing with the standard educational systems of our country. They have also been useful in predicting success in vocational pursuits whenever job requirements depend upon educationally based knowledge and skills. And specific measures of abilities, although somewhat more controversial, have nevertheless had some utility in predicting competence in those specific situations where special abilities could be expected to be of importance. A reasonable argument could be made for the proposition that motivational and other personality variables are of greater potency in predicting adjustment and competence in midlife than is intelligence, but the empirical evidence is less than convincing. When dealing with the elderly, however, it becomes readily apparent that assessment of intellectual competence again reaches paramount importance. Questions such as who shall be retired for cause (in the absence of mandatory retirement at an early age), whether there is sufficient remaining competence for independent living, or whether persons can continue to conserve and dispose of their property clearly involve the assessment of intellectual functions.

If we agree that the preceding issues are important to our society, it then becomes necessary to study in detail the factual issues involved in the development of intelligence beyond young adulthood. We must begin to differentiate intraindividual changes (IACs) of a decremental nature from interindividual differences which result in the obsolescent behavior of older cohorts when compared with their younger peers. In this context, it is necessary to know at what age developmental peaks occur and to assess generational differences as well as within-generation age changes. In addition, we must give careful attention to the question of why some individuals show intellectual decrement in early adulthood while others maintain or even increase their level of functioning well into old age.

The programmatic inquiry reported in this chapter has tried to address these questions more or less systematically. In particular, it has asked the following broad questions:

1. Does intelligence change uniformly or in different ability patterns?
2. At what age is there a reliably detectable age decrement in ability, and what is its magnitude?
3. What are the patterns of generational differences, and what is their magnitude?
4. What accounts for individual differences in IAC in intellectual function across adulthood?

The following section discusses more detailed objectives and gives a brief history of how the final design of the study emerged.

History and Objectives of the Study

The origins of the Seattle Longitudinal Study may be traced back to work done by me as an undergraduate at the University of California at Berkeley as part of directed studies under the supervision of Professor Read D. Tuddenham. After he introduced me to the basic concepts of factor analysis and to the writings of L. L. Thurstone, I inferred that, although the work of Wechsler on adult intelligence might be of great concern to clinicians, the Wechsler–Bellevue and its derivatives, because of their factorial complexity, were less than desirable for the exploration of developmental issues. I also learned that the more explicitly defined PMAs had not been explored beyond adolescence and concluded that this was a possibly fruitful topic for systematic pursuit. In an initial study, I explored whether the factorial independence of the five abilities measured in the most advanced form of the PMA test (Thurstone & Thurstone, 1949) was retained in adulthood and then proceeded to ask whether adults functioned at the same level as did adolescents and, more specifically, if there were ability-related differentials in adult PMA performance, I also questioned whether differences in pattern would be maintained if the PMA test were administered under nonspeeded conditions (Schaie, Rosenthal, & Perlman, 1953).

With my appetite having been whetted by some provocative results in this early pilot study, I continued to explore a variety of corollaries of intelligence in adulthood during my graduate work at the University of Washington (Schaie, Baltes, & Strother, 1964; Schaie & Strother, 1968a, 1968d; Strother, Schaie, & Horst, 1957). As part of this work, it also became necessary to develop a new factored test of behavioral rigidity (Schaie, 1955, 1960; Schaie & Parham, 1975). This work culminated in a doctoral dissertation designed to replicate the earlier work on differential ability patterns across a wider portion of the adult life span as well as to test the effect of rigidity–flexibility on maintenance or decline of intelligence (Schaie, 1958a, 1958b, 1958c, 1959a, 1959b). This dissertation, of course, became the base for the subsequent longitudinal and sequential studies.

The search for a suitable population frame for the base study was guided by the consideration that what was needed was a subject pool with known demographic characteristics, which had been established for reasons other than research on cognitive behavior. That is, if possible, the initial selection of volunteer subjects for the study should not be designed so as to maximize selection in terms of the subjects' interest in, concern with, or performance level on the dependent variables. When plans for the study matured, my mentor, Charles Strother, was, by coincidence, president of the board of the Group Health Cooperative of Puget Sound, one of the first broadly based health maintenance organizations. An arrangement was worked out with the managers of the health plan that permitted me to recruit research subjects who had been selected by a random draw from the age/sex stratification of plan members above the age of 21 years. The appeal to participate was made by the plan's managers as part of a membership satisfaction survey, the administration and analysis of which was my *quid pro quo* for gaining access to this population.

Results of the 1956 base study did not support a causal model involving differential patterns of intellectual performance across age for flexible and rigid individuals. The study did demonstrate a relationship between flexibility–rigidity and intelligence at all ages, but more important, provided a sound demonstration of differential patterns of intelligence across age, and by virtue of its design, serendipitously provided the basis for the following sequential studies.

Perhaps the final stimulation leading to the conversion of a one-time cross-sectional study into a series of longitudinal studies was my reading of the reports of longitudinal studies of individuals reaching middle adulthood, such as the papers by Bayley and Oden (1955); Jarvik, Kallmann, and Falek (1962); and Owens (1953, 1959). (See Chapters 2 and 3, this volume, for descriptions of the last two of these studies.) Taken together, these studies suggested maintenance of most intellectual abilities at least into middle age, and of some abilities beyond this point, findings that contrasted with the results of the earlier cross-sectional literature and my own dissertation data. What seemed to be called for, I was soon convinced, was the follow-up of a broad cross-sectional panel, such as the one I had examined, by means of a short-term longitudinal inquiry. Intensive discussions of such a project with Charles Strother were followed by a grant application to the National Institutes of Health (NIH), which was funded in time to collect the first set of follow-up data in the summer of 1963.

In addition to tracking down and retesting as many of the persons studied in 1956 as possible, we decided to draw a new random sample from the original population frame in order to provide controls for the examination of retest effects and to begin to address the possibility that sociocultural change affects intellectual performance, heeding the thoughtful admonitions previously voiced by Raymond Kuhlen (1940, 1963). The new sample extended over the original age range (22–70 years) plus an additional 7-year interval to match the range now reached by the original sample.

Whereas the second cross-sectional study provided essential replication of the earlier findings, the short-term longitudinal study disclosed substantially different information about peak levels and rate of decline. Publication of results was therefore delayed until a theoretical model could be built that accounted for the discrepancy between the longitudinal and cross-sectional data (Schaie, 1965, 1967). These analyses suggested that group mean comparisons ought to be conducted both for repeatedly measured samples and for successive independent samples drawn from the same cohorts. Results were reported that called attention to the large observed cohort differences and that questioned the universality and significance of intellectual decrement in community-dwelling persons (Nesselroade, Schaie, & Baltes, 1972; Schaie, 1970; Schaie & Strother, 1968b, 1968c). Availability of the longitudinal data also permitted a first pass at addressing the problems of experimental mortality (Baltes, Schaie, & Nardi, 1971) and regression effects in longitudinal studies (Baltes, Nesselroade, Schaie, & Labouvie, 1972).

It soon became clear that the conclusions based on a single 7-year interval required further replication, particularly because two occasions of measurement permit examination of cross-sectional, but not of longitudinal, sequences (cf. Baltes, Reese, & Nesselroade, 1977); the latter require a minimum of three occasions of measurement. It is the latter, however, that explicitly permit contrasting age and cohort effects. A third data collection was therefore conducted in 1970, with the retesting of as many persons as possible from the first two occasions, and the drawing of a third random sample from the residual members of the base population frame (Schaie, 1979; Schaie, Labouvie, & Buech, 1973; Schaie & Labouvie-Vief, 1974; Schaie & Parham, 1977).

Although results of the third data collection seemed rather definitive, a number of questions remained. Discrepancies between the repeated-measurement and independent-sampling studies argued for a replication of our 14-year longitudinal sequences, and it seemed of interest to take another look at our original sample. Consequently, a fourth data collection was conducted in 1977, again retesting the previous samples and adding a new random sample (this time from an expanded population frame). Continuous funding also made it possible to address collateral questions. These included an examination of the aging of tests (Gribbin & Schaie, 1977), an analysis of the effects of monetary incentives upon subject selection and characteristics (Gribbin & Schaie, 1976), and the beginning of the causal analysis of health and environmental factors upon change or maintenance of adult intelligence (Gribbin, Schaie, & Parham, 1980; Hertzog, Schaie, & Gribbin, 1978b).

A longitudinal study soon develops its own social network. None of the studies reported here could have occurred without the cooperation of many devoted graduate students and colleagues or without the enthusiastic cooperation of members and staff of our population source, the Group Health Cooperative of Puget Sound. Our study may be a good model for showing how long-range developmental studies can be conducted through meaningful collaboration with organizations that must maintain long-term panel membership for socially significant reasons. Over the past few years, results from this study have greatly affected my interpretative writing on adult intelligence addressed to a variety of target audiences (cf. Baltes & Schaie, 1974; Schaie, 1972, 1974, 1975a, 1980, 1981; Schaie

& Parr, 1981; Schaie & Willis, 1978, 1981). The remainder of the chapter will provide the reader with a basis for judging whether the assertions I have made in the interpretative writing are indeed justified.

Description of the Measurement Variables

Although the Wechsler scales have been most widely used with adults for purposes of clinical diagnosis (cf. Matarazzo, 1972; Schaie & Schaie, 1977) and have also received substantial attention in developmentally oriented studies (for reviews, see Botwinick, 1977; Schaie, 1980), they do not have a clear-cut factorial structure. The latter is necessary, however, if the objective of one's inquiry is to delineate the differential life course of human abilities. At the outset of my investigation, it therefore seemed reasonable to consider the factored tests provided by the work of the Thurstones (1941, 1949), even though this work had previously not extended beyond the life stage of adolescence. In addition, we required certain control measures related to cognitive style, which led to the development of the Test of Behavioral Rigidity (TBR; Schaie, 1955, 1960; Schaie & Parham, 1975). Other materials used in this study included regularly collected demographic data, indicators of health behavior (Hertzog, Schaie, & Gribbin, 1978b; Parham, Gribbin, Hertzog, & Schaie, 1975), and, since 1974, contextual data collected by means of the Life Complexity Inventory (LCI; Gribbin, Schaie, & Parham, 1980; Schaie & Gribbin, 1975b).

The Primary Mental Abilities

The PMA test battery was derived from a series of factor-analytic studies of some 56 mental tests, which resulted in the definition of relatively independent mental abilities (L. L. Thurstone, 1938). The test form used consistently in our studies was the 1948 PMA 11–17 version.[2] This version, which at the time was the most difficult form of the test, consists of five subtests designed to cover the abilities listed in this section. The descriptions given are slightly modified from those provided by the test manual (Thurstone & Thurstone, 1949).

[2]Illustrations in the following sections are from *SRA Primary Mental Abilities*, Ages 11–17, Form AM. Copyright 1948 by L. L. Thurstone and Thelma Gwinn Thurstone. Reprinted by permission of the publisher, Science Research Associates, Inc.

1. Verbal Meaning (V). This is a test of the ability to understand ideas expressed in words. It measures the range of a person's passive vocabulary used in activities where information is obtained by reading or listening to words. The task requires verbal recognition by means of a multiple-choice format. In the following example, the subject must select that alternative which is the best analogue of the capitalized stimulus word:

BIG A. ILL B. LARGE C. DOWN D. SOUR

The test contains 50 items in increasing order of difficulty, with a time limit of 4 minutes.

2. Space (S). This is a measure of the ability to think about objects in two or three dimensions. It may be described as the ability to imagine how an object or figure would look when it is rotated, to visualize objects in two or three dimensions, and to see the relations of an arrangement of objects in space. It is probably important in skills such as deducing one's physical orientation from a map or visualizing what objects would look like when assembled from pieces. The current technical term for this ability is often given as "spatial orientation." Space is measured by 20 test items, with a time limit of 5 minutes. In the example given here, every lettered figure that is the same as the stimulus figure, even though it is rotated, is to be marked. Figures that are mirror images of the stimulus figure are not to be marked.

3. Reasoning (R). This ability, which in current ability-factor taxonomies is often specifically identified as "inductive reasoning," involves the solution of logical problems—to foresee and plan. The Thurstones (1949) proposed that persons with good reasoning ability could solve problems, foresee consequences, analyze a situation on the basis of past experience, and make and carry out plans according to recognized facts. Reasoning is measured by items such as the following:

a b x c d x e f x g h x   h i̲ j k x y

The letters in the row form a series based on a rule. The problem is to discover the rule and mark the letter that should come next in the series. In this case, the rule is that the normal alphabetic progression is interrupted with an *x* after every second letter. The solution would therefore be the letter *i*. There are 30 test items, with a time limit of 6 minutes.

4. *Number* (*N*). This is the ability to work with figures and to handle simple quantitative problems rapidly and accurately. It is measured by asking subjects to check simple addition problems, with items of the following kind:

$$
\begin{array}{r}
17 \\
84 \\
\underline{29} \\
140
\end{array}
\quad \boxed{R} \quad \boxed{W}
$$

The sum for each column of figures is given. However, some of the solutions given are right (R) and others are wrong (W). The test contains 60 items with a time limit of 6 minutes.

5. *Word Fluency* (*W*). This ability is concerned with verbal recall involved in writing and talking easily. It differs from verbal meaning in that it focuses on the speed and ease with which words are used, rather than the degree of understanding of verbal concepts. The measurement task requires the subject to write as many words as possible beginning with the letter *s* during a 5-minute period.

Composite Indexes

In addition to the five ability-factor scores, we consistently reported data on two derived linear composites. Both of these were originally suggested by the Thurstones (1949). The first is an index of Intellectual Ability (*IA*), or a composite measure likely to approximate a conventional deviation IQ, obtained by summing subtest scores weighted approximately inversely to the standard deviation of each test:

$$IA = V + S + 2R + 2N + W$$

The second is an index of Educational Aptitude (*EA*), suggested by T. G. Thurstone (1958) as the best predictor, from the test battery, of performance in educational settings:

$$EA = 2V + R$$

Scaling of PMA Scores

No adult norms for the PMA test were available at the initiation of these studies. We therefore generally proceeded to obtain comparability across variables and age groups by expressing scores in *T*-score form, with a mean of 50 and a standard deviation of 10, using as the reference group all records at first test at the time of the particular analysis. Results reported for the total data base (four cycles) were scaled using all 2810 subjects at first test as the reference group.

The Test of Behavioral Rigidity

The TBR was developed as part of an inquiry concerned with determining the dimensions of the trait of rigidity (Schaie, 1955). Three factors were identified: Motor–Cognitive Rigidity (*MCR*), Personality–Perceptual Rigidity (*PPR*), and Psychomotor Speed (*PS*). These factors are measured by combinations of eight scores obtained from the three subtests described in the following paragraphs.

1. *The Capitals Test.* This test was adapted from Bernstein's (1924) study of quickness and intelligence and represents the Spearmanian, or "functional," approach to the study of perseveration or rigidity. Subjects spend 2½ minutes copying a printed paragraph, which contains some words starting with capital letters, others spelled entirely in capitals, and some starting with lower case letters and with the remainder in capitals. Subjects must copy the paragraph in writing, not printing. In the second half of the test, subjects must recopy the paragraph in writing, substituting capitals for lower case letters and lower case letters for capitals. The Psychomotor Speed score is the number of words correctly copied in the first series (*Cap*). The Motor–Cognitive Rigidity score is the ratio (rounded to integers) of the number of correctly copied words in the second series to that in the first series (*Cap-R*).

2. *The Opposites Test.* This was a newly constructed test, following the work of Scheier and Ferguson (1952). Subjects are given 2 minutes each to work on three lists of words (at a third-grade level of difficulty), the first of which requires providing the antonym, and the second the synonym, of the stimulus word. The third list contains selected stimulus words from the previous lists which must be responded to by an antonym if the stimulus word is printed in lower case letters, but by a synonym if printed in capitals. The Psychomotor Speed score is the sum of correct responses in the first two lists (*Opp*). There are two Motor–Cognitive Rigidity scores. List 3 is examined for responses that are incorrect, responses started incorrectly, or erasures. The first score (*Opp-R1*) is obtained by the formula

$$100 - \frac{\text{Series 3 errors}}{\text{Series 3 total}} \times 100$$

The second score (*Opp-R2*) involves the formula

$$\frac{\text{Series 3 correct}}{\frac{1}{2}\ (\text{Series 1 correct} + \text{Series 2 correct})} \times 100$$

3. *The Questionnaire.* This 75-item true–false questionnaire contains 22 rigidity–flexibility items (*R* scale) and 44 masking social responsibility items from the California Psychological Inventory (Gough, 1957; Gough, McCloskey, & Meehl, 1952; Schaie, 1959b). It also contains 9 items (*P* scale) obtained from the Guttman scaling of a 17-item perseveration scale first used by Lankes (1915). These items were selected to be suitable for adults of all ages.

Factor Scores

The eight raw scores from the TBR subtests are first transformed into standard score form and then converted, scaled to factor scores by multiplication with the appropriate factor weights determined in the original study:

$$MCR = .25\ Cap\text{-}R + .35\ Opp\text{-}R1 + .40\ Opp\text{-}R2$$
$$PPR = .50\ R \text{ scale} + .50\ P \text{ scale}$$
$$PS = .60\ Cap + .40\ Opp$$

For the purposes of the 1977 study, the resultant scaled scores (also see Schaie & Parham, 1975) were converted to *T* scores with a mean of 50 and a standard deviation of 10, based on the 2810 records of subjects at first test.

Demographic Information

Demographic information that was routinely collected in this study includes social status variables (years of education, income, and occupational level), marital status, family size, and measures of mobility (frequency in change of living quarters, number of job changes, and number of different occupations during the preceding 5 years).

Health Behavior Variables

Since all of our subjects received their health care from the plan that constituted the population frame, it became possible to gain access to health history charts. These were systematically abstracted using the

International Classification of Diseases (ICDA; USPHS, 1968). Each visit to the outpatient clinic or each day in the hospital was coded by diagnosis. Annual frequency counts were constructed by illness incidents (single visits) and illness episodes (continuous series of visits for a specific diagnostic code). Physician ratings were obtained on the relative severity (impact on future health and well-being) of diagnostic entities along a normally distributed 11-point scale, permitting the construction of severity-weighted indexes (Schaie, 1973a).

Life Complexity Inventory

Beginning in 1964, we expanded the contextual information available on our subjects by routinely administering a questionnaire (originally administered as a structured interview) surveying the person's microenvironment (cf. Schaie & Gribbin, 1975a, 1975b). The major topics include individual work circumstances (with homemaking defined as a job), friends and social interactions, daily activities, travel experiences, physical environment, and educational pursuits (including individualized programs such as reading and writing). A cluster analysis permits scoring of individuals on the factors of Social Status, Subjective Dissatisfaction with Life Status, Homemaker Characteristics, Disengagement, Semiengagement, Family Dissolution, Noisy Environment, and Maintenance of Acculturation.

Description of the Data Base

The data base for the Seattle Longitudinal Study consists of the results of four major testing cycles (1956, 1963, 1970, 1977). In addition, there were three pilot studies concerned with the characteristics of the PMA test and the TBR in work with adults (1952, 1953, 1954). And finally, there were two collateral studies concerned with the consequences of shifting to an expanded sampling frame (1974) and of dealing with the aging of our test battery (1975).

Age and Cohort Frequencies

All of our subjects (with the exception of those involved in the pilot studies) were members of the Group Health Cooperative of Puget Sound. Our original 1956 population frame consisted of approximately 18,000 potential subjects. These were stratified by age and sex, and 25 men and 25 women were randomly selected for each year of birth from 1880 to 1939. After removing individuals who were not in the area, 2818 persons were actually contacted, of whom 910 agreed to participate. Testing then proceeded in small groups of 10 to 30 persons, until 25 men and 25 women had been tested in each 5-year birth interval over the age range of 22 to 70 years (cf. Schaie, 1958c, 1959a).

For the 1963 cycle, in addition to the longitudinal follow-up, approximately 3000 names were again drawn randomly from the 1956 population frame, after deleting names of all individuals tested in 1956. Of these, 996 persons ranging in age from 22 to 77 years were successfully tested. A similar procedure was followed in 1970: retesting survivors of the 1956 and 1963 panels, and establishing a new randomly selected panel (aged 22 to 84 years), consisting of 705 individuals. Our population frame having been virtually exhausted, we determined, by means of a collateral study, (Gribbin, Schaie, & Stone, 1976) that it would be feasible to shift to a sampling-with-replacement basis. For the 1977 cycle, we therefore sampled approximately 3000 persons from what had now become a 210,000-member health plan. Of these, 609 new subjects were tested.

Because of our 7-year intervals, all data have been reorganized in 7-year age and cohort groupings. Tables 4.1 and 4.2 show that we now have, for purposes of analysis, ten different data sets. These are as follows:

1. A cross-sectional sequence consisting of four independent data sets: Aa ($n = 500$)—seven cohorts tested in 1956 (mean ages: 25 to 67; mean birth years: 1889 to 1931); Bb ($n = 996$)—eight cohorts tested in 1963 (mean ages: 25 to 74; mean birth years: 1889 to 1938); Cc ($n = 705$)—nine cohorts tested in 1970 (mean ages: 25 to 81; mean birth years: 1889 to 1945); and Dd ($n = 609$)—nine cohorts tested in 1977 (mean ages: 25 to 81; mean birth years: 1896 to 1952) (see Table 4.1).

2. Longitudinal sequences involving six data sets include three 7-year, two 14-year, and one 21-year follow-ups: Ab ($n = 303$)—seven cohorts followed from 1956 to 1963; Bc ($n = 420$)—eight cohorts followed from 1963 to 1970; Cd ($n = 340$)—nine cohorts followed from 1970 to 1977; Ac ($n = 162$)—seven cohorts followed from 1956 to 1970; Bd ($n = 337$)—eight cohorts followed from 1963 to 1977; and Ad ($n = 130$)—seven cohorts followed from 1956 to 1977 (see Table 4.2).[3]

Successively longer studies, of course, involve subsets of those examined earlier. Our total data base consequently consists of 4504 test records

---

[3]In data set Ac, 81 subjects missed the 1970 testing. Similarly, in data set Ad, 2 subjects missed the 1970 testing, and 8 subjects missed both the 1963 and the 1970 data collections.

TABLE 4.1. Distribution of Subjects at First Test in the Main Study, by Cohort, Sex, and Test Occasion

	Mean year of birth (cohort)									
	1889	1896	1903	1910	1917	1924	1931	1938	1945	1952
1956 Sample Aa										
Mean age	(67)	(60)	(53)	(46)	(39)	(32)	(25)	—	—	—
M	38	35	35	35	36	33	38	—	—	—
F	38	37	35	30	35	37	38	—	—	—
T	76	72	70	65	71	70	76	—	—	—
1963 Sample Bb										
Mean age	(74)	(67)	(60)	(53)	(46)	(39)	(32)	(25)	—	—
M	38	64	68	62	79	71	52	42	—	—
F	39	63	64	81	76	79	70	58	—	—
T	77	127	122	143	155	150	122	100	—	—
1970 Sample Cc										
Mean age	(81)	(74)	(67)	(60)	(53)	(46)	(39)	(32)	(25)	—
M	26	46	42	38	40	44	34	28	31	—
F	24	42	49	42	49	43	50	37	40	—
T	50	88	91	80	89	87	84	65	71	—
1977 Sample Dd										
Mean age		(81)	(74)	(67)	(60)	(53)	(46)	(39)	(32)	(25)
M		27	37	35	35	40	32	37	29	28
F		31	33	38	37	37	37	36	33	27
T		58	70	73	72	77	69	73	62	55
Cohort totals										
M	102	172	172	170	180	188	156	107	60	28
F	101	173	181	191	197	196	195	131	73	27
T	203	345	353	361	377	384	351	238	133	55
Age totals										
Mean age	(25)	(32)	(39)	(46)	(53)	(60)	(67)	(74)	(81)	—
M	139	142	178	190	177	166	179	121	53	—
F	160	177	200	186	192	180	188	114	55	—
T	299	319	378	376	369	346	367	235	108	—

involving 120 subjects tested four times, 300 subjects tested three times, 734 subjects tested twice, and 1656 subjects tested one time only.

Demographic Characteristics

Our subject source provided a population frame that was reasonably close to the demographic pattern of the community from which it was drawn, although somewhat sparse at the lowest socioeconomic levels. I report here data on educational and occupational levels for the four successive cycles and discuss shifts caused by nonrandom subject attrition. Data on

TABLE 4.2. Distribution of Repeatedly Tested Subjects in the Main Study, by Cohort, Sex, and Test Occasion

	Mean year of birth (cohort)								
	1889	1896	1903	1910	1917	1924	1931	1938	1945
1963 Sample Ab									
Mean age	(74)	(67)	(60)	(53)	(46)	(39)	(32)	—	—
M	25	13	21	22	23	19	19	—	—
F	23	27	23	18	24	25	21	—	—
T	48	40	44	40	47	44	40	—	—
1970 Sample Ac									
Mean age	(81)	(74)	(67)	(60)	(53)	(46)	(39)	(32)	—
M	8	3	13	17	11	11	10	—	—
F	6	12	15	15	15	15	11	—	—
T	14	15	28	32	26	26	21	—	—
1970 Sample Bc									
M	8	19	19	29	36	36	23	9	—
F	6	24	22	45	37	43	38	26	—
T	14	43	41	74	73	79	61	35	—
1977 Sample Ad									
Mean age	(88)	(81)	(74)	(67)	(60)	(53)	(46)	(39)	(32)
M	3	2	10	16	9	8	10	—	—
F	2	7	14	15	12	11	9	—	—
T	5	9	24	31	21	19	19	—	—
1977 Sample Bd									
M	1	11	11	27	31	32	19	10	—
F	3	16	12	40	38	35	36	15	—
T	4	27	23	67	69	67	55	25	—
1977 Sample Cd									
M	4	13	18	21	24	28	17	14	10
F	4	17	16	25	29	26	28	22	24
T	8	30	34	46	53	54	45	36	34

income were also collected, but because of inflationary factors, they are not directly comparable across occasions.

Table 4.3 provides percentage figures for our ten data sets by educational level (grade school, high school, college, and graduate training), and Table 4.4 gives similar data for occupational level (unskilled = cleaning services, maintenance services, laborers, factory workers, fishermen; semiskilled = protective services, personal services, bartenders, custodians; skilled = mechanical–technical and clerical occupations; semiprofessional = managers, proprietors, professions requiring less than an MA degree; professional = requiring MA or more). Inspection of these tables shows that we, too, experience an upwardly skewed socioeconomic

TABLE 4.3. Educational Levels for Data Sets in the Main Study as Proportions of Each Sample

	First test	Second test	Third test	Fourth test
	Sample Aa	Sample Ab	Sample Ac	Sample Ad
0–8 years grade school	11.0	9.2	4.3	4.2
9–12 years high school	42.4	38.2	41.0	38.7
13–16 years college education	32.6	35.6	36.6	38.7
17 years plus graduate training	14.0	16.8	18.0	18.5
	Sample Bb	Sample Bc	Sample Bc	
0–8 years grade school	12.9	7.4	4.2	
9–12 years high school	46.1	43.8	42.3	
13–16 years college education	30.9	37.4	40.6	
17 years plus graduate training	10.0	11.4	12.9	
	Sample Cc	Sample Cd		
0–8 years grade school	10.1	4.4		
9–12 years high school	40.4	37.4		
13–16 years college education	35.5	40.6		
17 years plus graduate training	14.0	17.6		
	Sample Dd			
0–8 years grade school	9.7			
9–12 years high school	32.8			
13–16 years college education	38.0			
17 years plus graduate training	19.5			

TABLE 4.4. Occupational Level for Data Sets in the Main Study as Proportions of Each Sample

	First test	Second test	Third test	Fourth test
	Sample Aa	Sample Ab	Sample Ac	Sample Ad
Unskilled	4.5	4.0	2.5	3.3
Semiskilled	10.9	8.6	3.7	4.2
Skilled	47.2	45.5	48.1	47.5
Semiprofessional	32.2	36.0	40.1	38.3
Professional	5.3	5.9	5.6	6.7
	Sample Bb	Sample Bc	Sample Bd	
Unskilled	5.1	2.9	2.0	
Semiskilled	11.3	7.2	7.1	
Skilled	56.5	57.7	56.0	
Semiprofessional	23.4	29.0	31.7	
Professional	3.8	3.1	3.2	
	Sample Cc	Sample Cd		
Unskilled	.6	.9		
Semiskilled	5.0	5.0		
Skilled	48.7	44.1		
Semiprofessional	38.0	39.7		
Professional	7.7	10.3		
	Sample Dd			
Unskilled	6.6			
Semiskilled	8.0			
Skilled	30.6			
Semiprofessional	32.8			
Professional	22.0			

distribution upon completion of the acquisition of volunteer subjects. Some further complications arise because of an upward socioeconomic tendency due to nonrandom retest attrition and nonrandom outflow of members of the population frame over the successive random draws. Nevertheless, our sample structure does represent a reasonable approximation of the urban population structure, and shifts across samples, although worthy of further investigation, would not seem to interfere seriously with the comparison to be reported.

Age Differences in Ability Patterns

Our inquiry began by questioning whether factorially defined measures of different intellectual abilities would show differential age patterns. Before this question could be examined parametrically, it was first necessary to examine the applicability of the PMA test to an older population, with respect to both its level of difficulty and the continuing low correlation among the several abilities. Two pilot studies concerned with these questions are described in this section, and then cross-sectional data at first test are presented from the four testing cycles.

The Pilot Studies

Sixty-one subjects, gathered from the geriatric practice of my family physician and from the membership of the small first cohort of the San Francisco Senior Citizen Center, were given the PMA test under standard conditions. For purposes of analysis, they were arbitrarily divided into four approximately equal groups: ages 53 to 58, 59 to 64, 65 to 70, and 71 to 78 years. In the absence of available adult norms, and to permit comparison across the different ability measures, raw scores were converted into percentiles using norms for 17-year-old adolescents (Thurstone & Thurstone, 1949). The results of this study are shown in Figure 4.1. For the group in its 50s, stability is suggested for Verbal Meaning and Number (by the members' performance being slightly above the 50th percentile for the adolescent-norm group), but there is substantial lowering of scores for the other three tests. This differential pattern was observed for all groups, with some further lowering of scores into the 60s and apparent maintenance of the lower level for the group in its 70s (Schaie, Rosenthal, & Perlman, 1953).

On the off chance that this pattern might be caused by the differential effect of the slightly speeded instructions for older individuals, four of the tests were administered to 31 subjects without a time limit. Results shown in Figure 4.2 indicate that, if anything, differential performance levels were greater and in the same order as under the standard conditions of instruction.

The first pilot study also investigated the construct validity of the PMA 11–17 when used with older individuals. Intercorrelations between the five tests were computed and shown to be quite low, ranging from .07 for the correlation between Space and Number to .31 for that between Space and Reasoning. These correlations did not differ significantly from those

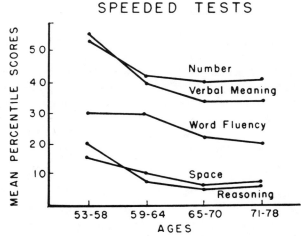

FIGURE 4.1. Performance of adult subjects on the *Primary Mental Abilities* test in percentile scores for an adolescent comparison group. (From "Differential Deterioration of Factorially 'Pure' Functions in Later Maturity" by K. W. Schaie, F. Rosenthal, and R. M. Perlman, *Journal of Gerontology*, 1953, *8*, 192. Copyright 1953 by the Gerontological Society. Reprinted by permission.)

obtained for an adolescent comparison group (Schaie, 1958d). Split-half reliabilities computed under the power-test condition were also quite satisfactory, all being above .92 after Spearman–Brown correction.

A second pilot study was conducted in 1954 as part of an investigation of the optimal limits of functioning of a small group of well-educated, community-dwelling older persons (more completely described in Schaie & Strother, 1968a). A campus and community appeal resulted in the selection of 25 men and 25 women, all college graduates with professional careers, ranging in age from 70 to 88 years (mean age 76.5 years). These subjects were all in fair to superior health and free of diagnosable psychiatric symptoms. The differential pattern of the first pilot study was replicated, with Number, Word Fluency, and Verbal Meaning substantially above values for Space and Reasoning. Also noteworthy was the finding that some of the octogenarians in the study still equaled or exceeded the adolescent mean on some of the verbal tests, even though it was most likely that this represented a decrement from a previous higher level suggested by their unusual population characteristics. Findings also suggested sex differences in favor of the males for the Space and Number tests and for the females for the three verbally oriented tests (Strother, Schaie & Horst, 1957).

Having satisfied ourselves that the test battery selected seemed appropriate for our questions, we next proceeded to design a parametric study for a representative sample across a broad spectrum of the adult age range in the context of investigating the relationship between intelligence and flexibility–rigidity (discussed later). This resulted in the first cross-sectional inquiry (Schaie, 1958c), the base of the main study.

The Cross-Sectional Studies

In this section, I review the findings of the first cross-sectional inquiry and its three successive replications. Having previously presented the first three of these studies in their historical sequence (Schaie, 1979), I here compare all four cross-sectional studies jointly, to see what can be learned from their simultaneous analysis.

FIGURE 4.2. The *Primary Mental Abilities* test administered as a power test to older adults. (From "Differential Deterioration of Factorially 'Pure' Functions in Later Maturity" by K. W. Schaie, F. Rosenthal, and R. M. Perlman, *Journal of Gerontology*, 1953, *8*, 194. Copyright 1953 by the Gerontological Society. Reprinted by permission.)

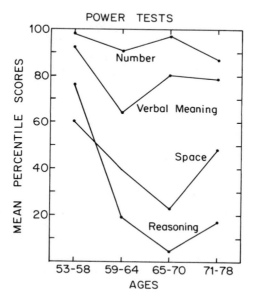

Differential Ability Patterns

Mean scores by age and sex for the five PMAs and the two composite measures of intellectual ability and educational aptitude are presented in Table 4.5. These values are graphed separately by sex for the 1956 and 1977 studies in Figure 4.3. The findings of the original pilot study were virtually replicated in our first cross-sectional inquiry. For the oldest groups, relative performance remains best for Word Fluency and Number; it is worst for the men for Reasoning, and for the women for Space. Age gradients appear to be steepest for Space and Reasoning, and flattest for Number. But note an interesting age/cohort-by-sex interaction. Young men are relatively superior on Space, Reasoning, and Word Fluency, but do less well on Verbal Meaning and Number. The earlier cohorts in advanced age, however, reverse this order for Reasoning and Number. Likewise, young women are relatively highest on Reasoning, Verbal Meaning, and Word Fluency, with lower performance on Space and Number. For them, Reasoning, Verbal Meaning, and Number reverse their positions.

Except for the age/cohort extremes, the 1956 study noted greater dispersion of the ability profile for women than for men. Another noteworthy finding was the differential attainment of peak performance levels by age. For example, age 25 is the peak age for Reasoning, but the peak for Word Fluency appears at age 46; for Number, women showed peak performance at age 53 (see Table 4.5).

By 1977, the pattern of ability at age 25 remained very similar to that found in the first study, conducted 21 years earlier, but the sex difference in profile dispersion was no longer found, and extension of the data base to more advanced ages resulted in a somewhat different ability pattern by the 80s. Examination of Figure 4.3 shows that the oldest male age/cohort does relatively best on Space and Reasoning, and worst on Verbal Meaning. The oldest women, by contrast, do best on Word Fluency, and worst on Space and Verbal Meaning.

Age-Difference Patterns across Time

It is commonplace to suggest that age-difference data are not directly relevant to testing propositions about ontogenetic change. Such data in the context of cross-sectional sequences, however, are quite relevant to testing the proposition that age-difference patterns remain invariant over time and, given certain assumptions, to evaluating the magnitude of cohort differences and time-of-measurement (period) effects. The issue of whether or not age-difference patterns remain invariant over time has been addressed previously, with the conclusion that there are indeed

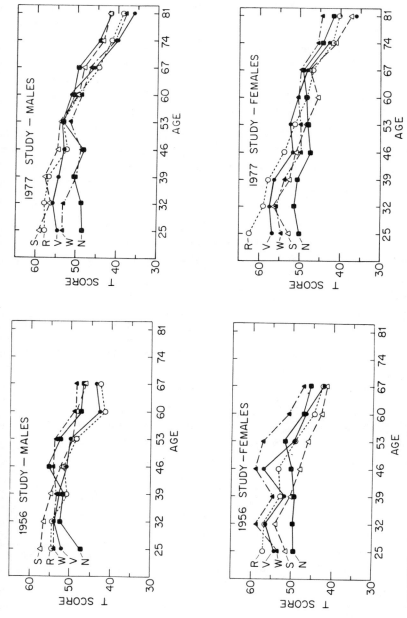

FIGURE 4.3. Mean scores for the five *Primary Mental Abilities* for the 1956 and 1977 cross-sectional studies, by sex.

87

TABLE 4.5. *T*-Score Means for the Cross-Sectional Data, by Age, Sex, and Study[a]

Age	1956			1963			1970			1977		
	M	F	T	M	F	T	M	F	T	M	F	T
						Verbal Meaning						
25	52.2	54.1	53.1	53.0	54.3	53.8	53.3	55.1	54.3	54.6	56.9	55.7
32	54.0[b]	56.5	55.3[b]	53.8	55.1[b]	54.5	52.8	55.3	54.2	55.8[b]	57.4[b]	56.7[b]
39	52.7	51.9	52.3	55.3[b]	54.0	54.6[b]	54.7	54.3	54.4	54.4	56.3	55.3
46	51.0	57.0[b]	53.8	51.1	53.2	52.1	54.1	55.7[b]	54.9	53.9	51.9	52.8
53	49.8	49.4	49.6	47.6	49.6	48.8	55.8[b]	54.1	54.9[b]	54.2	52.2	53.3
60	42.8	46.7	44.8	45.4	49.0	47.3	54.5	51.1	52.7	51.3	50.5	50.9
67	43.6	42.4	43.0	41.7	44.3	43.0	44.6	46.8	45.8	45.6	48.0	46.9
74	—	—	—	40.0	40.1	40.0	39.0	41.9	40.4	40.0	42.8	41.3
81	—	—	—	—	—	—	37.5	38.9	38.1	36.0	36.2	36.1
						Space						
25	57.2[b]	51.3	54.2	59.3[b]	56.5[b]	57.7[b]	6.2[b]	55.8[b]	58.1[b]	58.9[b]	52.9	55.9
32	56.6	53.9[b]	55.2[b]	56.9	52.8	54.6	60.2	55.6	57.6	56.5	56.3[b]	56.4[b]
39	54.7	50.1	52.4	56.7	50.3	53.4	57.5	51.0	53.6	57.7	52.8	55.3
46	52.7	48.0	50.4	54.3	48.9	51.6	56.0	52.0	54.0	54.5	51.0	52.6
53	49.9	45.9	47.9	51.1	47.2	48.9	53.4	49.1	51.0	53.9	48.3	51.2
60	48.3	42.7	45.4	49.4	45.4	47.3	52.2	47.3	49.6	49.7	45.6	47.6
67	46.3	41.6	43.9	45.3	41.8	43.6	47.0	41.3	44.0	48.2	47.4	47.8
74	—	—	—	43.2	40.1	41.6	43.0	40.0	41.6	43.7	41.0	42.4
81	—	—	—	—	—	—	42.9	37.8	40.4	42.0	37.2	39.4
						Reasoning						
25	54.6[b]	57.1[b]	55.8[b]	58.6[b]	59.7[b]	59.2[b]	60.8	60.2[b]	60.5[b]	57.7[b]	62.3[b]	60.0[b]
32	54.5	56.8	55.8	54.9	58.0	56.7	58.2	59.2	58.8	57.7	59.0	58.4
39	50.8	52.9	54.1	54.9	54.1	54.5	55.3	54.5	54.8	56.8	57.8	57.3
46	51.5	53.3	52.3	49.6	52.0	50.8	53.5	54.4	53.9	52.5	53.9	53.3
53	48.5	49.2	48.9	46.7	47.5	47.2	51.0	52.0	51.6	53.3	51.2	52.3
60	41.4	44.6	43.1	44.1	46.5	45.4	51.6	49.1	50.2	49.7	48.3	49.0
67	42.8	42.6	42.7	40.9	41.8	41.3	42.5	43.5	43.0	44.7	46.8	45.8
74	—	—	—	42.0	38.7	40.3	39.8	40.5	40.1	41.4	41.7	41.5
81	—	—	—	—	—	—	39.1	39.1	39.1	38.6	40.3	39.5
						Number						
25	47.2	49.6	48.4	50.0	50.5	50.3	51.7	50.1	50.8	48.5	50.0	49.2
32	52.7	49.8	51.2	54.5	52.1	53.2	57.2[b]	49.6	52.9	48.8	51.5[b]	50.2
39	52.0	49.4	50.7	55.8[b]	51.8	53.7[b]	53.3	50.8	51.8	50.7	50.7	50.7
46	55.3[b]	50.2	53.0[b]	52.3	52.6[b]	52.4	54.5	53.2	53.9	48.2	47.4	47.8
53	52.6	51.9[b]	52.2	50.6	48.4	49.3	54.2	53.5	53.8	53.5[b]	48.0	50.9[b]
60	47.4	47.1	47.2	49.0	48.2	48.6	55.4	53.7[b]	54.5[b]	50.8	48.4	49.5

TABLE 4.5. (*Continued*)

Age	1956 M	F	T	1963 M	F	T	1970 M	F	T	1977 M	F	T
						Number (*continued*)						
67	46.8	45.5	46.2	46.5	43.9	45.2	48.2	46.8	47.4	49.7	49.1	49.4
74	—	—	—	46.1	41.2	43.6	44.1	43.8	44.0	44.3	44.3	44.3
81	—	—	—	—	—	—	43.5	38.0	40.9	41.9	41.7	41.8
						Word Fluency						
25	53.9	53.7	53.8	51.1	53.1	52.2	52.5^b	53.9^b	53.3^b	53.4^b	54.5	53.9
32	53.9	58.9	56.6	49.3	54.8^b	52.5^b	47.8	52.8	50.7	53.2	56.0^b	54.7^b
39	53.4	54.9	54.1	52.4^b	51.2	51.8	49.0	51.1	50.3	50.2	53.8	51.9
46	54.3^b	59.0^b	56.5^b	49.5	51.9	50.7	50.7	53.6	52.1	48.9	49.9	49.4
53	53.7	57.3	55.5	45.9	48.9	47.5	52.1	53.3	52.8	51.6	49.9	50.8
60	48.9	50.9	49.9	47.0	50.9	49.0	50.4	50.2	50.3	48.9	50.4	49.7
67	48.6	47.2	47.9	44.0	45.0	44.5	42.4	45.3	44.0	46.5	48.5	47.5
74	—	—	—	44.8	44.2	44.5	39.9	43.0	41.4	40.4	45.7	42.9
81	—	—	—	—	—	—	41.2	43.5	42.3	38.0	44.5	41.5
						Intellectual Ability						
25	52.9	53.7	53.3	55.0	55.6	55.3	56.9	55.7^b	56.2^b	54.9^b	56.2	55.5
32	55.3^b	55.8^b	55.6^b	55.1	55.6^b	55.4^b	57.1^b	55.0	55.9	54.8	57.0^b	56.0^b
39	53.3	52.0	52.7	56.6^b	53.0	54.7	54.9	52.8	53.6	54.6	55.0	54.8
46	54.3	54.1	54.2	51.8	52.4	52.1	55.0	54.9	54.9	51.3	50.5	50.9
53	51.4	51.2	51.3	48.2	47.9	48.0	54.2	53.4	53.7	54.3	49.6	52.1
60	44.7	45.5	45.1	46.3	47.4	46.9	54.1	51.0	52.4	50.2	48.2	49.2
67	44.4	42.5	43.5	42.3	41.5	41.9	43.9	43.5	43.7	46.4	47.6	47.0
74	—	—	—	41.8	38.2	32.9	39.1	39.9	39.4	40.0	41.3	40.6
81	—	—	—	—	—	—	38.7	36.2	37.5	37.0	37.5	37.3
						Educational Aptitude						
25	52.8	55.1	53.9	54.5	56.0	55.4^b	55.4^b	56.8^b	56.2^b	55.5	58.6^b	57.0
32	54.4^b	57.0^b	55.7^b	54.3	56.1^b	55.3	54.4	56.6	55.7	56.7^b	58.3^b	57.5^b
39	52.4	52.3	52.4	55.5^b	54.4	54.9	55.1	54.5	54.8	55.3	57.1	56.2
46	51.3	56.5	53.7	50.8	53.1	52.0	54.2	55.7	55.0	53.9	52.6	53.2
53	49.5	49.2	49.3	48.3	47.3	49.1	54.9	53.9	54.3	54.3	52.1	53.3
60	42.0	45.9	44.0	44.8	48.3	46.6	54.1	50.7	52.3	51.1	49.9	50.5
67	42.9	42.0	42.5	40.9	43.3	42.1	43.6	45.7	44.8	45.1	47.6	46.4
74	—	—	—	39.7	39.2	39.5	38.4	41.0	39.7	39.7	42.0	40.8
81	—	—	—	—	—	—	37.2	38.2	37.7	35.9	36.3	36.1

^{a}For cell frequencies, refer to Table 4.1.
^{b}Peak performance level.

statistically significant shifts in such patterns. This conclusion was based in part upon the finding of significant age-by-time interactions in time-sequential analyses and of cohort-by-time interactions in cross-sequential analyses (Schaie, Labouvie, & Buech, 1973; Schaie & Strother, 1968c; Stone, Schaie, & Gonda, 1979).

To examine shifts in age profiles as well as peak ages across all four cross-sectional studies, mean scores for Verbal Meaning (to represent a verbal, or "crystallized," measure) and Reasoning (to represent nonverbal, or "fluid," abilities) have been graphed in Figure 4.4. What seems most apparent is that, until the 70s, means observed at the same ages tend to fall at progressively higher levels for successive cohorts attaining a given age. Most noteworthy for Verbal Meaning (see Figure 4.4) is the apparent shift in substantial age differences to older levels. For example, the first appearance of a noteworthy age difference disadvantaging the older group occurred in 1956 and 1963 between those aged 46 and those aged 53; a similar gap for the 1970 and 1977 studies does not appear until we examine the difference between those aged 60 and those aged 67. This phenomenon is not quite as pronounced for Reasoning (see Figure 4.4), since age differences follow a more linear pattern. Nevertheless, it is interesting to note that the largest age difference in 1956 occurred between those aged 53 and those aged 60, but in 1977, between those aged 60 and those aged 67. It is suggested that these age-difference shifts may have considerable impact on the public perception of ability differences between age groups and may affect the decision process with respect to the age at which an attempt should or must be made to rejuvenate the work force (whether by voluntary or mandatory retirement or by discharge for cause).

Although, in the absence of independent information, it is not possible to unconfound cohort and period effects unambiguously, it is possible, from data such as ours, to estimate cohort differences over fixed time periods by comparing the performance of successive cohorts over the age ranges for which both have been observed. These cohort differences will, of course, be confounded with period effects, but if computed over the same period, they will be equally affected. In our case, it is possible to generate nine cohort differences for ten 7-year birth cohorts born from 1889 to 1952.[4] Table 4.6 provides mean differences in T-score points computed for all cohort combinations in our study. This table should be read as follows: A positive value indicates that the performance of the cohort identified in the column exceeds, on average, by the value given at equivalent ages, the performance of the cohort identified by the row. A

[4]Cohort comparisons are based on three age levels, or an age range of 14 years, except for the cohorts born in 1945 and 1952, for which only two and one comparisons, respectively, are available.

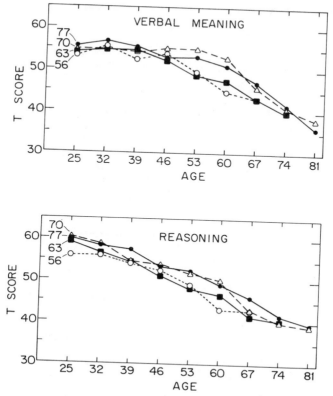

FIGURE 4.4. Comparison of mean scores for the abilities of Verbal Meaning and Reasoning for the four cross-sectional studies.

negative value, conversely, means that the performance of the row (earlier born) cohort exceeds that of the column (later born) cohort.

It is interesting to note that the composite index of Intellectual Ability will tend to obscure cohort differences because of differential cohort trends of the subtests; for this composite index, only the three earliest born cohorts differ significantly from later born cohorts. On the other hand, when the abilities are considered separately, it becomes clear from these data that there are systematic advances in cohort level for Space and Reasoning; a significant disadvantage with respect to later cohorts is apparent up to the cohort born in 1931! A similar pattern prevails for Verbal Meaning, but here only cohorts born in 1917 or earlier are at a significant disadvantage when compared with later born cohorts.

TABLE 4.6. Mean Advantage of Later Born Cohorts over Earlier Born Cohorts, in *T*-Score Points[a]

	Mean year of birth								
	1896	1903	1910	1917	1924	1931	1938	1945	1952
Verbal Meaning									
1889	−.28	1.77	2.93*	3.83*	4.98*	3.97*	4.21	5.70*	7.11*
1896		2.05*	3.21*	4.11*	5.26*	4.25*	4.49*	5.98*	7.39*
1903			1.16	2.06*	3.21*	2.20*	2.44*	3.93*	5.34*
1910				.90	2.05*	1.04	1.28	2.77*	4.18*
1917					1.15	.14	.38	1.87	3.28*
1924						−1.01	−.77	.72	2.13
1931							.24	1.73	3.14*
1938								1.49	2.90
1945									1.41
Space									
1889	−.44	.59	2.99*	3.37*	4.55*	3.98*	6.67*	6.30*	4.07*
1896		1.03	3.43*	3.81*	4.29*	4.42*	7.11*	6.74*	4.51*
1903			2.40*	2.78*	3.96*	3.39*	6.08*	5.71*	3.48*
1910				.38	1.56	.99	3.68*	3.31*	1.08
1917					1.18	.61	3.30*	2.93*	.70
1924						−.57	2.12*	1.75	−.78
1931							2.69*	2.32	.09
1938								−.37	−2.60
1945									−2.23
Reasoning									
1889	−.39	1.41*	3.39*	3.91*	6.08*	6.30*	8.95*	9.36*	8.87*
1896		1.80*	3.78*	4.30*	6.47*	6.69*	9.34*	9.75*	9.26*
1903			1.98*	2.50*	4.67*	4.89*	7.54*	7.95*	7.46*
1910				.52	2.69*	2.91*	5.56*	5.97*	5.48*
1917					2.17*	2.39*	5.04*	5.45*	4.96*
1924						.22	2.87*	3.28*	2.79
1931							2.65*	3.06*	2.57
1938								.41	−.08
1945									−.49
Number									
1889	.13	1.42	3.08*	2.73*	3.22*	1.23	1.39	1.33	−1.25
1896		1.29	2.95*	2.60*	3.09*	1.10	1.26	.20	−1.38
1903			1.66	1.31	1.80	−.19	−.03	−1.09	−2.67
1910				−.35	.14	−1.85	−1.69	−2.75*	−4.33*
1917					.49	−1.50	−1.34	−2.40*	−3.98*
1924						−1.99	−1.83	−2.89*	−4.47*

TABLE 4.6. (*Continued*)

	Mean year of birth								
	1896	1903	1910	1917	1924	1931	1938	1945	1952
Number (*continued*)									
1931							.16	−.90	−2.48
1938								−1.06	−2.64
1945									−1.58
Word Fluency									
1889	−2.44*	−2.39*	−3.45*	−3.84*	−4.80*	−7.57*	−8.20*	−5.65*	−4.28*
1896		.05	−1.01	−1.40	−2.36*	−5.13*	−5.76*	−3.21*	−1.74
1903			−1.06	−1.45	−2.41*	−5.18*	−5.81*	−3.26*	−1.79
1910				−.39	−1.35	−4.12*	−4.75*	−2.20	−.73
1917					−.96	−3.73*	−4.46*	−1.81	−.44
1924						−2.77	−3.40*	−.85	.52
1931							−.63	1.92	3.29
1938								2.55*	3.92*
1945									1.37
Intellectual Ability									
1889	−.76	.82	1.79	1.92*	2.92*	1.17	2.41*	2.89*	2.18
1896		1.58	2.55*	2.68*	3.68*	1.93*	3.17*	3.65*	2.94
1903			.97	1.10	2.10*	.35	1.59	2.07	1.36
1910				.13	1.13	−.62	.62	1.10	.39
1917					1.00	−.75	.49	.97	.26
1924						−1.75	−.51	−.03	−.74
1931							1.24	1.72	1.01
1938								.48	−.23
1945									−.71
Educational Aptitude									
1889	.57	2.70*	4.80*	5.64*	7.13*	7.38*	7.43*	8.97*	9.62*
1896		2.13*	4.23*	5.07*	6.56*	6.81*	6.86*	8.20*	9.05*
1903			2.10*	2.94*	4.43*	4.68*	4.73*	6.07*	6.92*
1910				.84	2.33*	2.58*	2.63*	3.97*	4.82*
1917					1.49	1.74	1.79	3.13*	3.98*
1924						.25	.30	1.64	2.49
1931							.05	1.39	2.24
1938								1.34	2.19
1945									.85

[a]Negative values indicate that the later born cohort is at a disadvantage compared to the earlier born cohort.

*$p < .01$.

Very different findings occur for Number and Word Fluency. The former shows positive cohort changes up to about the 1910 cohort. Then there is a plateau and a shift to successive lowering of performance level. As a consequence, the 1924 cohort is found to exceed both earlier and later born cohorts; both the youngest and oldest cohorts are now at a disadvantage compared to the middle cohorts. For Word Fluency, we find a successive lowering of cohort level until the 1938 cohort, but improvement for the last two cohorts. Earlier born cohorts consequently have an advantage over the later born ones, with the recent reversal noted previously.

Finally, on the issue of cohort differences, and possibly of considerable significance in terms of policy implications, are the findings for the composite index of Educational Aptitude. This index shows systematic positive cohort shifts, with a significant disadvantage to all cohorts born in 1917 or earlier. This would seem to be another convincing demonstration of the importance of taking generational differences into account in planning present and future adult education activities.

Estimates of Time-of-Measurement Effects

Just as we estimated cohort differences by matching across age and assuming equivalence of period effects across cohorts, so can we use these data to estimate time-of-measurement (period) effects by matching across age and assuming equivalence of cohort effects across periods. This computation has been done by considering the four sets of first-time tests totaled across the range of mean ages from 25 to 67 years (for which all sets are represented four times). The three period effects obtained are shown in Table 4.7 for the total sample, since no significant time-by-sex interactions were found. A significant negative time trend occurred from 1956 to 1963 only for Word Fluency. However, there was a positive trend for all variables to 1970. No further changes occur in the period to 1977, except for Number, which now shows a significant negative trend. For the two composite indexes, significant positive time trends are found only for the period from 1963 to 1970.

Several alternative explanations can be offered for these period effects. They may simply represent systematic testing effects, that is, small but systematic changes in test administration and scoring procedures, which, even with the best documentation, can readily slip into longitudinal studies. Although unlikely for large samples, it is nevertheless possible that these differences represent systematic sampling error, attributable to changes in the composition of the pool from which the successive samples were drawn. Another explanation would be a systematic cohort trend,

TABLE 4.7. Time-of-Measurement (Period) Effects for Three Periods, in T-Score Points

	Verbal Meaning			Space			Reasoning			Number		
	1963	1970	1977	1963	1970	1977	1963	1970	1977	1963	1970	1977
1956	.43	2.73	2.74*	.95	2.27*	2.27*	.57	2.87*	3.43*	.76	2.37*	−.04
1963		2.30*	2.31*		1.32	1.32		2.29	2.85*		1.61*	−.80
1970			.01			.00			.56			−2.41*

	Word Fluency			Intellectual Ability			Educational Aptitude		
	1963	1970	1977	1963	1970	1977	1963	1970	1977
1956	−3.66*	−2.99*	−2.39*	−.12	1.98*	1.31	.50	2.94*	3.11*
1963		.67	1.27		2.10*	1.43		2.43*	2.61*
1970			.60			−.66			.18

Note. n = 1956, 500; 1963, 919; 1970, 567; 1977, 481.
*p < .01.

95

although cohort differences should only minimally affect our period estimates since, for each estimate, five of the seven cohorts used were identical. Finally, these findings might represent true period effects caused by a systematic environmental impact such as the improvement of media, increased utilization of adult education opportunities, improved nutrition, and increased application of preventive health care principles.

These matters are not trivial because longitudinal data should be adjusted for period effects if generalizable age functions are to be adduced. In particular, this becomes an important problem when age functions are constructed from short-term longitudinal studies applying sequential data-gathering strategies. Data from cross-sectional sequences make it possible to consider certain adjustments to observed longitudinal data. If one assumes that there are no significant cohort differences, then it would be possible to adjust longitudinal change data by means of values such as were presented in Table 4.7. If cohort differences are presumed to exist, then more complicated corrections may be needed. In that case, one would compute age/time-specific time lags from the cross-sectional data in Table 4.5, subtract the appropriate cohort differences given in Table 4.6, and use the resultant age/cohort-specific estimates of period effect to correct age-change data. The first correction would be most appropriate in the case of testing effects or true period effects occurring across all age/cohort levels. The second correction would be appropriate for use in dealing with age/cohort-specific sampling fluctuations. Examples of such adjustments as applied to our longitudinal data are given later in this chapter.

Age Changes in Intellectual Abilities

In this section, I review the results of our longitudinal studies. As indicated in the discussion of the data base, these consist of three 7-year follow-ups, two 14-year follow-ups, and one 21-year follow-up. Again, I have not repeated the presentation of data and conclusions presented elsewhere (Hertzog, Schaie, & Gribbin, 1978a; Schaie, 1979; Schaie & Labouvie-Vief, 1974; Schaie & Parham, 1977; Schaie & Strother, 1968b; Stone & Schaie, 1979). Instead, I have tried to integrate the entire longitudinal data base in order to provide estimates of age change based on the largest available number of subjects for each age interval, to consider how such estimates are affected if one applies corrections for period and cohort differences (based on the estimates presented in the previous section), and to deal with the comparability of age changes obtained from the replications of the 7-year and 14-year studies.

Estimates of Age Changes Based on 7-Year Data

If one is interested in forecasting ontogenetic change within individuals and in generating normative data that would permit assessing whether a particular individual change is within the average range of individual differences in such change or is excessive and thus a possible clue to behavior pathology, it would seem best to obtain estimates averaged over as many cohorts and times of measurement as possible. I have therefore computed average IAC estimates for 7-year intervals from ages 25 to 88, based upon the 1601 test records for which measures were available for two points 7 years apart. Table 4.8 provides the resultant average IACs in *T*-score units, with positive values indicating gain from the age listed in the row to that listed in the column, and negative values indicating age decrement. The values in the diagonals of that table represent the observed within-group age changes. The off diagonals are the cumulated changes obtained by summing the appropriate successive within-group values. These estimates are needed in order to determine the ages at which decrement from some previous age reaches statistical significance. One can immediately see that statistically significant cumulative age decrement from any previous age was not observed for any of the variables prior to age 67. Several variables showed modest increment in young adulthood. Such increment above performance shown at age 25 remained significant for Verbal Meaning until age 60. It also led to the finding that cumulative age decrement, when taken from age 25, reached statistically significant magnitudes for Verbal Meaning, Reasoning, and Word Fluency only at age 74, and for Space as late as age 81.

To permit comparison of the longitudinal findings with the cross-sectional data reported earlier, I have computed estimated mean-level values for the most recent cohort, the one born in 1952. The average IACs were cumulated and added to the base values for the 1952 cohort that were empirically obtained when it was observed at age 25. These predicted values were computed for the total sample and separately by sex; they are given in Table 4.9. It is interesting to note that the resultant data suggest far later attainment of peak performance levels than was suggested by the cross-sectional studies. Peak performance ages for the total group occurred for Number at 32, for Reasoning at 39, and for Space and Word Fluency as well as the Index of Intellectual Ability at 46, but for Verbal Meaning and the Index of Educational Aptitude not until 53. There were also sex differences in peak-level ages, with Space peaking for men at 46, but for women at 53; Reasoning peaking for women already at 39, but for men not until 53; and Number peaking for men at 32, but for women at 46. Differences for the composite indexes indicated that men peaked on the

TABLE 4.8. Cumulative Age Changes from 7-Year Longitudinal Data, in *T*-Score Points

	Mean age								
	32	39	46	53	60	67	74	81	88
					Verbal Meaning				
25	1.60	2.98*	3.68*	4.02*	3.73*	1.75	−1.33	−4.95*	−14.01*
32		1.38	2.08*	2.42*	2.13*	.15	−2.93*	−6.55*	−15.61*
39			.70	1.04	.75	−1.23	−4.31*	−7.93*	−16.99*
46				.34	.05	−1.93	−5.01*	−8.63*	−17.69*
53					−.29	−2.27*	−5.35*	−8.97*	−18.03*
60						−1.98*	−5.06*	−8.68*	−17.74*
67							−3.08*	−6.70*	−15.76*
74								−3.52*	−12.58*
81									−9.06*
					Space				
25	1.31	1.45	1.97	1.88	1.58	−.14	−2.46	−4.92*	−8.76*
32		.14	.66	.57	.27	−1.45	−3.77*	−6.23*	−10.07*
39			.52	.43	.13	−1.59	−3.91*	−6.37*	−10.21*
46				−.09	−.39	−2.11*	−4.43*	−6.89*	−10.73*
53					−.30	−2.02*	−4.34*	−6.80*	−10.64*
60						−1.72	−4.04*	−6.50*	−10.34*
67							−2.32*	−4.78*	−8.62*
74								−2.46	−6.30*
81									−3.84
					Reasoning				
25	.65	1.04	1.07	.94	.77	−1.12	−3.80*	−5.89	−9.42*
32		.39	.42	.29	.12	−1.77	−4.45*	−6.54	−10.07*
39			.03	−.10	−.27	−2.16*	−4.84*	−6.93*	−10.46*
46				−.13	−.30	−2.19*	−4.87*	−6.96*	−10.49*
53					−.17	−2.06	−4.74*	−6.86*	−10.36*
60						−1.89*	−4.67*	−6.66*	−10.19*
67							−2.68*	−4.77*	−8.30*
74								−2.09	−5.62*
81									−3.53
					Number				
25	1.59	.97	1.15	.14	−.23	−2.73*	−5.37*	−9.56*	−16.44*
32		−.62	−.44	−1.45	−1.82	−4.32*	−6.96*	−11.15*	−18.03*
39			.18	−.83	−1.20	−3.70*	−6.34	−10.53*	−17.41*
46				−1.01	−1.38	−3.88*	−6.52*	−10.71*	−17.59*
53					−.37	−2.87*	−5.51*	−9.70*	−16.58*

TABLE 4.8. (*Continued*)

	Mean age								
	32	39	46	53	60	67	74	81	88
Number (continued)									
60						−2.50*	−5.14*	−9.33*	−16.21*
67							−2.64*	−6.83*	−16.71*
74								−4.19*	−11.07*
81									−6.88*
Word Fluency									
25	.69	.75	1.29	.49	−.34	−2.24	−4.67*	−8.06*	−10.40*
32		.06	.60	−.20	−1.03	−2.03	−5.36*	−8.75*	−11.09*
39			.54	−.26	−1.09	−2.99*	−5.42*	−8.81*	−11.15*
46				−.80	−1.63	−3.53*	−5.96*	−9.35*	−11.69*
53					−.83	−2.73*	−5.16*	−8.55*	−10.89*
60						−1.90	−4.33*	−7.72*	−10.06*
67							−2.43	−5.82*	−8.16
74								−3.39*	−5.73
81									−2.34
Intellectual Ability									
25	1.92	2.75*	3.66*	3.38*	3.41*	.90	−2.17	−6.37*	−12.55*
32		.83	1.74	1.45	1.49	−1.02	−4.09*	−8.29*	−14.47*
39			.91	.63	.66	−1.85	−4.92*	−9.12*	−15.30*
46				−.28	−.25	−2.76*	−5.83*	−10.03*	−16.21*
53					.03	−2.48*	−5.55*	−9.75*	−15.93*
60						−2.51*	−5.58*	−9.78*	−15.96*
67							−3.07*	−7.27*	−13.46*
74								−4.20	−10.38*
81									−6.18
Educational Aptitude									
25	1.49	2.29*	2.78*	2.87*	2.35*	.41	−2.72*	−5.98*	−14.33*
32		.80	1.29	1.38	.86	−1.08	−4.21*	−7.47*	−15.82*
39			.49	.58	.06	−1.88*	−5.01*	−8.27*	−16.62*
46				.09	−.43	−2.37*	−5.50*	−8.76*	−17.11*
53					−.52	−2.46*	−5.59*	−8.85*	−17.20*
60						−1.94	−5.07*	−8.33*	−16.68*
67							−3.13*	−6.39*	−14.74*
74								−3.26*	−11.61*
81									−8.35*

*$p < .01$.

TABLE 4.9. Predicted Mean Values, in T Scores, of Performance at Successive Ages for a Cohort Born in 1952 (from 7-Year Longitudinal Data)

Age	Verbal Meaning			Space			Reasoning			Number			Word Fluency			Intellectual Ability			Educational Aptitude		
	M	F	T	M	F	T	M	F	T	M	F	T	M	F	T	M	F	T	M	F	T
25	52.8	56.5	55.2	60.0	55.6	58.7	58.7	60.0	59.5	49.0	51.4	50.5	52.7	54.3	53.8	55.0	56.6	56.0	54.4	57.8	56.6
32	55.8	57.4	56.8	61.6	56.8	58.4	58.6	61.0	60.2	52.5[a]	51.9	52.1[a]	52.6	55.3	54.5	57.8	58.0	58.0	56.8	58.8	58.1
39	57.4	58.6	58.2	61.8	56.8	58.6	58.5	61.8[a]	60.6[a]	50.6	52.2	51.5	53.2	55.0	54.5	58.0	59.2	58.8	57.8	59.5	58.9
46	58.8	58.8	58.9	62.5[a]	57.2	59.1[a]	61.4	61.4	60.6	50.8	52.3[a]	51.7	53.4[a]	55.8[a]	55.1	58.8[a]	60.2	59.7[a]	59.0	59.5[a]	59.4
53	59.4[a]	58.9[a]	59.2[a]	62.3	57.3[a]	59.0	59.2[a]	61.0	60.5	50.1	51.1	50.7	52.5	55.1	54.3	58.6	59.8	59.4	59.4[a]	59.2	59.5[a]
60	58.8	58.8	59.0	61.7	57.2	58.7	58.8	61.3	60.3	49.1	51.2	50.3	51.9	54.1	53.4	58.2	60.3[a]	59.4	58.7	57.6	59.0
67	56.5	57.9	57.0	59.3	56.0	57.0	57.0	59.3	58.4	46.0	49.1	47.8	50.4	51.9	51.5	55.4	57.9	56.9	56.2	56.1	57.0
74	53.9	54.4	43.9	56.9	53.8	54.7	54.6	56.4	55.7	43.2	46.6	45.2	47.7	49.7	49.1	52.7	54.6	53.9	53.4	52.7	53.9
81	50.6	50.7	50.4	52.7	51.9	52.2	52.3	54.4	53.6	38.8	42.6	44.8	46.2	44.8	45.7	48.4	50.4	49.7	50.2	49.4	50.6
88	45.9	37.8	41.2	50.0	44.5	48.4	51.8	48.2	50.1	34.5	33.4	34.1	46.6	39.7	43.4	45.1	41.4	43.5	46.2	37.2	42.3

[a]Peak performance level.

summary score of Intellectual Ability at 46, but women at 60, while for Educational Aptitude, women peaked at 46, but men at 53.

Estimates of Age Changes Based on 14-Year Data

In addition to the longitudinal age-change estimates available from our replicated 7-year studies, it is also possible to obtain estimates that derive from the observation of the same individuals, albeit a smaller number of them, over 14 years. The data used for this analysis were obtained by combining 14-year retest observations for the samples followed from 1956 to 1970 and from 1963 to 1977, a total of 617 subjects. Table 4.10 gives average 14-year changes in T-score points. These data suggest significant 14-year gains in performance for Reasoning and Word Fluency to age 39 and for Verbal Meaning, Space, and the composite indexes to age 46. Significant 14-year loss is shown for Number by age 53, for Word Fluency by age 60, and for the remaining measures by age 67. Note again that absolute loss for the fluid abilities is less than for the crystallized and speeded measures.

Estimates of Age Changes Based on 21-Year Data

A final set of age-change data is provided from the 128 subjects who were observed over the entire 21-year duration of the study. This data set, of course, has been systematically attrited, and its subsets have small cell frequencies; the resultant estimates of age change must clearly be treated with much caution. They are reported here, however, because of the scarcity of longitudinal data for such an extended time span.

TABLE 4.10. Average 14-Year Longitudinal Age Changes, in T-Score Points

Age range	n	Verbal Meaning	Space	Reasoning	Number	Word Fluency	Intellectual Ability	Educational Aptitude
25–39	46	2.59*	.87	1.72*	1.09	2.26*	4.11*	.85
32–46	98	1.47*	.95	.17	−.65	−.39	1.04*	1.06*
39–53	109	.18	−.20	.01	−1.44*	−.04	−.31	−.16
46–60	122	.25	−.29	−.43	−1.81*	−1.38*	−.50	−.64
53–67	123	−2.36*	−2.52*	−1.76*	−2.13*	−2.68	−3.34*	−2.23*
60–74	61	−5.00*	−3.62*	−3.56*	−3.97*	−3.45*	−5.03*	−4.81*
67–81	49	−6.22*	−5.16*	−4.88*	−5.71*	−6.79*	−7.68*	−6.08*

*$p < .01$.

Table 4.11 shows significant gains over the 21-year span from 25 to 46 years for Verbal Meaning and the index of Educational Aptitude. Statistically significant age decrement over a 21-year interval is shown first for Word Fluency at age 60 and for Space, Number, and the index of Intellectual Ability at age 67; for Verbal Meaning, Reasoning, and the index of Educational Aptitude, however, such decrement is shown beginning at age 74.

Cumulative age decrement from the three data sources do not differ a great deal at most ages. The 14-year data generally show the least decrement, but in further discussions, I consider primarily the cumulated 7-year longitudinal data because of the larger sample size.

Adjustments for Cohort, Period, and Dropout Effects

The validity of the within-cohort estimates of ontogenetic age change in ability can, of course, be questioned by arguing that the age-change data are obviously specific to the cohorts from which they were gained, that the data are affected by idiosyncratic period effects, and that the unavoidable attrition (dropout) in longitudinal panels will largely lead to results generalizable only to the favorable subset remaining in this study. The first two confounds will affect primarily the estimated magnitudes of change, and the third will determine reported levels of functioning. I have already described, in the section on age differences, the approach used to estimate cohort and period effects. Some additional comments are in order with regard to dropout.

TABLE 4.11. Average 21-Year Longitudinal Age Changes, in *T*-Score Points

Age range	*n*	Verbal Meaning	Space	Reasoning	Number	Word Fluency	Intellectual Ability	Educational Aptitude
25–46	19	3.26*	3.10	1.26	1.00	−1.33	1.63	3.11*
32–53	19	.58	−.79	−.58	−.84	−3.05	−1.25	.33
39–60	21	−1.19	−1.38	−.57	−.219	−4.67*	−2.57	−1.00
46–67	31	−1.22	−3.84*	−2.08	−4.94*	−6.06*	−4.87*	−1.35
53–74	24	−4.42*	−3.13*	−4.42*	−4.42*	−7.30*	−6.63*	−4.66*
60–81	9	−7.11*	−1.89	−5.00*	−2.78	−10.00*	−6.67*	−6.99*
67–88	5	−9.80	−5.60	−6.20	−10.80*	−5.60	−10.60*	−9.60

*p < .01.

Dropout Effects

These effects were examined cross-sectionally by cohort after a single 7-year period (Baltes, Schaie, & Nardi, 1971) and by means of sequential analyses for two successive 7-year intervals (Schaie, Labouvie, & Barrett, 1973) and for three successive 7-year intervals (Gribbin & Schaie, 1977, 1979). What is at issue here is that, because of selective mortality and other factors (such as health and motivation), there has been selective attrition with respect to the dependent variables of interest. As a result, retest survivors are found to score higher at first test than individuals who drop out. This finding has been replicated and is consistent for all but the youngest cohorts. (See Figure 4.5 for an example of the dropout analysis reported for the 1970 data collection.) There are, however, a number of age-by-dropout interactions, and it was discovered more recently that selective dropout is particularly severe only upon the second test occasion. That is, once longitudinal participants are brought back for follow-up, it appears that further attrition then becomes reasonably random.

The findings on selective dropout suggest that age gradients, such as those shown in Figure 4.6, will have inflated base levels even when there is no age-by-dropout interaction. Most typically, they will lead to more favorable conclusions than are warranted regarding the magnitude of change as a function of base levels; that is, levels of functioning may be predicted that are higher than may be warranted. The first correction for longitudinal estimates, therefore, would seem to be the assignment of base levels to values obtained from the full, rather than the attrited, sample.

Correction for Period Effects

Since longitudinal estimates confound age and period effects, which may either attenuate or heighten age changes, it is desirable to correct estimates for known period effects. As shown in the preceding section, the least biased estimates of period effects will be the average time-lag difference between successive occasions across all available cohorts equating for age. To the extent that stable age estimates were obtained by averaging across several cohorts, this correction, however, will be excessive for some cohorts and too low for others, and a further adjustment is therefore needed.

Correction for Cohort Effects

Given the fact that time-lag estimates confound period and cohort effects, it is next necessary to subtract out the appropriate cohort differ-

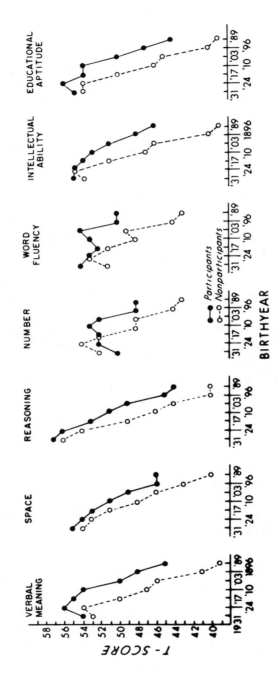

FIGURE 4.5. Cohort differences for retest participants and dropouts. (From "Selective Attrition Effects in a Fourteen Year Study of Adult Intelligence" by K. W. Schaie, G. V. Labouvie, and T. J. Barrett, *Journal of Gerontology*, 1973, *28*, 331. Copyright 1973 by the Gerontological Society. Reprinted by permission.)

104

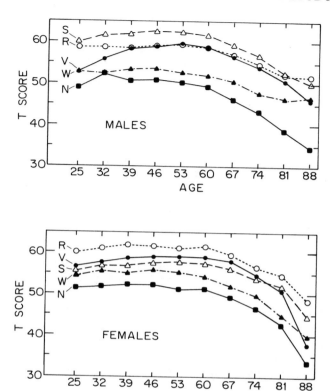

FIGURE 4.6. Longitudinal estimates of age changes for men and women for the *Primary Mental Abilities* from 7-year data.

ences, estimated across all available times of measurement. The final approach taken consequently involves longitudinal estimates obtained by averaging across all available age changes within individuals, adjusting for period effects weighted according to the size of subsamples involved for each period, and adding cohort adjustments weighted for the cohorts involved in each particular age change. In the following subsection, where we attempt to get a better understanding of the significance of age changes, data are reported both in their directly observed form and after correction for dropout, period, and cohort effects.

Estimates from Successive Independent Samples

As long as one's interest is primarily in age changes expressed as population parameters, it is possible to obtain estimates of age change by computing mean differences at successive ages within cohorts, where each measurement point is represented by a distinct random sample drawn from the same parent population. In this case, we assume, of course, that the population has remained stable, or that there has indeed been sampling with replacement, and further, that we have indeed succeeded in drawing comparable successive random samples. If these assumptions are justified (see Gribbin, Schaie, & Stone, 1976), then it is possible to compute age-change estimates that are controlled for the effects of testing and experimental mortality. Such estimates based upon successive independent samples have previously been reported for more limited data across a 7-year time interval (Schaie & Parham, 1977). Tables 4.12, 4.13 and 4.14 present estimates based upon the entire data set for within-cohort changes estimated over 7-, 14-, and 21-year intervals, respectively.

The 7-year estimates in Table 4.12 may be compared with the longitudinal panel data to be found in the diagonals of Table 4.8. They are generally quite comparable, except for small but statistically significant age decrements from age 46 to 53 for Reasoning, Word Fluency, and the composite indexes, decrements not seen in the repeated measurement data. Further, the gains into the 30s shown in the panel data fail to be significant in the independent-sample data except for the Number variable.

TABLE 4.12. Average 7-Year Age Changes Estimated from Independent Samples, in T-Score Points

Age range	n^a	Verbal Meaning	Space	Reasoning	Number	Word Fluency	Intellectual Ability	Educational Aptitude
25–32	247/249	1.40	−.51	−.54	2.25*	−.53	.81	1.02
32–39	257/307	.12	−1.68	−1.55	−.68	−1.90	−1.26	.69
39–46	305/311	−.50	−.38	−1.04	−.72	−1.31	−1.04	−.62
46–53	307/309	−1.28	−1.67	−2.00*	−1.75	−2.73*	−2.45*	−1.89*
53–60	302/274	−.80	−1.13	−1.02	−.90	−2.27*	−1.53	−.85
60–67	274/291	−3.08*	−2.34*	−2.86*	−2.76*	−4.39*	−3.95*	3.23*
67–74	294/235	−3.25*	−1.95*	−1.59	−2.34*	−2.54*	−3.01*	−3.14*
74–81	165/107	−3.07*	−1.64	−.91	−2.44	−1.04	−2.30*	−2.64*

^{a}First number indicates frequency at first age; second number indicates frequency at second age.
*$p < .01$.

TABLE 4.13. Average 14-Year Age Changes Estimated from Independent Samples, in T-Score Points

Age range	n^a	Verbal Meaning	Space	Reasoning	Number	Word Fluency	Intellectual Ability	Educational Aptitude
25–39	176/157	1.44	−1.51	−1.48	1.92	−1.93	−.09	2.32*
32–46	192/156	−1.04	−1.56	−2.63*	−1.68	−3.72*	−2.60*	−1.46
39–53	221/166	−.63	−1.76	−1.20	.16	−1.18	−.78	.18
46–60	220/252	−1.16	−2.50*	−1.96	−.66	−3.58*	−2.34	−1.42
53–67	213/164	−2.88*	−2.54*	−3.62*	−2.36	−5.74*	−4.30*	−3.28*
60–74	194/158	−5.23*	−4.19*	−3.40*	−3.78*	−7.32*	−6.00*	−5.10*
67–81	203/108	−5.88*	−3.81*	−2.70*	−4.38*	−4.28*	−5.27*	−5.36*

^{a}First number indicates frequency at first age; second number indicates frequency at second age.
*$p < .01$.

In a like manner, the 14-year estimates in Table 4.13 can be compared with the panel data in Table 4.10. Major discrepancies occur for Reasoning and Word Fluency, where the independent-sample data show a significant difference over the 32- to 46-year-old range, and for Space, where significant decrement is found by age 60. On the other hand, statistically significant decrement for number does not appear until age 74, much later than in the panel data.

Finally, comparison may be made between the 21-year data in Table 4.14 and the corresponding panel values in Table 4.11. Again, there is substantial correspondence, the major exceptions being, in the independent samples, an earlier appearance of decrement for Word Fluency and a later decrement for Number.

TABLE 4.14. Average 21-Year Age Changes Estimated from Independent Samples, in T-Score Points

Age range	n^a	Verbal Meaning	Space	Reasoning	Number	Word Fluency	Intellectual Ability	Educational Aptitude
25–46	76/79	−.29	−1.64	−2.53	−.64	−4.38*	−3.41	−.73
32–53	70/77	−2.01	−3.93	−3.49	−.31	−5.79*	−3.56	−2.47
39–60	71/72	−1.42	−4.81*	−2.86	−1.16	−4.47*	−3.52	−1.84
46–67	65/73	−6.91*	−2.76*	−6.56*	−3.59	−8.90*	−7.14*	−7.50*
53–74	70/70	−8.29*	−5.45*	−7.36*	−7.95*	−12.61*	−10.70*	−8.64*
60–81	72/58	−8.75*	−5.98*	−3.54*	−5.45*	−8.42*	−7.84*	−7.89*

^{a}First number indicates frequency at first age; second number indicates frequency at second age.
*$p < .01$.

Individual Differences in Intraindividual Change

Until recently, most analyses of intellectual change in adulthood (including our own) have confirmed themselves to the comparison of mean-level changes. One of the major rationales and the exclusive advantage of the longitudinal study is the possibility of tracking individual patterns of change. If we are simply interested in the range of talent at given ages, we do not need longitudinal data because only interindividual differences are involved. What we are concerned with here are the interindividual differences in IAC, that is, the differences in scores between successive occasions.[5] There are a number of different approaches that can be taken to summarize the resultant findings. Two indexes will be reported on here: The first is the standard deviation (SD) of the difference scores for successive longitudinal observations; the second involves creating a ratio in standard deviation units, obtained by dividing the observed mean differences for successive ages within the same group by the standard deviation of the difference scores.

Range of Individual Variability

Inspection of Table 4.15 immediately calls attention to the fact that individual differences of change scores are considerably smaller than those of the base scores ($SD = 10$). Although there is a predominant pattern for such differences to be smallest in midlife, with a subsequent increase in variability, there are exceptions. Thus variability once again declines for all abilities except Verbal Meaning as the 80s are reached. Also, it is apparent that different abilities show differential variability patterns, with the result that the greatest regularity is found in the composite indexes, which minimize the apparent age-by-ability interaction in variability.

Magnitude of Average Contrasted to Individual Differences

One way in which the significance of average IAC can be assessed is by contrasting the magnitude of mean changes to the range of individual differences of such change. Cohen (1977), in his work on power analysis, has proposed that one might distinguish between small, moderate, and large effects, depending upon the amount of overlap, as expressed in

---

[5] For detailed discussions of the differential information to be gathered from longitudinal studies with respect to intraindividual and interindividual differences, see Baltes and Nesselroade (1979) or Schaie and Hertzog (1982).

TABLE 4.15. Standard Deviations of Longitudinal 7-Year Difference Scores, in
T-Score Points

Age range	n	Verbal Meaning	Space	Reasoning	Number	Word Fluency	Intellectual Ability	Educational Aptitude
25–32	109	5.00	7.29	5.77	5.78	6.90	4.28	4.63
32–39	184	4.14	5.64	4.92	6.33	7.84	3.88	3.64
39–46	255	3.62	6.96	4.78	5.78	7.13	3.84	3.89
46–53	261	4.06	6.57	4.91	5.15	5.46	3.60	3.37
53–60	275	5.45	6.76	5.10	5.30	6.32	3.83	4.67
60–67	231	6.71	6.30	4.78	5.21	7.47	4.42	6.17
67–74	181	7.34	6.03	5.40	6.99	5.97	4.67	6.15
74–81	88	7.42	4.98	4.51	5.14	5.88	4.21	6.44

standard deviation units, between individuals in groups to be compared.
In the case of repeated measurement studies such as the longitudinal
investigation of age changes, the overlap in question refers to the proportion of individuals who would be identified as having shown reliable
change from one occasion to the next. By Cohen's definition, a difference
of .2 SD units reflects a small change (roughly 15% nonoverlap), a
difference of .5 SD a moderate change (33% nonoverlap), and .8 SD a
large change (47% nonoverlap).

Table 4.16, using these criteria, suggests small, positive changes for
Verbal Meaning through age 46 and for Number to age 32. The earliest

TABLE 4.16. Average Individual 7-Year Change as Expressed in Standard Deviations
of Individual Differences of IAC

Age range	n	Verbal Meaning	Space	Reasoning	Number	Word Fluency	Intellectual Ability	Educational Aptitude
25–32	109	+.32[a]	+.18	+.11	+.28[a]	+.10	+.45[b]	+.32[a]
32–39	184	+.33[a]	+.02	+.08	−.10	+.01	+.21[a]	+.22[a]
39–46	255	+.47[b]	+.07	+.01	+.03	+.08	+.24[a]	+.13
46–53	261	+.08	−.01	−.03	−.20[a]	−.15	−.08	+.03
53–60	275	−.05	−.04	−.03	−.07	−.13	+.01	−.11
60–67	231	−.30[a]	−.27[a]	−.40[a]	−.41[a]	−.25[a]	−.57[b]	−.31[a]
67–74	181	−.42[a]	−.38[a]	−.50[b]	−.38[a]	−.41[a]	−.66[b]	−.51[b]
74–81	88	−.47[b]	−.49[b]	−.46[b]	−.82[c]	−.58[b]	−1.00[c]	−.51[b]

[a]Small effect.
[b]Moderate effect.
[c]Large effect (see Cohen, 1977).

small decremental change occurs for Number by age 53, but it is not until age 67 that small or moderate changes are found for all abilities. Note that a large effect in terms of individual differences in IAC is detected for the index of Intellectual Ability by age 81; the only separate ability that shows such a sizable effect is Number.

Changes in Ability Structure with Age

What is labeled by some as "qualitative change with age" can, in the psychometric frame of reference, be most directly addressed by considering measurement models that can be fitted to the intercorrelations between abilities across age and cohort groups. Although a number of authors (e.g., Cohen, 1957) have addressed the question of factorial invariance of intelligence test batteries across different age groups, such work has been primarily cross-sectional in nature (but see Horn & McArdle, 1980). Until the seminal work by Joreskog and his associates (e.g., Joreskog, 1979; Joreskog & Sorbom, 1977) became available, there had also been conceptual and algorithmic obstacles to a careful analysis of this question. The powerful new methods developed by Joreskog and his associates were recently applied to part of our data base by Hertzog (1979), with his findings being substantially replicated by means of the LISREL IV and COFAMM algorithms.

Hertzog fitted both test-specific and occasion-specific models to our longitudinal sample tested in 1956, 1963, and 1970. He found reasonable fits for both approaches, using the entire sample. To study age-related changes in factor structure, he followed the occasion-specific model by merging the three-occasion data from the two panels first tested in 1956 and 1963. To obtain samples large enough for model fitting, he aggregated across sex and cohorts to obtain three subsamples: young adult (mean ages 30, 37, and 44), middle-aged (mean ages 42, 49, and 56), and old adult (mean ages 58, 65, and 72). Factor covariances remained high over the three occasions for all three samples, indicating consistency of individual differences across time. Group differences occurred primarily as a function of differences in factor variance, the youngest group having the least variance and the oldest the greatest. There were also differences in change in variability over time. Consistently with the between-group findings, within-group variance changes were in the direction of reduced variance from age 30 to 44, but increased variances were found from age 58 to 72. Hertzog's examination of the test-specific model showed greatest covariances in the older group, all above .5 when standardized, suggesting that the factor space had become more oblique as the sample aged. In addition, factor variability was greatest for Verbal Meaning, Reasoning, and Number, and least for Space.

The preceding analyses led me to conclude that the ability domain investigated in our studies does indeed retain its structural properties across the adult life span and that the conclusions based on our parametric findings cannot be questioned on the basis of possible changes in variable meaning over time. Nevertheless, the increase in factor variance with increasing age suggests that group norms for the older age levels may be less representative of individual change than is true at earlier ages.

Practical Significance of Age Changes and Cohort Differences

Scientists frequently become preoccupied with demonstrating the presence or absence of reliable differences and relationships. What is often ignored is the question of whether or not the obtained differences are substantial enough to warrant use of the data as the factual basis for implementing public policy decisions or in deciding practical matters. In this section, I provide an intuitive rationale on how to proceed in this matter, giving relevant estimates of age changes over 7-year intervals from 25 to 81 years and similar estimates of cohort differences for cohorts with average birth years from 1889 to 1952.

To be sure, one must first demonstrate that there are indeed statistically reliable differences within or between groups. Once this is done, however, we need some reasonable approach to determining effect size. One such approach, advocated by Cohen (1977), is to consider the amount of change or difference in standard deviation units, where .2 SD is considered a small effect, .5 SD moderate, and 1 SD large. The reader may wish to apply these criteria directly to the data presented in Tables 4.6, 4.7, 4.8, 4.10, and 4.11. It will be found that the differences reported there generally range from small to moderate.

Assessing the Practical Significance of Age Changes

The preceding approach is problematic because it assumes that a large difference on a variable having modest variability is equivalent to a much smaller change in a variable with large variability. In addition, the approach does not at all account for the fact that absolute performance at base age may be a psychologically more meaningful scaling base than taking one's departure from the overall population average. We think we have addressed these issues by the alternative approach of computing cumulative age changes as proportions of performance level at age 25. Obviously, our data permit similar computations using any other base ages within the range of our study. In the case of the repeated-measurement data, this approach leads to quite conservative estimates, actually favoring greater decrement than might be found in individuals monitored over their entire adult age span, because the favorably selected members of a panel will tend to have scores that regress toward the sample mean (cf. Baltes, Nesselroade, Schaie, & Labouvie, 1972).

Using this approach, it is possible to compute an index that represents average performance at an older age as a proportion of the base performance at a younger age, with 100 indicating the level at base. Table 4.17 provides a tabulation for this index for men, women, and all subjects combined, based on the 7-year data reported previously in the section on age changes in abilities. The reader may wish to apply these criteria directly to the data presented in Tables 4.6, 4.7, 4.8, 4.10, and 4.22. It will be found that the differences reported there generally range from small to moderate.

I have recently advocated that a reasonable approach to appraising the practical significance of cumulative age changes or cohort differences is to take recourse to the traditional psychometric assumption that one probable error (*PE*) about the mean defines the middle 50% (average) range of performance on mental abilities, assuming their normal distribution in the population (cf. Matarazzo, 1972, pp. 124–126). Given this premise, it follows that average cumulative decrement attains practical importance where such loss reduces the average performance of the older sample more than 1 *PE* below the mean of the younger comparison base, that is, a drop to the lower quartile of the base group. Table 4.17 indicates that a drop of such magnitude occurs for male panel members by age 74 for Number and by age 81 for Space, Reasoning, and the index of Intellectual Ability. For the female panel members, however, the criterion of a practically significant drop is reached for all parameters, except Space, by age 81.

As was previously indicated, our estimates may be inflated by favorable time-of-measurement effects, favorable cohort differences, and (for the panel members) favorable dropout effects. Table 4.18 therefore gives corrected values for all subjects across sex (to obtain more stable corrections from the resultant larger cell sizes). The corrections appear to affect primarily the variables of Reasoning, Number, and Word Fluency. As corrected, age decrement on Reasoning now attains practical significance by age 74, and decrement on Word Fluency as early as age 67. Number seems most heavily affected by these corrections. The adjusted scores suggest attainment of peak performance as late as age 60 and no drop of practical importance over the age range studied.

TABLE 4.17. Performance at Various Ages as a Proportion of Performance at Age 25

Age	Verbal Meaning	Space	Reasoning	Number	Word Fluency	Intellectual Ability	Educational Aptitude
				Males			
32	109	106	99	117	100	108	108
39	115	107	99	108	101	109	111
46	119	110	101	109	102	111	114
53	121	109	102	105	99	110	116
60	119	107	100	100	97	109	113
67	112	97	94	85	93	101	106
74	103	88	84	71^a	85	93	97
81	93	72^a	76^a	49^a	81	81^a	87
−1 PE at age 25	81	77	83	72	83	85	83
				Females			
32	102	105	104	102	103	104	103
39	106	106	106	104	102	108	105
46	106	107	105	104	104	110	105
53	107	108	104	99	102	109	104
60	107	107	105	99	100	110	103
67	104	102	98	90	93	104	99
74	94	92	87	79	87	94	89^a
81	84^a	83	80^a	61^a	73^a	83^a	80^a
−1 PE at age 25	89	71	83	76	85	87	89
				All subjects			
32	105	106	102	111	102	106	104
39	109	106	104	108	102	108	107
46	111	108	104	104	104	110	108
53	112	108	104	96	101	110	107
60	111	106	103	91	99	110	107
67	105	99	96	78	94	103	101
74	96	89	86	67^a	87	94	92
81	85	79	78^a	55^a	77^a	82^a	82^a
−1 PE at age 25	85	72	83	74	84	80	86

[a]Index is more than 1 PE below the mean of the 25-year-old base comparison group.

TABLE 4.18. Performance at Various Ages as a Proportion of Performance at Age 25, Corrected for Time Lag, Cohort Differences, and Dropout

Age	Verbal Meaning	Space	Reasoning	Number	Word Fluency	Intellectual Ability	Educational Aptitude
32	105	103	100	107	105	105	104
39	109	105	103	110	105	108	106
46	109	107	102	120	104	109	105
53	113	106	103	122	94	111	108
60	111	105	101	126	90	110	105
67	107	103	91	122	83^a	104	100
74	97	90	81^a	109	81^a	92	91
81	87	79	73^a	90	62^a	80^a	84^a
−1 PE at age 25	85	72	82	73	84	86	86

[a]Index is more than 1 PE below the mean of the 25-year-old base comparison group.

Assessing the Practical Significance of Cohort Differences

The approach we have taken to estimating the practical significance of age changes can also be applied to the evaluation of the impact of cohort differences. We can take the estimates of cumulative cohort differences given in Table 4.6 and express them as proportions of the performance level of the youngest cohort (born in 1952). Cohort obsolescence indexes can then be computed for each cohort with average birth years from 1896 to 1945. Once again, it is assumed that the value of 1 PE below the mean (the lower quartile) of the younger cohort can serve as an indicator that the obsolescence of the earlier born (older) cohort assumes practical importance. Since cohort differences are strictly interindividual difference variables, these data are based on the cohort-differences estimated from the unattrited samples at first test (see Table 4.19).

On the basis of these data, it becomes obvious that obsolescence effects on intelligence-test performance are also quite ability-specific. Older cohorts even seem to have an advantage over the more recent ones on both Word Fluency and Numbers skills. On the other hand, substantial obsolescence effects are noted on Reasoning, with obvious implications for effectiveness in decision-making situations. More modest obsolescence effects are noted as well for Verbal Meaning and Space. For the composite indexes, this results in a balancing out for the global index of intelligence (further evidence as to the questionable value of such indexes in studies of aging), while the index of Educational Aptitude shows a substantial disadvantage for cohorts born around the turn of the century.

Factors Affecting Change in Intellectual Performance

Our attempt to provide an accurate description of age change in intellectual abilities over the adult life span is obviously only a first step in our understanding of that process. Throughout our endeavors, we attempted to collect collateral data that might help us to discover some explanatory principles. That is, we wanted to know whether there are predictable causal factors that will distinguish between individuals who show rapid or slow decline in advanced age or that at least will permit us to describe differential patterns of aging. In this section, I briefly describe the result of our investigation of health history factors, of environmental factors, and of the relationships of certain personality variables to performance on the PMA test.

Health and Change in Intelligence

Since our research participants all received their health care in a single system throughout the period of our studies, it was possible to gain access to fairly complete health histories. We soon discovered, however, that although physicians were very good at recording their diagnostic findings, very little work had been done on retrieving and quantifying health

TABLE 4.19. Performance of Various Cohorts as a Proportion of the Performance of the Cohort Born in 1952

Mean year of birth	Verbal Meaning	Space	Reasoning	Number	Word Fluency	Intellectual Ability	Educational Aptitude
1945	96	110	102	108	96	102	98
1938	92	112	100	113	89	101	94
1931	91	100	91	112	90	97	94
1924	94	103	90	122	98	102	93
1917	90	97	82	120	101	99	88
1910	88	95	80^a	122	102	99	86
1903	85	84	73^a	115	105	96	80^a
1896	79^a	79	67^a	107	105	92	74^a
1889	79^a	81	68^a	107	112	94	72^a
−1 PE for 1952 cohort	85	75	81	70	83	85	85

^{a}Index is more than 1 PE below the mean of the 1952 base cohort.

history contents in such a manner that they could be meaningfully related to behavioral data. For this purpose, what was needed was a method of characterizing health trauma by specific type of disease as well as by the likely impact of such disease upon the individual's future life experience (Schaie, 1973a). Although we did not solve this problem to our complete satisfaction, we approached a solution by charting each clinic or hospital contact of our participants by the appropriate code from the ICDA (USPHS, 1968). Individual incidents of disease were further linked into "disease episodes," which refers to the entire set of consecutive physician contacts for a particular health problem.

The problem of determining the impact of illness was addressed by charting the health records of 150 participants over a 14-year period. Although the ICDA lists 8000 possible classifications, only approximately 800 diagnoses were actually encountered. After overlapping categories were collapsed, it was possible to reduce the diagnostic terms to a total of 448 classifications. These were then Q-sorted by 12 physicians (6 internal medicine and 6 psychiatry residents) on an 11-point scale ranging from benign to extremely severe with respect to the impact of each disease entity upon the future health and well-being of a patient encountering such conditions (Parham, Gribbin, Hertzog, & Schaie, 1975). When cumulative incident and episode illness scores were correlated, to our initial surprise, only minor relationships were found. Low-level negative correlations occurred between cumulative health trauma (limited to the episode-weighted scores) and Verbal Meaning and Word Fluency.

Although some variance associated with verbal behavior decrement could be attributed to cumulative disease, it is perhaps not unreasonable to expect only low-level relationships when a gross, cumulative grab bag of diseases is considered jointly. A more fine-grained analysis requires attention to specific disease entities in relation to cognitive function. This line of inquiry was therefore pursued with respect to individuals with known cardiovascular disease (CVD). A number of interesting findings occurred upon detailed analysis of 155 panel members followed over a 14-year period. At first glance, it appears that CVD can be implicated in lowered function on all of the variables included in our study. Further analyses, however, reduce the plausibility of this conclusion. For example, controlling for cohort membership (CVD is simply more prevalent in the older cohorts!) wipes out the effect for Space and Word Fluency. And when socioeconomic status (SES) is taken into consideration, the effect of CVD upon decremental change in intellectual performance remains significant for Number and the composite index of Intellectual Ability (Hertzog, Schaie, & Gribbin, 1978). Although these data suggest that CVD does indeed contribute to intellectual decline, the amount of variance accounted for is relatively small, and moreover, effects may be indirect rather than causally specific. That is, CVD may lead to life-style changes that in turn more directly affect cognitive behavior.

Further studies of the effect of disease upon cognitive function conducted with our data base more recently have utilized the LISREL approach to testing the model fit for certain hypothesized relationships and as a by-product have estimated path coefficients indicative of the proportion of variance predicted (Stone, 1980). These analyses were conducted separately for the younger and the older half of our longitudinal samples. Disease categories investigated included circulatory disorders, digestive disorders, genitourinary disorders, infective and parasitic diseases, disease of the musculoskeletal system and connective tissues, neoplasms, diseases of the nervous system and sense organs, and diseases of the respiratory system. No relationships were found for the younger group. For the older group, circulatory disorders, neoplasms, and musculoskeletal disorders were found to be significant predictors of intellectual change over 7-year intervals. The causal direction was verified by an appropriate falsification study, in which change in intelligence was not found to predict significantly changes in health status on the disease categories cited. The proportions of variance accounted for were small, ranging from 1.6% for neoplasms to 4.4% for CVD. These values must be evaluated, however, in the context of the massive stability of intellectual ability. That is, about 85% of the variance is predicted by prior ability level, and consequently, a maximum total of 15% of the variance could be attributed to ability extraneous factors.

Environmental Factors and Changes in Intelligence

The effect of environmental factors upon the maintenance or decline of intelligence was investigated by considering a number of variables present in the day-to-day experience of adults that might be assumed to make a difference with respect to intellectual functioning. These variables were assessed by means of a specially constructed survey instrument, LCI (cf. Gribbin, Schaie, & Parham, 1980). Initial analyses of this questionnaire for 140 participants for whom 14-year intellectual ability data were available yielded eight item clusters representing (1) Subjective Dissatisfaction with Life Status, (2) Social Status, (3) Noisy Environment, (4) Family Dissolution, (5) Disengagement from interaction with the environment, (6) Semipassive Engagement with the environment, (7) Maintenance of Acculturation, and (8) Female Homemaker Characteristics.

Negative correlations were found between age and the cluster scores for Social Status, and positive correlations occurred between age and the Disengagement and Family Dissolution patterns. Considering the relationship of LCI cluster scores and intellectual ability, we found that all ability variables correlated positively with the Social Status and negatively with the Disengagement cluster. Further, Verbal Meaning, Word Fluency, and Educational Aptitude correlated positively with Maintenance of Acculturation; Word Fluency correlated positively with Noisy Environment; Space correlated negatively with Female Homemaker Characteristics; and Number and the index of Intellectual Ability correlated negatively with Family Dissolution. Correlations were also computed between 7-year changes in intellectual ability and LCI scores. The results of the latter analysis suggest that a personal environment characteristic of Disengagement and Family Dissolution is associated with cognitive decrement, while Dissatisfaction with Life Status appeared to be associated with maintenance or improvement of cognitive functions (Gribbin, Schaie, & Parham, 1980).

An alternative approach to the study of the relationship between personal environment and cognitive change consists of the investigation of differential change in ability over time for individuals with different lifestyles. For this purpose, we examined cluster profiles for those persons who had been followed for the first 14 years of the study. Four major types emerged: Type 1 persons were mostly males of average social status and average level of acculturation, who lived with intact families in a relatively noise-free environment and who were quite engaged with life, but who voiced strong dissatisfaction with their life status. Type 2 persons had high social status, with which they were well satisfied; they had intact families, lived in noisy and accessible environments, and indicated above-average maintenance of acculturation. Type 3 persons were mostly women of average social status who were homemakers with intact family situations and average life-status satisfaction. These persons were low on maintenance of acculturation, but lived in accessible and noisy environments and reported activities reflecting passive engagement. Type 4 persons were almost all female, but, on average, older than the previous type. They had low social status, with which they were dissatisfied, and they were lowest on reported activities, whether active or passive. They lived in largely noise-free, but also inaccessible, environments and were highest on family dissolution. When a change in mental abilities is related to these life-style types, a pattern of relationship becomes evident. Table 4.20 lists average change scores for the PMAs over a 14-year period by life-style type. It is quite apparent that the first two engaged types generally show maintenance or gain, whereas the most disengaged type, the widowed homemakers, show clear evidence of decrement (cf. also Schaie & Gribbin, 1975b).

The LISREL approach has also been used to estimate effects accounted

TABLE 4.20. Cumulative Change in Mean Score on Cognitive Variables over a 14-Year Period, by Subject Type, in T-Score Points[a]

	Type 1	Type 2	Type 3	Type 4	All types
Verbal Meaning	+3.6	+1.4	−.2	−4.4	+.4
Space	+1.0	−1.1	+1.5	−.1	+.2
Reasoning	−.2	+1.1	−1.9	−3.1	−.7
Number	+1.0	+.8	−.9	−1.6	
Word Fluency	−3.5	−4.2	−6.2	−5.6	−4.8
Intellectual Ability	+.5	−.2	−1.9	−4.0	−1.1
Educational Aptitude	+2.8	+1.3	−.6	−4.3	+.1

[a]Positive values denote incremental change; negative values denote decremental change.

for in intellectual change by items surveyed in the LCI. Hertzog (1979) estimated the contribution of a latent SES variable (derived from the observed variables of years of education, family income, and occupational status) at initial testing to the initial level of intellectual ability. Regression coefficients under different model assumptions ranged from .50 to .60. Interestingly enough, SES predicted the initial level of ability, but not change in ability. With respect to the specific ability variables, SES was related to all but Space, with maximum correlation with Verbal Meaning. In a related study, Stone (1980) found significant path coefficients between initial ability levels and SES as well as an index of life-change events. However, falsification of the model showed these relationships to be reciprocal rather than causal.

In sum, it appears that there are substantial relationships among social status, life-styles, and the maintenance of intellectual ability. But these relationships seem to be interactive rather than causal. Thus early, favorable life experience may be implicated in attaining high levels of intellectual functioning in young adulthood; their maintenance into old age, however, may be related to an engaged life-style, but that life-style may also be a function of a high level of ability.

Personality Variables and Changes in Intelligence

Throughout our investigation, we collected data on our participants on measures of behavioral rigidity. In fact, our study began with the question whether there was an age-differentiated relationship between rigidity–flexibility and intelligence (Schaie, 1958a, 1958b). In this section, I describe the age-related patterns for the TBR (Schaie, 1960; Schaie & Parham,

1975) and discuss our findings on concurrent correlations between intelligence and rigidity–flexibility, as well as the data on the cross-lagged relationships based on longitudinal data.

Age Changes and Age Differences in Rigidity–Flexibility

Cross-sectional data for the rigidity-flexibility variables reported in Table 4.21 for each of the four studies show a nearly linear, negatively accelerating age-difference pattern. For these data, high values are scored in the flexible direction. Consequently, ages at which peak flexibility occurs appear to be 25 for both Motor–Cognitive and Personality–Perceptual Rigidity, and 32 for Psychomotor Speed. Sex differences on the whole point to men being more flexible than women, but to women at comparable ages demonstrating greater Psychomotor Speed than men. Time-of-measurement (period) trends are generally positive, except for a negative period effect for Psychomotor Speed from 1956 to 1963. As for the intellectual abilities, positive cohort trends are apparent.

Using the same method described earlier, we averaged across 7-year longitudinal data at all available ages to determine IACs. Table 4.22 provides the resultant cumulative age-change data from ages 25 to 88. Consistent with expectations, decremental changes appear in the 60s for Psychomotor Speed, becoming statistically significant by age 67. The rigidity–flexibility factor scores, however, differ dramatically from each other. Motor–Cognitive Rigidity does not increase to a statistically significant level until age 81, whereas Personality–Perceptual Rigidity shows an early trend in the rigid direction, with statistically significant cumulative change occurring by age 67.

For comparability with the intellectual ability data, we also computed rigidity–flexibility scores for a cohort born in 1952, estimated for mean ages from 25 to 88. Table 4.23 shows that the most flexible age (for our total sample) is 67 with respect to Motor–Cognitive Ridigity, but 32 for Personality–Perceptual Rigidity and 39 for Psychomotor Speed. Figure 4.7 graphically shows the virtually stable pattern for Motor–Cognitive Rigidity until the 70s, with obvious decline in the rigid direction occurring for Personality–Perceptual Rigidity from age 60, and for Psychomotor Speed from age 53. Attention should be called to some interesting sex differences. Although these data suggest that men are more flexible than women on the Motor-Cognitive dimension, women's peak flexibility occurs later. An even more complex pattern occurs for the Personality–Perceptual dimension. Here women start out less flexible than men, but peak later, and from the 60s on, they are more flexible than the men.

TABLE 4.21. *T*-Score Means for the Cross-Sectional Rigidity–Flexibility Data, by Age, Sex, and Study

Age	1956			1963			1970			1977		
	M	F	T	M	F	T	M	F	T	M	F	T
	Motor–Cognitive Rigidity											
25	54.8	57.4	56.1	59.1	57.1	58.0	56.2	57.1	56.7	59.9	58.0	58.9
32	54.4	54.0	54.2	56.9	56.1	56.4	55.2	56.0	55.6	58.6	57.8	58.1
39	50.9	48.1	49.5	55.0	54.2	54.6	53.9	51.6	52.5	57.2	56.9	57.1
46	49.2	52.4	50.7	51.8	52.1	52.0	53.4	52.7	53.1	55.8	53.2	54.4
53	49.9	46.9	48.4	59.5	49.9	49.7	52.9	49.4	51.0	53.9	51.6	52.8
60	41.1	45.8	43.5	46.7	47.1	46.9	52.8	48.4	50.5	52.6	48.9	50.7
67	42.6	41.3	42.0	43.9	44.0	44.0	43.2	42.2	42.7	46.2	46.9	46.6
74	—	—	—	44.8	40.9	42.8	41.3	41.8	41.5	44.1	47.6	45.8
81	—	—	—	—	—	—	43.9	38.0	41.0	43.0	41.9	42.4
	Personality–Perceptual Rigidity											
25	54.6	55.0	54.8	54.6	52.6	53.5	54.9	56.0	55.5	57.1	55.8	56.4
32	53.0	53.7	53.4	54.2	51.9	52.9	57.2	54.8	55.9	58.1	53.2	55.4
39	52.8	49.1	50.9	53.5	51.9	52.7	50.9	51.1	51.0	54.0	52.2	53.1
46	51.5	51.9	51.7	50.4	51.5	50.9	56.3	53.9	55.1	56.1	51.6	53.7
53	49.4	50.4	49.9	48.5	49.2	48.9	53.4	51.7	52.4	51.9	50.2	51.8
60	47.2	47.7	47.4	47.1	48.4	47.8	50.4	47.9	49.1	53.8	50.8	52.3
67	44.9	45.4	44.3	43.7	44.6	44.1	47.2	47.7	47.5	44.4	49.6	47.1
74	—	—	—	40.7	40.6	40.7	42.4	45.1	43.7	46.8	46.4	46.6
81	—	—	—	—	—	—	45.0	45.0	45.0	41.2	44.8	43.1
	Psychomotor Speed											
25	52.5	58.5	55.5	51.5	55.5	53.8	55.4	60.2	58.1	54.3	59.2	56.7
32	50.8	58.0	54.6	50.0	55.0	52.8	57.0	58.3	57.8	58.8	61.5	60.2
39	52.4	54.6	53.5	50.4	52.9	51.7	53.8	54.8	54.4	54.0	59.8	56.9
46	52.7	55.0	53.7	46.5	52.6	49.5	54.3	58.0	56.1	51.5	53.5	52.6
53	49.6	54.3	52.0	44.7	48.8	47.0	54.3	56.5	55.5	51.3	50.3	50.8
60	45.2	51.3	48.3	43.5	46.6	45.1	50.2	51.7	51.0	47.4	50.4	48.9
67	44.0	46.2	45.1	40.7	44.0	42.3	42.5	47.3	45.1	45.8	48.6	47.3
74	—	—	—	41.7	42.0	41.9	39.1	45.0	41.9	36.8	43.6	40.0
81	—	—	—	—	—	—	38.6	41.8	40.1	37.5	40.3	39.0

TABLE 4.22. Cumulative Age Changes from 7-Year Longitudinal Data for the Rigidity–Flexibility Variables, in T-Score Points[a]

From mean age	To mean age								
	32	39	46	53	60	67	74	81	88
Motor–Cognitive Rigidity									
25	1.26	1.65	1.77	1.08	2.23*	2.29*	1.51	−1.39	−3.34
32		.39	.51	−.18	.97	1.03	.25	−2.65	−4.60
39			.21	−.57	.58	.64	−.14	−3.04*	−4.99
46				−.69	.46	.52	−.26	−3.16*	−5.11
53					1.15	1.21	.43	−2.47	−4.42
60						.06	−.72	−3.62*	−5.57
67							−.78	−3.68*	−5.63
74								−2.90	−4.85
81									−1.95
Personality–Perceptual Rigidity									
25	.69	−.10	−.33	−1.20	−1.33	−2.57	−5.41*	−8.52*	−14.58*
32		−.79	−1.02	−1.89	−2.02	−3.26*	−6.10*	−9.21*	−15.27*
39			−.23	−1.10	−1.23	−2.47*	−5.31*	−8.42	−14.48*
46				−.87	−1.00	−2.24*	−5.08*	−8.19*	−14.25*
53					−.13	−1.37	−4.21*	−7.32*	−13.38*
60						−1.24	−4.08*	−7.19*	−13.25*
67							−2.84*	−5.95*	−12.01*
74								−3.11	−9.17*
81									−6.06
Psychomotor Speed									
25	.11	1.08	.91	.69	−.62	−2.75*	−6.13*	−9.49*	−14.84*
32		.97	.80	.58	−.73	−2.86*	−6.24*	−9.60*	−14.95*
39			−.17	−.39	−1.70	−3.83*	−7.21*	−10.57*	−15.92*
46				−.22	−1.53	−3.66*	−7.04*	−10.40*	−15.75*
53					−1.31	−3.44*	−6.82*	−10.18*	−15.53*
60						−2.13	−5.51*	−8.87*	−14.22*
67							−3.38*	−6.74*	−12.09*
74								−3.36*	−8.71*
81									−5.35

[a]Positive values indicate gains; negative values indicate decrements.
*$p < .01$.

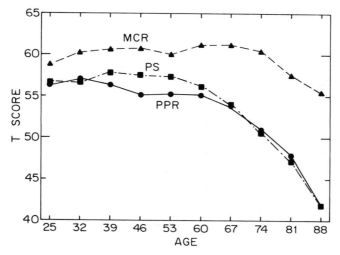

FIGURE 4.7. Longitudinal change on the rigidity–flexibility measures from 7-year data, estimated for a cohort born in 1952.

TABLE 4.23. Predicted Mean Values of Performance on the Rigidity–Flexibility Variables from 7-Year Longitudinal Data for a Cohort Born in 1952, in *T* Scores

Age	Motor–Cognitive			Personality–Perceptual			Psychomotor Speed		
	M	F	T	M	F	T	M	F	T
25	59.9	58.0	58.9	57.1	55.8	56.4	54.3[a]	59.2	56.7
32	61.9	58.8	60.2	58.4[a]	55.6	57.1[a]	53.9	59.5	56.8
39	62.5	59.1	60.6	58.2	55.1	56.4	55.3	60.3	57.8[a]
46	62.8	59.7	60.7	56.4	56.0[a]	55.1	53.9	61.1[a]	57.6
53	62.7	58.5	60.0	55.2	55.6	55.2	53.5	61.0	57.4
60	63.3[a]	60.1	61.2	55.5	55.0	55.1	52.1	59.8	56.1
67	62.6	60.7[a]	61.2[a]	53.6	54.3	53.9	49.9	57.7	54.0
74	62.1	58.6	60.4	50.5	51.5	51.0	46.0	54.8	50.6
81	61.3	55.1	57.5	46.6	50.0	47.9	43.2	51.0	47.2
88	55.9	55.6	55.5	38.6	45.7	41.9	38.5	45.1	41.9

[a]Age of most flexible performance.

Finally, on Psychomotor Speed, women perform better at all ages and peak considerably later than do the men.

Concurrent Relationship between Rigidity–Flexibility and the Intellectual Abilities

Our first question concerning the relationship between rigidity–flexibility and the intellectual abilities deals with the amount of variance shared by the two domains. Table 4.24 provides correlations for all ages investigated at first test. Note that there are moderate to substantial correlations between Psychomotor Speed and all ability measures except for Space. Motor–Cognitive Rigidity correlates moderately with all measures, with the most substantial relationships found with Verbal Meaning and Reasoning. Somewhat lower correlations, mostly during midlife, were found between Personality–Perceptual Rigidity and Verbal Meaning, Reasoning, and Word Fluency. Of considerable interest is the finding that, for all three correlates, values typically increased to about age 60 and then showed some decline. It might be inferred, therefore, that cognitive styles have their major impact upon ability performance in midlife.

Rigidity–Flexibility as a Predictor of Future Ability Level

From the longitudinal data on rigidity–flexibility and the intellectual abilities, it is possible to estimate cross-lagged correlations, which permits a cautious test of time-dependent causal relationships between the two domains. A study by Witt and Cunningham (1979) implied that intellectual performance on crystallized-type measures at a later point could be predicted from intellectual speed at an earlier point. Obviously, our Psychomotor Speed measure lends itself to an independent test of their conclusions. Data from our four-occasion sample ($n = 120$) were employed for this analysis, with subjects' average age being 43 years on the first occasion and 64 years on the final occasion. All four occasions were utilized in an analysis using Humphreys and Parsons's (1979) approach, while only the first and last occasions were considered when computing cross-lags corrected for changes in reliability according to Kenny's (1975) method. Analyses were conducted for the relationship between all three rigidity–flexibility factor scores and the ability measures.

Table 4.25 shows the corrected cross-lagged correlations coefficients (according to Kenny's procedures) that appeared to be most readily interpretable. The results shed some doubt upon Witt and Cunningham's (1979) findings. Psychomotor Speed predicted significantly later performance on Number, probably our most highly speeded test. On the other

TABLE 4.24. Concurrent Correlations between the Rigidity–Flexibility and Intellectual Ability Measures at First Test

Age	n	Verbal Meaning	Space	Reasoning	Number	Word Fluency
			Motor–Cognitive Rigidity			
25	302	.22	.36	.30	.21	.18
32	319	.32	.30	.32	.24	.10
39	378	.38	.27	.43	.21	.21
46	376	.53	.32	.48	.27	.34
53	379	.45	.33	.50	.37	.28
60	346	.48	.30	.48	.39	.37
67	366	.47	.32	.48	.34	.35
74	234	.39	.19	.41	.34	.29
81	104	.39	.31	.33	.34	.12
			Personality–Perceptual Rigidity			
25	302	.21	.03	.09	−.02	.20
32	319	.20	.18	.24	−.01	.11
39	378	.12	.10	.10	−.01	.07
46	376	.30	.03	.21	.02	.14
53	379	.28	.18	.24	.17	.27
60	346	.29	.14	.30	.13	.25
67	367	.23	.10	.22	.15	.14
74	235	.22	.12	.24	.13	.12
81	107	.03	.07	−.01	.00	−.01
			Psychomotor Speed			
25	302	.60	.16	.57	.46	.49
32	319	.55	.19	.48	.30	.43
39	378	.54	.09	.53	.34	.45
46	376	.64	.27	.57	.39	.49
53	379	.64	.21	.60	.48	.61
60	346	.65	.25	.57	.54	.52
67	367	.62	.23	.57	.48	.54
74	234	.54	.18	.40	.45	.49
81	105	.53	.15	.33	.35	.56

hand, Verbal Meaning and Reasoning predicted significantly later performance on the Psychomotor Speed measure. Reasoning also predicted significantly later performance on the measure of Motor–Cognitive Rigidity. But Motor–Cognitive Rigidity predicted later performance on Word Fluency. To our surprise, Personality–Perceptual Rigidity predicted

TABLE 4.25. Cross-Lagged Correlation Coefficients between the Rigidity–Flexibility Measures and the Intellectual Ability Variables after Correction for Changes in Reliability

	Motor–Cognitive Rigidity	Personality–Perceptual Rigidity	Psychomotor Speed
	1956	1956	1956
Verbal Meaning, 1977	.31	.56**	.58
Space, 1977	.34	.27*	.20
Reasoning, 1977	.34	.55**	.46
Number, 1977	.25	.33*	.59*
Word Fluency, 1977	.36*	.40*	.46
	1977	1977	1977
Verbal Meaning, 1956	.37	.20	.68*
Space, 1956	.27	.06	.32
Reasoning, 1956	.50*	.27	.61**
Number, 1956	.24	.12	.41
Word Fluency, 1956	.12	.23	.42

Note. Cross-lags followed by asterisks are significantly greater than their falsification (Pearson–Filon test); $*p > .05$, $**p > .01$.

significantly later performance on all ability measures, with the proportion of variance accounted for ranging from about 7% for Space to 31% for Verbal Meaning. Keeping in mind all the cautions about the limitations of cross-lagged correlations (cf. Rogosa, 1979), it might still be concluded that the progression of intellectual ability from middle to old age is not so much related to earlier speed of performance as it is to behavioral flexibility. That is, it appears that persons who at midlife show flexible personality styles are more likely to perform at high ability levels in early old age.

Summary and Conclusions

The reader has by now accompanied me through most of the highlights of the 21-year scientific journey that was required to gain a clear understanding of the progress of adult development of the psychometric abilities. What remains is for me to state succinctly what I think can be concluded from these studies in response to the four major questions raised in the introduction.

Does Intelligence Change Uniformly or in Different Ability Patterns?

The answer to this first question is quite unambiguous: There clearly is no uniform pattern across the abilities, and although some overall index of intellectual aptitude may be of theoretical interest, such a global measure is not likely to be of practical utility in monitoring changes in function across the adult life span for individuals or groups. Although our data do lend some support to the notion that fluid, or active (Cunningham, 1980), intellectual abilities decline earlier than the crystalized, or passive, abilities, there are important ability-by-sex and ability-by-cohort interactions that complicate matters. For example, in the most recent study, it appears that women decline first on the active abilities, but men do so on the passive abilities. It may well be, then, that patterns of socialization unique to a given sex role within a historical period may be the major determinant of the pattern of change in abilities across the adult life span.

At What Age Is There a Reliably Detectable Age Decrement in Ability and What Is Its Magnitude?

At the risk of possible overgeneralization, it is my general conclusion that reliably replicable age changes in psychometric abilities of more than trivial magnitude cannot be demonstrated prior to age 60, but that reliable decrement can be shown to have occurred for all abilities by age 74. This statement must be further qualified by noting that, when IACs are examined, a few individuals show reliable change over a 7-year period prior to age 60, but that even at age 81, less than half of all observed individuals have shown such reliable change in the preceding 7 years. If we consider the magnitudes of change, we may note that, prior to age 60, no decrement in excess of .2 SD can be observed, whereas by age 81 the magnitude of decrement is approximately one population standard deviation for most variables. In other words, it is typically the period of the late 60s and the 70s during which many individuals seem to experience significant ability decrement. Even so, it is typically only by age 81 that one can show that the average older person will fall below the middle range of performance for young adults.

What Are the Patterns of Generational Differences and What Is Their Magnitude?

Our studies clearly demonstrate that there are substantial generational trends in psychometric intelligence. Because the effects of cohort trends differ across abilities, these effects are least noticeable for composite ability indexes. Even here, though, persons born prior to World War I appear to be at a disadvantage when compared to those born at a later time. For the abilities of Space and Reasoning, the disadvantage for the older cohorts extends to those born as late as 1931. That is, cohort differences affect persons now in their 50s or older. For Verbal Meaning, cohorts born in 1917 or earlier are at a disadvantage compared to those born later. On the other hand, Number skills reach the highest level for cohorts with mean birth years from 1910 to 1924, with more recently born cohorts at some disadvantage at comparable ages to their elders. And for Word Fluency, there is actually a negative cohort gradient; that is, more recent cohorts are at a disadvantage compared to those born earlier, except for a reversal in the positive direction for those born after World War II. Equally important was the finding that these generational differences equal or exceed in magnitude age changes across comparable time intervals. Notice in particular that apparent age differences on the active (fluid) abilities prior to the 60s are largely a function of generational differences and that age differences on the passive (crystallized) abilities in advanced age appear smaller than would be warranted by actual within-individual age changes because of the generational trends favoring, to some extent, the earlier-born cohorts.

What Accounts for Individual Differences in Intraindividual Change across Adulthood?

As has been stressed throughout this chapter, there are vast individual differences in intellectual change across adulthood, ranging from early decrement for some persons to maintenance of function into very advanced age for others. Our studies have begun to shed some light on what factors might be implicated in such individual differences. First, it appears that CVD and arthritis lead to an earlier lowering of performance, the former probably through its disruption of optimal synchrony between cortical and autonomous nervous system functions, and the latter through its impact upon motor behavior involved in test performance. Second, it is clear that a favorable environment as characterized by an advantaged SES is related not only to high levels of intellectual functioning, but also to the maintenance of such functioning into late life. The mechanism involved here is likely to be the maintenance of varied opportunities for environmental stimulation. I find myself concluding that the use-it-or-lose-it principle applies not only to the maintenance of muscular flexibility, but to the maintenance of flexible life-styles and a related high level of intellectual performance as well. Third, it appears that a flexible personality style in midlife tends to predict a high level of performance in old age. Some of these variables are clearly subject to genetic control, but others may be subject to environmental and educational intervention. I believe that such intervention holds inordinate promise (cf. Schaie & Willis, 1978; Willis & Schaie, 1981).

Some Final Comments

This presentation of an extensive and detailed inquiry into the course of psychometric abilities over the adult life span must be ended with certain cautions. First, the reader must be reminded that all our work has been descriptive or in the nature of quasi-experiments. Whatever causal inferences were made must therefore be taken as based upon what has been observed to have happened in the past; it may not necessarily be predictive for future generations. Second, we have described intellectual change across adulthood measured by means of devices that were originally developed for adolescents and young adults. It has been shown that such measures, though not inappropriate, may place older study participants at a disadvantage for reasons unrelated to their actual competence with respect to the dependent variables of interest (cf. Schaie, 1978; Schaie, Gonda, & Quayhagen, 1980). Third, the abilities here discussed are synthesized abstractions of behavioral competence; their expressions in socially significant contexts will differ, depending upon the situation in which they are exercised (Scheidt & Schaie, 1978). Nevertheless, I believe that this body of evidence at the present state of the art, provides a reasonable base for making policy recommendations on such diverse issues as determining the age ranges for which adult education may be most profitable or specifying the ages at which workers in industries requiring certain abilities may start to be at a disadvantage. I am fully cognizant that the projections made will be time limited and that new evidence will have to be collected continuously to account for the impact on behavior of our rapidly changing technological environment. I hope that new studies will profit from the insights gained by the successes as well as the failures of the efforts described here.

Acknowledgments

Research reported in this chapter was most recently supported by Research Grant #AG-480 from the National Institute on Aging. Earlier phases of the study were supported by grants from the National Institute of Child Health and Human Development (HD-367 and

HD-4476). The enthusiastic cooperation of the staff and members of the Group Health Cooperative of Puget Sound is gratefully acknowledged.

References

Adam, J. Sequential strategies and the separation of age, cohort, and time-of-measurement contributions to developmental data. *Psychological Bulletin*, 1978, *85*, 1309–1316.

Baltes, P. B. Longitudinal and cross-sectional sequences in the study of age and generation effects. *Human Development*, 1968, *11*, 145–171.

Baltes, P. B., & Nesselroade, J. R. History and rationale of longitudinal research. In J. R. Nesselroade & P. B. Baltes (Eds.), *Longitudinal research in the study of behavior and development*. New York: Academic Press, 1979.

Baltes, P. B., Nesselroade, J. R., Schaie, K. W., & Labouvie, E. W. On the dilemma of regression effects in examining ability level-related differentials in ontogenetic patterns of adult intelligence. *Developmental Psychology*, 1972, *6*, 79–84.

Baltes, P. B., Reese, H. W., & Nesselroade, J. R. *Life-span developmental psychology: An introduction to research methods*. Monterey, Calif.: Brooks/Cole, 1977.

Baltes, P. B., & Schaie, K. W. Aging and IQ: The myth of the twilight years. *Psychology Today*, May 1974, pp. 35–40.

Baltes, P. B., & Schaie, K. W. On the plasticity of intelligence in adulthood and old age: Where Horn and Donaldson fail. *American Psychologist*, 1976, *31*, 720–725.

Baltes, P. B., Schaie, K. W., & Nardi, A. H. Age and experimental mortality in a seven-year longitudinal study of cognitive behavior. *Developmental Psychology* 1971, *5*, 18–26.

Bayley, N., & Oden, M. H. The maintenance of intellectual ability in gifted adults. *Journal of Gerontology*, 1955, *10*, 91–107.

Bernstein, E. Quickness and intelligence. *British Journal of Psychology Monograph Supplement* 1924, *3*(7).

Binet, A., & Simon, T. Méthodes nouvelles pour le diagnostic du niveau intellectuel des anormaux. *L' Année Psychologique*, 1905, *11*, 191.

Botwinick, J. Intellectual abilities. In J. E. Birren & K. W. Schaie (Eds.), *Handbook of the psychology of aging*. New York: Van Nostrand Reinhold, 1977.

Botwinick, J., & Arenberg, D. Disparate time spans in sequential studies of aging. *Experimental Aging Research*, 1976, *2*, 55–61.

Brooks, J., & Weintraub, M. A history of infant intelligence testing. In M. Lewis (Ed.), *Origins of intelligence*. New York: Plenum, 1976.

Buss, A. R. Methodological issues in life-span developmental psychology from a dialectical perspective. *Journal of Aging and Human Development*, 1979/1980, *10*, 121–163.

Cohen, J. The factorial structure of the WAIS between early adulthood and old age. *Journal of Consulting Psychology*, 1957, *21*, 283–290.

Cohen, J. *Statistical power analysis for the behavioral sciences*. New York: Academic Press, 1977.

Cronbach, L. J. *Essentials of psychological testing* (3rd ed.). New York: Harper & Row, 1970.

Cunningham, W. R. *Is it aging or is it something else? Methodological considerations*. Paper presented at the annual meeting of the American Psychological Association, Montreal, August 1980.

Galton, F. *Hereditary genious*. London: Macmillan, 1869.

Gough, H. G. *The California Psychological Inventory*. Palo Alto, Calif.: Consulting Psychologists' Press, 1957.

Gough, H. G., McCloskey, H., & Meehl, P. E. A personality scale for social responsibility. *Journal of Abnormal and Social Psychology*, 1952, *47*, 73–80.

Gribbin, K., & Schaie, K. W. Monetary incentive, age, and cognition. *Experimental Aging Research*, 1976, *2*, 461–468.

Gribbin, K., & Schaie, K. W. *The aging of tests: A methodological problem of longitudinal studies.* Paper presented at the meeting of the Gerontological Society, San Francisco, November 1977.

Gribbin, K., & Schaie, K. W. Selective attrition in longitudinal studies: A cohort-sequential approach. In H. Orino, K. Shimada, M. Iriki, & D. Maeda (Eds.), *Recent advances in gerontology*. Amsterdam: Excerpta Medica, 1979.

Gribbin, K., Schaie, K. W., & Parham, I. A. Complexity of the life style and maintenance of intellectual abilities. *Journal of Social Issues*, 1980, *21*, 47–61.

Gribbin, K., Schaie, K. W., & Stone, V. *Ability differences between established and redefined populations in sequential studies.* Paper presented at the annual meeting of the American Psychological Association, Washington, D.C., August 1976.

Hall, G. S. *Senescence, the last half of life*. New York: Appleton, 1922.

Hertzog, C. K. *A structural equations analysis of adult intellectual development.* Unpublished doctoral dissertation, University of Southern California, 1979.

Hertzog, C. K., Schaie, K. W., & Gribbin, K. *Age and cohort effects in cognitive behavior: A cohort-sequential replication.* Paper presented at the annual meeting of the Gerontological Society, Dallas, November 1978. (a)

Hertzog, C. K., Schaie, K. W., & Gribbin, K. Cardiovascular disease and changes in intellectual functioning from middle to old age. *Journal of Gerontology*, 1978, *33*, 872–883. (b)

Hollingsworth, H. L. *Mental growth and decline: A survey of developmental psychology.* New York: Appleton, 1927.

Horn, J. L., & Donaldson, G. On the myth of intellectual decline in adulthood. *American Psychologist*, 1976, *31*, 701–719.

Horn, J. L., & McArdle, J. J. Perspectives on mathematical/statistical model building (MASMOB) in research on aging. In L. W. Poon (Ed.), *Aging in the 1980's*. Washington, D.C.: American Psychological Association, 1980.

Humphreys, L. G., & Parsons, C. K. A simplex process model for describing differences between cross-lagged correlations. *Psychological Bulletin*, 1979, *86*, 325–334.

Jarvik, L. F., Kallmann, F. J., & Falek, A. Intellectual changes in aged twins. *Journal of Gerontology*, 1962, *17*, 289–294.

Jones, H. E., & Conrad, H. S. The growth and decline of intelligence: A study of a homogeneous group between the ages of ten and sixty. *Genetic Psychology Monographs*, 1933, *13*, 223–298.

Joreskog, K. Statistical estimation of structural models in longitudinal-developmental investigations. In J. R. Nesselroade & P. B. Baltes (Eds.), *Longitudinal research in the study of behavior and development*. New York: Academic Press, 1979.

Joreskog, K. G., & Sorbom, D. Statistical models and methods for analysis of longitudinal data. In D. J. Aigner & A. S. Goldberger (Eds.), *Latent variables in socioeconomic models*. Amsterdam: North-Holland, 1977.

Kamin, L. J. *The science and politics of IQ*. Hillsdale, N.J.: Erlbaum, 1974.

Kenny, D. A. Cross-lagged panel correlations: A test for spuriousness. *Psychological Bulletin*, 1975, *76*, 887–903.

Kuhlen, R. G. Social change: A neglected factor in psychological studies of the life span. *School and Society*, 1940, *52*, 14–16.

Kuhlen, R. G. Age and intelligence: The significance of cultural change in longitudinal vs. cross-sectional findings. *Vita Humana*, 1963, *6*, 113–124.

Lankes, W. Perseveration. *British Journal of Psychology*, 1915, *7*, 387–419.

Matarazzo, J. D. *Wechsler's measurement and appraisal of adult intelligence*. Baltimore: Williams & Wilkins, 1972.

Nesselroade, J. R., Schaie, K. W., & Baltes, P. B. Ontogenetic and generational components of structural and quantitative change in adult behavior. *Journal of Gerontology*, 1972, *27*, 222–228.

Owens, W. A., Jr. Age and mental abilities: A longitudinal study. *Genetic Psychology Monographs*, 1953, *48*, 3–54.

Owens, W. A., Jr. Is age kinder to the initially more able? *Journal of Gerontology*, 1959, *14*, 334–337.

Parham, I. A., Gribbin, K., Hertzog, C. K., & Schaie, K. W. *Health status change by age and implications for adult cognitive change*. Paper presented at the 10th International Congress of Gerontology, Jerusalem, Israel, July 1975.

Pressey, S. L., Janney, J. E., & Kuhlen, R. G. *Life: A psychological survey*. New York: Hayer, 1939.

Rogosa, D. Causal models in longitudinal research: Rationale, formulation and interpretation. In J. R. Nesselroade & P. B. Baltes (Eds.), *Longitudinal research in the study of behavior and development*. New York: Academic Press, 1979.

Schaie, K. W. A test of behavioral rigidity. *Journal of Abnormal and Social Psychology*, 1955, *51*, 604–610.

Schaie, K. W. Differences in some personal characteristics of "rigid" and "flexible" individuals. *Journal of Clinical Psychology*, 1958, *14*, 11–14. (a)

Schaie, K. W. Occupational level and the Primary Mental Abilities. *Journal of Educational Psychology*, 1958, *40*, 299–303. (b)

Schaie, K. W. Rigidity–flexibility and intelligence: A cross-sectional study of the adult life span from 20 to 70. *Psychological Monographs*, 1958, *72*(462, Whole No. 9). (c)

Schaie, K. W. Tests of hypotheses about differences between two intercorrelation matrices. *Journal of Experimental Education*, 1958, *26*, 241–245. (d)

Schaie, K. W. Cross-sectional methods in the study of psychological aspects of aging. *Journal of Gerontology*, 1959, *14*, 208–215. (a)

Schaie, K. W. The effect of age on a scale of social responsibility. *Journal of Social Psychology*, 1959, *50*, 221–224. (b)

Schaie, K. W. *Manual for the Test of Behavioral Rigidity*. Palo Alto, Calif.: Consulting Psychologists' Press, 1960.

Schaie, K. W. A general model for the study of developmental problems. *Psychological Bulletin*, 1965, *64*, 92–107.

Schaie, K. W. Age changes and differences. *Gerontologist*, 1967, *7*, 128–132.

Schaie, K. W. A reinterpretation of age-related changes in cognitive structure and functioning. In L. R. Goulet & P. B. Baltes (Eds.), *Life-span developmental psychology: Research and theory*. New York: Academic Press, 1970.

Schaie, K. W. Can the longitudinal method be applied to psychological studies of human development? In F. Z. Moenks, W. W. Hartup, & J. DeWitt (Eds.), *Determinants of human behavior*. New York: Academic Press, 1972.

Schaie, K. W. *Cumulative health trauma and age changes in adult cognitive behavior*. Paper presented at the meeting of the American Psychological Association, Montreal, August 1973. (a)

Schaie, K. W. Methodological problems in descriptive developmental research on adulthood and aging. In J. R. Nesselroade & H. W. Reese (Eds.), *Life-span developmental psychology: Methodological issues.* New York: Academic Press, 1973. (b)

Schaie, K. W. Translations in gerontology—From lab to life: Intellectual functioning. *American Psychologist,* 1974, *29,* 802–807.

Schaie, K. W. Age changes in adult intelligence. In D. S. Woodruff & J. E. Birren (Eds.), *Aging: Scientific perspectives and social issues.* New York: Van Nostrand, 1975. (a)

Schaie, K. W. Research strategy in developmental human behavior genetics. In K. W. Schaie, E. V. Anderson, G. E. McClearn, & J. Money (Eds.), *Developmental human behavior genetics.* Lexington, Mass.: D. C. Heath, 1975. (b)

Schaie, K. W. Quasi-experimental design in the psychology of aging. In J. E. Birren & K. W. Schaie (Eds.), *Handbook of the psychology of aging.* New York: Van Nostrand Reinhold, 1977.

Schaie, K. W. External validity in the assessment of intellectual functioning in adulthood. *Journal of Gerontology,* 1978, *33,* 695–701.

Schaie, K. W. The primary mental abilities in adulthood: An exploration in the development of psychometric intelligence. In P. B. Baltes & O. G. Brim, Jr. (Eds.), *Life-span development and behavior* (Vol. 2). New York: Academic Press, 1979.

Schaie, K. W. Intelligence and problem solving. In J. E. Birren & R. B. Sloane (Eds.), *Handbook of mental health and aging.* Englewood Cliffs, N.J.: Prentice-Hall, 1980.

Schaie, K. W. Psychological changes from midlife to early old age: Implications for the maintenance of mental health. *Journal of Orthopsychiatry,* 1981, *51,* 199–218.

Schaie, K. W., & Baltes, P. B. Some faith helps to see the forest: A final comment on the Horn and Donaldson myth on the Baltes–Schaie position on adult intelligence. *American Psychologist,* 1977, *32,* 1118–1120.

Schaie, K. W., Baltes, P. B., & Strother, C. R. A study of auditory sensitivity in advanced age. *Journal of Gerontology,* 1964, *19,* 453–457.

Schaie, K. W., Gonda, N. N., & Quayhagen, M. *The relationship between intellectual performance and perception of everyday competence in middle-aged, young-old and old-old adults.* Paper presented at the meeting of the International Congress of Psychology, Leipzig, German Democratic Republic, July 1980.

Schaie, K. W., & Gribbin, K. Einfluesse der aktuellen Umwelt auf die Persoenlichkeitsentwicklung im Erwachsenenalter [Environmental influences upon personality development in adulthood]. *Zeitschrift fuer Entwicklungpsychologie und Paedagogische Psychologie,* 1975, *7,* 233–246. (a)

Schaie, K. W., & Gribbin, K. *The impact of environmental complexity upon adult cognitive development.* Paper presented at the meeting of the International Society for the Study of Behavioral Development, Guildford, England, 1975. (b)

Schaie, K. W., & Hertzog, C. Longitudinal methods. In B. B. Wolman (Ed.), *Handbook of developmental psychology.* Englewood Cliffs, N.J.: Prentice-Hall, 1982.

Schaie, K. W., Labouvie, G. V., & Barrett, T. J. Selective attrition effects in a fourteen-year study of adult intelligence. *Journal of Gerontology,* 1973, *28,* 328–334.

Schaie, K. W., Labouvie, G. V., & Buech, B. U. Generational and cohort-specific differences in adult cognitive functioning: A fourteen-year study of independent samples. *Developmental Psychology,* 1973, *9,* 151–166.

Schaie, K. W., & Labouvie-Vief, G. Generational versus ontogenetic components of change in adult cognitive behavior: A fourteen-year cross-sequential study. *Developmental Psychology,* 1974, *10,* 305–320.

Schaie, K. W., & Parham, I. A. *Manual for the test of behavioral rigidity* (2nd ed). Palo Alto, Calif.: Consulting Psychologists' Press, 1975.

Schaie, K. W., & Parham, I. A. Cohort-sequential analyses of adult intellectual development. *Developmental Psychology*, 1977, *13*, 649–653.

Schaie, K. W., & Parr, J. Intellectual development. In A. W. Chickering (Ed.), *The modern american college*. San Francisco: Jossey-Bass, 1981.

Schaie, K. W., Rosenthal, F., & Perlman, R. M. Differential deterioration of factorially "pure" mental abilities. *Journal of Gerontology*, 1953, *8*, 191–196.

Schaie, K. W., & Schaie, J. P. Clinical assessment and aging. In J. E. Birren & K. W. Schaie (Eds.), *Handbook of the psychology of aging*. New York: Van Nostrand Reinhold, 1977.

Schaie, K. W., & Strother, C. R. Cognitive and personality variables in college graduates of advanced age. In G. A. Talland (Ed.), *Human behavior and aging: Recent advances in research and theory*. New York: Academic Press, 1968. (a)

Schaie, K. W., & Strother, C. R. The cross-sequential study of age changes in cognitive behavior. *Psychological Bulletin*, 1968, *70*, 671–680. (b)

Schaie, K. W., & Strother, C. R. The effects of time and cohort differences on the interpretation of age changes in cognitive behavior. *Multivariate Behavioral Research*, 1968, *3*, 259–293. (c)

Schaie, K. W., & Strother, C. R. Limits of optimal functioning in superior old adults. In S. M. Chown & K. F. Riegel (Eds.). *Interdisciplinary topics in gerontology*. Basel, Switzerland: S. Karger, 1968. (d)

Schaie, K. W., & Willis, S. L. Life-span development: Implications for education. *Review of Research in Education*, 1978, *6*, 120–156.

Schaie, K. W., & Willis, S. L. Maintenance and decline of adult mental abilities: I. Descriptive data and explanatory models. In F. W. Grote & R. Feringer (Eds.), *Adult learning and development*. Bellingham, Wash.: Western Washington University, 1981.

Scheidt, R. J., & Schaie, K. W. A situational taxonomy for the elderly: Generating situational criteria. *Journal of Gerontology*, 1978, *33*, 848–857.

Scheier, I., & Ferguson, G. A. Further factorial studies of tests of rigidity. *Canadian Journal of Psychology*, 1952, *6*, 18–30.

Stone, V. *Structural modeling of the relations among environmental variables, health status, and intelligence in adulthood*. Unpublished doctoral dissertation, University of Southern California, 1980.

Stone, V., & Schaie, K. W. *A cross-sequential study of cognitive behavior spanning 21 years*. Paper presented at the annual meeting of the American Psychological Association, New York, August 1979.

Stone, V., Schaie, K. W., & Gonda, J. N. *Intergenerational differences in adult cognitive behavior: Results for a 21-year independent samples study*. Paper presented at the annual meeting of the Gerontological Society, Washington, D.C., November 1979.

Strother, C. R., Schaie, K. W., & Horst, P. The relationship between advanced age and mental abilities. *Journal of Abnormal and Social Psychology*, 1957, *55*, 166–170.

Terman, L. M. *The measurement of intelligence*. Boston: Houghton, 1916.

Thurstone, L. L. *The primary mental abilities*. Chicago: University of Chicago Press, 1938.

Thurstone, L. L., & Thurstone, T. G. *Factorial studies of intelligence*. Chicago: University of Chicago Press, 1941.

Thurstone, L. L., & Thurstone, T. G. *Examiner manual for the SRA Primary Mental Abilities Test*. Chicago: Science Research Associates, 1949.

Thurstone, T. G. *Manual for the SRA Primary Mental Abilities 11–17*. Chicago: Science Research Associates, 1958.

U.S. Public Health Service. *Eighth revision international classification of diseases. Adapted for use in the United States* (U.S. Public Health Service Publication No. 1693). Washington, D.C.: U.S. Government Printing Office, 1968.

Wechsler, D. *The measurement of adult intelligence.* Baltimore: Williams & Wilkins, 1939.

Willis, S. L., & Schaie, K. W. Maintenance and decline of adult mental abilities: II. Susceptibility to intervention. In F. W. Grote & R. Feringer (Eds.), *Adult learning and development.* Bellingham, Wash.: Western Washington University, 1981.

Witt, S. J., & Cunningham, W. R. Cognitive speed and subsequent intellectual development: A longitudinal investigation. *Journal of Gerontology*, 1979, *4*, 540–546.

Yerkes, R. M. Psychological examining in the United States Army. *Memoirs of the National Academy of Sciences*, 1921, *15*, 1–890.

5 Psychological Aspects of the Duke Longitudinal Studies

ILENE C. SIEGLER

Introduction

The Duke Longitudinal Studies are two large-scale, multidisciplinary studies that have focused on providing information that describes normal aging during the later half of the life span. The first longitudinal study began in 1955 with a panel of 270 community volunteers aged 60 to 94. The second longitudinal study was started in 1968 with a stratified random sample of 502 community volunteers aged 46–70. The second study developed from the first and was designed to have a special emphasis on studying adaptation to significant life challenges during middle and later life.

Psychological constructs played an important role in both studies. There were four major laboratories involved in the data collection and organization of the studies: psychology, psychiatry, medicine, and sociology. The data collection on the studies was completed in 1976. The purposes of this chapter are to describe both studies fully, to review selected findings from both studies that pertain to the psychology of adult development and aging, and to put in perspective the knowledge gained about normal aging.

Description of the Studies

The first longitudinal study was developed by E. W. Busse in 1954 and grew out of his interest in understanding the problem of standardizing the electroencephalogram (EEG) in normal aging persons. As EEG changes common to later life were characterized, Busse and his colleagues at Duke

ILENE C. SIEGLER. Department of Psychiatry and Center for the Study of Aging and Human Development, Duke University Medical Center, Durham, North Carolina.

University decided to expand the study to include relevant medical, psychological, psychiatric, and social variables that could lead to an understanding of the complex, multiple processes involved in normal aging. The title of the original project was "The Effects of Aging on the Central Nervous System: Physiological, Psychological, and Social Aspects of Aging."[1] This has remained the title of the longitudinal studies. In contrast to other longitudinal studies of aging, the Duke studies, from their inception, have had a special emphasis on medical and psychiatric functioning. The first longitudinal study is perhaps most similar to the Human Aging Study started in 1955 at the National Institute of Mental Health (NIMH; Birren, Butler, Greenhouse, Sokoloff, & Yarrow, 1963; Granick & Patterson, 1971). The Human Aging Study initially controlled more stringently for physical health and had a much smaller, more intensively studied sample; however, as Granick and Patterson (1971) stated, "these two studies complement each other, and where their findings are similar, their validity may merit much confidence" (p. 4).

Planning for the second longitudinal study was begun in 1965.[2] The study was influenced by then-recent developments in methodology (Harris, 1963; Schaie, 1965) and was designed as a short-term longitudinal study with five 5-year cohorts ranging in age from 46 to 70 and four times of measurement. The purposes of the study were to understand normal development during the middle years and to consider responses to normative life transitions (Palmore, 1974a).

Overview of the Samples and Psychological Variables

An overview of both study populations is presented in Table 5.1. In the longitudinal studies, data were characterized by the laboratory that had responsibility for the data collection. As can be seen from Table 5.1, the number of subjects seen at a particular round, or wave, of data collection varied by the requirements of the particular laboratory. Figures are provided for the total number of subjects seen and for the number of subjects seen in the psychological laboratory.

The two studies were similar in that the same group of investigators studied both populations in the same laboratory setting. The first longitudinal study was initially designed to follow the subject population until death. However, in 1973, during the 17th year of the study, the decision was made to end data collection at the same time that data collection was

[1]Grant M900C, 10/1/54, E. W. Busse, principal investigator. See the final report (Duke University, 1980, pp. 20–23) for a fuller description of the history of the longitudinal studies.
[2]Grant HD00668-09, 12/29/65, E. W. Busse, principal investigator.

TABLE 5.1. Duke Longitudinal Study Populations

Wave	Dates seen	Number seen	Number with psychological data	Age range
		Longitudinal I		
1	3/55–5/59	270[a]	267	59–94
2	9/59–5/61	183	182	
3	1/64–3/65	178	140	
4	10/66–6/67	138	110	
5	6/68–1/69	110	93	
6	2/70–8/70	108	92	
7	1/72–5/72	81	60	
8	2/73–8/73	68	57	
9	4/74–9/74	57	52	
10	12/74–8/75	56	47	
11	3/76–8/76	44[b]	42	76–102
		Longitudinal II		
1	8/60–4/70	502	502	46–70
2	8/70–3/72	443	438	
3	6/72–7/74	386	383	
4	8/74–10/76	375	331	51–77

[a]Three subjects did not complete Wave 1.
[b]Twenty-six subjects were still living as of December 1980.

scheduled to end for the second longitudinal study. At the writing of this chapter, 26 subjects are alive. In 1977, all surviving subjects were contacted about participating in an autopsy study. Twelve subjects and their families agreed, and two subjects have been autopsied.

The study population for the first longitudinal study was recruited from the Research Triangle area (Durham, Orange, and Wake Counties, North Carolina) and selected so that the age, sex, race, and socioeconomic characteristics of the sample reflected the distribution of these factors in the community. The initial sample included 270 individuals; however, 3 subjects did not complete the first examination and are not included in any of the analyses. Of the 267 participants at the first examination, 47.56% were male, and 52.44% female; 65.17% were white, and 34.83% were black. At the final measurement point in 1976, 33.3% of the sample were male, and 66.7% female; 54.76% were white, and 45.24% were black. Maddox (1962) evaluated the sample characteristics in comparison to (1) data on health from the National Health Survey, (2) epidemiological surveys of mental health, (3) a random sample of white elderly drawn from the same geographic area, and (4) in terms of selective dropout between the first and second examinations. The sample was found to be quite similar to the other samples of older persons on mental and physical health characteristics. The major difference between the longitudinal sample and the Durham community survey was the higher proportion of males and of married persons in the sample. Although the sample was not a random one, study participants were quite similar to other elderly volunteer subjects. Dropout between the first two examinations was selective and continued to be so throughout the rest of the study.

The study population for the second longitudinal study was drawn from the membership lists of a local health insurance association. Subjects were sampled in five 5-year cohort groups (1898–1922), and men were deliberately oversampled. Few individuals over 65 belonged to the insurance group, so the group was augmented with 32 subjects sampled from older patients at Duke Hospital. The sample was compared to 1970 Census statistics, and its subjects were found to be somewhat more married (85% vs. 79%), somewhat more employed (66% vs. 59%), better educated (12.5 vs. 11.1 median years of education completed), and in higher occupational categories (35% vs. 25% professional or managerial). The subjects were initially aged 46–70, and more were men (52% male vs. 48% female). All subjects in the study were white. At the end of the study, the age range was 51–77, and the sexes were balanced. More detailed information on the samples can be found in Palmore (1974a) and in the final report that summarizes both studies (Duke University, 1980).

The major psychological variables and their times of measurement are listed in Table 5.2. As can be seen from the table, the measures in the two studies are different, except for four subtests of the Wechsler Adult Intelligence Scale (WAIS) and the measures of pure-tone audiometry.

TABLE 5.2. Psychological Constructs in the Longitudinal Studies

	Tests used and dates given			
Constructs	Longitudinal I	Waves	Longitudinal II	Waves
Intelligence	Full WAIS	1–11	Short WAIS[a]	1–4
Personality	Rorschach	1,2,4	Form C of the Cattell 16 PF	1–4
RT	Simple and choice RT	2–11	CPT	1,3 or 2,4
Audition	Pure-tone audiometry, spondee words	1–11	Pure-tone audiometry	1–4
Vision	—[b]		Eye chart Reading card	1–4
Memory	Modified WMS[c]	2–11	—	

[a]Information, Vocabulary, Picture Arrangement, DSS.
[b]A complete ophthalmologic examination was given in Longitudinal I.
[c]Logical Memory (Immediate and Delayed Recall), Paired-Associate Learning, Visual Reproduction.

Measures in the areas of health and electroencephalography were similar between the two studies. A detailed social history was designed for each study, reflecting the current social psychological measures of attitudes and activities. Measures of mental health were included in the social history of the second study. Except for the addition of variables at Wave 2 and the dropping of the Rorschach after Wave 4, the psychological data collected were consistent throughout the study.

The Longitudinal Studies in Perspective

Many variables with psychological content were included in the social histories of both studies and in the mental status and psychiatric data collected in the first study. Because of the differences in the psychological measures, findings from the two studies are reviewed separately here.

In many ways, longitudinal studies are essentially institutional enterprises: Each study developed procedures to handle changes in personnel, committees to make decisions, and strategies for maintenance of the study population. Information about the administrative and managerial aspects of the Duke studies can be found in Busse (1965). These studies were coordinated by a set of committees, with regular Monday-night meetings, where senior investigators reviewed progress and made what decisions were required. A careful balancing act was required between the needs of the study and the desires of individual investigators. Senior investigators, or laboratory heads in a specific disciplinary area, were given official responsibility for supervising the collection and preparation of the data for inclusion in the computer files of the longitudinal study. Ramm and Gianturco (1974) have reviewed the history of the computing laboratory. It is interesting to note that the requirements of the longitudinal data set were instrumental in the development of the TSAR statistical package (see Ramm & Gianturco, 1974).

Each senior investigator was given the first right of refusal on analysis of the data collected by his or her lab and the responsibility of collaborating with colleagues from other disciplines who wished to use data from the particular area. However, simultaneously, each senior investigator was given complete academic freedom to pursue or not pursue particular analyses from the full data set. As a longitudinal investigator who joined the team at the time of data collection on the ninth examination of the first study and the fourth examination of the second, I was given the responsibility for the psychological data collection and final data "cleaning," as well as the opportunity to use the longitudinal data sets to pursue my own reseach interests.

The First Longitudinal Study

Measures

Intelligence was assessed with the WAIS (Wechsler, 1955). Hearing was assessed for pure tones at frequencies ranging from 125 Hz to 8000 Hz, and for speech perception with spondee words. Spondee words, a measure of speech perception, were added during the first examination, which took 4 years to complete. At the time of the second evaluation, a reaction time (RT) task and three subtests from the Wechsler Memory Scale (WMS; Stone, Girdner, & Albrecht, 1946; Wechsler, 1945) were added. Personality was assessed by the Rorschach, which was given at the first, second, and fourth examinations and then dropped from the study protocol. The other psychological variables were repeated at each succeeding time of measurement.

The rest of the longitudinal test battery included extensive medical data. Briefly, these data included a complete medical history and physical examination, an electrocardiogram (ECG), a laboratory analysis of blood and urine, a chest X ray, and special examinations in ophthalmology, neurology, and dermatology. The psychiatric data base included extensive interviews focused on depression, dementia, hypochondriasis and an EEG, and cerebral blood flow (CBF). The social history covered sociodemographic factors, attitudes about retirement, and a large variety of attitude and adjustment scales developed at the University of Chicago (Burgess, Cavan, & Havighurst, 1948; Cavan, Burgess, Havighurst, & Goldhamer, 1949). Many of the findings from the first longitudinal study were reported in two volumes edited by Palmore, *Normal Aging I* (1970) and *Normal Aging II* (1974b). Major reviews that have appeared since then are those by Gianturco and Busse (1978) and by Busse (1978) reviewing psychiatric functioning; by Busse and Wang (1979) reviewing findings from the EEG and CBF; and by Palmore (1981) on the social aspects of aging. At the fourth examination, a satellite study was started in order to look at changes in the immune system, and at the sixth examination, the psychiatric interview was revised (Wang, 1980).

Sample Maintenance

The issue of sample maintenance is important in any longitudinal study. In the first Duke study, tremendous care and attention were given to developing relationships with the study participants so that their cooperation over the length of the study would be maximized. As an inducement to participation, the results of the physical examination were communicated to study participants and to their personal physicians shortly after completion of a given round of the study. Medical treatment was not provided by the longitudinal physicians. This referral back to subjects' physicians was important in ensuring their cooperation. Special attention was paid to keeping in contact with subjects by sending birthday and Christmas cards and to continuing to stay in touch by mail, even if the subjects had moved away from the Durham area. The maintenance of the sample was due to the excellent efforts of the longitudinal study's social workers, Frances Jeffers and Dorothy Heyman. It was not uncommon for subjects who had moved away to come in for testing when they were back visiting family and friends in the Durham area.

Participation Patterns

The study protocol took 2 full days in the laboratory to complete. Two subjects were seen at a time. Home visits were started during the third wave of the study (1964–1965) for those who were too ill to come in. Generally, the physical examination and the social history were conducted in the home. Home visits did not include psychological data collection until the fifth examination (1968–1969). The WAIS, the WMS, and pure-tone audiometry were conducted on home visits; RT and spondee words were not. For individuals who were able to complete the psychological tests during the home visit, the results were not different, as a group, when compared to age-matched controls; thus home-visit data were included in the regular data files, but were noted as such. Thus the number of subjects seen at a particular wave also varied by test. The number of subjects seen per wave and complete data on the psychological variables are given in Table 5.3.

In 1977, all data were checked and rescored, if necessary, and reasons for missing data were ascertained. Differences, among waves, in the number of subjects seen within a visit are due to equipment failures, a subject's refusal of a particular test, a visual or psychomotor problem that prevented the administration of a test, or the subject's being available for only 1 day of testing.

The number of subjects listed in Table 5.3 does not necessarily correspond to the number of subjects used in a particular analysis or research report because more than one variable is often involved, and this table does not indicate the repeated participation patterns of complete data at multiple waves.

TABLE 5.3. Participation Pattern Regarding Psychological Variables

Variable/condition	Wave 1	Wave 2	Wave 3	Wave 4	Wave 5	Wave 6	Wave 7	Wave 8	Wave 9	Wave 10	Wave 11
WAIS: complete/office	246	184	130	102	89	76	50	43	32	35	30
WAIS: complete/home	—	—	—	—	1	9	9	8	16	4	3
Total WAIS	246	184	130	102	90	85	59	51	48	39	33
Audiometry: complete/office	72	189	134	106	91	79	51	45	31	38	31
Audiometry: pure tone only/office	155	2	2	1	—	1	1	—	1	1	1
Audiometry: pure tone only/home	—	—	—	—	1	11	8	12	17	7	7
Total audiometry	227	191	136	107	92	91	60	57	49	46	39
WMS: complete/office	—	174	132	106	88	78	50	46	35	36	31
WMS: complete/home	—	—	—	—	1	8	9	9	15	5	3
Total WMS	—	174	132	106	89	86	59	55	50	41	34
RT: complete	—	166	130	104	88	75	50	43	28	34	29
Subject alive; did not see	—	33	18	19	30	21	22	21	17	16	11
Subject dead	—	42	79	110	127	139	164	180	194	197	212

Note. The number of subjects seen and alive plus those not seen and dead does not always add up to 267 because some subjects had only partial data on the psychological variables.

143

Specific Procedures in Test Administration

The specific procedures used in the psychology laboratory are detailed in the *Technician's Handbook* (Siegler, Murray, Johnson, & Rusin, 1976). Divergences in our procedures from standard administration of published tests and more detailed descriptions of nonstandard procedures are detailed here.

Wechsler Adult Intelligence Scale

The WAIS was always given in the morning, and the instructions in the manual were followed. All WAISs were scored by the examiner and then checked by a second technician. Any discrepancies were resolved. In 1976–1977, all original WAIS forms were checked for accuracy of scoring and interpretation in order to assess whether scoring criteria had changed over the 20 years of testing. It appeared that little probing of the subjects had been done during the first three examinations (1955–1965), and occasionally a subtest was stopped too early; however, on scoring, the interpretations were liberal, and the subject was given the benefit of the doubt. Starting with the fourth examination (1966–1976), more exact procedures were followed during test administration, and more questioning of subjects was done; simultaneously, the scoring criteria tightened. Thus these two patterns appeared to cancel each other out. A few addition and keypunching errors were discovered and corrected. All of the actual forms used for data collection, including the WAIS protocols, were microfilmed for permanent storage. Raw-score data were not keypunched. All of the analyses were done with scaled scores, unless otherwise noted.

Wechsler Memory Scale

Three scales were adopted from the WMS. Logical Memory and Paired-Associate Learning were taken from Form I (Wechsler, 1945), and Visual Reproduction from Form II (Stone *et al.*, 1946). A second recall of the Logical Memory paragraphs was required after the hearing test (20 to 30 minutes) in order to provide a measure of Delayed Recall.

Auditory Functioning

Thresholds for pure tones were tested with a Belltone audiometer at 125, 250, 500, 1000, 1500, 2000, 3000, 4000, 6000, and 8000 Hz for each ear separately. Mean decibel loss for combined hearing loss was calculated by the formula

$$\frac{7 \text{ (smaller db loss)} + \text{higher db loss}}{8}$$

Thresholds for spondee words were determined for each ear separately.

Reaction Time

The subject sat before a vertical panel containing three lights: a centrally located warning light and two signal lights, one on either side of the warning light. The subject depressed a large, central rest button with his or her dominant hand. There were two response buttons, one on either side of the rest button. On each trial, the warning light was illuminated for 3 sec, following which one of the signal lights was lit. The signal light stayed on until the subject responded by pressing the response button on the same side as the light.

The final 20 trials in each session measured simple RT, with only one signal light (the right in the first 10 trials, the left in the next 10) being used. The next 44 trials measured choice RT, with both lights being used, alternating in a predetermined random order. On 4 of these trials (numbers 21, 28, 35, and 44), both signal lights were lit simultaneously. This allowed RT to be examined before and after this conflict situation.

The available measures on this task are (1) lift time (from the signal until the subject lifted the hand from the rest button), (2) movement time (from the lift until the response button was pressed), and (3) total time (from signal to press). The decision component of the task is presumably reflected mainly in the lift time, while visuomotor factors are more prominent in movement time.

Major Findings

The first longitudinal study has served as the data base for many publications. In this review, I discuss in detail only analyses that are based on data from the psychological laboratory or from multidisciplinary studies that included one or more of the variables from the psychological laboratory. The studies listed as cross-sectional studies may, at first glance, appear to be confusing. They are of three types:

1. Analyses that report data from the first wave of the study and that are thus cross-sectional in the traditional sense of the word.
2. Analyses that use data from a single point of data collection (typically the first examination), but that are concerned with sample attrition or

the prediction of survival and thus include a measure of survival or distance from death that required that time elapse until the criterion could be established. Because the data typically compare subjects all of whom were measured at the first time of measurement (the only time when all subjects are available for comparison purposes), the groups compared are essentially a cross-sectional analysis stratified on the basis of later outcomes.

3. A traditional cross-sectional analysis on later waves of the data. For example, data on RT and the WMS, which were first given at the second examination, can be analyzed cross-sectionally; however, all of the subjects differ from those in a traditional cross-sectional study because they have survived an additional 4 years since the first examination. Thus any data collected after the first time of measurement is based on subjects with additional experience.

Appropriate control groups for participation and/or dropout effects were not added to the longitudinal panel as the study progressed, and this needs to be taken into account in the interpretation of the data. The longitudinal analyses compare the same individuals across a specific time interval and vary in the particular times of measurement employed.

Major findings from the psychological laboratory are reviewed in three sections. The first set of studies constitutes those that were concerned with the psychological variables themselves. The second set relates psychological functioning to health. The third set used data from the range of variables included in the study and focused on more integrated questions such as successful aging and survival.

Psychological Variables Singly and in Combination

Wechsler Adult Intelligence Scale. As can be seen in Table 5.4, the WAIS was the most often studied variable in the psychological battery. This is perhaps not surprising, given the prominent role that studies of adult intelligence have played in the psychology of aging (Riegel, 1977).

The early cross-sectional analyses of the WAIS (Eisdorfer, Busse, & Cohen, 1959; Eisdorfer & Cohen, 1961) were concerned with norms of the WAIS for older persons. Only individuals through the age of 64 were included in the standardization sample; thus the norms for individuals aged 65 and older were based on a special sample of 352 older persons drawn from a stratified sample in Kansas City, Missouri, and Kansas City, Kansas (Dopplett & Wallace, 1955; Wechsler, 1955). The data developed from the norming sample are important because the conversion of the scaled scores (common for all ages to the norm group aged 20–34)

TABLE 5.4. Psychological Variables Singly and in Combination

Author/date	Variables[a]	Waves at which cross-sectional analyses were conducted	Waves at which longitudinal analyses were conducted
Eisdorfer, Busse, & Cohen (1959)	W	1	
Eisdorfer (1960a, 1960b)	R,A,V	1	
Eisdorfer & Cohen (1961)	W	1	
Eisdorfer (1963a)	W	1	1–2
Eisdorfer (1963b)	W,R	1	
Busse & Eisdorfer (1970)	W,R,MH	1	
Eisdorfer & Wilkie (1972)	A		1–3
Eisdorfer & Wilkie (1973)	W	1	1–4
Wilkie & Eisdorfer (1973a, 1973b)	W		1–7
Siegler, Harkins, & Thompson (1974)	W		1–9
Wilkie, Eisdorfer, & Siegler (1975)	RT		2–5
Fox (1979)	R		1, 2, 4
Siegler & Botwinick (1979)	W	1	1–11
Botwinick & Siegler (1980)	W	1, 2, 3, 5	1, 2, 3, 5
Siegler (1981)	W,WM,RT	1, 2	1–4, 2–4, 5–11
McCarty, Siegler & Logue (1982)	WM	2	2–3, 2–6, 2–11
Siegler, McCarty, & Logue (1982)	W,WM	2	

[a]W = WAIS; R = Rorschach; A = audition; V = vision; MH = marital happiness; RT = reaction time; WM = Weschler Memory.

to IQ scores were developed on the standardization samples. Comparisons of the Kansas City data with the Duke data indicated that the Duke sample was consistently higher on the Verbal subtests. When data from the Duke sample were analyzed by sex, race, socioeconomic status (SES), and mental health status (with the inclusion of a group of mental patients' data in the anlaysis), the Verbal–Performance discrepancy compared to the Kansas City data remained (Eisdorfer et al., 1959).

Longitudinal comparisons of WAIS performance focused on the assessment of stability versus changes in performance, selective attrition, and survival (Botwinick & Siegler, 1980; Eisdorfer, 1963a; Eisdorfer & Wilkie, 1973; Siegler, 1981; Siegler & Botwinick, 1979; Siegler, Harkins, & Thompson, 1974). Eisdorfer (1963a) compared performance at the first and second measurement times. Stability of performance in both the younger (60–69) and the older (70+) participants was observed, regardless of initial level of functioning. Those who failed to return for the second testing were not significantly different from the returns, except for the 70–79-year-olds in the middle range of the IQ scale (85–115). These attrition effects became stronger as the study progressed. Siegler and Botwinick (1979) evaluated the attrition through the entire study. The impact of repeated participation is shown in Figure 5.1. Although the age grouping was different than that used by Eisdorfer (1963a), the lack of a difference for the younger subjects was still evident.

Longitudinal changes in WAIS performance were reported by Eisdorfer and Wilkie (1973) through 1967 (Wave 4), and by Siegler (1981) and Siegler and Botwinick (1979) through 1976 (Wave 11). Eisdorfer and Wilkie (1973) illustrated the importance of evaluating survivors and non-survivors separately. When the data on the WAIS were analyzed for

FIGURE 5.1. Mean intelligence test scores at the time of first testing as a function of the number of longitudinal test sessions. Only subjects who were tested on all test sessions, up to and including the abscissa test number, are represented. (From "A Long-Term Longitudinal Study of Intellectual Ability of Older Adults: The Matter of Selective Attrition" by I. C. Siegler and J. Botwinick, *Journal of Gerontology*, 1979, *34*, 243. Copyright 1979 by the Gerontological Society. Reprinted by permission.)

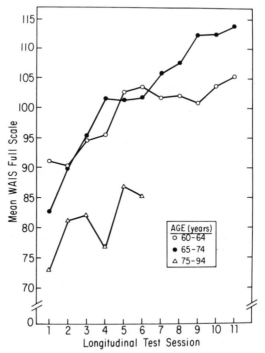

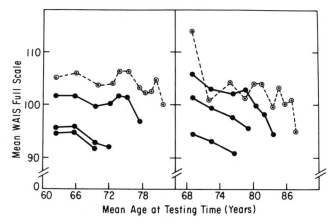

FIGURE 5.2. Subjects aged 60-64 (left half of figure) and 65-74 years (right half of figure) at the start of the study; each curve represents the mean performance of the subjects for only those measurement points indicated. (From "A Long-Term Longitudinal Study of Intellectual Ability of Older Adults: The Matter of Selective Attrition" by I. C. Siegler and J. Botwinick, *Journal of Gerontology*, 1979, *34*, 244. Copyright 1979 by the Gerontological Society. Reprinted by permission.)

just those present at each of the first four waves, it appeared that mean Full-Scale scores increased for both those initially aged 60-69 and those aged 70-79 across the 10 years of testing. When the survivors and non-survivors were analyzed separately, the pattern of change indicated decline in all four groups (see Eisdorfer & Wilkie, 1973, Figure 4.1, p. 23), which is similar to the patterns shown in Figure 5.2 (from Siegler & Botwinick, 1979, which shows the mean performance of the surviving participants at the 3rd, 5th, 7th, and 11th examinations).

The data were analyzed with respect to initial levels of performance, with scaled scores converted to IQ scores and classified as high (116+), middle (85-115), and low (under 85). At the time of the fourth examination, approximately 10 years later, 38.6% of the high-IQ subjects, 51.4% of the middle-IQ subjects, and 72% of the low-IQ subjects were no longer participating in the study (Eisdorfer & Wilkie, 1973).

Siegler (1981) evaluated stability and changes in WAIS performance in the young-old versus the old-old. These two cohorts were defined by a split at age 70 at the first time of measurement. Through the fifth examination, there were no significant cross-sectional differences between the 46 young-old persons (aged 64.56 vs. 75.82 years) and the 26 old-old persons (aged 72.36 vs. 84.00 years). However, both groups had small, but statistically significant, declines on Verbal ($F = 4.01$, $p < .004$), Performance ($F = 11.14$, $p < .001$), and Full-Scale scores ($F = 9.21$, $p < .001$) over time. Similarly, when performance of the 19 subjects from the young-old group who completed the study as the second old-old group (aged 78.47 vs. 84.58 years, Waves 6–11) was tested, their scores were similar in level to those of the previous groups, with significant small declines over time ($F = 5.14$ Verbal, $F = 3.32$ Performance, $F = 6.02$ Full-Scale, p's $< .001$). These changes are shown in Figure 5.3.

Wilkie and Eisdorfer (1973) compared performance at Wave 1 with performance at Wave 7, about a 15-year interval, for the 50 subjects with complete data at both measurement points. They reported significant losses of 3.2, 4.4, and 7.6 points in Verbal, Performance, and Full-Scale weighted scores, respectively. Performance on the WAIS subtests was also evaluated; of the 7.6-point loss reported, 5.4 points reflected loss on the speeded subtests, and 2.3 points on the untimed tests.

Siegler, Harkins, and Thompson (1974) evaluated (1) WAIS performance at the first examination as a function of the distance of that measurement from death and (2) the average rate of change in Full-Scale per-

FIGURE 5.3. Verbal, Performance, and Full-Scale weighted scores for three groups of subjects, by age.

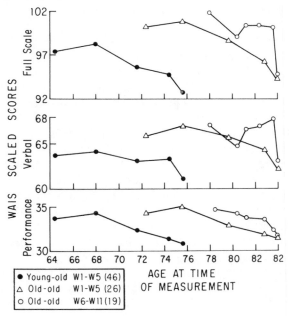

formance for the various groups. The data from that study are presented in Table 5.5. These data differ slightly from the attrition data because some subjects dropped out of the study for reasons other than death. While the change in Full-Scale scores as a function of distance from death was statistically significant, the rate of change averaged across individuals was not. Work in progress on the question of terminal changes in intellectual functioning has used a polynomial regression procedure to model the individual curves over time for all subjects with four or more data points. The results indicate that 76% of the sample decline before death, and 24% do not. Of the 76% who decline, 80% of that group show primarily linear decline, while 20% show a curvilinear decline.

Botwinick and Siegler (1980) examined stability and change in the WAIS in a select subset of the longitudinal panel. Seventy subjects were chosen so that approximately equal time-of-measurement intervals were achieved, and then subjects were stratified into age/cohort groups on the basis of the same 4-year width. Thus approximately 12 years of real time were represented by the cross-sectional age or cohort comparisons at each of the four measurement times, as were included in the longitudinal comparisons. The data were analyzed with the cross-sectional age/cohort comparison as the between-subject factor and with the longitudinal or time change as the within-subject factor in a repeated-measures analysis of variance (ANOVA). Only the longitudinal time change was statistically significant. This is perhaps not as surprising as it might seem when it is recognized that, for the subjects to be available for the cross-sectional comparison at each of the times of measurement, they had to share the same survival and participation requirements as the longitudinal subjects; in addition, the educational level of the four age groups was also found to be equivalent across the age range for these 70 subjects. Thus, when the major variables that cause longitudinal and cross-sectional analyses to diverge are controlled (e.g., survival, sample attrition, and level of formal education), then the cross-sectional comparisons are not significant.

Audition. Longitudinal changes in the auditory system were evaluated by Eisdorfer and Wilkie (1972). The analysis was based on 92 subjects who had complete data on the first and third measurements approximately 7 years apart; the data were analyzed separately for subjects initially in their 60s and in their 70s. The results indicated that hearing acuity diminished significantly above frequencies in the speech range (average of 500, 1000, and 2000 Hz). Declines were more severe for men and for whites. Auditory functioning was also used in analyses that evaluated personality functioning as assessed by the Rorschach (Eisdorfer, 1960a, 1960b). Rorschach rigidity was found to be related to hearing impairment, independent of level of visual functioning (Eisdorfer, 1960a), as

TABLE 5.5. WAIS Performance as a Function of Distance from Death[a]

Subjects	Full-Scale			Verbal			Performance				n	Age at T1[e]	Age at death	Mean Full-Scale change per year
	Wtd.[b]	IQ_a[c]	IQ_{25}[d]	Wtd.	IQ_a	IQ_{25}	Wtd.	IQ_a	IQ_{25}					
Survivors[f]	91	102	88	59	105	98	31	96	76		74	66.27	—	−.28
15–19	88	106	87	59	111	98	30	101	74		36	70.08	86.47	−.57
10–14	86	105	86	57	109	96	30	101	74		50	71.44	83.40	−.39
5–9	72	97	77	50	102	89	23	91	65		58	73.00	79.77	−.41
0–4	68	95	75	48	100	87	20	88	61		40	74.40	76.57	−.40

[a]From Siegler, Harkins, and Thompson (1974, Tables 1 and 2).
[b]Wtd. = weighted.
[c]IQ_a = IQ at age of testing.
[d]IQ_{25} = IQ converted on the basis of the 25–34-year-old standardization group.
[e]T1 = first examination.
[f]Survivors as of August 1974.

well, significantly lowered developmental level as defined by vocabulary level and functional integration scores was related to hearing impairment, and not to visual impairment, although those subjects impaired on both senses were the most impaired. Subjects in each study numbered 48 and were those who had participated with normal levels of hearing in the first examination.

Personality. Eisdorfer (1963b) evaluated the Rorschach performance of 242 subjects at the first examination who had both complete WAIS and complete Rorschach protocols. The results indicated that intellectual level, rather than age *per se*, was important in interpretation of Rorschach results. Indexes derived from the Rorschach were also used to investigate marital happiness in 30 couples in the first round of the study (Busse & Eisdorfer, 1970).

Fox (1979) evaluated stability and change in Rorschach performance in a subset of the longitudinal population. Indexes of psychological rigidity, ego energy, and interiority were developed from Holt's (1970) manual for the scoring of primary process manifestations in Rorschach responses and from Fisher and Cleveland's (1958) barrier score. Seventy-eight of the original 267 subjects had complete Rorschach protocols across the three times of measurement at which the Rorschach was administered. From this group, 35 subjects were randomly selected for this analysis. The data were analyzed with a four-cohort (1881, 1885, 1890, 1895) by three-times-of-measurement (1955, 1959, 1967) repeated-measures ANOVA. In addition to this cross-sequential analysis, the data were also analyzed with two time-sequential strategies: (1) with two age levels (70–74 vs. 75+) and the three times of testing and (2) with three age levels (65–69, 70–74, 75+) and two times of testing (1955, 1959). No significant differences were found in any of the sequential analyses for measures of psychological rigidity or ego energy. The predicted increase in interiority was not found; rather, there was a significant increase in the percentage of barrier responses for subjects across time, regardless of cohort affiliation, suggesting a significant increased orientation toward mastery behavior.

Reaction Time. Longitudinal RT was investigated by Wilkie, Eisdorfer, and Siegler (1975) and by Siegler (1981). Wilkie *et al.* compared performance on the RT task of a group of younger subjects ($n = 151, \bar{x}$ age $= 20.5$) who had a single measurement on the same task with the 135 longitudinal subjects who had complete data on two examinations 7 years apart. Sex differences favoring males were found for the younger subjects, but no sex differences were found for the older subjects. There were no significant differences in RT between those subjects who were seen at the 7-year follow-up and those who were not. Among the older subjects who returned, little slowing was evident, except on the responses after the conflict trials.

The young and old at the first measurement time had conflicting patterns postconflict (the young initially slowing their responses postconflict and then returning to speed, the old doing the reverse). Seven years later, the older subjects had a pattern of responding to the conflict trials similar to that of the younger subjects.

Siegler (1981) looked at choice RT performance averaged over the 20 choice RT trials before the first conflict trial was introduced. Mean lift time (decision component), mean press time (visuomotor component), and total RT were evaluated for young-old (60–90 years) and old-old (70 + years) cohorts at the second through the fifth times of measurement, and for a second old-old group (the survivors of the young-old group, who completed the 11 waves of the study). There were no significant cohort/age differences between the young-old and old-old groups through the first four times of measurement; however, significant time effects were found for lift ($F = 3.69, p < .013$) and press ($F = 12.49, p < .001$) times. The lift times decreased significantly from approximately 505 msec to 469 msec, while press times increased significantly from 360 msec to 450 msec, with changes in total RT nonsignificant. For the second old-old group, there were no significant differences for the press component, while both lift and total RT changed significantly in a nonlinear fashion, with the slowest RTs at the final measurement point. These results suggest that the changes in RT observed longitudinally may well be less than the traditional cross-sectional paradigms would suggest.

Wechsler Memory Scale. Performance on the WMS of subjects evaluated in two age cohorts across 2, 5, and 10 times of measurement is shown in Figure 5.4, taken from McCarty, Siegler, and Logue (1982). All differences were tested in a repeated-measures ANOVA. Significant age/cohort differences between the subjects aged in the 60s and in the 70s (mean ages 67.61 and 76.16, respectively, at Wave 2) were found only for Immediate and Delayed Recall ($F_{114} = 4.70, p < .05$; $F_{114} = 4.90, p < .05$); significant time effects were seen on all variables except easy Paired Associates. At Waves 2–6 (middle panel, Figure 5.4) there were no significant age/cohort effects, and time effects were significant except for the easy Paired Associates, as was true for the previous comparison with very similar F values. In the right-hand panel (Figure 5.4), the only time effect that was significant was that for Visual Reproduction ($F = 4.01, p < .001$). Thus considerable stability of performance was seen on all of the verbal memory functions for the long-term surviving participants.

The data shown in Figure 5.5 compare WMS and WAIS scores as a function of distance from death. The data are from 1960 (Wave 2) for both WMS and WAIS scores. Group means were tested by ANOVA. Although all four of the comparisons are highly significant, Duncan's

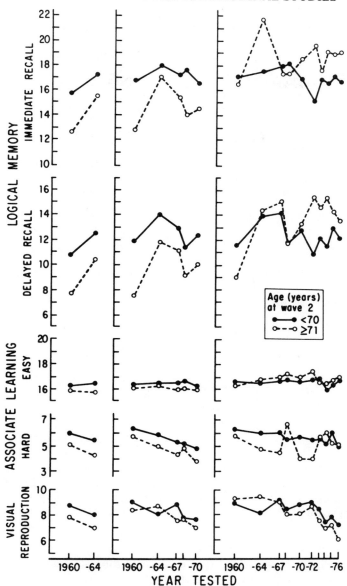

FIGURE 5.4. Longitudinal WMS curves for subjects present at Waves 2–3 (left), 2–6 (middle), and 2–11 (right). (From "Cross-Sectional Patterns of Three Wechsler Memory Scale Subtests" by S. M. McCarty, I. C. Siegler, and P. E. Logue, *Journal of Gerontology*, 1982, *37*, 170. Copyright 1982 by the Gerontological Society. Reprinted by permission.)

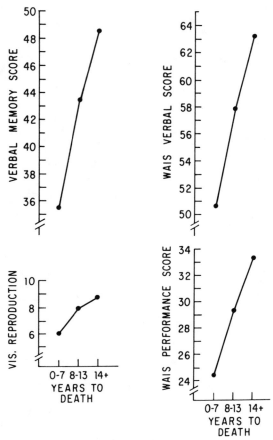

FIGURE 5.5. Mean WMS and WAIS composite scores by years to death. (From "Wechsler Memory Scale Scores, Selective Attrition, and Distance from Death" by I. C. Siegler, S. M. McCarty, and P. E. Logue, *Journal of Gerontology*, 1982, *37*, 180. Copyright 1982 by the Gerontological Society. Reprinted by permission.)

multiple-range tests revealed that the significant differences in all cases were between the first two groups (Siegler, McCarty, & Logue, 1982).

As a group, these studies have provided a picture that reveals relatively few age differences when the two larger cohorts in the decade of the 60s and the decade of the 70s are compared, but modest, albeit statistically significant, longitudinal changes. When data for the surviving subjects in the later waves of the study are analyzed, the declines are seen; however, these are most often found to occur in the late 70s and in the 80s. Although these estimates may overestimate the level of functioning achieved by age peers without repeated testing, they suggest a much more optimistic picture of normal aging, in subjects who remain capable of participating. As will be seen in the next section, changes in health help to explain the observed declines. These data also point to the special sensitivity of these measures to the problems of selective subject attrition and the strong relationship of the data to distance from death.

Psychological and Health Variables

A major purpose of the first longitudinal study was to evaluate normal aging in a group of noninstitutionalized older persons, as well as to be able to explore, with a single population, the interactions among variables from a variety of disciplines. The studies reviewed here are those that included data from the psychological laboratory in conjunction with variables that assessed central nervous system (CNS) functioning (primarily blood pressure [BP], indexes of cardiovascular disease [CVD], physical health ratings, and immunoglobulins).

Relationships among psychological functioning, measures of CNS functioning, and health have been a major focus of the first longitudinal study and are briefly summarized in Table 5.6.

Obrist, Busse, Eisdorfer, and Kleemeier (1962) evaluated the relationship between levels of intellectual functioning and patterns of EEG classifications in three samples of older persons. Subjects from the first cycle of the longitudinal study formed the community group and were compared to a group of older persons who were psychiatric inpatients and to a second group of older persons who resided in a home for the aged. In the longitudinal sample, no significant relationship was found between intellectual functioning and diffuse, slow EEG activity as had been observed in the other two samples studied. Similarly, significant correlations between alpha frequency and level of intellectual functioning were observed only in the institutionalized groups; the presence of arteriosclerosis was required for the appearance of a significant relationship between alpha frequency and intelligence, which was not observed in institutionalized subjects without arteriosclerosis who were matched for age. The relationships were stronger for the performance than for the verbal subtests. In summary, the study indicated little or no relationship between intelligence and EEG in healthy community elderly. Focal slow activity and excess fast activity were unrelated to intellectual functioning in any of the groups studied. Thus the presence of a health problem, particularly CVD, was necessary in order to observe the relationship.

TABLE 5.6. Psychological Variables, CNS Function, and Health

Author/date	Variables[a]	Waves at which cross-sectional analyses were conducted	Waves at which longitudinal analyses were conducted
Obrist, Busse, Eisdorfer, & Kleemeier (1962)	W,EEG,Ath	1	
Thompson, Eisdorfer, & Estes (1966)	W,CVD		1–2
Wang, Obrist, & Busse (1970)	W,EEG,CBF		1–5
Busse & Wang (1971)	W,EEG,BP,ACT,H	1	1–3
Wilkie & Eisdorfer (1971)	W,BP	1	1–4
Wilkie & Eisdorfer (1972)	RT,BP		2–4
Wilkie & Eisdorfer (1973b)	W,BP		1–2
Wilkie & Eisdorfer (1974)	W,CVD		1–6
Wang & Busse (1974b)	W,CVD,EEG	1	
Roseman & Buckley (1975)	W,Ig's	8	4–8
Wilkie, Eisdorfer, & Nowlin (1976)	WM,BP		2–4
Prinz (1977)	W,WM,SEEG		1–8
Woodbury & Manton (1983)	W,BP,Chol		1–11

[a]W = WAIS; R = Rorschach; A = audition; V = vision; MH = marital happiness; RT = reaction time; WM = Weschler Memory; BP = blood pressure; CVD = cardiovascular disease; Ig's = immunoglobulins; Chol = cholesterol; Ath = atherosclerosis; CBF = cerebral blood flow; ACT = activities; H = health status; SEEG = sleep EEG.

Thompson, Eisdorfer, and Estes (1966) evaluated verbal and performance intelligence in the first two examinations as a function of the presence or absence of CVD. Only the WAIS Performance scores were higher for those without CVD, which was true at both the first and the second examinations. However, there was no relationship between CVD and changes in intellectual functioning over the 3–4-year interval. Similarly, changes in RT and on the WMS were not related to CVD status.

Wang, Obrist, and Busse (1970) evaluated the neurophysiological correlates of intellectual functioning with two subsamples from the first longitudinal study. The first group included 32 subjects selected because they were free of any symptoms of cardiopulmonary and neurological diseases for both the first and the second examinations. A second group of 24 subjects from the fifth examination was selected at random from the returning subjects and was evaluated by the xenon-inhalation method of measuring CBF. Although there was no association between occipital frequency and initial WAIS performance, there was a significant correlation between slower frequencies and the Verbal–Performance discrepancy score (see Wechsler, 1958). In addition, slower frequencies at the first examination were related to a greater decline in the Performance scales of the WAIS between Wave 1 and Wave 2. Subjects were then classified on the presence or absence of focal abnormalities in the EEG. Declines between Wave 1 and Wave 2 were greater in the group with focal abnormalities for both Verbal and Performance scales. The WAIS scores were then compared for the 24 subjects who had blood-flow data. There were no significant differences on measures of intelligence taken when the blood-flow measures were done (Wave 5) nor when changes over the 12-year period were calculated. However, when SES and level of education were taken into account, a significant relationship was found between blood flow and the Performance scale of the WAIS.

Busse and Wang (1971) divided the sample at the first examination into six groups on the basis of the presence or absence of heart and lung disease. Approximately half of the sample was disease free. These six groups were then evaluated for the percentage classified as having diffuse, slow tracings on the EEG, the mean occipital dominant frequency of the EEG, and the percentage diagnosed by a neurological examination and WAIS performance. The results indicated that decompensated heart disease rather than lung disease was related to indexes of brain impairment. The patterns of intellectual functioning were not as clear. Main differences among the groups were found on mean arterial blood pressure (MABP) and in amount of daily activities. Thus subjects with mildly elevated BP and high degrees of activity appeared to do the best. These two hypotheses were tested by comparing change in MABP and in average EEG occipital frequency over a 7-year period (Waves 1–3). The development of heart disease was related to MABP in a linear fashion, such that only 6% of subjects with MABP below 95 mm Hg developed heart disease, while 44% with MABP above 114 mm Hg developed heart disease.

Changes in intellectual functioning were evaluated as a function of the individuals' activity profiles. Three activity profiles were identified: many activities of both types; many locomotor, but few sedentary, activities; and few activities of either type. Changes in intellectual performance at the first and third visits were calculated for Verbal and Performance scales and for the WAIS deterioration quotient (DQ). Those high on both types of activities had a significant increase in the Verbal scaled score, whereas those low on both had a significant decrease in the Verbal scaled score. The Performance scaled score significantly decreased only for those low on both activities. The DQ was stable for those high on both types of activity and increased for other activity groups.

Wang and Busse (1974b) evaluated the relationship among heart disease, intelligence, and activity patterns. The study included 227 subjects who were free of any pulmonary disease and who were divided into 4 groups: (1) no heart disease ($n = 105$); (2) questionable heart disease ($n = 27$); (3) definite and compensated heart disease ($n = 47$); and (4) definite and decompensated heart disease ($n = 48$). Groups were first compared on sociodemographic indexes (age, sex, race, occupation, and education). The first two groups were similar. The third group had a higher percentage of black subjects, and the fourth group was older and had more blacks, fewer subjects in low-status occupations, and subjects with lower educational attainment. The WAIS Verbal and Performance scaled scores were lower in the two groups with significant disease, even when the sociodemographic factors were controlled. Evidence of brain disorder on the basis of the neurological exam was 9.5% for Group 1, 7.4% for Group 2, 2.1% for Group 3, and 27% for Group 4. Mean systolic BP and mean diastolic BP were also high for the third and fourth groups.

Wilkie and Eisdorfer (1972) evaluated changes in intellectual functioning related to death and distance from death in a subsample of the first longitudinal study. The analyses were completed after the sixth evaluation and were limited to subjects with at least three complete examinations. Subjects who had died were included if they had died within 3 years of their final testing. The subsample included 66 survivors and 37 nonsurvivors, divided into three groups: those who died within 1 year, those who died within 2 years, and those who died from 25 to 32 months after the final examination. The survivors had survived 4 years after the third measurement point. Analyses of variance indicated no significant differences among groups on WAIS performance and no significant correlation between test scores and distance from death. However, significant differences were observed on the magnitude of change across the three measurement occasions. The change was significant on Full-Scale, Verbal, and Performance components for the two nonsurviving groups, at 2 and 3 years, respectively; however, the significant change was between the first two measurement points only. Individual differences were large, since 24% of the nonsurvivors had no changes of less than 6 points in the Full-Scale weighted scores. Survivors and nonsurvivors were then compared on initial level of IQ and change in score between the first and third examinations. Only the middle- and high-IQ groups had significant differences that discriminated survivors from nonsurvivors. Survivors and nonsurvivors were then compared on degree of CVD as assessed by a physician's rating of no CVD, mild CVD, or moderately severe CVD. In this group, 59% of the survivors and 62% of the nonsurvivors had moderately severe CVD. Changes in Full-Scale scores were significantly different only for the group without CVD.

Medical records were checked next to assess the contributions of chronic and acute diseases. Included in chronic diseases were CVD, emphysema, arthritis, diabetes, and epilepsy; acute illnesses were infections, injuries, or other minor illnesses, including surgery. The survivors were relatively free of chronic diseases except for CVD, with only about 17% having any of the acute illnesses. For nonsurvivors, those with only chronic diseases indicated about a 5-point loss between Waves 1 and 3; those with both chronic and acute diseases, a loss of about 13 points.

Wilkie and Eisdorfer (1973b) evaluated the relationship between BP and intellectual performance at the first two examinations. The study included 122 subjects at Wave 1 and 91 subjects at Wave 2 who were initially aged 60–69 years and 107 subjects at Wave 1 and 76 subjects at Wave 2 who were initially aged 70–79 years. Blood pressure was indexed by the systolic BP, with subjects classified into three groups: low (96–125 mm Hg), medium (126–185 mm Hg), and high (186–300 mm Hg). There was no relationship between BP and intellectual performance for the 60-year-old cohort at the first examination as indexed by ANOVA or by correlations of all subtests and weighted scores with the systolic BP. However, in the 70-year-old cohort, significant differences were found at the first examination. Approximately 3 years later, at the second examination, BP was significantly related only to the Performance weighted score for the younger cohort; but to all three weighted scores for the older cohort. In all cases, increased systolic BP was related to poorer intellectual functioning.

Psychological performance on the WAIS, the WMS, and RT as a function of BP has been studied by Wilkie and her colleagues (Wilkie & Eisdorfer, 1971, 1972; Wilkie, Eisdorfer, & Nowlin, 1976) and has recently been reviewed by Wilkie (1980). In these three studies, diastolic BP was used to divide the subjects into three groups: normal, or between 66 and 95 mm Hg; borderline high, with 96 to 105 mm Hg; and high, or above 105 mm Hg. The high-BP group had significantly greater evidence of end-organ change.

This same grouping of subjects was used by Wilkie and Eisdorfer (1973b): a 60–69-year-old cohort versus a 70–79-year-old cohort, at the first examination for the WAIS, at the second examination for the WMS and RT, and at the fourth evaluation for the longitudinal follow-up. Wilkie and Eisdorfer (1972) reported that, at initial evaluation, RT was not related to BP; at the fourth examination, none of the older hypertensives were available for testing. For those in the borderline-high group, slowing was observed, while little change was observed among those in their 70s in the normal diastolic group. For the younger cohort, a significant slowing in RT was observed only for the hypertensive group. Wilkie and Eisdorfer (1971) replicated the findings reported by Wilkie and Eisdorfer (1973b) by extending the analysis through Wave 4 of data collection. Most interesting was the finding that, for the borderline-hypertensive group in the 60s, a significant increase in performance score was observed; this increase was interpreted as reflecting stability of performance that had been related to additional practice on the test. The relationship among WAIS performance, BP, and selective attrition was evaluated. For the younger cohort, the subjects who completed the 10-year study had higher WAIS scores at the first examination, independent of BP categories. However, when the BP groups were looked at separately, the main difference was between the returning and the nonreturning hypertensives only; this same relationship was observed for the normotensive and borderline-hypertensive groups in the older cohort.

Wilkie, Eisdorfer, and Nowlin (1976) evaluated the impact of diastolic BP on memory as assessed by the WMS. No significant relationships were observed at the initial evaluation (Wave 2); however, at follow-up (Wave 4), the hypertensive group indicated declines on all tasks, with significant declines only on visual reproduction. Thus degree of hypertension was shown to be related to cognitive performance across a variety of measures, and for the younger cohort (aged in the 60s), borderline hypertension was not related to decreased performance as it was in the older cohorts.

Woodbury and Manton (1983) evaluated risk profiles for the occurrence of CVD in the first longitudinal study population using methods for risk analysis in longitudinal studies based on the Framingham data (Woodbury, Manton, & Stallard, 1979a, 1979b). They found that maintenance of intellectual function as indexed by the WAIS performance score was related to reduced risk of CVD, even in the context of elevated physiological risk factors.

Roseman and Buckley (1975) investigated the relationship between intellectual functioning and serum immunoglobulin levels for IgG, IgA, and IgM in 97 subjects with complete data on both measures. Blood samples were taken for later immunological analysis starting with Wave 4 (1966–1967). Only the relationship between WAIS scores and IgG was significant ($r = -.332$, $p < .005$). The finding for IgG was replicated with the adaptation study sample. The high levels of IgG may be an index of poorer health, and thus the negative relationship reported is consistent with other findings.

Prinz (1977) investigated the relationship between sleep patterns and intellectual performance in 12 of the longitudinal subjects. Sleep EEGs were recorded at home near the time of the eighth examination (1973). The subjects ranged in age from 76 to 82 years and had a mean age of 82 at the time the sleep EEGs were measured. Time spent in rapid-eye-movement (REM) sleep was found to be positively correlated with the WAIS Performance score measured contemporaneously ($r = .764$) and with the change per year ($r = .841$). The WAIS Verbal score was not related to REM sleep. Of the measures available from the WMS, only the change in performance on the hard-paired-associates task was related to REM sleep ($r = .605$). The subjects were then classified into two groups on the basis of amount of REM sleep time, and the longitudinal patterns of WAIS scores were evaluated. For the high-REM group ($\bar{x} = 89$ minutes), the scores were stable over the 18-year period; whereas for the low-REM group ($\bar{x} = 64.6$ minutes), a significant decline was observed after the sixth examination.

The studies reviewed in this section suggest that observed patterns of stability and change in intellectual performance are related to indexes of the integrity of the CNS, the immune system, and the cardiovascular system. Ongoing analyses are exploring these relationships further. For example, in February 1977, after the major data collection had been completed, subjects were interviewed about their current life situation. Permission for autopsy was given by 12 members (of 25 contacted) of the longitudinal panel and their families so that the morphological changes observed could be correlated with the longitudinal test battery (Vogel, Burger, Siegler, & Nowlin, 1977).

Two subjects have been autopsied thus far. Both subjects completed all 11 examinations. The first subject joined the study at age 66 (Full-Scale WAIS of 118), had her final WAIS given at age 86 (Full-Scale of 119), and died at age 88. During the course of the study, her scores varied from a high of 124 achieved at the fifth examination to a low of 104 at the tenth. When interviewed in 1977, her health was beginning to fail, and she was worried about her ability to continue to live in her own home. Nine brain areas were evaluated microscopically, revealing six senile plaques (two inferior frontal, four amygdala) and 62 neurofibrillary tangles in the hippocampus; however, a fair degree of cortical atrophy was noted. The second subject joined the study at age 72 (Full-Scale WAIS of 132) and had his final WAIS at age 92 (Full-Scale WAIS of 113). His scores varied, with a high of 134 at the fourth measurement, and linearly declined after Wave 7 (130, 119, 118, 114, 113). He died at age 94. When seen for the interview, his vision had deteriorated badly, as had his memory, and although a formal mental status examination was not given, he appeared to be severely impaired and would not have been able to complete a WAIS. On examination, senile plaques were found in all nine brain areas, ranging from 52 to 160 plaques per area. Neurofibrillary tangles were found in seven areas and ranged from 1 tangle to 35 tangles per area. Data on cell counts in these areas are not yet available, and the remaining subjects who have given autopsy permission are still alive; however, this analysis indicates the potential use of the data in comparing the data base with the pathological findings as they become available. These data are discussed more fully in the final report of the study (Duke University, 1980).

Survival, Successful Aging, and Special Topics

This final set of analyses from the first longitudinal study constitutes those that represent data from the entire data base and that tend to be organized around specific questions. Although there are many other reports on the first longitudinal study that deal with important issues in aging, such as disengagement theory (see Maddox, 1965, 1966), and reviews of other substantive areas that have already been cited, the set of reports discussed here used psychological data in conjunction with other data to address specific problems. Maddox and Douglass (1974) investigated the question of stability and change in variance in selected social, psychological, and physical health measures. Nowlin (1977) derived a measure of successful aging; Palmore (1969, 1971, 1974c), Pfeiffer (1970), and Wang and Busse (1974a) evaluated the predictors of survival; and Palmore and Cleveland (1976) evaluated the questions of terminal decline and terminal drop.

Maddox and Douglass (1974) studied the 106 survivors from the first longitudinal panel who participated in the study through the sixth examination. They evaluated a variety of social, psychological, and health measures for stability or change in variance when comparing the first and sixth examinations or the first and third. The statistical technique employed was Pitman's test for correlated variances (see Maddox & Douglass, 1974, p. 559).

The number of subjects available for each comparison ranged from 33 to 72. The results indicated considerable stability of variance across both measurement times and for most variables. Significant increases in variance were found only for life satisfaction and concern about health, cardiovascular health status, and visual acuity for Waves 1 versus 6; significant decreases in variance were found for self-assessment of health and diastolic BP. The same test, made in comparing Waves 3 and 6, found no significant coefficients for any of the social or psychological variables, but significant increases in variance for an overall health rating and percentage hearing loss. None of the significant coefficients yielded by comparing Waves 1 and 6 were observed when Waves 3 and 6 were compared. Although most of the signs of the coefficients were negative, indicating increased variance, most of them also did not differ significantly from zero. Spearman's rank-order correlations for the psychological variables indicated the extreme stability of these measures between Waves 1 and 6 ($\pi = .92$ for Full-Scale WAIS; .93 for WAIS Verbal scaled score; .85 for WAIS Performance scaled score; .76 for percentage hearing loss; and .64 for lift RT, Waves 3 and 6). All of these coefficients were significant at $p < .01$. A special analysis on the lift RTs was conducted, which indicated stability of variance in RT as well; however, analyses in progress with the same data indicate that this finding is unlikely to be replicated.

Nowlin (1977) defined "successful aging" as achievement of age 75 with maintenance of physical health. Thus, at the tenth examination, in 1975, the subjects were divided into three groups: 51 subjects who were defined as successful agers; 105 who had survived to 75 years of age, but whose health was compromised; and 99 nonsurvivors. Data from the second examination were used to expore the predictors of successful aging. At Wave 2 (1960), the groups were significantly different on measures of serum cholesterol, educational attainment, Cavan Activity Scale, and Full-Scale WAIS. No differences were observed for measures of BP, height and weight, CVD rating, visual and hearing acuity, and hemoglobin. There were no significant race or sex differences in the composition of the three criterion groups. However, race and sex differences were found in the total sample at Wave 2 on many of the variables. The variables as a set were then used in a discriminant analysis to predict successful aging. The Cavan Activity Scale, serum cholesterol, and CVD rating successfully discriminated the successful aging groups from the other two groups.

The final set of analyses reviewed here were concerned with the prediction of survival. Palmore (1969) developed the longevity index (LI). The LI was defined as either the number of years survived for subjects still alive or the number of years of predicted survival based on the appropriate life tables. Palmore (1971) also presented a longevity quotient (LQ). The LQ was defined as a ratio of the LI divided by the actual life expectancy of the individual. The LQ had a value of greater than 1 if the individual achieved a greater-than-predicted survival and a value of less than 1 if the individual died before the life tables would have predicted. In this set of studies, either LI, LQ, or both were used as the dependent variable in a series of multiple-regression equations that used various social, psychological, and health variables, with various subsets of the data as predictors. For the total sample, four variables—life expectancy at Time 1 (LET1), physical function rating (PFR), work satisfaction (WS), and Performance scaled score (PSS)—had a multiple R of .64 with the LI and accounted for a total of 40% of the variance. Stepwise regressions on these variables were then calculated for subsets of the data separately: men, women, men and women aged over and under 70 years, blacks, and whites. There were between-group variations on the prediction equations developed for each subsample, but for the total sample, the equation developed was

$$\text{Longevity} = 12.7 + .87_{\text{LETI}} + 1.07_{\text{PFR}} + .71_{\text{WS}} + .06_{\text{Pss}}$$

Palmore (1971) reported the zero-order correlations of 39 variables with the LI and the LQ and used five variables in stepwise regression equations to predict LQ: the PFR ($r = .21$), work satisfaction ($r = .26$), and Performance scaled scores ($r = .21$) used in the previous analyses, and a happiness rating ($r = .25$) and a use-of-tobacco measure ($r = .19$). For the total sample, 17% of the variance in LQ was accounted for by four of the measures (Performance scaled scores did not enter the equation). Palmore (1974c) focused on the LQ and found that, for the total sample in the stepwise regression analysis, CVD rating, work satisfaction, cigarette smoking, PFR, and happiness rating account for 27% of the variance in LQ.

Pfeiffer (1970) looked at the same question by matching 37 of the long-lived subjects with 37 of the shortest lived subjects. The long-lived men had an LI of 17.22 years and an LQ of 1.56 compared to 2.42 years and .24 for the short-lived men. The values of the LI and the LQ for the long-lived women were 19.3 years and 1.34, and for the short-lived women 5.5 years and .44. The groups were then compared on a large number of variables; all comparisons for men and women were done separately, and the groups had been matched on age and race. Results indicated that, for both sexes, the significant relationships to survival were found for Full-Scale WAIS, Verbal scaled score, Performance scaled score, self-rated health, and perceived change in self-rated health. For men only, self-health concerns, number of days in bed, PFR, education, financial self-evaluation, and change in financial self-evaluation were related to survival; for women, marital status and occupation were the only variables related to survival. Stepwise regression equations predicted 38% of the variance for women and 58% of the variance for men, with the variables in slightly different orders for the two sexes.

Wang and Busse (1974a) used EEG dominant frequency, WAIS DQ, neurological evidence of CNS disorder, and EEG focal disturbance as predictors for LI and LQ. Twenty-three percent of the variance in LI was predicted by EEG frequency, WAIS DQ, and evidence of CNS disorder, while 10.2% of the variance in LQ was predicted by WAIS DQ, CNS disorder, and EEG frequency. Thus, as a group, these studies indicate that the predictions for LI account for more variance than the predictions for

LQ, even when the life expectancy is not a variable in the LI analysis, and that social, physical, and psychological factors all play a role in the prediction of survival.

Palmore and Cleveland (1976) chose 21 variables from the data set, which included physical functioning, intelligence, activities, and attitude measures. The analysis was based on two sets of multiple-regression equations. In the first set of analyses, the value of the variable at the first measurement point for the 178 subjects who had died by December 1974 was analyzed by stepwise regression, with age at Wave 1 and time before death at Wave 1 as the two independent variables. The proportions of variance accounted for were reported for each of the 21 equations. The amounts of variance accounted for were not large, with five variables shown to be related to age (PFR, hearing, and three types of activities) and six variables related to distance from death (PFR, self-rated health, Full-Scale WAIS, and three attitude measures).

In the second set of analyses, 85 subjects who had died and who had from three to eight measurements, or 368 person examinations, formed the data base, so that age at wave and distance from death squared (a measure of curvilinear decline or terminal drop) were tested with the same 21 variables used as the dependent variables in the regressions. In these analyses, age accounted for significant amounts of variance in 17 of the 21 predictors (2 activities and 2 attitudes were nonsignificant), and time before death squared explained significant variance for only two variables, Full-Scale WAIS (an additional 2%) and the personal adjustment attitude (an additional 2%). Thus Palmore and Cleveland concluded that effects of distance from death (or "terminal decline," in their terminology) were much stronger than the evidence for terminal drop. These findings are consistent with the individual patterns of change observed in intelligence, which suggest that a greater proportion of the subjects showed linear, rather than curvilinear, declines; however, the relatively small amounts of variance explained may be related to the 25% of the sample who had stable or increasing patterns.

The Second Longitudinal Study

Measures and Procedures

Concomitant with the increase in sample size was the cutting in half of the time for examination of each subject: subjects were seen for only 1 day. The major psychological variables (see Table 5.2) were four subtests of the WAIS. The four subtests chosen were Information, Vocabulary,

Picture Arrangement, and Digit Symbol Substitution (DSS), all of which took about half an hour to administer. These were chosen because they had the highest correlations with the Verbal and Performance scales in the youngest part of the first longitudinal population. Personality was assessed by Form C of Cattell's 16 Personality Factors (16PF) Questionnaire (Cattell, Eber, & Tatsuka, 1970). Form C was chosen because of the simpler reading level and reduced time required for administration. Hearing was assessed by pure-tone audiometry at frequencies ranging from 500 Hz to 6000 Hz. Vision was assessed in the psychological laboratory with the American Optical Company's reading card and a Snellen eye chart. A continuous performance task (CPT) was added to the psychological data collection in order to get observations of subjects' behavior while under stress in an experimental setting. The procedures were smiliar to those described by Thompson, Opton, and Cohen (1963). Heart rate (HR) and basal skin conductance (GSR) were recorded during the task, and the Nowlis Mood Adjective Check List (MACL; Nowlis, 1956) was administered at baseline, after each experimental set of trials, and at the conclusion of the task. The CPT was given only twice during the study per subject and was alternated with measurements made in the EEG laboratory. Thus subjects had the CPT on either their first and third visits or their second and fourth visits. (For more detailed information on specific procedures, see Siegler et al., 1976).

The medical examination given during the second longitudinal study was similar to that given during the first study, except that the examinations in ophthamology and dermatology were not done by specialists. Reviews of these systems were added to the physician examination, and vision was tested in the psychological laboratory. A chest X ray and an assessment of medications were added. Similar laboratory tests were performed, as were evaluations of the immune system. There was no psychiatric interview per se because the social history section was expanded to include measures of mental health and psychological well-being. Aside from sociodemographic variables, social contacts, and activities, the social history also included questions about self-rated health, sexual functioning, leisure, and attitudes toward time and death. Of particular psychological interest is a set of self-report scales including locus of control (Jessor, Graves, Hanson, & Jessor, 1968), semantic differential ratings of self-concept (Back & Guptill, 1966), achievement value orientation (Rosen, 1956, anomie (McClosky & Schaar, 1965), affect balance (Bradburn, 1969; Bradburn & Caplovitz, 1965), a checklist of psychosomatic symptoms (Bradburn & Caplovitz, 1965), and a ladder measure of life satisfaction (Cantrill, 1965). The Social Readjustment Rating Scale (Holmes &

Rahe, 1967) was added during the third examination. These measures are fully discussed in George (1976a, 1976b).

One satellite study has developed from the second longitudinal study. One hundred of the 331 long-term participants with complete psychological data were interviewed for a study of coping mechanisms (Siegler, Gatz, Tyler, & George, 1979; George & Siegler, 1982).[3] This study (the coping study) is concerned with the individual's perceptions of significant life events. The data include a fifth measurement point on many of the social psychological scales used in the social history and a 2-hour tape-recorded interview designed to assess coping strategies and perceptions of life events.

The data from the second longitudinal study are now available for secondary analysis, and four code books with frequency distributions on all variables have recently been published.[4]

Sample Maintenance and Participation Patterns

As in the first longitudinal study, the results of subjects' physical examination were communicated to them and to their physicians shortly after each visit. However, since many more of the subjects were working full time, it was more difficult to schedule appointments even though the study required only 1 full day in the laboratory. The participation patterns of the total sample are shown in Table 5.7. Categories of participation and dropout for major psychological variables, summed for the entire study, are shown in Table 5.8. As both of these tables indicate, dropout, rather than death, was the major reason for attrition in the second longitudinal study.

Major Findings

The second longitudinal study was designed to explore the patterns of normal aging that had been observed in the first longitudinal study. Implicitly, as can be seen from the choice of variables just described, there

[3]This satellite study has been supported by Grant 90-A-1022 from the Administration on Aging (M. Gatz and I. C. Siegler, coprincipal investigators) and by a grant from the NRTA-AARP Andrus Foundation, (L. K. George and I. C. Siegler, coprincipal investigators).

[4]The data tapes and code books are available from the Data Archive and Adult Development and Aging, Box 3003, Duke University Medical Center, Durham, N.C. 27710. Data tapes and code books of the first longitudinal study are currently in preparation.

TABLE 5.7. Participation Patterns in Longitudinal II

	Wave of study			
	W1 (1968–1970)	W2 (1970–1972)	W3 (1972–1974)	W4 (1974–1976)
Subjects seen	502	438	383	375
Subjects who dropped out		50	87	79
Subjects who died		14	32	48

was a shift away from exploration of psychological constructs (e.g., intelligence, RT, and memory) and the normative patterns of stability and change observed to exploration of the behavior of the individuals in context. The shortened version of the WAIS was used to develop an estimate of adult intelligence. The first longitudinal study, as well as data from other studies, had suggested little reason to expect large changes in intellectual performance in the middle years. The main emphasis on cognitive performance shifted to looking at performance of the subjects in the stressful laboratory situation of the CPT. The Cattell 16PF was used to evaluate stability and change in personality during the middle years and to evaluate the relationships among personality, health, and behavioral performance. Many psychological constructs (e.g., locus of control and self-concept) and measures of psychological well-being (affect balance and life satisfaction) were included in the social history as measures of adaptation. Findings from the second longitudinal study are reviewed in two sections. The first section is concerned with personality

TABLE 5.8. Summary of Participation Patterns with Psychological Data

Category of participation	Number of subjects	Number of subjects who took WAIS	Number of subjects who took Cattell
Seen at all four waves	350	348	346
Dropouts			
Seen/dropped out/seen	27		
Dropped out	77	104	98
Dropped out and died	9		
Died	39	48	47
	502	500[a]	491[a]

[a]These numbers do not add up to 502 because of incomplete data at first examination on these variables.

and social psychological factors during the middle years, and the second section with studies that consider stress, health, and the adaptation to significant life events experienced during the course of the study.

Personality and Social Factors

Personality. Siegler, George, and Okun (1979) evaluated the age/cohort and time effects observed in personality by employing a cross-sequential design with 12 2-year cohort groups. All subjects analyzed had complete data at all four waves. The results indicated that, over the 6-year study period, personality tended to be stable. The most frequent finding was the stability of sex differences, which varied neither by age/cohort nor by time. Five traits displayed this picture: A (Reserved vs. Outgoing), E (Submissive vs. Dominant, I (Tough-minded vs. Tender-minded), N (Naive vs. Shrewd), and Q_4 (Relaxed vs. Tense). Only one factor, B, a verbal intelligence, problem-solving factor, had significant time effects (an increase through the third examination, then a level equivalent to that achieved at the second examination) and a significant age/cohort effect, where the oldest cohort had a mean of 4.2. Only the two youngest cohorts (born 1919-1922, aged 46-49) had values near the mean of the scale (5.5), 5.41 and 5.60, respectively. There was one significant sex-by-time interaction for Factor O (Guilt-prone vs. Confident)—men became more confident, women more guilt-prone—and a significant sex-by-cohort interaction for Factor Q_1 (Liberal vs. Conservative Thinking)—no difference for the younger cohorts and a large difference for the older cohorts, that is, older women were more conservative, older men more experimenting. Thus most of the observed differences in personality were the sex differences, most of which were stable and in the direction of traditional sex-role stereotypes.

Rusin and Siegler (1975) examined personality predictors of dropout and death through the first three examinations and reported that the dropouts and deaths were not significantly different from each other, but that as a group they could be characterized as significantly more anxious than those who participated in the study, with a significant finding for Q_{II} (Anxiety-Adjustment) and, not surprisingly, lineup for the three factors that constitute it ($C-$, $O+$, Q_4). Factor B (Brightness) was significant only for females. A reanalysis of these data after the study had been completed indicated that C and Q_4 were no longer significantly related to dropout, but that O and Q_{II} remained significant. Factors B and Q_1 (Extraversion) were related to participation. Special efforts were made at the final examination to schedule all surviving subjects, and thus some of those who had earlier refused were recruited back into the study.

George (1978), using multiple-regression techniques, evaluated personality factors and social status and health indicators to predict social activity levels and psychological well-being assessed with the After Balance Scale at the third measurement point. The Cattell 16PF accounted for 10.4% of the variance in social activities, and the set of social status variables accounted for 11.2%. Both sets of variables accounted for 18.8% of the variables. The largest single predictor was employment status ($\beta = -.24$), followed by Q_2 (Group-dependent, $\beta = -.13$), in the joint equation. For psychological well-being, the relative variances were reversed, with more variance accounted for by the personality measures (18.3% of variance vs. 5.7% of the variance accounted for by social status variables). In the joint equation, 21.8% of the variance was accounted for, with the major contributors to the explained variance being $G+$ (Conscientious, $\beta = .14$), $I+$ (Tough-minded, $\beta = .14$), $M-$ (Practical, $\beta = -.15$), Q_4 (Tense, $\beta = -.25$), and Q_{III} (Alertness, $\beta = .36$). The main social indicator was "being married" ($\beta = .13$). The relationship between the personality traits assessed by the Cattell 16PF and the measure of affect balance suggests that a significant amount of the variance in what was designed to be a mood indicator was predictable on the basis of supposedly more stable personality traits.

Locus of Control. Siegler and Gatz (in press) evaluated the stability of locus of control by comparing the longitudinal patterns of locus of control with the observed patterns for affect balance scores and verbal intelligence. Affect balance and verbal intelligence were chosen for comparison because they were thought to represent theoretically a state variable that would be expected to be responsive to environmental change and life events (affect balance) and a trait variable expected to be stable (verbal intelligence). Stability for the three variables was assessed by Heise's (1969) procedures for evaluating stability and reliability. The data are given in Table 5.9.

As can be seen in Table 5.9, the cross-wave correlations suggest that locus of control is midway between affect balance and verbal intelligence. When these are converted to stability coefficients, it can be seen that locus of control is closer to verbal intelligence, which is extremely stable. A repeated-measures ANOVA that used sex and the occurrence of five significant life events (retirement of self and/or spouse, empty nest, widowhood, and a major medical event requiring hospitalization) as between-subject factors and that included the 375 subjects studied by Palmore, Cleveland, Nowlin, Ramm, and Siegler, (1979) indicated that, although all three variables changed significantly across the time of the study, the only variable that responded to the event condition was affect balance.

TABLE 5.9. Cross-Wave Correlations, Stability Coefficients, and Reliability Coefficients for Three Variables

Coefficient	Affect balance	Locus of control	Verbal intelligence
Cross-wave correlations			
r_{12}	.399	.604	.964
r_{13}	.403	.568	.956
r_{23}	.528	.600	.964
Stability coefficients			
s_{12}	.76	.94	.99
s_{13}	.77	.94	.99
s_{23}	1.01^a	.89	.98
Reliability	.52	.63	.95

$^a s_{23} = r_{13}/r_{12}$.

The Jessor measure of locus of control is an 11-item version that was designed for nonstudent populations. The relationship between the Jessor scale and the more widely used Rotter scale was evaluated in the coping study. The correlation between the two scales was .65; thus they have only 42% of the variance in common. Some of the difficulty in understanding the locus of control relationships as a function of age may result from the proliferation of scales used to measure it.

Palmore and Luikart (1972) evaluated 18 predictors of life satisfaction in the first wave of the data. The predictor set included locus of control and intelligence as well as health, social status, and activity variables. Internal control was found to be significantly correlated with life satisfaction ($r = .16$) and in the regression equation, was a predictor of life satisfaction only for women and for subjects over 60 years of age. When locus of control was used as the dependent variable, only 9.3% of the variance was explained, with the major variable being the sex of the subject ($\beta = -.342$) since the men in the sample have been shown to have more internal control than the women when analyzed for each sex separately. For men, 7.1% of the variance was accounted for, with employment status ($\beta = .414$) and presence of a confidant ($\beta = .233$) as major predictors. For women, 8.1% of the variance was accounted for, with the major contributor being degree of sexual enjoyment ($\beta = .168$).

Siegler and Gatz (in press) compared members of the adaptation study panel to a group of undergraduates on the Jessor measure. Two groups were selected from the adaptation study: 101 men and women aged 46–54 and 106 men and women aged 63–70. The student group consisted of 101 undergraduates at the University of Maryland, aged 18–26. The three groups had equivalent sex ratios and at least a high school education. When compared to the younger subjects, the middle-aged and older subjects from the adaptation study had significantly more internal control than the undergraduate subjects and were not significantly different from each other. The sex differences remained, but did not interact with age. In the younger subjects, the Rotter scale was also included and had a correlation of .58 with the Jessor scale.

Thus the observed age differences in the Jessor measure of locus of control appear to occur relatively early in the life cycle and to show consistent sex differences throughout the adult life cycle and stability in the fact of life events.

Self-Concept. Back and his colleagues (Back, 1971; Back & Morris, 1974) explored measures of self-concept. The seven-item semantic differential scale was included at all four times of measurement and was analyzed for three separate dimensions of self-concept: involvement (busy, effective, useful), evaluation or optimism (effective, looking to the future, satisfied with life), and freedom (a single item, free to do things), which rated three separate concepts: "What I really am," "How I appear to others," and "What I would like to be." A second index of self-concept, the Who-Are-You Test (Kuhn & McPartland, 1954), was included at the first examination. The discrepancy between real and ideal self was calculated at the first measurement point in five 5-year age cohorts. Significant cross-sectional age differences were found, although there were no significant sex or age-by-sex interactions. The pattern with age was not linear, suggesting that events and experiences most probably account for the differences. Each dimension of self-concept was then evaluated by age, sex, and whether the respondent had children still at home or was working. In this set of cross-sectional analyses, sex differences were important in understanding the many specific findings that emerged (Back, 1971).

Back and Morris (1974) evaluated changes in self-image with changes in life conditions between the first two examinations. Dimensions evaluated were self-concept discrepancies, locus of control, time–death metaphors (Knapp, 1960), and parameters developed from a life graph (Back & Bourque, 1970). All of the self-image measures were factor-analyzed, and no general factors emerged. When comparisons across the 2-year measurement interval were made, no significant differences emerged. Life conditions were assessed by evaluating any changes in work status, income, and presence of children in the home. Measures of self-image interacted with the changes in life conditions, and the patterns observed were more often related to sex than to age.

Health, Stress, and Life Events

Health Factors and Stress. Given the age range of the second longitudinal study, important questions assessed by the data are the prediction of CVD and the understanding of the role of risk factors. Nowlin (1974) evaluated obesity in the sample with the Quetelet index, which is weight divided by height squared. A regression analysis found that only diastolic BP was significantly related to the Quetelet index, while HR, CVD rating, overall health, serum cholesterol, and serum triglyceride were not This relationship was true for both men and women and was not related to age. Nowlin, Williams, and Wilkie (1973) evaluated predictors of a myocardial infarction (MI) in the men in the study. Of the 261 men, 19 had an MI between 1968 and 1972. These 19 were matched in age with the remaining healthy subjects ($n = 48$), and a stepwise multiple-regression analysis was used to evaluate the significant predictors of MI. Those who had MIs were significantly different from their healthy, age-matched controls by having had higher systolic BP and serum cholesterol ratings, lower resting HR, and higher scores on factor $O+$ (apprehensive).

Siegler and Nowlin (1979) evaluated stability and change in intellectual functioning and personality in groups defined by stability of health status across the 6 years of the study. Of the 502 subjects seen initially, 159 had no evidence of hypertension or CVD on the basis of a complete physical examination and ECG findings (at all four waves), 24 had hypertension throughout the study, 32 had coronary artery disease (CAD), and 8 had both hypertension and CAD. For the latter three groups, if disease was present consistently after Wave 1, those subjects were included in the consistent disease group.

One hundred and two subjects had unstable patterns of health and disease across the study, and 177 (114 dropouts, 63 deaths) subjects were not included because they had dropped out of the study or had insufficient data. Thus the analysis was based on 64 subjects with disease that was stable and on the 159 healthy subjects. The four experimental groups did not differ in sex composition, but did differ in age. The normal controls and the hypertensive group had mean ages of 56 and 55.5 years, respectively; those with CAD only had a mean age of 60.1 years; and those with both diseases were aged 63.4 at the first examination. However, when initial age was covaried, the results of the analysis did not change. This special selection of subjects raises an important problem in longitudinal studies, particularly where the variables of concern are related to dropout.

When the analysis was done in 1979, of the 63 subjects who were known to have died, 68% died from CVD. When all 502 subjects were analyzed at the first measurement point, the effect of this selective dropout could be seen clearly. Four groups were included in the analysis: (1) the 218 subjects who participated in the study, including the healthy subjects as well as those who survived with hypertension and CAD; (2) the 107 with inconsistent findings relating to disease status; (3) the 114 who dropped out of the study; and (4) the 63 who died. A one-way repeated-measures ANOVA indicated significant group differences for systolic BP; physician's health rating; age; WAIS Full-Scale, Verbal, and Performance scaled scores; extraversion; and anxiety. Duncan's multiple-range tests indicated significant differences among the four groups for the physician's health rating, systolic BP, and age at T1. Participants, independent of the stability of cardiovascular status, were significantly different from the dropout and death groups on intelligence and personality. Compared to the total sample, all of the surviving participants whose health status could be unambiguously classified as a group were brighter, less anxious, and less introverted than the deaths and dropouts. However, even within the restricted ranges included in the analysis, significant differences were found.

In relationship to type of disease, levels of intelligence, anxiety, and introversion were significantly different between disease groups. Verbal, Performance, and Full-Scaled measures of intelligence changed significantly over time, whereas the personality measures were stable across the four measurement times. Interactions between the CAD groups and change in intelligence were not significant; however, those with consistent hypertension who survived had significantly higher levels of intellectual functioning than those without disease, the latter of whom were higher than those with CAD, independent of hypertension. The pattern for all groups tended to increase significantly over the course of the study. The groups with any disease were more anxious than those without disease, and those with CAD appeared to be more introverted than normals, who were more introverted than those with hypertension, who were the most extraverted.

In summary, anxiety was related only to having disease, and extraversion, to the types of disease; both factors were stable over time. Relationships to intellectual functioning were related to both types of disease. Interestingly enough, none of these findings were related to the sex of the subject. As discussed in Siegler, Nowlin, and Blumenthal (1980), even starting with a relatively large population, the numbers of subjects were such that it was impossible to test all of the important differences simultaneously. However, the information on the deaths and dropouts suggests that findings would probably have been even stronger since the dropouts biased against the finding of differences.

Harkins, Nowlin, Ramm, and Schroeder (1974) evaluated the performance of the subjects tested on the CPT at Wave 1 of data collection (165 men and 161 women) compared to the performance of a group of younger subjects (aged 18 to 25 years) on the same task. Average percent correct detections, false positive responses, and RT to correct detections were analyzed by multivariate ANOVA by age and sex. The older subjects were divided into three age groups, with approximately 50 men and 50 women in each group, with mean ages of 51, 59, and 67 years. The cross-sectional age effect was significant for all three dependent variables, but the age-by-sex interaction was not significant. The univariate analysis indicated that, with age, percent correct detections decreased (mainly in the 20-year-olds as opposed to the three older groups) and the number of false positive responses increased. For RT to correct detections, there was a monotonic linear increase in response times with age. The task was then divided into thirds to get an estimate of performance across time during phases of the task. For the younger subjects, performance declined during the second phase of the task and then stabilized; for the older subjects as a group, performance declined throughout the task. The patterns were true of all three indexes of performance.

This cross-sectional analysis suggests that important changes in performance on the CPT most probably occur between the ages of 21 and 46, but that for percent correct detections, there are no additional changes through the decade of the 60s. For both false positive responses and for RT, there appears to be change during middle and later life. The young subjects were not included in the follow-up. As has been mentioned previously, only half of the sample had the CPT at any one visit; thus the subjects had the first measurement at Waves 1 or 2 and the second at Waves 3 or 4.

Longitudinal analysis of the returning subjects with complete data on two measures of the CPT and on the variables of interest has been started. While the initial task had three 10-minute experimental sessions, the later measurements had only two 10-minute sessions. Thus only the first two blocks of trials are considered in the longitudinal analysis. The two times of measurement compare the parts of the sample first tested in 1969 and 1971 with the same subjects retested in 1973 and 1975, respectively, so that for any individual subject, the time-of-measurement difference was 4 years. In this preliminary analysis, the figures for trials are averaged across the two times of measurement, and the figures for the two times of measurement are averaged across the trials given during any one session.

Three performance measures—percent correct detections, false alarms (or commission errors), and RT to correct detections—and two physiological measures—HR and GSR—as well as the percentage change in HR and GSR from baseline to task were evaluated with an age-by-sex repeated-measures ANOVA for trials and time of measurement.

The observed means for the performance measures are presented in Table 5.10. Individuals also were asked for self-report measures of the degree of stress experienced during the experimental task. The degree of stress reported was generally high and was negatively correlated with effective performance on the task. The main age difference seen cross-sectionally was between the middle-aged and older persons on the number of commission errors. The older subjects made fewer commission errors, perhaps indicating an increased cautiousness in responding. Reaction time for correct responses decreased significantly both during the task and across the 4-year measurement interval. The significant age by time-of-measurement interaction is interesting in that both the older and the middle-aged subjects increased their performance to the same level; however, the increase for the older subjects was less because they had initially scored higher on the task.

The physiological indexes of arousal are presented in Table 5.11. The measures of arousal were sensitive to the task when compared to baseline levels on both measures. In addition, during the study and between examinations, the significant changes are in the direction of lowered arousal during the second block of trials and at the second time of measurement. The CPT was the least favored, by the subjects, of all the longitudinal tasks, and the rate of incomplete data is quite high when compared to other parameters in the study (e.g., 331 subjects with complete 16PFs across all four waves of the study). Analyses that compare these 72 subjects to the initial study population, and analyses that look at the individual correlates of effective performance, are currently under way.

Life Events. The Schedule of Recent Events (SRE) was added to the second longitudinal study protocol at the third time of measurement. Subjects were asked to check which events they had experienced in the past 12 months and also since the start of the study. Wilson (1980) was concerned with methodological and measurement issues as well as with substantive findings about the impact of life events on a set of social psychological and health outcomes. Briefly, the study used data at the second measurement as baseline indicators and the same variables at the third measurement as outcome variables. The variables were a psychosomatic symptoms index, affect balance, and a physical health index that was a combination of ratings made by the longitudinal study's physician

TABLE 5.10. Longitudinal Performance on the CPT: Performance Indexes, Means, and Significant Differences

	Age		Sex		Trial		Time of measurement	
	Middle	Older	Male	Female	Block 1	Block 2	1969/1971	1973/1975
Percent correct detections	59.8	62.2	52.5	59.4	59.9	61.8	56.9	64.8**[a]
False alarms (commission errors)	26.5	18.0*	19.4	26.5*	25.6	20.8*	21.8	24.6
RT correct responses	862	842	847	859	865	842*	869	840*

[a]There was also a significant age by time-of-measurement interaction: For the middle-aged subjects, it was 54.9 at T1 and 64.8 at T2; for the older subjects, it was 59.6 at T1 and 64.7 at T2. No other interactions were statistically significant.
*$p \leq .05$.
**$p \leq .01$.

TABLE 5.11. Physiological Responses to CPT

	Age		Sex		Activity		Trials		Time of measurement	
	Middle	Older	Male	Female	Rest	Task	Block 1	Block 2	1969/1971	1973/1975
HR[a]	78.9	77.6	76.7	79.7*	76.2	80.4*	79.1	77.5*	80.9	75.9*
Percentage change in HR, baseline to task	5.7	5.0	5.1	5.6	—	—	6.4	4.6*	6.2	4.6*
GSR	17.1	14.4*	16.1	15.6	14.5	17.1**	15.4	16.3	17.0	14.9*
Percentage change in GSR, baseline in task	20.8	30.5*	26.6	24.2	—	—	36.3	14.6*	23.3	27.0

[a]Age-by-sex interaction for middle-aged men was 78.5, and for older men, 74.9; for middle-aged women, it was 79.2, and for older women, 80.3.
*$p \leq .05$.
**$p \leq .01$.

on the musculoskeletal and cardiovascular systems and an overall index of the degree to which health status impaired performance. In addition, a set of social status indexes known to be related to the dependent variables were included: age, sex, income, marital status, and work status. In a series of multiple-regression models, the baseline variable was always entered first so that the measure of change controlled for the initial level of the variable. The analyses were based on the 317 subjects who had complete data at Waves 2 and 3 on the variables of interest.

The SRE used in the second longitudinal study was modified from the original Holmes and Rahe (1967) formulation in that it included 36, rather than 39, life events (pregnancy, starting and stopping school, and Christmas were excluded from the list). When weightings for the life events are used, the weighted measures constitute the Social Readjustment Rating Scale. In this sample, the correlation between the sum representing the total number of events experienced and the Social Readjustment Rating Scale score was .95; thus only the total number of events, or SSRE (Sum SRE), or individual events were used in the analyses. The SSRE ranged from 0 to 15 in the sample, with the range of the scale from 0 to 36. Three events were not observed (being fired or laid off from work, divorce, or marital reconciliation).

The time scale used in this analysis was during the past 12 months. Thus all events noted occurred sometime after the second examination and before the third, with the average time between visits for individuals being 2 years. The most frequent event was a vacation ($n = 217$), followed by the death of a close friend ($n = 36$), the death of a family member ($n = 36$), and a son or daughter leaving home (marriage, attending college, etc.) ($n = 33$). Death of a spouse ($n = 7$), retirement ($n = 10$), change in spouse's work ($n = 16$), and major personal illness or injury ($n = 16$) were relatively infrequent, even though these are seen as a set of normative events for this age group. A series of regression equations were then calculated for each of the five dependent variables. Total number of events (SSRE) accounted for no additional variance in the change from baseline to outcome.

Wilson then looked at life events separately. All of the events were dummy-coded ("experienced," "not experienced") and then correlated with the five dependent variables, resulting in a set of 12 events that were related to change in the dependent variables. These events varied in frequency and included death of a close friend, major change in living conditions, change in financial status, marriage, change in arguments with spouse, widowhood, outstanding personal achievement, major change in social activities, personal illness, change in sleeping habits, change in eating habits, and change in personal habits. It is not surprising that these events were the significant correlates of dependent variables that related to affect, psychosomatic symptoms, and physical health status.

In the second set of analyses, the events were added to the regression equations after the baseline and social status variables. Different events were related to the different outcome variables, but only for psychosomatic symptoms, negative affect, and physical illness did the proportion of explained variance increase when the events were added to the prediction equations. For psychosomatic symptoms, the variance explained ranged from 34% to 38%; for negative affect, from 21% to 26%; and for the health index, from 47% to 50%. At least in this restricted time frame, covering events occurring within a 12-month period, the contribution of the events was modest compared to the predictability of a residualized change score. However, it is most interesting that the specific events experienced, rather than the number of events experienced, was related to change in the outcome variables.

Palmore et al. (1979) took a very different approach to examining the impact of five specific life events on adaptation throughout the course of the study. First, the SRE was not used to define events; rather, changes in subjects' reports compared across waves defined the occurrence of an event. The five events chosen were retirement, retirement of spouse, empty nest, widowhood, and a major medical event requiring hospitalization. Individuals without events were compared to individuals eligible for the event. The 375 subjects who were present at both the first and the last measurement points (1969, 1975) were included in the analysis; data on the observed occurrence of events are presented in Table 5.12. As can be seen from the table, despite the use of the entire 6-year period of observation, the events observed were relatively low in frequency, and not the entire sample was at risk for the event during the course of the study.

It is important that the appropriate control group be used when the impact of life events is analyzed. Of the 375 subjects included in this analysis, 137, or 36.5%, experienced none of the events chosen for study. In addition, the status of the subject in terms of the resources available for use in adapting to the events was studied. Resources in health, psychological functioning, and social functioning were defined such that they included different variables than those chosen as indexes of adaptation. Health resources were an index of the degree to which physical health conditions impaired everyday activities. Psychological resources were a combination of intellectual functioning and adjustment as measured by a second-order factor on the Cattell 16PF (Q_{II}), and social resources were a combination of income, education, and the richness of the social network. The resources were found not only to influence the adaptation to the events, but also to be related to the occurrence of an event, in expectable

TABLE 5.12. Distribution of Events Observed during Longitudinal II

Event versus no-event control groups

Event	Number eligible	Number observed	Percent eligible	Percent of eligible experienced
Retirement	231	78	61.6%	33.76%
Spouse's retirement	169	78	45.06%	46.15%
Widowhood	318	25	84.80%	7.86%
Empty nest	112	57	29.86%	50.89%
Major medical event	375	92	100.00%	24.53%

ways. Those with lower health resources were more likely to retire and to experience subsequent hospitalization, and those with lower psychological resources were more likely to become widowed. In addition, when compared to the total sample of 502 subjects who formed the original second longitudinal population, those who completed the study and were included in the analysis were those with higher levels of all three types of resources, which would be expected to reduce the impact of the resource variables in the analysis. Of the seven social psychological outcome indexes of adaptation, only two, psychosomatic symptoms and active hours, were related to participation, with the participants having fewer symptoms and more active hours than the nonparticipants; however, five of the ten medical variables were related to participation status, indicating, as expected, that those who participated were initially in better health in a variety of dimensions (Siegler, 1977).

To a certain extent, the selection of the subjects who survived and participated repeatedly for four visits may be a measure of successful adaptation in and of itself, but it also biases against the detection of significant differences within the analyses. Overall, the results of the analyses presented in Palmore et al. (1979) illustrate the impact of these events and their interactions with the resource variables, concluding that the adaptive potential of this group of subjects was generally high. The analyses were limited in that the time between the event and the adaptive outcome measures could not be assessed directly. For example, of the events that did occur, there were 28 individual combinations of events, and of those with multiple events, no more than two to five subjects experienced any of the combinations; thus there were insufficient data to look at differences as a function of the special event combinations and their impact on measures of health and psychological well-being.

Summary

Findings from the second longitudinal study indicate considerable stability of personality and social factors with age when assessed cross-sectionally and across time when assessed longitudinally. For many of the psychological variables, stability or increased levels of performance were seen, and for the social psychological variables, sex, rather than age, appeared related to the different patterns observed. The importance of understanding the differential life experiences of men and women in middle and early old age is heightened by the findings from the study. The adaptive potential of this sample of middle-aged and older persons appeared to be high when assessed by indexes of well-being or by performance on the CPT. There were many fewer sex differences in the area of health and behavior relationships.

Comparisons between the psychological findings of the two longitudinal studies are difficult to evaluate because the particular analyses have not yet been done. Except in areas where the relationships between CVD and intellectual performance have been evaluated, the same questions have really not been asked. Because of the differences in ages of the two study populations, CVD has been shown to be related to poorer performance in both studies; in the second study, however, it was related to the lack of an increase in intellectual performance over time, which was observed in the healthy subjects, rather than to an accelerated decrease in intellectual performance as seen in the first longitudinal study. Second, moderate levels of hypertension were related to increased levels of intellectual functioning in both studies.

Concluding Comments

The aim of this chapter has been to review findings from the Duke Longitudinal Studies that have relevance to the psychology of adult development and aging. There have been tremendous recent advances in the development of methods appropriate to the analysis of longitudinal data (e.g., Nesselroade & Baltes, 1979) that have not yet been applied to the Duke data. However, the intention of this chapter has been to carefully describe the study populations, the psychological data collected, and the reports published and unpublished that have been concerned with psychological development. As in most large-scale data sets, much of the data remains unanalyzed or underanalyzed, and except for the methodological strategies developed by Woodbury and his colleagues, the applications of newer multivariate strategies to this data set remain to be done.

As Schaie's work on the developmental model has focused attention on cohort and time-of-measurement effects in the study of aging, so, too, do studies need to be evaluated with reference to the historical time frames in which they were designed, the particular operationalization of the constructs chosen, and the particular data-analytic techniques employed.

Two ongoing projects, the autopsy study and the coping study, will build on the rich data archives that each study now represents. In addition, plans are under way to continue to follow the survival patterns of the subjects from both studies, which will allow for further exploration of the data sets and of their usefulness in understanding the relationships among various indexes of psychological, social, and medical predictors of survival and death.

Acknowledgments

The research reported in this chapter has been supported by grants from the National Institute on Aging, AG00364 (HD00668), to the Duke University Center for the Study of Aging and Human Development.

I would like to thank my colleagues, the current senior investigators on the longitudinal studies: Drs. Ewald W. Busse, C. Edward Buckley, Linda K. George, Daniel T. Gianturco, George L. Maddox, John B. Nowlin, Erdman Palmore, Dietolf Ramm, H. Shan Wang, and Max A. Woodbury; and Robert D. Nebes and Kenneth G. Manton for their help in preparing the manuscript of this chapter.

Special thanks are due to my predecessors, who were the psychologists responsible for the psychological laboratory from 1955 to 1974: Drs. Carl Eisdorfer, Frances Wilkie, and Larry Thompson.

References

Back, K. W. Transition to aging and the self-image. *Aging and Human Development,* 1971, *2,* 296–304.

Back, K. W., & Bourque, L. Life graphs: Aging and cohort effect. *Journal of Gerontology,* 1970, *25,* 249–255.

Back, K. W., & Guptill, C. S. Retirement and self-ratings. In I. H. Simpson & J. C. McKinney (Eds.), *Social aspects of aging.* Durham, N.C.: Duke University Press, 1966.

Back, K. W., & Morris, J. D. Perception of self and the study of whole lives. In E. Palmore (Ed.), *Normal aging II.* Durham, N.C.: Duke University Press, 1974.

Birren, J. E., Butler, R. N., Greenhouse, S. W., Sokoloff, L., & Yarrow, M. *Human aging* (Public Health Service Document No. 986). Washington, D.C.: U.S. Government Printing Office, 1963.

Botwinick, J., & Siegler, I. C. Intellectual ability among the elderly: Simultaneous cross-sectional and longitudinal comparisons. *Developmental Psychology,* 1980, *16,* 49–53.

Bradburn, N. *The structure of psychological well-being.* Chicago: Aldine, 1969.

Bradburn, N., & Caplovitz, D. *Reports on happiness.* Chicago: Aldine, 1965.

Burgess, E. W., Cavan, R. S., & Havighurst, R. J. *Your attitudes and activities.* Chicago: Science Research Associates, 1948.

Busse, E. W. Administration of the interdisciplinary research team. *Journal of Medical Education*, 1965, *40*, 832–839.

Busse, E. W. Duke longitudinal study I: Senescence and senility. In R. Katzman, R. D. Terry, & K. L. Bick (Eds.), *Alzheimer's disease: Senile dementia and related disorders* (*Aging*, Vol. 7). New York: Raven, 1978.

Busse, E. W., & Eisdorfer, C. Two thousand years of married life. In E. Palmore (Ed.), *Normal aging*. Durham, N.C.: Duke University Press, 1970.

Busse, E. W., & Wang, H. S. Multiple factors contributing to dementia in old age. In *Proceedings of the Fifth World Congress of Psychiatry*, Mexico City, 1971. (Reprinted in E. Palmore [Ed.], *Normal aging II*. Durham, N.C.: Duke University Press, 1974.)

Busse, E. W., & Wang, H. S. The electroencephalographic changes in later life: A longitudinal study. *Journal of Clinical and Experimental Gerontology*, 1979, *1*, 145–158.

Cantrill, H. *The pattern of human concerns*. New Brunswick, N.J.: Rutgers University Press, 1965.

Cattell, R. B., Eber, H. W., & Tatsuka, M. M. *Handbook for the Sixteen Personality Factor Questionnaire (16PF)*. Champaign, Ill.: Institute for Personality and Ability Testing, 1970.

Cavan, R. S., Burgess, E. W., Havighurst, R. J., & Goldhamer, H. *Personal adjustment in old age*. Chicago: Science Research Associates, 1949.

Dopplett, J. E., & Wallace, W. L. Standardization of the Wechsler Adult Intelligence Scale for older persons. *Journal of Abnormal and Social Psychology*, 1955, *51*, 312–330.

Duke University Center for the Study of Aging and Human Development. *The Duke longitudinal studies: An integrated investigation of aging and the aged, ancillary studies and research support services: 1955–1980* final report). Bethesda, Md.: National Institute on Aging, November 1980.

Eisdorfer, C. Developmental level and sensory impairment in the aged. *Journal of Projective Techniques and Personality Assessment*, 1960, *24*, 129–132. (a)

Eisdorfer, C. Rorschach rigidity and sensory decrement in a senescent population. *Journal of Gerontology*, 1960, *15*, 188–190. (b)

Eisdorfer, C. Rorschach performance and intellectual functioning in the aged. *Journal of Gerontology*, 1963, *18*, 358–363. (a)

Eisdorfer, C. The WAIS performance of the aged: A retest evaluation. *Journal of Gerontology*, 1963, *18*, 169–172. (b)

Eisdorfer, C., Busse, E. W., & Cohen, L. D. The WAIS performance of an aged sample: The relationship between verbal and performance IQ's. *Journal of Gerontology*, 1959, *14*, 197–201.

Eisdorfer, C., & Cohen, L. D. The generality of the WAIS standardization for the aged. *Journal of Abnormal and Social Psychology*, 1961, *62*, 520–527.

Eisdorfer, C., & Wilkie, F. Auditory changes. *Journal of American Geriatrics Society*, 1972, *20*, 377–382.

Eisdorfer, C., & Wilkie, F. Intellectual change with advancing age. In L. F. Jarvik, C. Eisdorfer, & J. E. Blum (Eds.), *Intellectual functioning in adults*. New York: Springer, 1973.

Fisher, S., & Cleveland, S. E. *Body image and personality*. New York: Van Nostrand Reinhold, 1958.

Fox, C. F. *A cross-sequential study of age changes in personality in an aged population*. Unpublished doctoral dissertation, University of Florida, 1979.

George, L. K. *Review of measures in the adaptation study social history: Life events and self-concept*. Unpublished manuscript, Duke University, 1976 (a)

George, L. K. *Review of measures in the adaptation study social history: Measure of well-being and attitudes.* Unpublished manuscript, Duke University 1976. (b)

George, L. K. The impact of personality and social status factors upon levels of activity and psychological well-being. *Journal of Gerontology*, 1978, *33*, 840–847.

George, L. K., & Siegler, I. C. Stress and coping in later life. *Educational Horizons*, Summer 1982, pp. 147–154.

Gianturco, D. T., & Busse, E. W. Psychiatric problems encountered during a long-term study of normal aging volunteers. In A. D. Issacs & F. Post (Eds.), *Studies in geriatric medicine.* Chichester, UK: Wiley, 1978.

Granick, S., & Patterson, R. D. (Eds.). *Human aging II. An eleven-year follow-up: Biomedical and behavioral study* (DHEW Publication No.(HSM) 71-9037). Washington, D.C.: U.S. Government Printing Office, 1971.

Harkins, S. W., Nowlin, J. B., Ramm, D., & Schroeder, S. Effects of age, sex, and time-on-watch on a brief continuous performance task. In E. Palmore (Ed.), *Normal aging II.* Durham, N.C.: Duke University, 1974.

Harris, C. W. (Ed.). *Problems in measuring change.* Madison: University of Wisconsin Press, 1963.

Heise, D. R. Separating reliability and stability in test–retest correlation. *American Sociological Review*, 1969, *34*, 93–101.

Holmes, T. H., & Rahe, R. H. The Social Readjustment Rating Scale. *Journal of Psychosomatic Research*, 1967, *11*, 213–218.

Holt, R. R. *Manual for scoring primary process manifestations in Rorschach responses.* Unpublished manuscript, 1970.

Jessor, R., Graves, T. S., Hansen, R. C., & Jessor, S. L. *Society, personality and deviant behavior*, New York: Holt, Rinehart & Winston, 1968.

Knapp, R. H. A study of the metaphor. *Journal of Projective Techniques*, 1960, *24*, 389–395.

Kuhn, M. H., & McPartland, T. S. An empirical investigation of self-attitudes. *American Sociological Review*, 1954, *19*, 68–76.

Maddox, G. L. Selected methodological issues. In *Proceedings of the Social Statistics Section of the American Statistical Association*, 1962. (Reprinted in E. Palmore [Ed.], *Normal aging.* Durham, N.C.: Duke University Press, 1970.)

Maddox, G. L. Fact and artifact. *Human Development*, 1965, *8*, 117–180.

Maddox, G. L. Persistence of life style among the elderly. In *Proceedings of the 7th International Congress of Gerontology*, 1966. (Reprinted in E. Palmore [Ed.], *Normal aging.* Durham, N.C.: Duke University Press, 1970.)

Maddox, G. L., & Douglass, E. Aging and individual differences. *Journal of Gerontology*, 1974, *29*, 555–563.

McCarty, S. M., Siegler, I. C., & Logue, P. E. Cross-sectional patterns of three Wechsler Memory Scale subtests. *Journal of Gerontology*, 1982, *37*, 169–175.

McClosky, H., & Schaar, J. H. Psychological dimensions of anomy. *American Sociological Review*, 1965, *30*, 14–40.

Nesselroade, J. R., & Baltes, P. B. (Eds.). *Longitudinal research in the study of behavior and development.* New York: Academic Press, 1979.

Nowlin, J. B. Obesity and cardiovascular function in a middle-aged and older population. In E. Palmore (Ed.), *Normal aging II.* Durham, N.C.: Duke University Press, 1974.

Nowlin, J. B. Successful aging: Health and social factors in an interracial population. *Black Aging*, 1977, *2*, 10–17.

Nowlin, J. B., Williams, R., & Wilkie, F. Prospective study of physical and psychologic factors in elderly men who subsequently suffered myocardial infarction. *Clinical Research*, 1973, *21*, 465.

Nowlis, V. The description and analysis of mood. *Annals of the New York Academy of Science*, 1956, *65*, 345-355.

Obrist, W. D., Busse, E. W., Eisdorfer, C., & Kleemeier, R. W. Relation of the EEG to intellectual functioning in senescence. *Journal of Gerontology*, 1962, *17*, 109-122.

Palmore, E. Physical, mental and social factors in predicting longevity. *Gerontologist*, 1969, *9*, 103-108.

Palmore, E. (Ed.). *Normal aging*. Durham, N.C.: Duke University Press, 1970.

Palmore, E. The relative importance of social factors in predicting longevity. In E. Palmore & F. Jeffers (Eds.), *Prediction of life span*. Lexington, Mass.: D. C. Heath, 1971.

Palmore, E. Design of adaptation study. In E. Palmore (Ed.), *Normal aging II*. Durham, N.C.: Duke University Press, 1974 (a)

Palmore, E. (Ed.). *Normal aging II*. Durham, N.C.: Duke University Press, 1974. (b)

Palmore, E. Predicting longevity: A new method. In E. Palmore (Ed.), *Normal aging II*. Durham, N.C.: Duke University Press, 1974. (c)

Palmore, E. *Social patterns in normal aging*. Durham, N.C.: Duke University Press, 1981.

Palmore, E., & Cleveland, W. P. Aging, terminal decline and terminal drop. *Journal of Gerontology*, 1976, *31*, 76-81.

Palmore, E., Cleveland, W. P., Nowlin, J. B., Ramm, D., & Siegler, I. C. Stress and adaptation in later life. *Journal of Gerontology*, 1979, *34*, 841-851.

Palmore, E., & Luikart, C. Health and social factors in life satisfaction. *Journal of Health and Social Behavior*, 1972, *13*, 236-242.

Pfeiffer, E. Survival in old age. *Journal of the American Geriatrics Society*, 1970, *18*, 273-285.

Prinz, P. N. Sleep patterns in healthy aged: Relationship with intellectual function. *Journal of Gerontology*, 1977, *32*, 179-186.

Ramm, D., & Gianturco, D. T. Data processing in longitudinal studies. In E. Palmore (Ed.), *Normal aging II*. Durham, N.C.: Duke University Press, 1974.

Reigel, K. F. History of psychosocial gerontology. In J. E. Birren & K. W. Schaie (Eds.), *Handbook of the psychology of aging*. New York: Van Nostrand Reinhold, 1977.

Roseman, J. R., & Buckley, C. E., III. Inverse relationship between serum IgG concentrations and measures of intelligence in elderly persons. *Nature*, 1975, *264*, 55-56.

Rosen, B. C. The achievement syndrome: A psychocultural dimension of social stratification. *American Sociological Review*, 1956, *21*, 203-211.

Rusin, M., & Siegler, I. *Personality differences between participants and drop-outs in a longitudinal study*. Paper presented at the meeting of the Gerontological Society, Louisville, November 1975.

Schaie, K. W. A general model for the study of developmental problems. *Psychological Bulletin*, 1965, *64*, 92-107.

Siegler, I. C. Description of study population sample, major life events and resources. In E. W. Busse (Chair), *Stress and adaptation in late life*. Symposium presented at the meeting of the Gerontological Society, San Francisco, 1977.

Siegler, I. C. Intelligence, reaction time and memory in young-old vs. old-old participants in the first longitudinal study. In K. W. Schaie & G. Rudinger (Chairs), *Consistency and change in the cognitive functioning in the young old and the old old*. Symposium presented at the XIIth International Congress of Gerontology, Hamburg, Germany, 1981.

Siegler, I. C., & Botwinick, J. A long-term longitudinal study of intellectual ability of older adults: The matter of selective attrition. *Journal of Gerontology*, 1979, *34*, 242–245.

Siegler, I. C., & Gatz, M. Locus of control. In E. Palmore, J. B. Nowlin, E. W. Busse, I. C. Siegler, & G. L. Maddox (Eds.), *Normal aging III*. Durham, N.C.: Duke University Press, in press.

Siegler, I. C., Gatz, M., Tyler, F., & George, L. K. *Aging competently* (final report). Washington, D.C.: Administration on Aging, April 1979.

Siegler, I. C., George, L. K., & Okun, M. A. Cross-sequential analysis of adult personality. *Developmental Psychology*, 1979, *15*, 350–351.

Siegler, I. C., Harkins, S. W., & Thompson, L. W. *Stability and change in intellectual performance: An examination of the terminal drop hypothesis in the later years of life*. Paper presented at the meeting of the Gerontological Society, Portland, November 1974.

Siegler, I. C., McCarty, S. M., & Logue, P. E. Wechsler Memory Scale scores, selective attrition, and distance from death. *Journal of Gerontology*, 1982, *37*, 176–181.

Siegler, I. C., Murray, P., Johnson, M., & Rusin, M. *Technician's handbook*. Unpublished technical report, Longitudinal Studies Laboratory, Duke University Medical Center, 1976.

Siegler, I. C., & Nowlin, J. B. The interaction of health and behavior in the Duke longitudinal studies. In I. G. Wittels (Chair), *Longitudinal studies in the psychology of aging*. Symposium presented at the meeting of the American Psychological Association, New York, August 1979.

Siegler, I. C., Nowlin, J. B., & Blumenthal, J. A. Health and behavior: Methodological considerations for adult development and aging. In L. W. Poon (Ed.), *Aging in the 1980's: Selected contemporary issues*. Washington, D.C.: American Psychological Association, 1980.

Stone, C. P., Girdner, J., & Albrecht, R. An alternate form of the Wechsler Memory Scale. *Journal of Psychology*, 1946, *22*, 193–206.

Thompson, L. W., Eisdorfer, C., & Estes, E. H. Cardiovascular disease and behavioral changes in the elderly. In *Proceedings of the 7th International Congress of Gerontology*, 1966. (Reprinted in E. Palmore [Ed.], *Normal aging*. Durham, N.C.: Duke University Press, 1974.)

Thompson, L. W., Opton, E., & Cohen, L. D. Effects of age, presentation speed, and sensory modality on performance of a "vigilance" task. *Journal of Gerontology*, 1963, *18*, 366–369.

Vogel, F. S., Burger, P. C., Siegler, I. C., & Nowlin, J. B. *An integrated investigation of aging and the aged: Autopsy supplement* (NIA Grant 5 P01 AG00364-20S1). 1977.

Wang, H. S. *Duke longitudinal studies: Psychiatric data*. Unpublished technical report, Duke University, 1980.

Wang, H. S., & Busse, E. W. Brain impairment and longevity. In E. Palmore (Ed.), *Normal aging II*. Durham, N.C.: Duke University Press, 1974. (a)

Wang, H. S., & Busse, E. W. Heart disease and brain impairment among aged persons. In E. Palmore (Ed.), *Normal aging II*. Durham, N.C.: Duke University Press, 1974. (b)

Wang, H. S., Obrist, W. D., & Busse, E. W. Neurophysiological correlates of the intellectual function of elderly persons living in the community. *American Journal of Psychiatry*, 1970, *126*, 39–46.

Wechsler, D. A standardized memory scale for clinical use. *Journal of Psychology*, 1945, *19*, 87–95.

Wechsler, D. *Wechsler Adult Intelligence Scale manual.* New York: Psychological Corporation, 1955.

Wechsler, D. *The measurement and appraisal of adult intelligence.* Baltimore: Williams & Wilkins, 1958.

Wilkie, F. L. Blood pressure and cognitive functioning. In S. G. Haynes & M. Feinlab (Eds.), *Second conference on the epidemiology of aging* (NIH Publication No. 80–696). Bethesda, Md.: National Institutes of Health, 1980.

Wilkie, F. L., & Eisdorfer, C. Intelligence and blood pressure in the aged. *Science*, 1971, *172*, 959–962.

Wilkie, F. L., & Eisdorfer, C. *Blood pressure and behavioral correlates in the aged.* Paper presented at the 9th International Congress of Gerontology, Kiev, USSR, July 1972.

Wilkie, F. L., & Eisdorfer, C. *Intellectual changes: A 15 year follow-up of the Duke sample.* Paper presented at the meeting of the Gerontological Society, Miami, November 1973. (a)

Wilkie, F. L., & Eisdorfer, C. Systemic disease and behavioral correlates. In L. F. Jarvik, C. Eisdorfer, & J. E. Blum (Eds.), *Intellectual functioning in adults.* New York: Springer, 1973. (b)

Wilkie, F. L., & Eisdorfer, C. Terminal changes in intelligence. In E. Palmore (Ed.), *Normal aging II.* Durham, N.C.: Duke University Press, 1974.

Wilkie, F. L., Eisdorfer, C., & Nowlin, J. B. Memory and blood pressure in the aged. *Experimental Aging Research*, 1976, *2*, 3–16.

Wilkie, F. L., Eisdorfer, C., & Siegler, I. C. Reaction time changes in the aged. *Proceedings of 10th International Congress of Gerontology*, 1975, *2*, 177. (Abstract)

Wilson, R. W. *Assessing the impact of life change events.* Unpublished doctoral dissertation, Duke University, 1980.

Woodbury, M. A., & Manton, K. G. A theoretical model of the physiological dynamics of circulatory disease in human populations. *Human Biology*, 1983.

Woodbury, M. A., & Manton, K. G., & Stallard, E. Analysis of the components of coronary heart disease risk in the Framingham Study: New multivariate procedures of the analysis of chronic disease development. *Computers and Biomedical Research*, 1979, *12*, 109–123. (a)

Woodbury, M. A., Manton, K. G., & Stallard, E. Longitudinal analysis of the dynamics and risk of coronary heart disease in the Framingham Study. *Biometrics*, 1979, *35*, 575–585 (b)

6 Constancy and Change of Behavior in Old Age: Findings from the Bonn Longitudinal Study on Aging

REINHARD SCHMITZ-SCHERZER AND
HANS THOMAE

Introduction

The planning and design of the Bonn Longitudinal Study on Aging (BLSA) was influenced by three different sources: the findings on the great amount of interindividual variability (IEV) in physiological and psychological variables in old age, the rise of cognitive theories of behavior since the mid-1950s, and the advantages of a global–empirical (compared to a hypothetical–deductive) approach as demonstrated by the Berkeley Longitudinal Studies on Life-Span Development.

Interindividual variability in cognitive functioning and adjustment received prominent attention in the conclusions drawn from longitudinal studies such as the Bethesda Study on Aged Men (Birren, Butler, Greenhouse, Sokoloff, & Yarrow, 1963, p. 314) and the Duke Study on Aging (Palmore, 1974, p. 290) and from cross-sectional studies such as those by Birren and Morrison (1961), Granick and Friedman (1973), Green (1969), Kuhlen (1963), Nehrke (1972), and Rudinger (1974).

Baltes and Schaie (1974, 1976) and Baltes and Willis (1979) confirmed our interpretation of these trends in psychogerontological research by pointing to the large interindividual differences in cognitive functioning, which require a multidimensional and multidirectional approach. Another label for this trend in research on aging is "differential gerontology,"

REINHARD SCHMITZ-SCHERZER. Department of Social Work, Gesamthochschule und Universität Kassel, Kassel, Federal Republic of Germany.

HANS THOMAE. Department of Psychology, Universität Bonn, Bonn, Federal Republic of Germany.

which tries to define the range of IEV in terms of different aspects of the aged persons and their interaction with the environment. Within the framework of a differential gerontology, longitudinal studies cannot be accused of providing distorted information on development due to selective dropout or repeated measurement effects. This kind of approach emphasizes the search for different patterns of aging rather than the establishment of age norms. Longitudinal studies do offer *valid* data as far as these data are related to interindividual differences in constancy and change within a sufficiently defined sample or to the biological and environmental correlates of such clusters of constancy and change.

So long as longitudinal studies define their aim to be the analysis of patterns of development, they will avoid problems such as those raised by Schaie (1965) and Baltes (1968) regarding uncautious generalizations from single-cohort studies. Nevertheless, we heeded the developmental model of Schaie (1965) by including in our design two cohorts (born 1890 to 1895 and 1900 to 1905) which are defined by differential socialization history during adolescence and young adulthood.

The rise of cognitive theories of personality largely influenced the choice of our research instruments. Instead of looking for traits and their constancies, we were interested in the life space of our subjects as their perceived environment, their perceived self, and their response to their own life space. For our purposes, the perceived situation can be regarded as the main determinant of behavior (cf. Baldwin, 1969; Kelly, 1955). The assessment of these perceptions by structured interviews, therefore, was our main instrument, although the usual intelligence tests and questionnaires were also included in our test battery.

Although the differential and cognitive theoretical framework had its impact upon the design and planning of the study, we still tried to be as "open" toward future theoretical development as had been the case in the Berkeley longitudinal studies. In 1952, the senior author had the privilege of being the first German visitor to work on the files of the Child Guidance Study and the Oakland Growth Study. At that time, there was no emphasis on ego psychology and on problems of coping and defending such as that which appeared in later data analyses by Haan (1977) and others. Nevertheless, it was because of the "global" approach emphasized by McFarlane (1938) and Jones (1959) that data collected in 1935 could be analyzed some 30 years later in the context of theories that emerged after 1955.

We hope that the records of the Bonn studies will likewise enable future generations of gerontologists to test their theories by use of our longitudinal data.

Methods

The schedule of our procedures at each of the first six measurement points (1965 to 1976/1977; see Table 6.1.) shows that the major part of the week during which our subjects were available was assigned to the interview. This decision was based, first, upon methodological preferences similar to those found in the Berkeley studies (Jones, 1959). Our decision was further supported by theoretical considerations arising from a "cognitive theory of personality" (Thomae, 1968) and of aging (Thomae, 1970), which placed special emphasis on behavior as a dependent variable of the situation as perceived by the individual. Our subjects' responses in the interviews can be regarded as rather valid cues to their perceptions of their present, past, and future life situation since they were well motivated to cooperate in our study. On the other hand, intelligence and personality tests were applied to get information as objective as possible on their psychological situation. Because cognitive and motivational aspects of behavior are related to each other in a complex manner, it was decided to assess as many variables as possible in order to be able to identify different patterns of aging and to determine the cognitive, motivational, social, and biological correlates of these patterns.

The design of the study was also influenced by the senior author's experience as psychological director of the German Longitudinal Study on Children (Coerper, Hagen, & Thomae, 1954; Hagen & Thomae, 1962), of longitudinal studies on middle-aged white-collar employees (Lehr & Thomae, 1959), and of a study of a sample of men and women born between 1885 and 1930 (Lehr & Thomae, 1965; Lehr, 1969). The final design was further discussed with many colleagues at Bonn and other universities.

Time Limits for the Measurement Points

In accord with the global orientation, the time schedule for each measurement point allowed a week per subject (see Table 6.1). The Volkswagen Foundation, which supported the project between 1964 and 1969, made this arrangement possible. At Measurement Point 5 (1972), the schedule had to be reduced to 2½ days because of increasing difficulty in finding support for basic research in social gerontology in the Federal Republic of Germany. The reduction of time principally affected the interview procedures, but may also have influenced other measures.

TABLE 6.1. Weekly Schedule for the Interviewing and Testing Program in the BLSA[a]

	Measurement Point[a]				
	1 (1965)	2 (1966)	3 (1967)	4 (1969)	6 (1976/1977)
Monday	Informal meeting between staff and subjects				
Tuesday					
a.m.	Interview on present life situation, social participation, changes in situation, and main life events in preceding year				
p.m.	Medical examination				Free
Wednesday					
a.m.	Interview on life history of perceived stress around 1945/1948, 1955, 1965, and on reactions to stress	Interview on life history of perceived stress between 1960 and 1965 and on reactions to stress and perceived changes in personality and achievement	Interview on perceived stress and reactions to stress during the past year and in the present situation and on the most relevant stages in life		Interview on perceived stress during the past year and on reactions to stress
p.m.	Free	Free	Free	Free	Free
Thursday					
a.m.	WAIS (Hamburg), Thematic Apperception Test, Z test, Riegel inventories	Raven Colored Progressive Matrices, Rorschach, Rosenzweig Picture Frustration Test, Goodenough Draw a Man Test, Riegel inventories	WAIS, Rorschach, Interpersonal Checklist, Rosenberg Self-Concept, Riegel inventories		Raven, WAIS (Hamburg), Rueppell Creativity Test, Riegel inventories
p.m.	Tour to the Rhine or Ahr Valley (participant observation techniques)				Medical examination
Friday					
a.m.	Interview on future time perspective	Bergius–Schreiner Inventory on Future Time Perspective			Life-Satisfaction Scale
p.m.	Free	Free	Free	Free	Free

[a]Measurement Point 5 was not included in this analysis.

194

At Points 6 (1976/1977) and 7 (1980), increased funding once again permitted implementation of the original schedule. This chapter reports on data collected at all measurement points except for Point 7 (1980).

Variables Measured by the Bonn Study

1. The first set of variables is related to social conditions existing immediately before the interview. In addition to careful assessment of the socioeconomic situation, we used the interview schedules of the Cross-National Study on Adjustment to Retirement (Havighurst, Munnichs, Neugarten, & Thomae, 1969) to assess the degree and quality of social participation of our subjects. This schedule was supplemented by inventories related to leisure-time activities and so on.

2. A second set of information was related to the past. We collected data on the subjects' life history from childhood to their marriage and/or the conclusion of their vocational training. We also inquired systematically about the time during and after World War II, when most of the "younger" men (born between 1900 and 1905) served in the armed forces. The time of the West German currency reform in 1948 served as a reference point for eliciting quite detailed retrospective reports regarding income, job, housing conditions, health, and family. The interviewers not only covered the situations as they were experienced, but also asked for detailed descriptions of how our subjects coped with different aspects of their situations.

The identical procedure was followed for the reference points 1955 (i.e., 10 years prior to the first interview), 1965, 1966, 1967, 1972, and 1976. These reference points enabled most subjects to remember a particular stressful situation and to report the ways they coped with it. Our data on perceived stress from 1948 to 1972 showed a continuous decrease, resulting in decreased amounts of information regarding problem-coping behavior.

3. A third set of data was related to the subjects' plans for the year following the interview and in the more distant future. From a complete set of items, ratings were made of the extension and quality of future time perspectives, attitudes toward health and death, and so on.

4. Our formal test data included the Hamburg–Wechsler test for the measurement of intelligence in adults (German standardization of the Wechsler Adult Intelligence Scale [WAIS]) at Measurement Points 1, 3, 4, 5, 6, and 7. The Raven Progressive Matrices were given at Points 2, 5, 6, and 7. As a test of psychomotor performance at high speed, we applied the Mierke apparatus (Kieler Determinationsgeraet), in which subjects have to react to irregular patterns of colored flashes and sounds with increasing speed. Two other tests of psychomotor adjustment were used only in the first and last years, respectively, of the study: a Pursuit Rotor learning task and the Beck apparatus.

5. Projective techniques used especially during the first years were the Rorschach and Behn–Rorschach, and Wilde's Wunsch-Probe ("wish test").

6. Questionnaires adapted for aged persons from the lower middle class were not available at the beginning of our study. We therefore used the Riegel inventories (Riegel, 1960), which had been developed with an aged population in northern Germany in the late 1950s. These inventories assess several aspects of attitudinal rigidity, dogmatism, and attitudes toward present and future time.

7. Data on health and standard medical data were recorded at each measurement point in a standardized situation. At Measurement Points 5, 6, and 7, a half-day clinical examination was added.

Sampling Procedures

Most longitudinal studies on aged persons use volunteers who are motivated by their association with organizations or agencies (Birren *et al.*, 1963, p. 7) or by their cooperative attitude toward friends, colleagues, or relatives who ask them to participate (snowball technique; Palmore, 1970, p. 4; see also Stone & Norris, 1966, p. 575).

We tried very hard to draw a random sample of subjects from the western part of West Germany (Ruhr area, Cologne, Bonn and suburbs, Frankfurt, Mannheim, Heidelberg) for our study. However, like many previous researchers, we faced many difficulties in doing so. Sampling procedures for a simple 2-hour interview are quite different from those used in a study that involves complex psychological and medical examinations and that requires travel to, and residence at, a university institute for a whole week. Our random sample was therefore completed with referrals from welfare organizations and industrial plants to whom we explained our aims and plans.

We required that the participants be in good health and live in their own household. The subjects we included had to be able to travel to Bonn by train and stay in a small hotel near the institute or, for those in the Bonn area, reach the institute every day using public transportation. Another selection requirement was lower middle-class or (for a very small percentage) middle middle-class status. We also tried to control the sample for religious background and place of birth (West Germany vs.

East Germany and former German provinces that now belong to Russia, Poland, and Czechoslovakia).

A major decision had to be made regarding the age cohort. To analyze possible effects of retirement, we ensured that one-half (about 110) of our subjects (59 men, 51 women) were expecting to retire or had retired no more than 2 years prior to the first point of measurement. A second cohort consisted mainly of persons who had retired 3 to 12 years before our study began. The design therefore included four groups of men and women of lower middle-class status: (1) men born between 1900 and 1905, (2) women born between 1900 and 1905, (3) men born between 1890 and 1895, and (4) women born betwen 1890 and 1895.

This design made it possible to combine longitudinal and cross-sectional comparisons. The two cohorts did not differ in regard to socioeconomic status (SES), but differences were found for the group of older women at the beginning of the study: Older women had poorer health.

Original Sample and Dropout Problems

Our sample consisted of 222 men and women at the first measurement point (108 women, 114 men). At Point 6 (1976/1977), 81 had survived; at Point 7 (1980), 48 were able to participate. As had to be expected, the number of dropouts was greater for the older cohort and for men.

Subjects were lost because of death in about 50% of the cases and because of illness or impairment in 50% of the original sample. There were no refusals to continue participation in the study for reasons other than poor health. The attrited sample did differ significantly in SES. The percentage of married persons dropped from 63% to 43%, while that of widowers and widows increased from 22% to 37%.

Findings

Cognitive Functioning

In an analysis of the data from Measurement Points 1 through 4, Schmitz-Scherzer (1977) pointed to a high degree of constancy in the WAIS (Hamburg) scores. The distribution of the WAIS (Hamburg) Verbal scores (weighted score) at the different points indicates some shifts, especially for individuals who were close to the group average. Generally, however, a high degree of constancy was observed for those persons who received 51 to 60 points at the beginning, although some scored lower at Measurement Points 3 and 4 (see Table 6.2). In any case, we do not observe any systematic changes.

For the Performance scores, on the other hand, we find an accumulation of subjects in the lower (up to 50) score groups (see Table 6.3). Although cognitive functioning remained fairly constant up to Measurement Point 5, there was a decrease from Point 5 to Point 6 in the Performance score. A similar trend can also be concluded from inspection of mean scores at the different measurement points (see Table 6.4).

There were no significant changes in Verbal scores from 1965 to 1976/ 1977 for the whole sample or for the younger cohort. The older cohort dropped significantly by almost 5 points. When evaluating this finding, it should be remembered, however, that the rank ordering implicated in the Friedman test can result in some leveling of the data. Men always scored higher than women, subjects coming from higher SES levels scored higher than those from lower SES levels, and those with poorer health scored lower than those with better health.

The Performance scores yielded significant group differences by cohort, sex, social class, and health (see Table 6.5). Decrease of WAIS Performance scores was found especially for those with lower social status and poorer health.

Similar analyses of the Raven Colored Progressive Matrices (CPM) scores support the preceding findings. For each cohort, sex, and social class group, there is a significant decrease in average scores, especially from Measurement Point 5 to Point 6. This decline is due mainly to performance on the B and AB series; there is no significant change on the

TABLE 6.2. Distribution of Weighted Verbal Scores on WAIS (Hamburg) Test at Five Measurement Points (1965 to 1976/1977)[a]

| Score | WAIS (Hamburg) | | | | |
	1	3	4	5	6
to 40	4	6	5	5	7
41–50	23	27	23	27	28
51–60	35	29	28	30	27
61 plus	18	16	16	14	17
n	80	78	72	76	79

[a]WAIS (Hamburg) was not administered at Point 2.

TABLE 6.3. Distribution of Weighted Performance Scores on WAIS (Hamburg) Test at Five Measurement Points (1965 to 1976/1977)[a]

	WAIS (Hamburg)				
Score	1	3	4	5	6
to 40	23	21	23	23	40
41–50	38	34	29	31	31
51–60	15	18	17	19	5
61 plus	3	4	3	3	3
n	79	77	72	76	79

[a]WAIS (Hamburg) was not administered at Point 2.

TABLE 6.4. Weighted Verbal Scores on WAIS (Hamburg) Test at Five Measurement Points

	WAIS (Hamburg)				
	1	3	4	5	6
Cohort 1					
Average score	53.6	53.4	54.0	53.5	52.7
Standard deviation	7.8	7.4	8.1	7.1	8.4
Cohort 2[a]					
Average score	54.1	52.5	52.7	51.2	49.4
Standard deviation	8.8	9.4	9.5	8.6	11.2
Men					
Average score	55.9	54.8	56.4	53.0	53.7
Standard deviation	8.0	7.4	8.5	7.1	9.1
Women					
Average score	52.2	51.8	51.4	52.2	49.7
Standard deviation	8.0	8.6	8.3	8.2	10.4
Lower SES					
Average score	52.1	51.2	51.2	50.8	49.1
Standard deviation	7.8	7.9	7.6	7.0	9.4
Higher SES					
Average score	60.6	60.5	63.6	59.6	60.5
Standard deviation	5.9	4.8	5.6	6.7	7.1
Poorer health					
Average score	55.4	54.6	55.2	54.5	53.6
Standard deviation	7.5	7.4	8.8	7.6	9.7
Better health					
Average score	52.3	51.7	51.9	50.7	49.5
Standard deviation	8.6	8.8	8.4	7.4	9.9

[a]Significance (Friedman): χ^2, 10.2; df, 4; and $p = .04$.

TABLE 6.5. Weighted Performance Scores on WAIS (Hamburg) Test at Five Measurement Points

	WAIS (Hamburg)							
						Significance (Friedman)		
	1	3	4	5	6	χ^2	df	p
Cohort 1								
Mean score	44.9	46.5	47.4	46.4	43.2	27.2	4	.00
Standard deviation	8.5	8.7	7.4	8.7	8.6			
Cohort 2								
Mean score	44.5	43.4	42.5	42.9	36.2	23.6	4	.00
Standard deviation	9.4	8.6	9.4	8.5	9.6			
Men								
Mean score	46.6	46.5	48.2	46.5	41.8	18.9	4	.00
Standard deviation	8.5	7.9	8.4	7.9	8.6			
Women								
Mean score	43.4	44.7	43.1	44.6	39.2	40.4	4	.00
Standard deviation	8.8	9.2	8.2	9.4	10.3			
Lower SES								
Mean score	43.7	44.2	43.9	43.9	38.6	36.8	4	.00
Standard deviation	8.3	8.4	7.9	8.5	9.3			
Higher SES								
Mean score	49.0	50.6	51.0	51.1	46.8	10.4	4	.00
Standard deviation	9.7	8.3	9.5	7.8	8.3			
Poorer health								
Mean score	45.9	47.6	47.8	48.6	43.2	23.9	4	.00
Standard deviation	8.1	7.9	8.6	7.7	9.4			
Better health								
Mean score	43.7	43.6	42.9	42.5	37.7	27.6	4	.00
Standard deviation	9.3	9.0	8.0	8.7	9.1			

AA series scores. For the Raven CPM, the standard deviation as well as the solution time increased, particularly for the groups of elderly with poorer health and lower SES, and for women.

Repeated measurement effects could be observed on the Mierke Psychomotor Performance Test when scores from the first to the third measurement point were compared. From Point 3 to Point 6, performance decreased, that is, the time needed to obtain at least 50% successful reactions increased, especially in women and in persons with lower SES and poorer health. Furthermore, the standard deviation increased with advancing age during the period of longitudinal observation (Mathey, 1976).

The preceding findings demonstrate the interaction among age, sex, SES, and health in the determination of cognitive functioning and psychomotor performance. Health and SES contributed decisively to interindividual and intraindividual variation of performance. Rudinger (1980) has previously called attention to the consistently different mean WAIS (Hamburg) scores of older persons coming from different educational backgrounds (see Figure 6.1). On the Verbal scores, persons with higher education showed a constant trend of increasing achievement, while those with less education had lower scores and greater decline. These trends are less clear for the longitudinal trends on the WAIS (Hamburg) Perform-

FIGURE 6.1. Changes of WAIS (Hamburg) scores in aged persons from different educational backgrounds. (Adapted from Rudinger, 1980.)

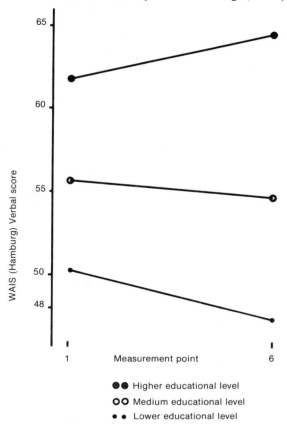

● ● Higher educational level
○ ○ Medium educational level
● ● Lower educational level

ance score. Differences in performance between the educational groups are constant, however. Rudinger and Lantermann (1980) fitted the data with a path-analytic model. They were able to demonstrate that 38% of the variance of WAIS (Hamburg) scores at Measurement Point 1 could be explained by the educational, occupational, and socioeconomic background of the parents of our subjects and by the subjects' own education and occupation. All these findings point to the complex conditions of constancy and change of cognitive functioning and psychomotor performance in aging, which have also been stressed by many other writers (Baltes & Willis, 1979, Schaie, 1974). The role of health would have been demonstrated more clearly if the criterion of good health had not been used for drawing the sample of the first measurement point. Although the range of variation regarding SES was reduced by our selection criterion, striking constant differences between socially defined groups were found.

The greater impact of chronological age on the Psychomotor Performance Test (Mierke) can be explained by the role of the speed factor in this test, which apparently is more closely related to a "primary process of aging" (Birren, 1965). However, even more striking is the degree of IEV on this test and the constant differences between the sexes and groups in better or poorer health.

Personality: Q Data

The main source for evaluating constancy and change in personality in our study were the scales developed by Riegel and Riegel for measuring rigidity, attitudes, and anxiety. Angleitner (1976) analyzed the data from the first four measurement points by means of a three-way analysis of variance (ANOVA), with sex, SES, and time as treatments. The scores for general rigidity decreased over time, whereas those for personal rigidity increased. Socioeconomic status had a significant effect on general as well as personal rigidity, with lower SES persons endorsing more stereotyped and rigid statements than those from somewhat higher SES. Sex did not significantly affect rigidity, but men showed a more positive orientation on attitudes toward their own lives.

Angleitner interpreted the results of his analysis of the rigidity data as failing to support the expectation of increased rigidity with advancing age (from Measurement Point 1 to Point 4). This conclusion is supported by the analyses of the longitudinal sample reported here. For the younger cohort, scores for general rigidity were almost identical at Points 1 and 6. Where there was a trend toward a slight increase in scores for men, the scores for women decreased. Scores for personal rigidity increased in the male group, especially from Points 4 to 6, and in the older cohort.

The scores for the scales on attitudes toward the present remained constant over time, but scores on attitudes toward the future became more positive at Measurement Point 6 in the men's group. Generally, our Q data support Mischel's (1973) criticism of trait-centered approaches as resulting in the leveling out of intraindividual and situation-specific variations.

Personality: L Data on Formal Aspects

During the 5 days the subjects spent at our center, there were many chances, at most of the measurement points, for making observations on formal aspects of behavior such as degree of activity, mood, responsiveness, adjustment, and feelings of security and insecurity. These aspects are relevant for any developmental assessment. They are especially important for studies on aging because the still-existing stereotypes held by some of the general public and by some "experts" like physicians imply that aging is equivalent to declining activity, adjustment, and responsiveness and to an increase in feelings of insecurity and depression.

The 9-point rating scales for these observations were tested for their generalizability (Cronbach, Gleser, Nanda, & Rajaratnam, 1972) by Rudinger and Feger (1970). Their ratings turned out to be "highly reliable." Only 9% of the total variance could be attributed to the "halo effect," that is, an interaction between subjects and judges.

Grombach (1975) computed stability coefficients between the rating scores on Activity, Mood, General Responsiveness, Adjustment, Ego Control, and Self-confidence for the several measurement points. The lowest stability was found for Ego Control (.38) and for Mood (.46) on Measurement Points 1 and 4. Relative stability of the behavioral aspects over a 5-year period was found for Activity (impulsive vs. controlled), General Responsiveness, Adjustment, and Self-confidence. In men, the Activity score drops from 6.7 to 5.5 ($p < .05$), whereas in women, this score remains constant (6.1 to 5.9). Change is also greater for the older cohort (6.3 to 5.4) and is significant for the older men in poorer health. A small, but significant, decrease can also be observed for Mood (from 5.7 to 5.2). Here the change is larger for men (from 5.9 to 5.1) than for women (from 5.5 to 5.2).

The General Responsiveness scores dropped by a half point from Measurement Point 1 to Point 6 for the total sample, but from 6.5 to 5.5

for the older cohort. These changes were not significant. Adjustment ratings changed significantly. They increased from 5.8 to 6.1 (at Point 4) and dropped to 5.4 at Point 6. Greater change was found for subjects with lower SES and for older women in poorer health. Scores for Ego Control dropped significantly, by .6 point from the first to the sixth measurement points. The greatest decrease (by .8 point) was observed in the lower SES group.

No change or an upward trend was observed in the ratings of Self-confidence. Our findings therefore do not confirm the stereotypes on the aging personality, in agreement with findings by Schaie and Parham (1976). High Mood decreases to average values, very high Activity to high Activity, and high degree of Adjustment and of Ego Control changes to good Adjustment and fair Ego Control. We simply do not know how those subjects who died might have reacted, aside from the fact that their scores were significantly lower in Activity at the first measurement point (Lehr & Schmitz-Scherzer, 1976).

Social Participation

Social participation was assessed with slight modifications in the interview schedule and with rating scales developed for the Cross-National Study on Adjustment to Retirement (Havighurst et al., 1969). The semi-structured interview assessed activity, satisfaction, involvement, and perceived stress in the roles of spouse, parent, grandparent, kin, friend, acquaintance, neighbor, club member, and citizen. "Activity" was defined by frequency of contacts during a week or a month in each of the roles. The score therefore depends not only on the elderly persons' behavior, but also on the relevant role of partnership. A nonsignificant increase was found in the high scores for activity in the spouse role as well as in the parent and grandparent roles. Increases of activity at a lower level could be observed also in the kin and citizen role.

Lehr (1979) analyzed the combinations of changes in role activities and satisfaction as postulated by the disengagement theory of aging (Cumming & Henry, 1960) or by activity theory (Maddox, 1965). Subjects supporting the disengagement theory of aging combine decreased role activity with increasing satisfaction, while aged persons confirming activity theory show increased satisfaction with increasing role activity. Lehr (1979) reported that disengagement-theory subjects differed most from activity-theory subjects on "central" roles, such as spouse, parent, grandparent, and friend, and less on more "peripheral" roles, such as kin, club member, or citizen. These differences were quite role-specific. In the spouse role, disengagement-theory subjects differed from activity-theory subjects by better health, lower degree of rigidity, and higher efforts to maintain a broad range of interests. Disengagement-theory subjects in the parent role had a higher degree of life satisfaction and of activity in the roles of parent and grandparent at the beginning of the study (1965). They generally had a more positive attitude toward the future. As in the grandparent role, they also were more active in the spouse role, had a more positive mood, were more responsive, and lived under less stressful economic conditions. On the other hand, these subjects in this role were less well off in terms of housing conditions, income, and health. Activity-theory subjects in the friend role had more problems with their families and with their spouses than did disengagement-theory subjects. They responded to these problems more often in an evasive way and had a lower degree of congruence between the desired and the achieved scales in the family.

This longitudinal analysis of different patterns of increase and decrease in role activity and satisfaction generally questions the value of global theories of aging such as disengagement theory or activity theory. Depending upon personal, health, economic, and other influences, changes in social participation, satisfaction with such change, and involvement can develop in the manner suggested by disengagement theory in some roles, while at the same time, changes in other roles can occur as would be predicted from activity theory. These findings consequently stress the relevance of differential aspects of gerontology.

Leisure-Time Activities

Leisure-time activities are principal sources for adjustment to retirement and to old age generally (Kleemeier, 1961; Schmitz-Scherzer, 1969, 1973). Furthermore, they may be indicators of the interests and the behavioral and cognitive competencies of the elderly. The analysis of constancy and change in these activities therefore contributes to the study of the aging personality and its interaction with the environment.

Data on leisure-time activities were gathered by use of a structured interview. Activities covered included reading books or newspapers, listening to the radio, watching television, gardening, entertaining visitors, visiting other people, taking walks and excursions with others, going to a tavern, walking, and attending church.

Activity frequencies were rated on scales from 1 (very rarely) to 7 (extremely frequent). Analysis of the mean rating scores did not yield any statistically significant changes in frequency of activities such as walking, reading books, reading newspapers or magazines, watching television, listening to the radio, and going to a tavern. Some of these activities structure the daily life of the elderly and point to a high degree of constancy of the everyday situation. This finding held true for all groups as defined by age, sex, health, and social class.

For another group of activities, a decrease in frequency was found especially in the elderly with lower SES. The latter finding occurred for taking a tour, gardening, visiting other people, and entertaining visitors. The decrease was not statistically significant, however, and was confined to the time between Measurement Points 5 and 6.

Perceived Life Space

Since we consider the *perceived* situation to be the main determinant of behavior (Kastenbaum, 1964; Thomae, 1970), we tried to assess the perceived present, past, and future aspects of the subjects' situations by means of two semistructured interviews. The cognitive appraisal of the last year before each measurement point along the dimension "unfavorable–favorable" indicated a trend toward more favorable perceptions (from 5.1 to 5.5). This favorable trend was truer for the younger cohort, whereas the older showed a modest trend in the direction of unfavorable perception. Everyday life was perceived by men as a little bit more monotonous at the end of the observation period compared to the beginning. In women, however, an opposite trend could be observed.

The perception of the "unchangeability" of the present situation with its advantages and disadvantages increased in a significant way, albeit at a very low level (scores from 1.6 to 3.0 on a 7-point scale). The change was not constant over the years of the study, with decreasing scores at Measurement Points 2 and 4, and rising scores at the last two measurement points.

Fisseni (1980) found significant correlations between the scores for perceived unchangeability and sex from Measurement Point 1 to Measurement Point 6. Women always scored higher compared with men. Those persons with poorer health and those with negative attitudes scored higher as well.

The relationship of perceived unchangeability to various variables became closer during the years of observation. From Measurement Point 5 to Point 6, the older cohort showed significantly higher scores compared with the younger cohort. Also from Point 5 to Point 6, low income correlated positively with the perceived unchangeability. Fisseni found correlations in the same direction between perceived unchangeability and poorer health (assessed by a physician) in Point 3 and between perceived unchangeability and less social participation in Point 5.

Fisseni (1980) concludes from these findings that the relationship between perceived unchangeability and social, biological, and psychological variables can be inconsistent. More difficult problems for the interpretation are raised by the decreasing correlations. Perhaps the impact of other variables is becoming decisive enough to effect the perception of unchangeability even in cases where there is higher SES, higher life satisfaction, and less conflict in family life.

In any case, it is shown in analyses such as these how longitudinal studies can help us understand the interaction among different aspects of the ever-changing life situation and cognitive as well as behavioral variables.

As far as other aspects of perceived life space are concerned, it should be mentioned that our subjects' perceptions of their life situations became significantly less disappointing and frustrating than they were at the beginning. This change was especially true for persons with lower SES and for those with better health. Fisseni (1976) examined constancy and change in the extension of perceived life space by means of "configural frequency analysis" (Lienert & Krauth, 1975). Special attention was given to the stress-related, satisfaction-inducing aspects. Four patterns of constancy and/or change were recognizable: one in which subjects scored high on all criteria for extension (perception of others as friendly vs. unfriendly, extension of future time perspective, number of plans for the future) and three patterns where subjects scored high on two of the criterion variables and low on the third. Generally, more changes were observed during the first measurement points, and constancy was observed after Measurement Point 3.

The general pattern was differentiated, however, by the effects of age, sex, health, and SES. Health as a discriminant variable pointed to three patterns: one in which subjects in good health scored high on all dimensions tested; one in which subjects with good health scored high on the future-related aspects of perceived life space and low on the perceptions of others as favorable; and a third, in which subjects were defined by poorer health, had more favorable perceptions of others, and had restricted future time perspective.

Perceptions of Self

At Measurement Point 3, we used the Interpersonal Checklist (ICL) of La Forge and Suczek (1955) to assess the self-concept at that part of the life space which is most decisive in determining constancy and change in behavior (Rogers, 1959). Angleitner (1975) found relatively healthy men to describe themselves as more "rebellious–distrustful" than men in poorer health. Women perceived themselves as most "rebellious–distrustful" when in poor health.

Fisseni (1981) analyzed data from Measurement Points 1 to 4 in terms of perceived change in one's own personality. His classification of patterns was based on interview data drawn from Measurement Point 2, when we asked our subjects whether they had become aware of any general change in themselves as well as of any specific change in achievement, physical strength, and attractiveness. One group (I) perceived less change and virtually no symptoms of aging in health, occupational and cognitive competence, and social participation. Another group (II) perceived more than average change in most of these areas.

These two groups with different self-concepts regarding change and symptoms of aging were compared at Measurement Points 1 to 4. Although there was no significant difference in WAIS scores at the beginning, the two groups showed very different changes over time. The scores of Group I increased, but there was a significant decrease in scores for Group II, from Measurement Point 1 to Point 3. A similar developmental trend was observed for Activity and Mood. Again, ratings for these variables did not differ at Measurement Point 1, but were lower at Point 3 for Group II. Life Satisfaction decreased rather steeply in Group II, while the degree of Perceived Stress increased in this group. Subjects who reported no change and no symptoms of aging at Measurement Point 2 (Group I) showed smaller changes in Life Satisfaction and decreasing scores for Perceived Stress.

An important factor in the differentiation of the two patterns of self-concept was that of sex: Men belonged mainly to Group I, women to Group II. Fisseni (1981) believes that the differences in self-concept are aspects of more global cognitive systems, which include a greater expectation of negative aspects of aging for women (Lehr, 1978). Fisseni also points to the interaction between global cognitive orientation and feedback from the environment. Increasing or constant scores for Morale, Adjustment, Feelings of Security, and Ego Control shown by Group I members suggest that they had received reinforcing responses from the social environment. The less stable Mood, Adjustment, Feelings of Security, and Ego Control observed in Group II may have resulted in responses from the environment that confirm a more negative self-concept.

Reactions to Life Stress

There is general agreement that reactions to stress are defined by the cognitive evaluation of stressors rather than by their objective quality

(Haan, 1977; Lazarus & Launier, 1978; Renner & Birren, 1980; Thomae, 1970). However, there still exist great differences in the classification and theoretical interpretation of these reactions. On the one hand, models of coping with stress have been derived from neopsychoanalysis or egopsychology, such as those of Haan (1977) and Vaillant (1977), who analyze response to life stress in the framework of a response hierarchy. People reacting to stress are classified into those who use more mature or immature, more realistic or unrealistic, more active or passive responses. This kind of classsification evaluates any response to life stress in terms of a normative model of humans whose main values are active mastery, objective thinking, and control of emotions and affect.

On the other hand, there are those authors who define coping with stress as adaptation under very difficult conditions (White, 1974) and who suggest a formal system of classification similar to that of Lazarus and Launier (1978). We should avoid applying a classificatory system derived from psychotherapy or from other clinical studies because we have little knowledge as to how elderly people perceive stress and how they cope with it. Rather, we should focus on the manner in which old people report stress in everyday life and on how they cope with such stress. Only then can descriptive-stage theories and taxonomies of stress reactions in old age be formulated.

We have previously studied reactions to stress in juvenile delinquents (Thomae, 1953), displaced persons (Haupt, 1959), and handicapped war veterans (Hambitzer, 1962) from this empirical, rather than nomothetic, point of view. When designing the BLSA, findings of these previous studies were applicable. The ultimate scoring system, however, was formulated after careful analysis of reports of persons on the ways in which they experienced the time of currency reform (1948) in Western Germany and on their reactions to it. At that time, every person in our country lost his or her savings and received only 40 DM cash. Subjects remembered this period very well and included in their reports their whole life histories at the end of and subsequent to World War II. The structured interview assessed degree of stress as perceived in the following areas of life: occupation, income, housing, family, and health. We also asked our subjects to describe carefully the ways in which they reacted to each of these stress areas. By ordering responses in terms of their semantic content rather than according to a theoretical or formal model, it was possible to define approximately 25 types of responses, of which 18 could be traced in the majority of subjects and situations, for example, cultivating social contacts, revising expectations, and hoping for change (Thomae, 1968). This interview was conducted at the first measurement point of the BLSA, in 1965, that is, about 18 years after the currency reform. We also asked our subjects to report on their life situations of

10 years earlier (1955) and at the present time. The same scoring system was applied to these reports (von Langermann & Erlenkamp, 1970). We repeated these interviews and ratings for each of the following years, or measurement points: 1966, 1967, 1969, 1976/1977, and 1980.

Reactions to Health Problems

Increases in perceived health problems were also validated by the data from the medical examination: Problems regarding vision, hearing, and mobility were increasingly indicated for the older cohort. Symptoms of sclerosis and cardiac insufficiency as well as of hypertension were significantly more frequent at the last than at the first measurement points.

The overall scores for active coping with health problems increased in all groups, but this increase was statistically significant only for the group of younger men with fewer health problems. These ratings also included the degree to which the situation was perceived as stressful. As shown in Figure 6.2, during the period 1966–1976/1977, there was an increase in perceived stress concerning health problems, a small decrease for family and housing problems, and a sizable decrease for economic problems. This finding must be treated with caution. It most likely reflects the improving conditions of life of our lower middle-class population and their increasing tendency to cope with stress by controlling the primary appraisal thereof (Lazarus, 1966). Because perceived stress was fairly moderate, reactions to it were very often absent or very weak. The mean scores (on a 7-point scale) for most of the types of reactions were very low. The discussion of our findings focuses, therefore, upon similarities or different rank orders of reaction patterns related to health and family problems at the different measurement points.

As shown in Table 6.6, there was a high degree of constancy in the ten patterns of reaction to health problems that were mentioned by at least 10% of our subjects at Measurement Points 2 and 6.[1] The first two reaction patterns involve active coping by influencing the external world. Adjustment to institutions and legal regulations in the areas of health problems refers to skills in obtaining the most out of health insurance, in finding the best doctor or treatment, or in gaining the means for vacations at a health resort. It also includes adjustment to the regulations of a hospital or rehabilitation center in regard to smoking or consumption of alcohol.

Achievement-related behavior here refers to any expenditure of energy or effort in obtaining a goal. In 1966, it could have consisted, at least for

[1]Reactions to health problems were rated at Measurement Point 2 for the first time.

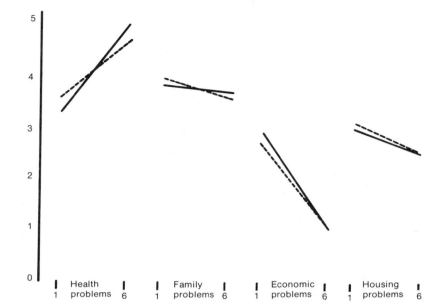

FIGURE 6.2. Degree of perceived stress (———) and reactions to stress (------) in different problem areas at Measurement Points 1 (1965) and 6 (1976/1977).

the younger cohort, of doing odd jobs to pay for the next vacation trip, of gardening (because it was "healthy"), or of engaging in some kind of physical activity such as walking (following the physician's advice). In 1976/1977, achievement-related behavior was confined primarily to the third kind of activity, especially in the older group, for some of whom walking really was quite a strenuous effort.

A depressive reaction or resignation represents in our scoring system a descriptive, rather than a clinical, category and defines a state rather than a constant trait. The average scores throughout the years of observation point to this dynamic character of depressive reactions in a nonclinical assessment. Such a reaction, however, is mentioned by different subjects as frequently as the more active ways of coping mentioned so far.

Nevertheless, we would like to stress that the rank order of average scores for depressive reactions did not increase during the 10 years we took for this comparison. According to clinical as well as cognitive-learning interpretations of reactive depression (cf. Seligman, 1975), we should have expected a sharp increase in the incidence of these reactions with increasing age. But for populations like the survivors of a lower middle-class longitudinal panel, clinical or cognitive-learning labels (such

TABLE 6.6. Rank Order of the Ten Most Important Patterns of Response to Health Problems, 1966 and 1976/1977

1966	1976/1977
1. Adjustment to institutional aspects of the situation	1. Achievement-related behavior
2. Achievement-related behavior	2. Adjustment to institutional aspects of the situation
3. Depressive reaction	3. Accepting the situation as it is
4. Hope for change	4. Depressive reaction
5. Accepting the situation as it is	5. Revision of expectancies
6. Relying on others	6. Relying on others
7. Active resistance	7. Asking for help
8. Using chances	8. Using chances
9. Asking for help	9. Hope for change
10. Revision of expectancies	10. Active resistance

as "learned helplessness") are misleading if they are replacing any connotations of well-organized coping styles with health problems. The depressive–resignative reaction pattern is woven into the complex structure of human reactions to life stress and is found in studies on adolescent, young, and middle-aged persons.

Another way of coping with perceived poor health is by acceptance, as is verbalized in statements such as "Well, even if I am bad off, there are many whose health is worse." It is a cognitive way of coping that may lead to a reappraisal (Lazarus & Launier, 1978) of the stressful situation and that apparently contributes increasingly to the restoration of emotional balance. Even more important is a cognitive restructuring of the situation, which we labeled "revision of expectancies." This restructuring is often represented by remarks such as "Well, I am not too well off, but what can you expect for a woman of my age?" As a response to physical impairment or chronic disease, this reaction shifted from tenth to fifth place. On the other hand, irrational cognitive reactions to stress, such as hope for change, apparently lose influence since they may turn out to be less successful in enabling one to deal with longer lasting stress.

Another reaction pattern that shifted from an intermediate to the lowest rank was labeled "active resistance." It refers to resistance against recommendations to go for a medical examination or to undergo surgery, but also to the failure to accept recommendations on diet, physical activity, consumption of alcohol, or smoking of cigarettes.

Reactions to Problems in Family Life

Problems or stress in family life can be related to poor health, to unfriendly behavior by one's spouse or other family members, to the economic or marital problems of one's children, and sometimes also to the educational or vocational problems of one's grandchildren. They can be related to loss of contact with children or to tensions arising from excessive contact when the grandparent lives in the household of a son or daughter and his or her children.

The impact of the type of problem on the selection of responses is demonstrated by the high rank order of some reaction patterns (see Table 6.7): adjustment to needs and/or peculiarities of others, cultivating social contacts, and identification with the aims and interests of children and/or grandchildren. The first of these response groups is defined by the adaptation of the subject's expectations and desires to those of a very egocentric or mentally deteriorated spouse, those of less family-centered grandchildren, or those of a daughter, son, or grandchild whose life-style is not quite in congruence with the traditional family norms. The difference in rank order for this pattern in 1966 and in 1976/1977 reflects achievement of a balance attained in between these measurement points.

Cultivating social contacts is mainly related to endeavors to contribute to the integration of the extended family by invitations, visits, telephone

TABLE 6.7. Rank Order of the Ten Most Important Patterns of Coping with Problems (Stress) in Family Life, 1966 and 1976/1977

1966	1976/1977
1. Adjustment to needs and/or peculiarities of others	1. Achievement-related behavior
2. Achievement-related behavior	2. Identification with the aims and interests of children and/or grandchildren
3. Cultivating social contacts	3. Cultivating social contacts
4. Identification with the aims and interests of children and/or grandchildren	4. Adjustment to needs and/or peculiarities of others
5. Depressive reaction	5. Depressive reaction
6. Active resistance	6. Relying on others
7. Delay of gratification	7. Accepting the situation as it is
8. Accepting the situation as it is	8. Delay of gratification
9. Evasive reaction	9. Evasive reaction
10. Relying on others	10. Active resistance

calls, or writing letters. The reaction pattern of identifying with the aims and interests of children and/or grandchildren is a form of adaptation in which the elderly person completely introjects plans, future perspectives, or worries and norms of the offspring and regulates his or her behavior from these introjected standards. Although this coping device was not helpful in response to health problems, it certainly contributed much to the solving of conflicts with children and grandchildren, although often by the older person's sacrificing his or her own interests. A similar pattern occurred in the reaction to economic and housing problems, albeit in a less exploitative manner than for family problems. Identification with the aims and interests of children helps to solve problems arising from a low degree of congruence between desired and attained goals in occupation, income, or housing. It is represented by verbalizations such as "Well I always had bad luck, but Robert [the son], he made it, he is well off" and "Why should I complain about my own fate?"

Aside from several minor shifts in the rank order of these reactions between 1966 and 1976/1977 and more sizable shifts for active resistance and reliance on others, there was a great degree of constancy in rank order of response patterns over a 10-year span. Achievement-related behavior became even more important in 1976/1977. It might have consisted of financial contributions to the household of one's children or frequent gifts to one's grandchildren, but also of taking care of the household of a daughter or daughter-in-law who was a working mother or of caring for a frail spouse or other kin. Generally, we can observe a rich repertoire of reactions which should not be obscured by aggregation into one dimension such as active–passive or external–internal action.

Determinants of Choice of Responses

The differences in rank order of the most relevant response patterns to stress, as well as the great similarities, point to the interaction of situation and person in the selection of responses. Among the personality variables that may be involved in the selection of responses, we studied, especially, the impact of cognitive representations of the situation and of transsituational cognitive systems. Olbrich and Thomae (1978) used a series of pathanalyses (Boudon, 1968) to compare the relationship between objective life conditions regarding housing, income, health, and so on, and reactions to these conditions on the one hand, and the relationship between the cognitive representations of these life conditions and reactions to these cognitive representations on the other hand.

According to one of these analyses, monthly income had very small, insignificant path coefficients with life satisfaction (the emotional reaction), while the cognitive representation of the economic situation in terms of perceived economic stress yielded highly significant path coefficients with both income and life satisfaction. In the same way, we found trivial path coefficients between several objective indicators of health problems (such as sclerosis and cardiac insufficiency) and degree of coping with health problems, while the path coefficients between perceived health and coping with health problems at different measurement points ranged from .56 to .70.

Pfoetsch (1979) used path analysis to test hypotheses related to antecedents of future time perspective. One of her hypotheses concerned the causal relationships between perceived stress and conflict in the family and achievement as independent variables, and attitude toward the future and life satisfaction as dependent variables (see Figure 6.3). The path coefficient between perceived stress and conflict in the family and achievement-related behavior increased from Measurement Point 1 to Point 4. But attitude toward the future and life satisfation did not have any connections with the selection of achievement-related behavior. Apparently, the constancy of a state such as that of stress and conflict in the family can contribute to the elicitation of achievement-related behavior without any interaction with general emotional dispositions such as life satisfaction or attitude toward the future. A similar pattern was shown by Pfoetsch for the relationships between perceived economic stress, achievement-related behavior, attitude toward the future, and life satisfaction.

FIGURE 6.3. Path-analytic diagram of coefficients between perceived stress in family life, attitude toward the future, and responses to perceived stress. MP = measurement point. (Adapted from Pfoetsch, 1979.)

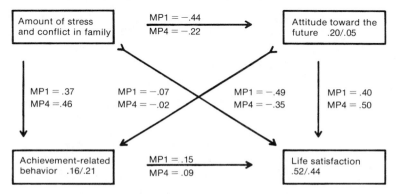

In connection with our studies on the perceived unchangeability of a stressful situation, we augmented our sample for a cross-sectional study of aged persons with health and economic problems with a control group having fewer problems of this kind (Thomae, 1981). We developed a scale to measure the generalized expectation of the unchangeability of stress (EU scale). The scale consists of ten items such as "All of my plans are getting more and more restricted due to poor health"; "A person of my age should not expect that hard times will change for the better"; and "If I would pay more attention, I would not forget so many things." Subjects were asked to indicate if they agreed or disagreed with these statements. Responses were scored in the direction of EU. Generalized expectations of the unchangeability of the situation should have reduced the probability of selection of active ways of coping and increased the chances of passive, depressive, or maladjusted reactions.

No significant correlations of EU were found with any of the more active ways of coping, such as achievement-related behavior or adjustment to institutional aspects of the situation (see Table 6.8), with regard to economic deprivation. Negative correlations were found between EU score and adjustment to relatives and friends, cultivating social contacts, and positive evaluation of the situation. Highly significant correlations

TABLE 6.8. Significant Correlations (r) between EU Scores and Scores for Patterns of Reaction to Economic and Health Problems

	Area of problem	
Pattern of reaction	Economic	Health
Adjustment to relatives and friends	−.204**	
Adjustment to institutional aspects of the situation		.119*
Asking for help	.167**	.212**
Achievement-related behavior		.236**
Cultivating social contacts	−.216**	
Delay of gratification	.174*	.329**
Positive evaluation of the situation	−.175*	
Relying on others	.123	−.206**
Hope for change	.293***	
Revision of expectations		.309***
Active resistance		.208**
Depressive reaction	.301***	.473***

*$p < .05$.
**$p < .01$.
***$p < .001$.

occurred between EU and depressive reaction, and significant correlation between EU and hope for change, asking for help, and delay of gratification.

The highest correlations between EU and poor health were found for depressive reaction, revision of expectations, and delay of gratification. However, there are highly significant correlations, too, between EU and active resistance and between EU and achievement-related behavior. Active resistance in this connection refers to behaviors that respond to physicians' prescriptions of diet, of giving up smoking, or of physical activity, for example. The resistance is expressed mainly to the spouse or other relatives who remind the respondent of the doctor's advice.

The pattern of reactions chosen by subjects with high EU scores diverges clearly from that of the total group, which reports achievement-related behavior (such as engaging in physical activity for improving health), adjustment to institutional aspects of the situation (e.g., finding the economic means for the best kind of treatment or rehabilitation), and asking for help as the most important ways of coping. The only form of reaction shared by high EU scorers with the whole group is delay of gratification. This may be due to classification problems; that is, different reactions may have been classified as delay of gratification by each group. It may be, too, that EU as a general expectancy does not interfere with situation-specific behaviors such as doing without drinking coffee, without drinking alcohol, or without smoking cigarettes.

The group with high EU scores diverges from the total group in the rank order of depressive reaction and active resistance. A high EU score is likely to facilitate depressive reactions and active resistance, which in the whole group hold the 7th and 11th ranks.

In the theoretical context of our study, the preceding findings point to relationships between transsituational cognitive systems (such as beliefs or expectancies) and the situation-specific cognitive representation of life in old age. Findings such as these supplement previous approaches to a cognitive theory of aging, which stress primarily the role or personality variables or motivational states, by pointing to the cognitive structures that are involved in constructing a specific cognitive representation.

Conclusions

In this chapter, we have presented only a selection of the problems, approaches, and findings of the BLSA. We have been asked why we have not described or defined "patterns" of aging since we desire to focus gerontology on the elaboration of such patterns and their origin

(Thomae, 1976). At present, it would be premature to present a new "typology" of aging such as that of Williams and Wirths (1965) or that of Reichard, Livson, and Peterson (1962). There are many ways in which patterns of aging could be defined. Classifications by health, SES, education, sex, and cohort are those we chose especially for this chapter. Alternative approaches could start with the extremes in personality variables, such as activity or general expectancies, or with different patterns of coping. We may do so in the future. For the present, it seems more important to point to the many ways in which the numerous forms of aging could be studied.

Acknowledgment

We thank Mr. Ernest Johannes Zimmermann for conducting the statistical analysis reported in the section "Findings" in this chapter.

References

Angleitner, A. Effects of health and sex on self-perception as measured by the ICL. In *Proceedings of the Tenth International Congress of Gerontology,* 1975.

Angleitner, A. Changes in personality observed in the questionnaire data from the Riegel questionnaire on rigidity, dogmatism, and attitudes toward life. In H. Thomae (Ed.), *Patterns of aging.* Basel–New York: S. Karger, 1976.

Baldwin, A. A cognitive theory of socialization. In D. Goslin (Ed.), *Handbook of socialization theory and research.* Chicago: Rand McNally, 1969.

Baltes, P. B. Longitudinal and cross-sectional sequences in the study of age and generation effects. *Human Development,* 1968, *2,* 145–171.

Baltes, P. B., & Schaie, K. W. The myth of the twilight years. *Psychology Today,* March 1974, pp. 35–38.

Baltes, P. B., & Schaie, K. W. On the plasticity of intelligence in adulthood and old age: Where Horn and Donaldson fail. *American Psychologist,* 1976, *31,* 720–725.

Baltes, P. B., & Willis, S. L. The critical importance of appropriate methodology in the study of aging: The sample case of psychometric intelligence. In *Bayer Symposium VII, Brain Function in Old Age.* Berlin–Heidelberg: Springer, 1979.

Birren, J. E. Age changes in speed of behavior. In A. T. Welford & J. E. Birren (Eds.), *Behavior, aging and the nervous system.* Springfield, Ill.: Charles C. Thomas, 1965.

Birren, J. E., Butler, R. N., Greenhouse, S. W., Sokoloff, L., & Yarrow, M. R. *Human aging: A biological and behavioral study.* Bethesda, Md.: National Institutes of Health, 1963.

Birren, J. E., & Morrison, D. F. Analysis of the WAIS subtests in relation to age and education. *Journal of Gerontology,* 1961, *16,* 363–369.

Boudon, R. A new look at correlational analysis. In H. M. Blalock & A. B. Blalock (Eds.), *Methodology in social research.* New York: McGraw-Hill, 1968.

Coerper, C., Hagen, W., & Thomae, H. (Eds.). *Deutsche Nachkriegskinder.* Stuttgart: Thieme, 1954.

Cronbach, L. J., Gleser, G. C., Nanda, H., & Rajaratnam, N. *The dependability of behavioral measurements.* New York: Wiley, 1972.

Cumming, E., & Henry, E. *Growing old.* New York: Basic Books, 1960.

Fisseni, H. J. Perceived life space: patterns of consistency and change. In H. Thomae (Ed.), *Patterns of aging.* Basel–New York: S. Karger, 1976.

Fisseni, H. J. Erleben der Endgueltigkeit der Situation: Biographische Aspekte. *Zeitschrift fuer Gerontologie*, 1980, *13*, 491–505.

Fisseni, H. J. *Zum Konzept des subjektiven Lebensraums: Eine Studie zum Modell der Selbstregulation.* Goettingen: Verlag fuer Psychologie, 1981.

Granick, S., & Friedman, A. S. The effect of education on the decline of test performance with age. *Journal of Gerontology*, 1973, *22*, 191–245.

Green, R. F. Age–intelligence relationships between ages of sixteen and sixty-four: A rising trend. *Developmental Psychology*, 1969, *1*, 618–627.

Grombach, H. *Konstanz und Variabilitaet von Persoenlichkeitsmerkmalen.* Unpublished doctoral dissertation, University of Bonn, 1975.

Haan, N. *Coping and defending.* New York: Academic Press, 1977.

Hagen, W., & Thomae, H. *10 Jahre Deutsche Nachkriegskinder.* Muenchen: Barth, 1962.

Hambitzer, M. *Schicksalsbewaeltigung und Daseinsermoeglichung bei Koerperbehinderten.* Bonn: Bouvier, 1962.

Haupt, K. Formen der sozialen Eingliederung Vertriebener. *Vita Humana*, 1959, *2*, 35–64.

Havighurst, R. J., Munnichs, J. M., Neugarten, B., & Thomae, H. (Eds). *Adjustment to retirement: A cross-national study.* Assen, The Netherlands: Van Gorcum & Comp. N. V., 1969.

Jones, H. E. Consistency and change in early maturity. *Vita Humana*, 1959, *1*, 43–51.

Kastenbaum, R. *New thoughts on old age.* New York: Springer, 1964.

Kelly, G. *Psychology of personal constructs* (2nd ed.). New York: W. W. Norton, 1955.

Kleemeier, R. W. (Ed.). *Aging and leisure.* New York: Wiley, 1961.

Kuhlen, R. G. Age and intelligence. *Vita Humana*, 1963, *6*, 56–64.

La Forge, R., & Suczek, R. F. The interpersonal dimension of personality: III. An interpersonal checklist. *Journal of Personality*, 1955, *24*, 94–112.

Lazarus, R. S. *Psychological stress and coping process.* New York: McGraw-Hill, 1966.

Lazarus, R. S., & Launier, R. Stress-related transactions between person and environment. In L. A. Pervin & M. Lewis (Eds.), *Internal and external determinants of behavior.* New York: Plenum, 1978.

Lehr, U. *Frau im Beruf: Eine psychologische Analyse.* Frankfurt: Athenäum, 1969.

Lehr, U. (Ed.). *Seniorinnen: Zur Situation der aelteren Frau.* Darmstadt: Steinkopff, 1978.

Lehr, U. *Patterns of social participation in old age—Findings from the Bonn Longitudinal Study on Aging.* Paper read at Scientific Meeting of the Gerontological Society, Washington, D.C., July 1979.

Lehr, U., & Schmitz-Scherzer, R. Survivors and nonsurvivors—Two fundamental patterns of aging. In H. Thomae (Ed.), *Patterns of aging.* Basel–New York: S. Karger, 1976.

Lehr, U., & Thomae, H. Eine Laengsschnittuntersuchung bei 30–50 jaehrigen Angestellten. *Vita Humana*, 1959, *1*, 100–110.

Lehr, U., & Thomae, H. *Konflikt, seelische Belastung und Lebensalter.* Forschungsberichte des Landes Nordrhein-Westfalen Nr. 1455. Köln–Opladen: Westdeutscher Verlag, 1965.

Lienert, G. A., & Krauth, J. Configural frequency analysis as a statistical tool for defining types. *Educational Psychological Measurement*, 1975, *35*, 231–238.

Maddox, G. Fact and artifact: Evidence bearing on disengagement theory. *Human Development*, 1965, *8*, 117–130.

Mathey, F. J. Psychomotor performance and reaction speed in old age. In H. Thomae (Ed.), *Patterns of aging.* Basel–New York: S. Karger, 1976.

McFarlane, J. W. Studies in child guidance. I. Methodology of data collection and organization. *Monographs of the Society for Research in Child Development*, 1938, *3* (24), 1–254.

Mischel, W. Toward a cognitive social learning reconceptualization of personality. *Psychological Review*, 1973, *80*, 252–283.

Nehrke, F. M. Age, sex, and educational differences in syllogistic reasoning. *Journal of Gerontology*, 1972, *27*, 466–470.

Olbrich, E., & Thomae, H. Contributions to a cognitive theory of aging. *International Journal of Behavioral Development*, 1978, *1*, 67–82.

Palmore, E. (Ed.). *Normal aging*. Durham, N.C.: Duke University Press, 1970.

Palmore, E. (Ed.). *Normal aging II*. Durham, N.C.: Duke University Press, 1974.

Pfoetsch, C. *Der Lebensraumbereich "Zukunftsperspektive" im hoeheren Alter*. Unpublished doctoral dissertation, University of Bonn, 1979.

Reichard, S., Livson, F., & Peterson, G. *Aging and personality*. London: Wiley, 1962.

Renner, V. J., & Birren, J. E. Stress: Physiological and psychological mechanisms. In J. E. Birren & R. B. Sloane (Eds.), *Handbook of mental health and aging*. Englewood Cliffs, N.J.: Prentice-Hall, 1980.

Riegel, K. F., & Riegel, R. M. A study of changes of attitudes and interests during later years of life. *Vita Humana*, 1960, *3*, 177–206.

Rogers, C. A. A theory of therapy, personality, and interpersonal relationships as developed in the client-centered framework. In S. Koch (Ed.), *Psychology: A Study of a science* (Vol. 3). New York: McGraw-Hill, 1959.

Rudinger, G. Eine Querschnittuntersuchung zur Intelligenzleistung im Altersbereich 20 bis 90 Jahre. *Zeitschrift fuer Gerontologie*, 1974, *7*, 323–333.

Rudinger, G. Intelligenzentwicklung unter unterschiedlichen sozialen Bedingungen. In *Proceedings of the 22nd International Congress of Psychology*, Leipzig, 1980.

Rudinger, G., & Feger, H. Die Beurteilung formaler Verhaltensmerkmale durch Rating-Skalen: Eine Generalisierbarkeitsstudie. *Zeitschrift fuer Entwicklungs—und Paedagogische Psychologie*, 1970, *2*, 96–112.

Rudinger, G., & Lantermann, E. D. Soziale Bedingungen der Intelligenz im Alter. *Zeitschrift fuer Gerontologie*, 1980, *13*, 433–441.

Schaie, K. W. A general model for the study of developmental problems. *Psychological Bulletin*, 1965, *64*, 92–105.

Schaie, K. W. Translations in gerontology—From lab to life: Intellectual functioning. *American Psychologist*, 1974, *29*, 802–807.

Schaie, K. W., & Parham, I. A. Stability of adult personality traits: Facts or fable? *Journal of Personality and Social Psychology*, 1976, *34*, 146–158.

Schmitz-Scherzer, R. *Freizeit und Alter*. Unpublished doctoral dissertation, University of Bonn, 1969.

Schmitz-Scherzer, R. *Freizeit im Alter*. Duesseldorf: Deutsche Gesellschaft fuer Freizeit, 1973.

Schmitz-Scherzer, R. Konstanz und Veraenderung der psychischen Leistungsfaehigkeit. *Aktuelle Gerontologie*, 1977, *7*, 369–383.

Seligman, M. E. P. *Helplessness—On depression, development, and death*. San Francisco: W. H. Freeman, 1975.

Stone, J. L., & Norris, A. Activities and attitudes of participants in the Baltimore Longitudinal Study. *Journal of Gerontology*, 1966, *21*, 575–580.

Thomae, H. Ueber Daseinstechniken sozial auffaelliger Jugendlicher. *Psychologische Forschung*, 1953, *23*, 11–33.

Thomae, H. *Das Individuum und seine Welt*. Goettingen: Verlag fuer Psychologie, 1968.

Thomae, H. Theory of aging and cognitive theories of personality. *Human Development*, 1970, *13*, 1–10.

Thomae, H. (Ed.). *Patterns of aging*. Basel–New York: S. Karger, 1976.

Thomae, H. Expected unchangeability of life stress in old age. *Human Development*, 1981, *24*, 229–239.

Vaillant, G. E. *Adaptation to life*. Boston: Little, Brown, 1977.

von Langermann, K., & Erlenkamp, B. *Reaktionsformen auf Belastungssituationen bei älteren Menschen: Eine Analyse der Daseinstechniken*. Unpublished doctoral dissertation, University of Bonn, 1970.

White, R. Strategies of adaptation: An attempt at systematic description. In. G. V. Coelho, D. A. Hamburg, & S. E. Adams (Eds.), *Coping and adaptation*. New York: Basic Books, 1974.

Williams, R. H., & Wirths, C. G. *Life through the years*. New York: Wiley, 1965.

7 Recent Longitudinal Research on Personality and Aging

PAUL T. COSTA, JR., ROBERT R. McCRAE, AND
DAVID ARENBERG

Methods and Models in the Study of Personality and Aging

Alternative Approaches to Personality

Personality psychology as a discipline is more unified by history than by
common methods, theories, or even goals. Psychoanalysis, social learning
theory, and measurement-based trait psychology all share the pages of
introductory texts on personality, but little else. In the more specialized
field of personality and aging, this problem is magnified. The psycho-
dynamic thinking of Jung and Erikson and, more recently, of Gould
(1978) and Levinson (Levinson, Darrow, Klein, Levinson, & McKee,
1978) has represented the major theorizing in the area, but most research
has been based on the use of trait measures, with little or no relationship
to these conceptions.

The significance of these circumstances is that no fully integrated
review of "personality and aging" is really possible. The reviewer must
choose either an eclectic presentation of the diverse work in the field or an
incomplete, but focused, synthesis of some specific approach to personality
and aging. In reviewing our own longitudinal work, we must necessarily
choose the latter. The reader, however, should bear in mind that this
chapter does not pretend to be an exhaustive survey of the field. In
particular, when we speak of the empirically demonstrated stability of

PAUL T. COSTA, JR., AND ROBERT R. McCRAE. Section on Stress and Coping,
Laboratory of Behavioral Sciences, Gerontology Research Center, National Institute on
Aging, National Institutes of Health, Baltimore, Maryland.

DAVID ARENBERG. Section on Learning and Problem Solving, Laboratory of Behavioral Sciences, Gerontology Research Center, National Institute on Aging, National
Institutes of Health, Baltimore, Maryland.

personality, we are referring to only one definition of personality. We do not know if ego functions, instinctual impulses, cognitive constructs, approach–avoidance gradients, needs for achievement, or psychophysiological expressions of emotion change with age. Relatively little research has been done in these areas, and conclusions would be premature. We can, however, speak about the tradition in personality research that identifies personality with individual differences in dispositions, including interpersonal relations, emotional responsiveness, and receptivity to experience.

The choice of a measurement-based trait approach to the study of aging was an outgrowth of longitudinal research strategies that have been widely adopted. Large-scale interdisciplinary studies of aging that included personality variables adopted the convenient self-report trait inventories as a way of gathering standardized data on subjects. Interviews and projective methods, which might yield either trait content or process data, depending on the way they are scored and analyzed, have been used in some studies (Berkeley, Duke), but they require an extraordinary investment of time and effort. By contrast, self-report inventories with their objective scoring procedures eliminate both the necessity for clinical expertise in interpretation and the possibility of interpretative bias. The rapid, uniform quantification from such personality inventories permits rigorous assessment of reliability and validity of the measures, which can then provide valuable baseline data on the condition of the individual at some particular time. The standardization of these measures makes possible the meaningful readministration of the same measures at a later time, so that longitudinal comparisons are straightforward. Finally, most of the cross-sectional studies comparing adults of different ages have used self-report measures, and comparison of longitudinal with cross-sectional results is most readily handled within the trait perspective.

A Model of Personality Traits

Within the trait approach to the study of personality and aging, the major obstacle to an understanding of the literature is the lack of shared conceptual models. Most theories of personality do not define the elements of personality or specify the major variables to which attention should be given. Instead of a systematic enumeration of the elements of personality, most personologists content themselves with the elaboration of one or a few constructs that they feel are important. In the absence of a shared definition of personality, constructs simply proliferate. Anxiety (Spielberger, 1972), Sensation Seeking (Zuckerman, 1979), Dogmatism (Rokeach, 1960), Repression–Sensitization (Byrne, 1964), Ascendance (All-port & Allport, 1928), Absorption (Tellegen & Atkinson, 1974), Depression (Beck, 1972), Activity (Buss & Plomin, 1975), and Authoritarianism (Adorno, Frenkel-Brunswik, Levinson, & Sanford, 1950) are among the more widely recognized traits. Scores of additional trait measures could be enumerated, but to do so would only confuse the issue. Is each of these to be regarded as a separate dimension of personality? If so, then each would need to be studied separately, and conclusions about the relation-ships of aging and personality would be impossible. Probably none has been the subject of enough studies to warrant a review and conclusion.

But if it were possible to group these traits into a handful of larger domains, then separate studies using ostensibly different trait measures could be compared, and generalizations about the whole domain might be drawn. In his classic paper "Traits Revisited," Gordon Allport (1966) acknowledged "the powerful contributions of Thurstone, Guilford, Cattell and Eysenck, based on factor analysis . . . [which] should provide eventually a satisfactory taxonomy of personality and of its hierarchical structure" (p. 3). The factor-analytic personality tradition provides an empirical basis for this kind of organizational simplification. Thus Anxiety, Depression, and Repression–Sensitization all covary within the domain of Neuroticism; Sensation Seeking, Ascendance, and Activity are classed as Extraversion; and Dogmatism, Absorption, and Authoritarianism are all elements of Openness to Experience. Our experience has convinced us of the utility of this three-domain model of personality. While some personality variables (such as locus of control) probably do not fall in any of our domains, a great many do. As a basis for organizing the literature on personality and aging, we find this model invaluable and rely on it explicitly in this review.

The bulk of research summarized in this chapter is also tied to self-report procedures, which have always been peculiarly associated with trait systems. However, the conceptualization of traits and their organiza-tion into domains is not a function of the method of assessment used. Our current program of research in the Baltimore Longitudinal Study of Aging employs performance tests of cognitive style; projective methods, including the Thematic Apperception Test (TAT) and the Holtzman Inkblot Test; semistructured interviews with Q-sort ratings; and spouse ratings. The data from these sources are conceptualized within the same three-domain model, but may also allow the application of different approaches to personality and aging in future years.

Most of the uniquely longitudinal research that we have conducted has dealt with the question of stability or change in personality, and a large section of this chapter is devoted to a discussion of the findings on this issue. Since all this research employs self-report methods, a consideration of their limitations is in order, and some new longitudinal analyses on response sets are presented in the subsequent section. But the real utility of personality research is in explaining phenomena outside of personality proper, and thus the last major section highlights some of the unique contributions of longitudinal research to an understanding of the relationships between personality and other variables such as well-being and perceptions of health. Finally, we indicate some of the new directions for longitudinal research to which a stable trait model of personality leads.

The Research Context

Much of the research described in this chapter has been conducted as a part of the Baltimore Longitudinal Study of Aging. Personality research represents only a small part of the overall Baltimore study program, which is an intensive, interdisciplinary study of the aging process. Since 1958, volunteers have been seen every 1 to 2 years, with regular medical examinations and periodic cognitive and psychological testing. Subsets of subjects have participated in a variety of special studies, and the data from all these sources can be used to characterize subjects.

Until 1977, the Baltimore study looked at men only, and thus longitudinal data are available only for them. Beginning with an initial pool of scientists who volunteered for the study, subjects have been continuously recruited, usually by friends or relatives who were already participants. New subjects are accepted from a waiting list of volunteers, and an attempt to maintain roughly even numbers of subjects in each age decade from the 20s to the 80s has been the primary basis for selection from the list. For the intensified study of personality, which began in 1978 with the creation of a section on stress and coping, additional subjects were needed. The spouses of volunteers were invited to participate in a stress-and-coping project, which involved only responses to questionnaires by mail. In this way, the number of women available for study was substantially increased.

A number of distinctive features of the Baltimore study result from these sampling procedures. Because subjects entered the study continuously over a 20-year period, it is possible to conduct sequential analyses on independent samples for many of the measures. The sample itself is also distinctive. Participants in the study are a community-dwelling, generally healthy group of volunteers who are committed to the research goals of the program. Among the men, the majority (80%) work in or are retired from scientific, professional, or managerial positions. Almost all (93%) are high school graduates, and 71% are college graduates. The women who have joined the study and the wives of the male subjects who participate in the mail studies generally share these economic and educational advantages.

The Stability of Personality in Adulthood

Statistical Definitions of Stability or Change

The term "stability" has two different and largely independent meanings. A trait may be considered stable for a group if the mean level of the trait in a group of individuals is constant over time. This can occur if all individuals remain at the same level, or if increases offset decreases over the interval. Analysis of variance on repeated administrations is the usual way to determine if significant changes in mean level have occurred. However, stability can also be assessed in terms of a test–retest correlation coefficient. These coefficients will be higher if individuals maintain the same relative ordering on the trait over time, regardless of the level of the trait. If some developmental process leads to a *uniform* increase or decrease of a variable over time, it would have no effect on the retest coefficient.

The implication of these considerations is that, except in the artificial case in which all individuals score identically on repeated administrations of a test, the issues of mean-level stability and retest stability must be addressed separately.

There is one final way in which stability or change in personality might be seen across the life span. Personality is often conceptualized in terms of the relationship between discrete variables, and these variables might change with age. The pattern of intercorrelations among a group of traits might alter with maturation; although this kind of change is least familiar, it is logically prior to the other kinds of stability or change. From the point of view of construct validity, what a test measures is determined by what it is correlated with. If the correlates of a test change, then the test itself, or the construct it represents, has somehow changed. If this has happened, then problems of interpretation of retest coefficients or mean levels arise.

The most common method of comparing patterns of intercorrelations is by factoring the battery of tests and showing that the same (or different) factors emerge in different age groups or administrations. This method has been used more frequently in studying cognitive abilities than personality dispositions, but the logic is similar. "Age-comparative factor analysis" is a term occasionally used to designate this kind of analysis (Cunningham, 1978). Considering the relationships between traits as the "structure" of personality, we have usually referred to this kind of problem as one of "structural stability."

Differences or changes in personality-test factor structure would have methodological as well as theoretical implications for gerontologists. Theoretically, a large number of distinguishable factors might be taken as a sign of personality differentiation, a hallmark of development. Different organizations of personality variables, or different "syndromes," may appear with age, as traits take on new meanings or new functions and significance. Methodologically, if major differences were found in the factor structure of standard personality tests in older samples, the use and interpretation of the tests in these groups could be challenged. The major personality inventories, such as the Eysenck Personality Inventory (EPI), the Guilford–Zimmerman Temperament Survey (GZTS), and Cattell's 16 Personality Factors Questionnaire (16PF), relied explicitly on factor analysis in their development, and age invariance is required for maintaining their factorial validity across age. All tests must demonstrate their validity by consistent patterns of convergent and divergent relationships. In the extreme case, all previous test-development efforts (except that conducted on elderly samples) would be called into question in application to elderly populations, as would all research that has employed these tests in the study of aging.

Beginning with structural stability, we review in this chapter our findings, which point to constancy of structure, stability of mean levels, and consistency of individual differences across time. Together, these results lead to the conclusion that adult age *per se* has no noticeable effect on any of the domains of personality we have studied.

But let us make it quite clear that these findings do *not* prove that personality is unchangeable. Some individuals do change in one or more characteristics, for reasons not yet understood. It is reasonable to suppose that psychotherapeutic interventions can make real changes in personality, and a host of techniques, from cognitive-behavior modification to biochemical interventions, may have profound effects as yet undocumented. What we can say is that such changes, for better or worse, are not likely to happen to anyone simply as a result of growing older.

Age Invariance of Personality Structure

The Quest for Change in Cattell's
16 Personality Factors Questionnaire

Our first research efforts, in fact, concerned looking for structural differences in personality within different age groups. In 1975, cluster analysis appeared to be a "cutting-edge" methodological technique for examining personality structure, and we conducted cluster analyses of the 16PF scales within three age groups using the male subjects of the Veterans Administration's Normative Aging Study (NAS). The cross-sectional results first presented at an American Psychological Association (APA) symposium in 1975 were attended with great interest and even greater hope that, at last, using objective standardized measures and sophisticated statistics on a very large sample, a developmental lodestone had been uncovered. Instead, the results were actually the first formulation of an age-invariant, three-domain model of personality.

Cluster analyses of 16PF scales were conducted within each of three age groups: 140 men aged 25–34 ($M = 32$), the young group; 711 men aged 35–54 ($M = 44$), the middle-aged group; and 118 men aged 55–82 ($M = 60$), the old group. Three clusters were found for each age, accounting for about 21%, 14%, and 6%, respectively, of the total variance in each group (Costa & McCrae, 1976).

The first cluster, which accounted for nearly half the common variance in all age groups, contained Scales (low) C (Stable), Q_4 (Tense), O (Guilt-prone), L (Suspicious), and (low) Q_3 (Controlled). Originally we labeled it an Anxiety–Adjustment cluster, following Cattell's convention, although we now prefer to interpret the first cluster as representing Neuroticism. The composition of the Neuroticism cluster was identical or invariant in the three age groups. Similarly, the second cluster, containing Scales A (Outgoing), F (Happy-go-lucky), H (Adventurous), and Q_2 (Group-dependent), was constant across all three age groups. What captured our imagination were the differences in the third and smallest cluster. The third cluster in the young and middle-aged groups had two scales as its elements, with Scale M (Practical vs. Imaginative) common to both. The second element in the young group's cluster was Scale I (Tough-minded vs. Tender-minded). In the middle-aged group, Scale I was "replaced" by Scale Q_1 (Conservative, Respecting Established Ideas vs. Experimenting, Free-Thinking). In the old group, the third cluster contained Scale B (Bright) as well as Scales I, M, and Q_1.

If we examine momentarily the details of these age differences in the third cluster, the reader may be able to appreciate how we were swept along by the apparent "lawful changes" (even though they were only differences) in experiential phenomena. We interpreted the young group's third cluster as an openness to feelings and aesthetic sensitivity. The adjectival descriptions for high scorers on Scale I include "sensitive" and "intuitive"; for Scale M, they include "unconventional" and "imaginative." It seemed reasonable to infer that the combination of high I and high M

represented openness to feelings, whereas low I and low M ("unsentimental, logical, practical, narrow interests") represented affective closedness. The high pole of this cluster dimension seemed to characterize the idealism and romanticism of youth.

In the middle-aged group, M again appeared, but this time in conjunction with Q_1 (Liberal Thinking). For these men, openness seemed to appear more in the realm of ideas and values than feelings. We speculated that the familial and professional obligations of the middle-aged man had transformed his concern from impractical feelings to more consequential ideas. Finally, the third cluster in the old group suggested even more tempting interpretations. The feelings cluster and the ideas cluster were merged, along with Scale B, which measures intelligence. This appeared to be the marvelous developmental synthesis of opposing psychological functions that C. G. Jung (1933) had promised us, and perhaps this synthesis was the basis of wisdom, at least for those old men who remained open to experience. Indeed, the integration of these processes might well be the end point of psychological development. The differences in cluster structure were certainly consistent with such an explanation.

We attempted to rule out the possibility that the cluster structure differences we observed were statistical artifacts of the particular age groups we constructed and were able to replicate roughly the third cluster differences in two repartitionings of the sample. But we recognized and stated in the 1976 article an even more important limitation and caution: The data were cross-sectional and did not provide direct evidence of structural changes in individuals.

Needless to say, we were greatly encouraged by the publication of these findings and by the enthusiastic reception they received from many of our colleagues. However, we felt an urgent need to document longitudinally these important changes in personality organization and structure. In 1975, we had administered the 1967 edition of the 16PF as a longitudinal retest, but major changes in the item composition of the scales had occurred since the 1962 edition, making direct longitudinal comparisons impossible. We therefore decided to readminister Scales I, M, and Q_1 from the 1962 edition, Form A, in 1977. Our original cross-sectional data had been based on combination A and B forms, so it was necessary to separate A from B scales in the original data. An examination of the new data showed no evidence of the cluster changes we had hypothesized and hoped for, and, to make matters worse, the clusters could not be located in the original data when only the A form was analyzed. Only a simple I-and-M cluster could be identified at any age.

It turned out to be the case that the variations in the original cluster analyses on combined A and B forms were largely the result of error due to the unreliability of the 16PF scales. Our conclusion was that the age-specific clusters should not be regarded as successive phases in a developmental sequence, but as a series of crude approximations to an underlying age-invariant dimension of Openness to Experience.

We published a letter to the editor of the *Journal of Gerontology* (Costa & McCrae, 1978a) to inform readers of that journal of our results, as well as a full report in another journal (Costa & McCrae, 1977), and we have cited these corrective findings in several other articles. Yet even several years later, the original finding is still discussed, while the failures to replicate are ignored (e.g., Thomae, 1980). Bad news apparently travels slowly.

The good news to us was that a third dimension, Openness to Experience, had been identified, and subsequent research using more reliable measures of openness to fantasy, aesthetics, feelings, actions, ideas, and values continued to form a third dimension of personality alongside the ever-present Extraversion and Neuroticism. Subsequent cross-sectional analyses (Costa & McCrae, 1980c) provided clear evidence that the composition of this domain of personality was invariant across the adult age range.

Constancy of Structure in the Guilford–Zimmerman Temperament Survey

It was, therefore, with an expectation of invariance that we approached the personality data of the Baltimore Longitudinal Study of Aging, where the GZTS had been given to subjects over a period of 20 years. In addition to cross-sectional comparisons of the factor structure of the GZTS scales in three different age groups, we performed longitudinal and time-of-measurement analyses as well (McCrae, Costa, & Arenberg, 1980). Data were obtained from men who entered the study from late 1958 through 1978). The age range of the 769 men at the first time of administration was from 17 to 97, with a mean of 50 years. Second-administration data (5.0 to 7.9 years later) were obtained from 346 men aged 26–91 ($M = 57.6$ years); third-administration data (11.0 to 15.4 years after first administration) were from 171 men aged 33–86 ($M = 62.0$ years). To assess possible structural differences stemming from time-of-measurement effects, the sample was divided into two groups: 455 men who completed the GZTS before July 1968 (age range = 17–83, $M = 52.1$ years) and 314 men who first completed the GZTS after that date (age range = 18–96, $M = 45.6$ years). To avoid possible confounding with practice effects, these last analyses were limited to first-administration data. All factor analyses were restricted to subjects with valid scores on all ten GZTS scales.

Both principal components and principal axes factor analyses were examined. Three factors had eigenvalues greater than unity and accounted for similar amounts of variance in all eight analyses: 28.3% to 30.3% for the first factor; 20.8% to 22.6% for the second; and 11.8% to 13.7% for the third. After Varimax rotation, comparison of the two methods of factoring showed highly similar results. Only the principal components solutions are presented because these results are somewhat clearer.

Table 7.1 shows factor loadings across analyses of data from three administrations, three age groups, and two times of measurement. Emotional Stability, Objectivity, Friendliness, Personal Relations, and Masculinity are consistent definers of this Emotional Health versus Neuroticism factor; low Thoughtfulness is marginal. The post-1968 analysis shows small contributions from Restraint and Sociability. The inclusion of low Masculinity among the definers of Neuroticism is somewhat unusual; it may result either from the use of an exclusively male sample or from the fact that 10 of the 30 items in this scale concern susceptibility to the emotions of fear and disgust.

The pattern of General Activity, Ascendance, and Sociability seen in the second factor in all eight analyses has been labeled "Social Activity" by Guilford, but could also be identified as Social Extraversion. Emotional Stability, low Restraint, and occasionally low Friendliness show small contributions to this factor.

The third factor has been designated "Thinking Introversion" by Guilford, but it is not to be confused with the Introversion–Extraversion factors of Eysenck (1960) or Cattell (1973). Clearly composed of Restraint and Thoughtfulness across all eight analyses, it shows a small contribution from low Masculinity in some cases. On psychological grounds, the meaningfulness of the third factor is questionable. Typically, other personality tests do not yield such a factor, nor do Guilford, Zimmerman, and Guilford (1976) discuss any clinical significance or counseling application of the factor. As a measure of Sensation Seeking or Impulsivity, Restraint may more properly belong in the domain of Extraversion, and small, but consistent, negative loadings of Restraint on the second factor are consistent with this hypothesis.

Maturational changes in personality structure should appear in both longitudinal and cross-sectional comparisons. As is clear from Table 7.1, the major definers are the same at each time and in each age group. Small variations in loadings do occur, but they do not show a clear direction or pattern replicated across longitudinal and cross-sectional analyses.

To quantify these impressions of invariance, coefficients of factor

TABLE 7.1. Factor Loadings for GZTS Scales across Administrations, Age Groups, and Times of Measurement

	Longitudinal administrations			Cross-sectional age groups			Times of measurement	
	1st (n = 769)	2nd (n = 346)	3rd (n = 171)	17 to 45 (n = 314)	46 to 59 (n = 242)	60 to 97 (n = 213)	Pre-1968 (n = 455)	Post-1968 (n = 314)
	Factor I: Emotional Health versus Neuroticism							
General Activity	-12	-14	-03	-15	-06	-16	-10	-16
Restraint	28	18	16	22	27	23	23	33
Ascendance	07	09	13	07	09	-01	06	13
Sociability	22	17	12	22	16	21	12	32
Emotional Stability	73	73	72	67	76	73	76	69
Objectivity	86	84	85	85	87	87	87	84
Friendliness	77	76	72	78	76	76	74	79
Thoughtfulness	-25	-31	-36	-33	-24	-34	-30	-19
Personal Relations	73	71	67	72	71	72	74	71
Masculinity	46	50	57	56	48	49	46	44
	Factor II: Social Activity or Extraversion							
General Activity	68	68	76	70	66	63	66	72
Restraint	-33	-36	-34	-19	-32	-37	-31	-34

Ascendance	86	88	86	85	87	84	86	87
Sociability	80	78	77	81	82	77	80	79
Emotional Stability	30	30	38	40	27	31	31	28
Objectivity	17	25	24	23	19	14	17	17
Friendliness	−30	−31	−36	−24	−28	−23	−31	−28
Thoughtfulness	21	19	23	16	11	14	16	07
Personal Relations	04	−01	03	13	06	−01	−01	14
Masculinity	−08	−05	00	−11	−10	−12	−09	−06

Factor III: "Thinking Introversion"

General Activity	−10	−09	02	−11	−03	−15	−03	−17
Restraint	71	76	79	79	69	73	76	67
Ascendance	07	05	07	18	−04	07	05	10
Sociability	−04	−06	−31	−09	−02	−05	−10	−02
Emotional Stability	−13	−10	−09	−17	−12	04	−01	−24
Objectivity	−12	−07	−10	−09	−07	−03	−04	−22
Friendliness	15	12	−07	13	23	11	14	12
Thoughtfulness	81	80	74	79	78	82	78	84
Personal Relations	08	03	−17	15	03	−07	00	11
Masculinity	−33	−10	17	−13	−32	−12	−21	−44

Note. Varimax-rotated principal components. Decimal points omitted.

congruence (Gorsuch, 1974) were calculated between corresponding factors for administrations, age groups, and times of measurement. Used with principal components, as they are here, these coefficients are equivalent to the product–moment correlations between factor scores. All coefficients are above .98 for the first two factors; for the third and smallest factor, they range from .83 to .98.

Additional analyses were conducted on data from the second administration for subjects aged 25–45 ($n = 60$), 46–59 ($n = 154$), and 60–91 ($n = 132$), and on data from the third administration for subjects aged 32–62 ($n = 84$) and 63–86 ($n = 87$). In all five analyses, three factors had eigenvalues above 1.0, and, despite small sample sizes, generally similar structures were observed. These are reflected in congruence coefficients (when compared with the full first administration solution) ranging from .96 to .99 for the Neuroticism factor, .91 to .99 for the Extraversion factor, and .58 to .99 for the "Thinking Introversion" factor.

Finally, in order to parallel traditional longitudinal designs in which the same subjects are tested on successive occasions (mean intervals = 6.6 and 12.9 years), comparisons were made between different administrations, restricting subjects to those with complete data on all administrations. Although the number of subjects meeting this qualification at all three administrations was relatively small ($n = 123$), the same general pattern of definers was replicated at each administration. The congruence coefficients were .99, .98, and .83 for the first, second, and third factors, respectively. When analyses were conducted for the 324 subjects who had complete data on both first and second administrations, coefficients of congruence for the corresponding factors across the two administrations were .98, .99, and .98.

The age-invariance of factor structure in the GZTS in the sample cited was clearly evident. Definers of factors stand out in each case from the marginal elements that show slight variations from one analysis to another. Despite aging, attrition, and possible practice effects, the same pattern is seen at each administration. The only divergence from high factor congruence is found in the case of the third factor at the third administration, when a coefficient of .83 is observed. Although this slight structural variation could result somehow from repeated exposure to the test, it is interpreted more simply as the result of error in the smallest factor and smallest sample. In the data presented here, no meaningful difference can be seen when comparing measurements before and after 1968, yet the decades of the 1960s and 1970s are surely different enough to make a difference if the structure of the GZTS and similar personality tests were particularly sensitive to historical and cultural shifts.

Stability of Mean Levels

Cross-Sectional Studies: Minnesota Multiphasic Personality Inventory

Until recently, most of our knowledge concerning the descriptions of adult personality has come from one-time administration of various personality questionnaires to a variety of adult samples. Much of the literature on assessment of age differences in adult personality has compared nonmatched extreme groups of old and young on measures that often lack reliability or validity. The Minnesota Multiphasic Personality Inventory (MMPI), which has more desirable psychometric properties, is less relevant to normal personality-trait descriptions than to mental health or psychopathology. But since it is a widely used instrument, we shall briefly and critically review the literature on age differences in the MMPI.

Lawton, Whelihan, and Belsky (1980) review 11 studies that compare MMPI clinical scale score ranks of elderly to younger subjects. Seven of the 11 studies contain either older psychiatric patients, institutional residents, or medical patients. One study contains job applicants over the age range of 19–56 years; the remaining three studies include older community residents. Lawton *et al.* assert that depression is clearly elevated among the elderly along with hypochondriasis, while the "acting out" scales (*Pd* and *Ma*) are clearly lower. Scores of the elderly on the "psychotic triad" scales (*Pa, Pt, S*) were either similar to or lower than scores of younger people, with minor exceptions only in the Newcastle-upon-Tyne community sample.

In his excellent review of age and the MMPI, Gynther (1980) arrives at broadly similar conclusions to the effect that certain pathological features decline with age. From youth to young adulthood, there are declines in admission of rebelliousness towards authority, suspiciousness, autistic thinking, and impulsivity. Since scale ranks are ipsative, the apparent increase in certain neurotic features, particularly depression, is interpreted as a consequence of age-linked *decreases* in the scores for Scales 4 (*Pd*), 6 (*Pa*), 8 (*Sc*), and 9 (*Ma*). Along with dysphoric affect, health problems are said to be salient for the elderly, and health and happiness seem to emerge as characteristic personality problems for the elderly. Yet these results are not beyond challenge.

Zemore and Eames (1979) reported a most instructive set of findings that question the widely held belief that the aged are more depressed than any other group. They noted that studies based on symptom counts find greater evidence of depression over age 65 in contrast to studies based on clinical judgments, which find depressive disorder most frequently between the ages of 25 and 65. They hypothesized that symptom checklists for depression invariably include a variety of somatic complaints more likely to reflect declining physical health than depression. They argued that clinicians would not diagnose as depressive elderly who have few cognitive or affective symptoms of depression, but who admit to fatigue, constipation, and sleep disturbances. In a simple and straightforward study, they compared psychic (cognitive and affective) versus somatic symptoms of depression on the Beck Depression Inventory (BDI) among 424 first-year psychology students, 48 elderly long-term residents of an old-age home, and 31 community-residing elderly awaiting entrance to an old-age home. The results supported their hypothesis: Namely, the BDI scores of the elderly were significantly higher than those of the students only when the 7 somatic items were included, that is, using all 21 items. When only the 14 psychic item scores were compared, the mean scores (4.47 vs. 4.43) were virtually identical. Thus even institutionalized elderly and those awaiting entrance to institutions for the elderly did not show any more psychic symptoms of depression, although they did report more somatic complaints. The latter are likely to covary with the physiological changes that accompany aging.

The Zemore and Eames results should serve to remind us that findings of age-associated differences need to be interpreted correctly. Even the apparent age-associated increases in physical complaints need to be scrutinized carefully. In our longitudinal studies of symptom reporting, we have not found generalized increases in somatic complaints due to aging (as the cross-sectional literature would suggest). Instead, specific age-related symptoms, namely, sensory, cardiovascular, and genitourinary problems, were seen to increase (Costa & McCrae, 1980b). Interestingly, Gynther (1980) reports similar findings from MMPI studies for non-psychiatric patients.

Cross-Sectional Studies: Factor-Based Inventories

Eysenck's two-dimensional model of personality, operationalized successively in the Maudsley Personality Inventory, the EPI, and (with the addition of a third dimension, Psychoticism) the Eysenck Personality Questionnaire, has occasionally been the object of cross-sectional studies. Eysenck (e.g., Eysenck & Eysenck, 1975) has consistently reported that younger subjects are higher in both Neuroticism and Extraversion than are older subjects, including both men and women. Older subjects score higher on the Lie scale, which may indicate greater social desirability, but might also be interpreted as showing higher levels of socialization.

Some of these cross-sectional trends for the EPI are paralleled by the cross-sectional results of Sealy and Cattell (1965), who gave the 16PF to a large sample of men and women aged 16–70. They found a significant decrease on the F (Happy-go-lucky) scale, which is a facet of Extraversion; an increase on the C (Stable) scale, which suggests lowered Neuroticism; and increases on the G (Conscientious) scale, showing higher Superego Strength or Socialization for the older subjects. The pattern of scale scores indicated statistically significant, but small, differences on the second-order factors of Anxiety and Extraversion.

Schaie (1959) found similar, but later occurring, introversion with his Social Responsibility scale. Fozard and Thomas (1975) observed that the decrease in Scale F (Happy-go-lucky) toward a more sober, serious, glum disposition is the most consistently observed age difference with the 16PF. Other studies have reported decreases in Scales A (Outgoing), H (Adventurous), and E (Assertive). These are recognized as signifying shifts away from extraversion, toward introversion. The first-order scales making up the Neuroticism domain from the 16PF (Scales C, O, L, Q_3, and Q_4) have shown inconsistent trends from one study to another. From Lawton et al.'s (1980) review of six cross-sectional studies using the 16PF, only Scale G (Conscientious) shows higher scores for older subjects across all studies.

The last group of cross-sectional studies discussed here employed the GZTS (Guilford et al., 1976), showing generally similar findings. Bendig (1960) examined the GZTS mean score differences of men in four age groups, finding significantly lower scores on General Activity, Ascendance, Sociability, and Masculinity. Significantly elevated scores were observed for Restraint and Personal Relations. Wagner (1960) compared 150 male executives 45 years and older with 150 who were 35 years or younger, with results consistent with those of Bendig (lower Ascendance, lower Sociability, and higher Restraint scores for older executives). Unlike Bendig, Wagner also found significantly lower scores for the Emotional Stability and Objectivity scales, which are components of Emotional Health, as Guilford et al. (1976) call this second-order factor.

Cross-sectional findings for the ten GZTS scale on a very large sample of men covering a wide age range have been reported by Douglas and Arenberg (1978) on the Baltimore study participants. Five of the ten scales were significantly related to age in two subsamples defined in terms of the date of first administration of the GZTS: Sample A, 605 men (aged 17–98) tested prior to July 1968; and Sample B, 310 men tested between July 1968 and June 1974. Like both Wagner and Bendig, Douglas and Arenberg found Ascendance to be negatively correlated with age. General

Activity and Masculinity were also negatively correlated with age, as only Bendig previously showed. The other component of the Social Activity or Extraversion factor, Sociability, was not significantly correlated with age in both samples. Restraint and Friendliness scale scores were positively correlated with age ($r = .28$ and .17, respectively). The General Activity decade means decreased consistently after the 30s from 18.78 to 16.92 for the 60s, while mean scores of 14.79 and 13.46 were observed for the 70- and 80-year-old groups, respectively. Means for Ascendance decreased monotonically from 18.35 (20s) to 14.35 (80s) for Sample A (pre-1968), but less consistently in Sample B (post-1968). The differences in Masculinity were not apparent in either sample until age 60. As for the increases with age, Restraint means increased monotonically in Sample A from 17.40 (20s) to 21.93 (70s), but less consistently in Sample B. Friendliness mean scores showed a similar pattern to the Restraint scores for Sample A; that is, the 20s group mean of 14.95 increased to 19.13 for the 70s group.

Consulting the GZTS *Handbook* (Guilford *et al.*, 1976), one finds that the most consistent finding with regard to GZTS scores and age is the decrease in Ascendance (Scale *A*) reported in 12 different samples. The second most consistent finding was an increase (cross-sectionally) in Restraint (*R*) scores observed in nine different samples. Seven samples demonstrated decreases in Sociability with age, while four samples showed General Activity decreases with age. Age differences for the other GZTS scale scores are inconsistent and "conflict markedly" (1976, p. 107).

Guilford *et al.* conclude that "there would seem to be little risk in using the same GZTS norms with any age group despite the consistency of the scale score differences with age, since the correlations and mean differences are small" (p. 105).

Repeated-Measures Analyses

Because all of the previous studies mentioned are cross-sectional, they do not answer the question of whether the obtained differences in personality-score levels are actually maturational–developmental or simply cohort effects. As has been so often stated, cross-sectional studies confound maturation with generational differences. "Generational differences," or "cohort effects" as they are also called, refer to the effects of the different socialization of successive birth cohorts. Resolution of this question of developmental versus cohort effects is of practical as well as theoretical importance. In a previous publication (Costa & McCrae, 1978b), we pointed out that cohort norms might be more appropriate and meaningful than age norms in the interpretation of certain test results.

To ascertain directly whether any consistent age differences observed were maturational rather than cohort or generational differences, we readministered, in 1975, the 16PF to a subsample of 139 men from the original 969 in the NAS. By measuring the same subjects at a later time (i.e., 10 years later), we hoped to generate data useful for resolving this question of maturational change in personality-trait levels (Costa & McCrae, 1978b).

Table 7.2 presents the results of repeated-measures analysis of variance (ANOVA) on all 16 scales. We used three age groups—25–40, 41–46, and over 47—as one of the two classifying variables, and administration as the second. Cross-sectional age differences, or cohort/aging differences, were found for Scales G (Conscientious), I (Tender-minded), and Q_1 (Liberal Thinking), all showing an increase across age groups. Two different scales, B (Bright) and Q_2 (Group-dependent), showed longitudinal changes (but not cohort differences), with increases over time. There were no significant time-by-cohort interactions. Because the conventional longitu-

TABLE 7.2. Group Means Averaged across Two Administrations

Scale	Age at first administration			F for age	F for time
	25 to 40 ($n = 46$)	41 to 46 ($n = 51$)	47+ ($n = 42$)		
A (Outgoing)	−5.94	−5.28	−5.78	1.48	2.64
B (Bright)	6.07	5.76	5.74	12.80	13.78***
C (Stable)	7.04	5.91	6.50	1.93	.59
E (Assertive)	−5.15	−5.25	−6.26	1.37	.36
F (Happy-go-lucky)	−2.32	−1.54	−3.00	1.57	2.73
G (Conscientious)	.47	1.06	1.92	5.49**	2.59
H (Adventurous)	−1.17	−.52	−.49	.54	.21
I^a (Tender-minded)	7.29	7.99	8.45	5.18**	1.27
L (Suspicious)	−2.85	−2.69	−2.55	.30	2.94
M^a (Imaginative)	11.98	12.03	12.53	1.92	2.48
N (Shrewd)	1.97	2.42	2.63	2.96	.06
O (Guilt-prone)	1.19	1.76	1.31	1.28	.05
Q_1^a (Liberal Thinking)	9,37	9.81	10.08	3.35*	.96
Q_2 (Independent)	−3.40	−3.45	−2.92	.88	19.33***
Q_3 (Controlled)	1.08	.59	1.07	1.83	.04
Q_4 (Tense)	−4.69	−3.91	−5.01	1.38	1.26

Note. Scales based on items common to 1962 and 1967 editions, Form A; scale norms do not apply.
[a] Based on full-scale retest in 1977, with $n = 134$, 101, and 169, respectively, for three age groups.
*$p < .05$.
**$p < .01$.
***$p < .001$.

dinal design we employed tested the same subjects at a later time and not a different subsample of the same age cohort, it is not possible to separate further the maturational changes from time-of-measurement or practice effects. Only by use of the sequential designs discussed later can this be approximated.

A simple maturational effect would be seen in both cross-sectional differences and longitudinal changes. That no scale showed this pattern of results leads to the suggestion that some other source of variation was responsible for the observed effects. The cross-sectional results can be attributed to cohort differences, but an explanation of the longitudinal findings is more difficult. It is possible that the changes were due to repeated exposure to the test or to cultural changes in the intervening 10 years. The change in Scale Q_2 is particularly difficult to understand, and since no comparable changes were found on any of the other scales in the Extraversion domain, perhaps the most parsimonious explanation is sampling error.

Yet another rival hypothesis can be mentioned as a likely explanation for the change in Scale B (Intelligence), which is, in fact, an ability scale rather than a personality scale. The 16PF was first administered in small groups, and implicit time pressure may have prevented some people from performing at their best. On the second administration, at home, individuals may have taken more time (or consulted the dictionary) and thus improved their scores. Thus, in addition to time-of-measurement and practice effects, we must be aware of changes in the assessment conditions or situations.

In the conventional longitudinal analysis of the GZTS scales by Douglas and Arenberg (1978), two aspects of the approach to measuring change are worthy of note. First, the authors presented an accounting of subject attrition, assessing the effects of subject loss by dividing their original sample ($n = 605$) into repeats (336 men who appeared in both the original sample and the longitudinal sample) and nonrepeats (269 men who appeared only in the original sample). Using a 2×3 (age groups 17–39, 40–59, 60–98) unweighted means ANOVA, significant main effects (differences) were found for the repeats versus the nonrepeats on four scales. In all age groups, men who were retested on the GZTS (repeats) were lower in Ascendance and higher in Objectivity, Friendliness, and Emotional Stability than nonrepeats. Although statistically significant, the differences were small in magnitude. Nevertheless, repeat subjects tended to be less neurotic (Emotional Stability, Objectivity, Friendliness) and less assertive.

The second notable aspect is that an attempt was made to determine whether the *magnitude of change* was related to age by computing part

PERSONALITY AND AGING / 241

correlations between age and residual of the second measure adjusted for the first. Analyses of such longitudinal change scores showed overall decline in General Activity, Friendliness, Thoughtfulness, Personal Relations, and Masculinity. The magnitude of change was related to age for the General Activity scale, suggesting an accelerated change in this variable, but not for the other four scales that showed significant changes. Table 7.3 shows the longitudinal changes for the five scales that showed significant changes.

Thus, as the men in the Baltimore study aged approximately 7 years (ranging from 5.6 to 9.9 years on retest), their General Activity, or pace of activity, declined, as did their scores on Scales F (Friendliness), T (Thoughtfulness), PR (Personal Relations), and M (Masculinity). This last maturational change might be expected by theorists such as David Gutmann (1974) who hypothesize a sex-linked shift or crossover in sex roles with advancing age.

Sequential Evidence for Stability

As discussed earlier, conventional longitudinal analyses, whether of test–retest or repeated-measures variety, are susceptible to rival interpretations other than maturational effects, including time-of-measurement and practice effects. More adequate data-gathering and data-analytic designs involve the use of cross-sequential and time-sequential analyses, which provide a more comprehensive identification of change phenomena (Baltes, 1968; Baltes, Reese, & Nesselroade, 1977; Schaie, 1965, 1977). Cross- and time-sequential analyses were performed on the GZTS scores for the Baltimore study sample by Douglas and Arenberg (1978). In cross-sequential analyses, independent samples of individuals born in the same historical period are compared at different times of testing. Since

TABLE 7.3. Longitudinal Changes from First to Second Administration on Five GZTS Scales

| GZTS scales | Age decades at first administration | | | | | |
	20s	30s	40s	50s	60s	70s
General Activity	1.67	−.10	−.01	−1.08	−2.04	−1.28
Friendliness	−.25	.00	−.88	−.44	−.07	−.92
Thoughtfulness	−2.33	−.78	−.54	−.07	−.48	−.65
Personal Relations	−.33	−1.13	−.38	−.78	−.74	−2.38
Masculinity	−.33	.14	−.61	−.61	.00	−.96

recruitment into the Baltimore study was continual, the Douglas and Arenberg study (as all our other sequential analyses) contrasted two successive intervals of testing (January 1958 through June 1968 with July 1968 to December 1974) rather than two distinct time points and thus only approximated a true cross-sequential design. Birth cohorts were defined in 8-year intervals from 1892–1899 to 1940–1947 in order to approximate the 7-year period between testing. Practice effects are eliminated in the cross-sequential design, as are main effects of cohort. But aging is confounded with time-of-measurement effects, and sampling differences may also be present.

In time-sequential analyses, independent samples of individuals of the same age are compared at different times of measurement. Maturation is ruled out, but any obtained differences (effects) may be due to either cohort or time of measurement. The second time-of-measurement sample in the cross-sequential analysis consisted of 238 men from Sample B (the later GZTS sample, described earlier) born during the same periods (i.e., 1892–1899, 1900–1907, 1908–1915, . . . , 1932–1939), but varying in age from 30 to 81 years. The second time-of-measurement sample in the time-sequential analyses again employed a subset of Sample B ($n = 240$), including men born between 1900 and 1947.

In the cross-sequential design, different-aged individuals from the same cohorts or historical periods are compared at different times of testing. The birth-cohort effect confounds cohort and aging and can be referred to as "cohort/aging." The time effect confounds secular changes between the times of measurement and aging and can be referred to as "time/aging." In the time-sequential design (independent samples of same-aged individuals, compared at different times of measurement), we can identify the effects as aging/cohort and time/cohort.

By comparing the consistency of results for different effects on various personality scales, one can make interpretations concerning the effects of maturation, generation, and cultural changes, although these interpretations are never unequivocal (see Adam, 1978). Table 7.4 summarizes the results of the sequential analyses along with the cross-sectional and longitudinal (repeated-measures) analyses of the GZTS scales. The only consistent maturational effect from the four types of analyses were found for Masculinity. Older age groups or cohorts in both samples showed declines in Masculinity over the seven decade groups from the 20s to the 80s. Within-subject changes over a 7-year time interval similarly showed declines for Masculinity. The absence of a time/cohort effect in the time-sequential analyses for Masculinity indicates that neither cohort differences nor cultural change from the first interval of measurement to the

TABLE 7.4. Summary of GZTS Results for Four Different Analyses

Scale	Cross-sectional cohort/aging[a]	Longitudinal time/ practice/aging	Cross-sequential time/aging	Time-sequential time/cohort
General Activity	Declined (A,B)	Declined	NS	—
Restraint	Increased (A,B)	—	—	NS
Ascendance	Declined (A,B)	—	—	—
Sociability	Declined (A)	—	—	NS
Emotional Stability	No difference	—	Declined	Declined
Objectivity	No difference	—	—	—
Friendliness	Increased (A,B)	Declined	NS	Declined
Thoughtfulness	Increased (A)	Declined	—	Declined
Personal Relations	Increased (B)	Declined	Declined	Declined
Masculinity	Declined (A,B)	Declined	Declined	—

[a]A = effect significant in Sample A; B = effect significant in Sample B.

second accounts for the observed decreases in Masculinity. A small, but significant, decline in Masculinity found for the time/aging effect in the cross-sequential analysis confirms the interpretation that the observed cohort differences and the longitudinal declines are probably maturational in nature. Practice effects are unlikely to account for the longitudinal decline; in both the cross-sectional and sequential results, only first administration results are used.

General Activity score changes were interpreted as reflecting the operation of maturation since both cross-sectional and repeated-measures longitudinal results showed declines, and there were no significant time/ cohort effects on the time-sequential analyses. The time/aging effect in the cross-sequential analysis showed a decrease, but it did not reach statistical significance. Thus the General Activity changes can be interpreted as maturational, but seem to occur predominately later in life.

The major import of these sophisticated, quasi-experimental statistical designs and analyses should be clearly recognized. None of the eight other personality traits (GZTS Scales R, A, S, E, O, F, T, and P) showed maturational changes. The T, P, and F scores reflected cultural changes and not maturational ones. The R and A scores reflected simple generational differences, with later born cohorts less restrained and more assertive than earlier born and therefore older cohorts.

We have devoted considerable time and space to these cross-sectional, longitudinal, and sequential analyses, so it is quite important that we not let the crucial facts slip from our grasp. For only two of the scales was the evidence consistent with maturational change in mean level of personality traits. Although many researchers are aware of the Douglas and Arenberg findings, it would appear that few clearly recognize the evidence for trait (mean-level) stability provided by their analyses and results. Even those scales that showed maturational effects changed very little. The magnitude of the maturational declines in General Activity and Masculinity amounts to about one-eighth of a standard deviation over a 7-year period, a change that is not at all of practical significance. In a somewhat lighter mood, we calculated the length of time it would take the average man in the Baltimore study sample to become "feminized," that is, to reach the mean Masculinity score of college females. At the rate of decline of .41 items every 6.6 years, it would take the older man (average age of 75) 136 years to become "feminized" under the admittedly preposterous assumption that one could live to 211 years!

How do the present results and conclusions compare with the data and judgments of other researchers in the field? After all, the studies reviewed deal with men only and with only two measurement points from 7 years (Baltimore study) to 10 years (NAS). Although the longitudinal and sequential-type analyses are quite scarce in comparison to the more numerous, if less informative, cross-sectional studies, there are two sequential studies—by Schaie and Parham (1976) and by Siegler and her associates at Duke—that bear examination. Since Siegler, George, and Okun (1979) used Form C of Cattell's 16PF in a sample of both women and men and with more than two measurement points, the results of their cross-sequential analyses of adult personality are of particular relevance. From a sample of 502 white, middle-class, adult subscribers to a health insurance plan in the Durham, North Carolina, area, 331 adults were assessed four times over an 8-year period (1968–1976). The authors formed 12 2-year cohorts born between 1899 and 1922, with the youngest cohort 46–47 years old, and the oldest 68–69 in 1969. Using a repeated-measures ANOVA design with 12 age cohorts, two sexes, and four times of measurement, the authors found that none of the 16 personality scales showed changes over time consistent with a maturational explanation. The only scale that showed a main effect for cohort and for time was the intelligence scale, Factor *B*, which seemed to be influenced by generational differences (later born cohorts score higher) and practice effects (later administrations yield higher scores) rather than aging, since the two effects are in opposite directions. There were main effects for sex on 5 of the 16 factors, which were in the sex-stereotyped direction and stable over time, and also two significant interactions. Our earlier longitudinal analysis of Form A (Costa & McCrae, 1978b) and the Siegler *et al.* (1979)

analysis of Form C of the 16PF are in rather substantial agreement, then, that there is little evidence for age-related change in personality in the adult and later years.

Schaie and Parham (1976) extracted 19 factors from a 75-item Social Responsibility scale and applied sequential methods to an analysis of change in these factors. Seventeen of the 19 factors showed stability, with only small changes in the other two factors. They concluded that "within the domain of factors identified in our study, we can with confidence support the stability model" (p. 152).

Individual Consistency over Time

Retest Data from Cattell's 16 Personality Factors Questionnaire

Retest correlations, or stability coefficients, assess the magnitude of personality consistency or change in the relative ordering of individuals, regardless of absolute level. These are among the most important analyses for longitudinal studies, for although different samples at different times, or different cohorts at one time, can be used to estimate age changes in trait levels, only repeated testing of the same individuals can speak to the degree of stability of individual differences.

Our first line of evidence for stability of personality came from an examination of longitudinal data from the Cattell 16PF, administered in 1966 and 1975, and from a short form of the EPI (the EPI-Q) devised by Floderus (1974), administered in 1976 (Costa & McCrae, 1977). Earlier work with cluster analyses of the 16PF had identified three clusters, two of which showed the same scale composition across all age groups. Retest correlations between the 16PF Neuroticism cluster scores over a 9-year interval in three age groups—25–34, 35–54, and 55–82—were .58, .67, and .69, respectively. The Extraversion–Introversion cluster scores showed even greater stability: .75, .70, and .84, respectively, for the young, middle-aged, and old groups. Even when we employed an alternate personality instrument—the 18-item EPI-Q—to measure Neuroticism and Extraversion in 1976, significant stability coefficients were obtained over a 10-year interval. Correlations of 16PF cluster scores in 1966 with EPI-Q measures in 1976 in the three different age groups were .41, .49, and .54 for Neuroticism, and .46, .54, and .53 for Extraversion measures. These "alternate-form," or equivalence-and-stability, coefficients are quite remarkable when one considers that the equivalence coefficients (which are a measure of the interchangeability of the tests measured contemporaneously) average only .56 for Neuroticism and .55 for Extraversion.

Enduring Dispositions in the
Guilford–Zimmerman Temperament Survey

Recently we reported additional evidence directly related to the longitudinal stability of personality traits, with particular attention focused upon two specific hypotheses (Costa, McCrae, & Arenberg, 1980). The first hypothesis was that certain socially desirable traits, such as sociability, assertiveness, and others that define the broad domain of Extraversion, are particularly stable and that change is more characteristic of undesirable traits that might be interpreted as elements of the Neuroticism domain. The second hypothesis asserts that stability coefficients will increase with age. This hypothesis was based on evidence that stability coefficients increase for children (Nesselroade & Baltes, 1974) and on suggestions that personality is increasingly consolidated in old age (Neugarten, 1964).

We tested these hypotheses with the GZTS scale scores of the Baltimore study participants described earlier. The GZTS was administered to subjects approximately every 6 years. Because of complications in scheduling, a few subjects took the test 2 years in succession or failed to take the second retest. To maintain uniformity of time interval and number of administrations, longitudinal analyses were limited to subjects who took their second GZTS 5.0 to 7.9 years after their first ($M = 6.6$ years, $n = 460$) and to those who took their third GZTS 11.0 to 15.4 years after the first ($M = 12.9$, $n = 222$). Three age groups were formed: young (17–44 years, mean age 36.7, $n = 145$); middle (45–59 years, mean age 51.5, $n = 183$); and old (60–85 years, mean age 67.9, $n = 132$).

Table 7.5 gives the 6-year and the 12-year stability coefficients for the total samples, and the 12-year stability coefficients within each of the three age groups.

Under the hypothesis that stability should be greater in older age groups, one-tailed tests of the significance of differences between correlations were computed for each pair of age groups on each scale. Of the 30 comparisons at each interval, six were significant for the 6-year interval, three for the 12-year interval. Of these nine significant differences, four were in the predicted direction, five in the opposite direction. Not one of the specific findings for scales at the 6-year interval was replicated at the 12-year interval.

Finally, Table 7.6 gives the estimated reliability and stability of the "true" scores (Heise, 1969) in a subsample of 114 subjects of all ages who had complete data for all scales at all three times. Also in this table are simple retest coefficients for Times 1 to 2, 2 to 3, and 1 to 3. The similarity of correlations in the first and second 6-year periods is further evidence of the continuing stability of traits. It is also noteworthy that 6-year retest coefficients in this most select group are quite comparable to those

TABLE 7.5. Six- and 12-Year Retest Coefficients for GZTS Scales for Total Samples and 12-Year Retest Coefficients for Three Age Groups

| | 6-year retest | 12-year retest | 12-year retest | | |
| | Total sample (17 to 85 years) | Total sample (20 to 76 years) | Young group (20 to 44 years) | Middle group (45 to 59 years) | Old group (60 to 76 years) |
Scale					
General Activity	.83 (410)	.77 (192)	.77 (60)	.82 (93)	.78 (39)
Restraint	.71 (418)	.72 (193)	.61 (62)	.74 (94)	.76 (37)
Ascendance	.82 (401)	.83 (194)	.85 (62)	.85 (95)	.77 (37)
Sociability	.81 (393)	.74 (182)	.64 (62)[a]	.81 (88)	.66 (32)
Emotional Stability	.74 (427)	.70 (203)	.63 (68)	.81 (88)	.71 (39)
Objectivity	.71 (405)	.69 (191)	.66 (64)	.76 (87)	.59 (40)
Friendliness	.77 (418)	.74 (193)	.74 (64)[b]	.76 (87)	.87 (41)
Thoughtfulness	.72 (418)	.73 (199)	.78 (64)	.68 (88)[c]	.71 (41)
Personal Relations	.73 (385)	.68 (188)	.70 (62)	.71 (94)	.71 (41)
Masculinity	.75 (417)	.72 (200)	.73 (66)	.64 (89)	.73 (37)
Mean stability	.77	.73	.72	.71 (94)	.70 (40)
				.75	.73

Note. n's are given in parentheses; numbers in parentheses in column headings are age range at Time I. All correlations are significant at p < .001.
[a] Difference between young and middle groups is significant at p < .05.
[b] Difference between young and old groups is significant at p < .05.
[c] Difference between middle and old groups is significant at p < .01.

TABLE 7.6. Observed Retest Coefficients for Three Intervals and Estimated Reliability and Stability Coefficients for "True" Scores

Scale	Observed retest correlations			Estimated reliability	Estimated 12-year stability
	r_{12}	r_{23}	r_{13}		
General Activity	.83	.84	.80	.88	.92
Restraint	.75	.75	.71	.80	.89
Ascendance	.81	.85	.85	.82	1.00[a]
Sociability	.84	.82	.75	.91	.82
Emotional Stability	.77	.83	.71	.89	.80
Objectivity	.77	.82	.74	.86	.86
Friendliness	.81	.78	.77	.83	.93
Thoughtfulness	.73	.76	.71	.78	.91
Personal Relations	.70	.73	.68	.75	.91
Masculinity	.74	.77	.73	.79	.92

Note. Coefficients were calculated with formulas of Heise (1969) for a subsample of 114 men with complete data at three times.
[a] Observed 12-year retest coefficient is greater than estimated reliability.

presented in Table 7.1 for a more inclusive group of subjects who may have dropped out of the study after the second administration of the GZTS.

The retest coefficients presented here are among the highest in the literature for so long a period of time, comparable to the 2-week retest coefficients of many scales. When statistical corrections for unreliability are applied to obtain estimates of the "true" stability of the dispositions, even higher values are seen. These estimates, using Heise's (1969) formulas, are given in Table 7.6. Because they are only estimates, themselves subject to sampling error, anomalies such as the more-than-perfect stability of the Ascendance scale sometimes occur, and these coefficients must be regarded with due caution. Simple, uncorrected Pearson correlations are straightforward and familiar, and the correlations seen here reach impressively large magnitudes despite errors of measurement.

The question of increasing stability with age in adulthood seems to be clearly answered in the negative; 6- and 12-year stability coefficients are quite similar for three age cohorts whose members have an initial age range of nearly 70 years. Statistically significant differences in the magnitude of stability coefficients are scattered and inconsistent and do not support the hypothesis. Increased stability with age may be found among children and adolescents, but by young adulthood, stability in these dimensions of temperament is so high—near the limits of reliability of the instrument—that a ceiling effect diminishes the likelihood of any further increase in stability.

The question of differential stability for different traits is more difficult to answer since change and error of measurement are confounded in retest coefficients. It can be seen that, for the total sample, the three traits that constitute the extraverted factor of Social Activity—General Activity, Sociability, and Ascendance—have mean coefficients of .82 and .78 for 6- and 12-year intervals, respectively, whereas the neurotic traits of low Emotional Stability, Objectivity, Friendliness, and Personal Relations show corresponding coefficients of .74 and .70. The latter are certainly lower, accounting for only about three-fourths as much variance. The result is comparable to findings with the 16PF mentioned earlier, in which 9-year coefficients ranged from .70 to .84 for Extraversion and from .58 and .69 for Anxiety or Neuroticism. It may be the case that extraordinary stresses produce temporary neurotic tendencies in some people or that the distress attendant on neurotic traits leads some individuals to change, either by themselves or with the aid of friends or professional therapists.

On the other hand, it may also be the case that neuroticism is more difficult to measure reliably. The estimated stabilities of "true" scores, corrected for unreliability, are given in Table 7.6. These show an average value of .91 for the three Extraversion scales and .88 for the four Neuroticism scales, suggesting that there is little basis for inferring differential stability between these two domains of traits.

The data on which this study was based are taken from a single self-report instrument applied to a select male sample, and methodological artifacts, including sample selection and attrition, social desirability, and response sets, may have inflated the correlations. But a similar pattern of results in other samples using other objective measures (Costa & McCrae, 1977; Leon, Gillum, Gillum, & Gouze, 1979) as well as ratings (Block, 1971) argues that the results presented here cannot be dismissed wholly as method variance. Indeed, the theme of stability in personality is being heard with increasing frequency from a variety of sources. The conclusion seems to hold for women as well as men (Siegler et al., 1979), for Germans as well as Americans (Grombach, 1976), and for adolescents as well older adults (Bachman, O'Malley, & Johnston, 1978).

Eliminating Response Bias as an Explanation for Stability

Response Styles and Age

Test Artifacts in Self-Report Measures

By far the greatest number of studies conducted on personality and aging have employed self-report instruments as the primary or sole source of data. This strategy has both advantages and disadvantages. On the positive side, objective self-report inventories have a number of properties that make them preferable to observer ratings or projective techniques. Self-report scales (except purely empirical ones) generally rest on the following rationale: If the individual is asked a number of related questions about his or her thoughts, feelings, or actions, he or she can usually be trusted to answer with some accuracy. Since the questions can cover typical behavior or quantify the frequency as well as the intensity of behavior or feelings, it is possible to sample the individual's experience widely. Because identical questions are asked of each respondent, and because each test is scored identically, individuals' scores are maximally comparable. These properties hold whether the scale is self-administered or read to the respondent by an interviewer. The former method has the advantage of allowing the fast and economical gathering of data, which, in addition to its practicality, has the scientific merit of encouraging large sample research and frequent replications. Finally, there are a number of phenomena of interest to psychologists, such as daydreaming and sub-jective well-being, for which the subject is the only reliable observer.

In contrast, projective tests and observer ratings are usually based on extremely limited samples of behavior and require extensive judgment on the part of the rater. The relationship between the observed behavior (say, inkblot responses) and the inferred characteristic (say, ego strength) often depends on a tortuous chain of reasoning, and clinicians may draw quite different inferences from the same signs. Unstructured interviews provide the rater with a different basis for rating each individual, and peer ratings traditionally have relied on the use of one or a few adjective pairs or ratings scales which may carry different meanings to different raters. For all these reasons, self-report instruments have generally shown a better record of internal consistency, retest reliability, and construct validity than have ratings or projective tests.[1]

But self-report inventories are also prone to certain problems. The transparency of the items makes it possible for individuals so motivated to present themselves favorably or unfavorably. The use of a standard format for answering questions (yes–no, a Likert scale, a rating bar) makes it possible for consistencies in the style of responding to distort the scores obtained from the instrument, leading to spuriously high con-sistency or correlations. Issues of social desirability, acquiescence, and extreme responding have been the source of interminable debate among personality psychologists, and no definitive resolution has been reached.

[1]It would be possible to incorporate the advantages of the self-report inventories with those of ratings by employing raters long familiar with the subject and by using a large number of standard questions to measure each construct. Research along these lines is currently being conducted.

The nihilistic interpretation of self-report responses as nothing but response sets (Berg, 1955) has been repeatedly answered (Block, 1965; Wiggins, 1966), and sophisticated test constructors have learned to balance scales in order to reduce acquiescence effects and to guard against social desirability in constructing and interpreting scales.

Longitudinal Analyses of Response Sets in the Guilford–Zimmerman Temperament Survey

There has, however, been relatively little research on age trends in response sets. Some writers (Schaie & Schaie, 1977) have argued persuasively that there have been enormous changes in the amounts and kinds of testing that individuals of different generations have been exposed to and that this may introduce unwanted sources of variance in tests. Increased cautiousness may alter the responses of older subjects (Botwinick, 1969), or standards of social desirability may change with age, bringing shifts in the influences of that set. Age changes or cohort differences in responding could account for observed differences in scale scores or could mask real changes that are occurring. To date, all of these are speculations, with little empirical foundation. Clearly, before any conclusions are drawn about aging and personality based on the use of objective personality measures, some information on these issues would be useful. Recent analyses of data from the Baltimore study contribute to a resolution.

Over the past 20 years, subjects in the Baltimore study have been given the GZTS every 6 years. Since recruitment into the study has been continuous, new samples of individuals, ranging in age from the 20s to the 90s, have been tested at a succession of times. By dividing ages, birth cohorts, and times of measurement into 6-year intervals, a variety of analytic designs may be applied to aid in the interpretation of changes or differences.

The men in the Baltimore study sample are community-dwelling volunteers, most with a background in science or the professions. Their commitment to a longitudinal study shows them to be more conscientious than average, and comparison of their scores on the GZTS with college norms show that they are better adjusted than that group. As volunteers, they have no particular incentive to falsify their scores, and thus the results of this study should not be hastily generalized to other testing situations (such as counseling or employment) where incentives to distort may be involved.

The GZTS was given to all subjects with standard instructions. Answer sheets provide three response options—"yes," "no," and "?"—but subjects were instructed to use the "?" option only if they were completely unable to select "yes" or "no." Following the suggestion of Guilford and Zimmerman (1949), scales containing more than three "?" responses were invalidated. This criterion has been used in all previously reported applications of the GZTS conducted by the Baltimore study. However, this exclusionary principle may distort results. In particular, if age produces caution in responding, a disproportionate number of older subjects may be excluded, perhaps especially the most cautious. Because of that possibility, a new approach was adopted in the analyses reported here. All the GZTS answer sheets were keypunched, so that responses to individual items could be analyzed. In the original scoring system, "?" responses were not scored and thus tended to lower the score of the individual. In the new system, responses were assigned a value of -1, 0, or $+1$, with the "?" represented as a neutral, rather than a negative, value.

The handbook for the GZTS (Guilford et al., 1976) lists three scales that have been developed to estimate the influence of certain response sets: the Gross Falsification (GF) scale, the Subtle Falsification (SF) scale, and the Careless Deviancy (CD) scale. The first two are intended to screen individuals who may be attempting to present an unduly favorable impression; the third is a scale composed of relatively rare responses, and a high score is interpretable either as careless responding or deviancy in personality. In addition, it is possible to measure at least three other response sets on the GZTS. The number of blanks was summed across all scales to give an index, as was the number of "?" responses. Items in the GZTS are roughly balanced on most scales, so it is possible to sum up the number of "yes" responses and consider it an index, not of any substantive personality trait, but of the tendency to acquiesce to items indiscriminately.

For each of these variables, cross-sectional, longitudinal, cross-sequential, and time-sequential analyses were performed. In the repeated-measures analysis, 348 men ranging in initial age from 32 to 74 and retested after 4 to 8 years (mean interval = 6.6 years) were the subjects. They were classified into seven age groups, each spanning a 6-year interval. In the time-sequential analyses, 328 men who were tested in the period from 1958 to 1964 were compared with 278 men tested between 1965 and 1971. They were cross-classified by the same seven age categories used in the repeated-measures design. In the cross-sequential analysis, 345 men tested between 1958 and 1964 were compared with 285 men tested between 1965 and 1971. In this design, however, they were cross-classified according to their dates of birth, using seven birth cohorts of 6-year intervals from 1896 to 1932.

Repeated-measures analyses showed a significant ($p < .05$) effect on the repeated factor for number of question marks, which increased from 6.2 to 9.6; on acquiescence, which decreased from 132.1 to 128.9; on the

GF scale, which increased from 11.8 to 12.1; and on the SF scale, which decreased from 21.2 to 20.8. Age-group differences were seen for the number of question marks, which were highest in the 68–74-year-old group and lowest in the 50–55-year-old group. In addition, there were two interactions: Men aged 38–43 at first testing showed a decrease instead of an increase in question marks, and men aged 55–61 showed an increase instead of a decrease in acquiescence.

These results are somewhat puzzling; certainly they did not show a monotonic change in any of the response sets with age. Most of the changes were extremely small in magnitude, and if we require a significance level of $p < .01$, only two effects are significant: the increase in question marks and the decrease in acquiescence. Neither of these longitudinal changes was mirrored in cross-sectional differences, suggesting that the changes are due either to time-of-measurement effects (i.e., a cultural change during the testing period) or to "practice" (i.e., repeated exposure to the test).

Examination of the cross- and time-sequential analyses, conducted on samples of more than 600 men, is revealing. Analyses of number of blanks, number of question marks, acquiescence, GF, SF, and careless deviancy show *no* significant ($p < .05$) effects for aging/cohort, aging/time, cohort/time, or cohort/aging, nor were there any significant interactions. These data suggest that the marginal cross-sectional differences and interactions in the repeated-measures analyses are best regarded as unreplicable error and that the longitudinal changes in acquiescence and use of question marks are attributable to practice effects. That acquiescence decreased while use of question marks increased by three items is suggestive: Perhaps subjects felt pressured on the first administration to avoid question marks at all costs and agreed to a few items of which they were uncertain. Some years later, as experienced subjects no longer as reticent to assert themselves, they used the question marks when they felt they needed to.

In any case, these data imply that response sets are not ordered by age. The longitudinal researcher may want to consider the effects of repeated administration of the same instrument, but the particular effect seen here is small in its overall influence on scale scores and probably is unique to instruments like the GZTS, which provide a question-mark option, but fail to score it.

Response Sets in the Neuroticism–Extraversion–Openness Inventory

But what about questionnaires that use a different response format? Likert scales, for example, are subject to the influence of extreme responding—the tendency to "strongly agree" or "strongly disagree" to a variety of questions. And are aging women perhaps more susceptible to response sets than aging men? We have no longitudinal data on which to base answers to these questions, but cross-sectional data on a new personality instrument, the NEO Inventory, do provide some indirect evidence of the effect of age on response styles in the Likert format for men and women.

The Neuroticism–Extraversion–Openness (NEO) Inventory consists of 144 items measuring three broad domains of personality—Neuroticism, Extraversion, and Openness to Experience—and six more specific facets within each of these. Subjects are asked to respond to each item on a 5-point scale from "strongly disagree" to "strongly agree." They are instructed to use the middle, neutral category if they are undecided. The scales are balanced, so a count of the number of items to which a subject responds "agree" or "strongly agree" can be taken as a content-free measure of acquiescence. A "naysayer" index can be created by counting the "disagree" and "strongly disagree" responses. Neutral responses can also be counted. Finally, it is possible to count the number of extreme responses—"strongly disagree" and "strongly agree"—in order to index extreme responding.

Using the same 6-year age groups as were used previously, these scores were analyzed for a sample of 265 men and 191 women. There were no significant effects for age group or gender, nor were there any significant interactions. Once again, the evidence suggests that stability or change in mean level of self-report personality inventories is not likely to be an artifact of response sets. It also suggests that older men and women respond to questionnaires in much the same way as younger people do. These results are but one of many pieces of evidence that must be considered in evaluating the validity of self-report inventories when used with the elderly. The construct validity, factorial invariance, and predictive utility of trait measures discussed in other sections of this chapter also contribute to the conclusion that this approach to aging and personality has much to offer.

Retest Stability and Response Bias

We have shown that such extraneous sources of variance as acquiescence, extreme responding, and social desirability are not themselves age related. But it might be argued that the high level of stability of individual differences in personality dispositions is, in fact, better regarded as the stability of responding styles. If the influence of these variables were removed, would the stability coefficients be as high?

To test this, we calculated the retest coefficients of the GZTS, partialling out the variance due to response sets. Clearly, the response scales derived from the GZTS itself cannot be used for this since they are based on the same items as the temperament scales. If the individual endorses the same item on both occasions, we cannot tell whether that should be attributed to stability of trait or response style. An independent measure of response bias, however, could be used in this analysis, and the response-style indexes derived from the NEO Inventory just described were available. As a measure of social desirability or deliberate falsification, the Lie scale of the EPI was also available. Unfortunately, only 98 subjects had complete data on all these variables, so there is a substantial difference in sample from the original stability data.

Table 7.7 gives the retest coefficients for the ten GZTS scales over an interval of from 4 to 8 years (mean = 6.6 years), statistically controlling for acquiescence, naysaying, and extreme responding as measured by the response indexes of the NEO, and for falsification as measured by the EPI Lie scale. It should be noted that data on the response-set variables were collected in 1980, in some cases several years after the second administration of the GZTS. However, since the hypothesis under consideration is that response styles account for the observed stability of personality-scale scores, these styles must, by hypothesis, be themselves extremely stable. The point at which they are measured is therefore more or less immaterial.

An examination of this table shows that most of the stability coefficients

TABLE 7.7. Retest Correlations of GZTS Scales over a 6-Year Interval Partialing out the Effects of Acquiescence, Naysaying, Extreme Responding, and Falsification in a Sample of 98 Men

Scale	Corrected correlation	Partial correlation
General Activity	.85	.85
Restraint	.71	.70
Ascendance	.83	.83
Sociability	.83	.82
Emotional Stability	.73	.72
Objectivity	.66	.64
Friendliness	.74	.74
Thoughtfulness	.73	.71
Personal Relations	.73	.74
Masculinity	.73	.68

are unchanged after removing the effects of response set. Only Masculinity showed a noticeable change, and this can be attributed to a small correlation (−.31) between Masculinity and extreme responding at each time. The statistical procedure of partial correlation merely demonstrates a fact that is evident when the simple correlations are examined: None of the response sets is substantially related to any of the GZTS scales, and it is therefore not the case that stability in these response styles could account for stability in personality-scale scores. Incidentally, this is also additional evidence for the validity of the GZTS scales.

Personality Variables in Longitudinal Research

Eliminating the Effects of Mood States

One of the great advantages of many longitudinal studies is the accumulation of data from a variety of measures on the same set of subjects. Only from a study in which data collection is carried out over a period of years is it feasible to measure health, cognitive ability, personality, life events, well-being, perception, and so on, in a sufficiently large sample to allow multivariate analyses of all these variables. This wealth of data is one of the primary rationales for conducting longitudinal studies and explains why so many of them are interdisciplinary in scope.

But longitudinal studies also incorporate time intervals between the measures collected, and the imaginative use of data collected at different times can contribute enormously to an understanding of causal sequences and developmental progressions. Indeed, the study of stability or change in a single measured variable is only the simplest and most basic kind of longitudinal analysis. Many more interesting variations are possible.

One major use of longitudinal analysis is seen in the elimination of certain time-of-measurement effects. In personality and some kinds of cognitive testing, the transient state of the individual may influence the results of testing. Test conditions, fatigue, or a temporary dysphoric mood may contaminate the measurement of personality traits that are presumed to be enduring dispositions. Such influences not only would distort the measurement of the trait, but also might wholly account for observed relationships between variables measured at the same time and under the same conditions.

Consider the relationship between personality and subjective well-being. Since Wilson's (1967) review, it has been known that happiness, or subjective well-being, was correlated with personality. Contemporaneous studies using personality measures from the Buss and Plomin EASI-III Temperament Survey, EPI, and the 16PF, and well being measures from the Bradburn Affect Balance Scales, the Knutson Personal Security Inventory, the Beck Hopelessness Scale, and an index of life satisfaction showed clearly that Extraversion was associated with happiness, and especially with the Positive Affect scale, and that Neuroticism was negatively related to happiness, and especially the Negative Affect scale (Costa & McCrae, 1980a). Using this variety of measures and sample sizes of several hundred men, it was possible to conclude that the relationship was not an artifact of the particular measures used. But the causal interpretation, that personality influenced or contributed to the determination of happiness, could not be sustained on the basis of concurrent correlations alone. It could be argued that the mood of the individual at the time of the administration of the test might account for the observed correlation—that the responses to a personality test of a happy man resembled those of an extravert, whereas the responses of an unhappy man mimicked neuroticism.

However, 10-year longitudinal data speak directly to this question. If personality characteristics measured 10 years previously show significant relationships to well-being 10 years later, the causal attribution is much more easily made. In fact, we found that 16PF Extraversion scores were related to Bradburn's Affect Balance ($r = .14, p < .05$) and Positive Affect ($r = .23, p < .001$), but not to Negative Affect ($r = .03$, NS). The 16PF Neuroticism scores, also as predicted, were related to Affect Balance ($r = -.30, p < .001$) and to Negative Affect ($r = .39, p < .001$), but not to Positive Affect ($r = -.08$, NS). Analyses conducted on the same data set subsequent to the publication of these results show that, over a 10-year interval, 16PF Neuroticism also predicts Hopelessness ($r = .40, n = 376, p < .001$) and Personal Security ($r = -.38, n = 258, p < .001$). Corresponding correlations for 16PF Extraversion scores were $r = -.19, p < .001$, and $r = .33, p < .001$, respectively.

These findings were replicated using a different sample and different measures of both dependent and independent variables (Costa, McCrae, & Norris, 1981). In this study, personal adjustment to aging as measured by scales from the Chicago Attitude Inventory was predicted from Extraversion and Neuroticism factors of the GZTS. In addition to contemporaneous associations, GZTS factors were also shown to predict personal adjustment 6 and 12 years later.

Predicting across Periods of the Life Span

It is also possible that there are unwanted sources of variance that contaminate all measures taken in an entire period of time. A stressful life event, such as the loss of a spouse, may influence personality-inventory responses, mood measures, coping styles, and even cognitive performance for weeks or months. Even if researchers have gone to the trouble of measuring variables on different days or in different testing conditions, they cannot rule out the possibility of this kind of effect without employing a sufficiently long time lag.

An instance of this is provided by two analyses of the male midlife crisis (Cooper, 1977; Costa & McCrae, 1978b). In these two studies, a self-report measure of characteristics and concerns hypothesized to contitute the "midlife crisis" (the MLC scale) was found to have no relationship to age, but a marked correlation was observed between the MLC scale and the Eysenck Neuroticism scale administered at about the same time. One interpretation was that only men high in neuroticism suffered a midlife crisis, but an alternative was offered by developmental-stage theorists. Levinson had written that "because a man in this crisis is often somewhat irrational, others may regard him as 'upset' or 'sick.' In most cases, he is not" (Levinson et al., 1978, p. 199). Such individuals are supposed to be in the midst of "tumultuous struggles," in which they call into question their entire lives and are "horrified by much that is revealed. They are full of recriminations against themselves and others" (p. 199). It is entirely reasonable to suppose that a normal individual going through such a transition would appear high on a scale of neuroticism. That these persons did not cluster anywhere near the predicted age for a midlife crisis leads, however, to some skepticism, and the availability of longitudinal personality data made possible a clear test of these rival hypotheses. If the crisis were a continuation of long-standing maladjustment, we would expect a correlation between earlier measures of neuroticism and MLC scale scores. If the contemporaneous correlation were a distortion, caused by the developmental crisis of the midlife transition, then there should be no relationship—indeed, a Jungian theorist might even hypothesize that those apparently best adjusted in early adulthood might have the most difficult readjustment at midlife and that a negative correlation should be expected.

Using 16PF data collected 10 years previously, we showed significant positive correlations between the MLC scale and each of the five scales loading on the General Anxiety or Neuroticism cluster. Individuals who will one day experience something that is phenomenologically similar to a midlife crisis are those with a long history of maladjustment. It is possible that at certain times their emotional stability is particularly low, so contemporaneous correlations may somewhat inflate the actual relationship, but these longitudinal data provide compelling evidence that the midlife crisis is more a matter of neuroticism than of development.

Cause and Effect in Psychosomatic Research

The analysis just suggested, in which a predictive relationship is compared to a concurrent one, is chiefly of interest as a means of eliminating the possible effects of transient states and is usually based on the assumption that the true variable is constant and that variations from one time to another are the result of errors in measurement. It is also possible to entertain the possibility that real changes may occur in the variable. Consider the case of coronary heart disease (CHD). The psychic shock of discovering that one has heart disease, and the alterations in activity and life-style that the individual may be asked by his or her physician to make, could plausibly alter enduring personality dispositions. For that reason, research reporting associations of personality with any phase of CHD are inherently ambiguous.

In some preliminary results, it was noted that Baltimore study subjects who complained of angina were lower than average on two of the GZTS scales: Emotional Stability and Masculinity. Was this an example of personality change resulting from medical illness, or were personality variables diagnostic of and perhaps causally involved in the development of the disease? To tease out these possibilities, it was necessary to separate subjects into different groups and to take into consideration the temporal course of their disease (Costa, Flegg, Lakata, & McCrae, 1980). Eighty-eight subjects were measured on the GZTS during their first or second visit to the Gerontology Research Center, and all were free from both anginal complaints and certain ECG signs on these visits. Over the next 20 years, four groups emerged: those who developed CHD as evidenced by both anginal complaints and ECG signs; those who showed ECG signs of CHD, but who never reported angina in a follow-up period of from 5 to 15 years; those who reported angina, but who showed no ECG signs of CHD in the same follow-up period; and an age-matched control group (age-matched to the total of the three groups) that showed neither ECG signs nor angina in a follow-up period of 10–20 years. (All subjects were classified according to their status at last examination; the varying follow-up intervals reflect the fact that subjects entered and left the study at different times.)

The first group is easily diagnosed as having CHD. The second and third groups are more ambiguous: Those with only angina seem to be overly sensitive; those with only ECG signs appear undersensitive. Do any of these distinctions show up in personality measures taken before the development of disease?

Our results showed that there were no differences between the first and fourth groups, that is, between those who definitely did and did not develop CHD. Thus none of the traits measured by the GZTS appears to have etiological significance. But there were preexisting differences between the two intermediate groups. Individuals who complained of anginal pains, but who gave no ECG evidence of disease, were lower on Masculinity and less emotionally stable than those who reported no angina despite ischemic ECG signs.

It is well known (Hurst, Logue, Schlant, & Wenger, 1978; Froelicher, 1977) that resting and stress ECG signs in themselves are far-from-perfect indicators of CHD, and the number of subjects in this study (88) is too small to be conclusive. Nevertheless, some interesting interpretations are suggested by the data. Individuals (or at least men) high in Masculinity and Emotional Stability may be more likely to minimize minor chest pains, and the discovery of disease in them may depend on routine medical procedures. Without routine examinations, these men are likely to remain undiagnosed and untreated (cf. Berglund, Ander, Lindstrom, & Tibblin, 1975). On the other hand, men who are low in Masculinity and Emotional Stability are very sensitive to chest pains and may report anginal symptoms even in the absence of organic pathology. These people may request unnecessary medical attention. Taken together, these analyses suggest that the personality variables measured by the GZTS do not affect the development of CHD, but they do seem to affect the presentation of symptoms.

If these personality differences were found at the same time as the symptoms, several alternate interpretations could be offered. We might argue that the experience of angina was sufficiently traumatic to lower the individual's emotional stability and that the restraints on behavior, imposed by the patient or his physician, had diminished his sense of masculinity. Or we might argue that self-selection played the crucial role: Those individuals who were aware of chest pains and who were also predisposed to worry about their health (i.e., the more neurotic) would be most likely to join and remain in a longitudinal study that promised periodic monitoring of their health. Better adjusted men with angina, some of whom could be expected to show no ECG signs and thus be classified in the third group, would be less concerned with their health and less likely to volunteer for the study. These kinds of arguments have been supported in studies of the relationship between hypertension and personality (Costa, McCrae, Andres, & Tobin, 1980).

But in this case, we can rule out those alternatives. The measurement of personality preceded the development of angina and ECG signs, so it could not have been influenced by them. Likewise, self-selection on this basis is impossible, since the individuals were presumably unaware that they would experience angina in the next few years. Retrospective accounts of personality difference could not be trusted in this context; only the archives of a longitudinal study permit the kinds of inferences offered here.

These rather simple examples of the kinds of inferences that can be ruled out with longitudinal data are useful in part because they illustrate the logic involved. Path-analytic techniques, however, offer far more sophisticated statistical models, which estimate not only the direction of causal influence, but the degree of influence, expressed as a regression weight (see Kenny, 1979). Causal inferences based on these statistical techniques are subject to a number of restrictions, many of them related to the assumptions necessary to constructing the model. In general, fewer assumptions and more reliable results can be obtained by having more measurement points and by measuring more of the variables that might plausibly have an influence on elements in the model. Clearly, longitudinal studies are ideal for this type of analysis.

Conclusions

The Utility of a Trait Model

A chapter on longitudinal research on personality is not the place for a defense of self-report measures, the trait approach, or a particular model of personality dimensions. But since we began with a disclaimer alerting the reader to the wide variety of traditions in personality that are not reviewed in this chapter, it may be useful, in closing, to review the benefits of the approach we have adopted.

Within the scope of this chapter, we have shown that traits in the domains of Neuroticism, Extraversion, and Openness to Experience are indeed the "enduring dispositions" posited by trait theorists. This is a major contribution to the field of personality that only longitudinal studies could make. We have addressed the issue of the possible influence of response sets on stability of personality and have found that it is negligible. This helps to restore confidence in self-report methods, which in practice have always dominated empirical personality research. By aggregating traits into covarying clusters or domains, we have been able to structure a review of the literature and to formulate generalizations that may apply to many trait measures not hitherto used in longitudinal research. Further research will judge the adequacy of these generalizations. Finally, in the application to such problems as subjective well-being, the midlife crisis, and certain kinds of symptom reports, we have demonstrated the value of our trait model in predicting outcomes or criteria of interest to students of adulthood and aging.

Considerations of convenience contributed to the choice of implementing objective personality inventories in longitudinal studies, but the choice has turned out to be fortunate. Yet it must be remembered that the value of one approach does not imply the uselessness of others. Large-scale longitudinal studies of nontrait variables, such as ego functions or coping processes used to deal with chronic and acute stress, should be conducted. Perhaps the most fruitful longitudinal research will study such processes across the life span in conjunction with enduring personality dispositions.

Research on Personality and the Life Course

The major drawback to the use of a stable individual-difference approach to life-span development is that current conceptions and methods of research on aging and personality are designed primarily for the study of change. The elegant models for attempting to separate true maturational changes from cohort differences and cultural changes are not very useful if there is no meaningful maturational change. The widespread attempt to chart the developmental course of personality in adulthood no longer seems profitable, and it may not be immediately clear what direction future research should take.

We have argued elsewhere (McCrae & Costa, 1982) that personality dimensions may be more usefully construed as causes than as effects. Age, and its attendant social, cognitive, and biological changes, should be considered in conjunction with personality as joint shapers of the life course. Personality can help explain the choices (educational, career, familial) that must be made at specific life transitions. The stability of personality dispositions may contribute to the individual's sense of identity and to the continuity and coherence of the life course. Finally, adaptation to life at all ages is likely to be powerfully influenced by personality.

Prospective life histories collected by longitudinal studies can help to answer such questions as the following: How do the lives of introverts differ from the lives of extraverts? Does openness to experience lead to a more fluid and unpredictable life course? How is neuroticism typically manifested at each stage of life? Answers to these questions may help in integrating the insights of life-span developmental psychology with those of personality in the study of lives.

References

Adam, J. Sequential strategies and the separation of age, cohort, and time-of-measurement contributions to developmental data. *Psychological Bulletin*, 1978, *85*, 1309–1316.

Adorno, T. W., Frenkel-Brunswik, E., Levinson, D. J., & Sanford, R. N. *The authoritarian personality*. New York: Harper, 1950.

Allport, G. W. Traits revisited. *American Psychologist*, 1966, *21*, 1–10.

Allport, G. W., & Allport, F. H. *A-S reaction study*. Boston: Houghton Mifflin, 1928.

Bachman, J. G., O'Malley, P. M., & Johnston, J. *Adolescence to adulthood: Change and stability in the lives of young men*. Ann Arbor, Mich.: Institute for Social Research, 1978.

Baltes, P. B. Longitudinal and cross-sectional sequences in the study of age and generation effects. *Human Development*, 1968, *11*, 145–171.

Baltes, P. B., Reese, H. W., & Nesselroade, J. R. *Life-span developmental psychology: Introduction to research methods*. Monterey, Calif.: Brooks/Cole, 1977.

Beck, A. T. *Depression: Causes and treatment*. Philadelphia: University of Pennsylvania Press, 1972.

Bendig, A. W. Age differences in the interscale factor structure of the Guilford–Zimmerman Temperament Survey. *Journal of Consulting Psychology*, 1960, *24*, 134–138.

Berg, I. A. Response bias and personality: The deviation hypothesis. *Journal of Psychology*, 1955, *40*, 61–71.

Berglund, G., Ander, S., Lindstrom, B., & Tibblin, G. Personality and reporting of symptoms in normo- and hypertensive 50-year-old males. *Journal of Psychosomatic Research*, 1975, *19*, 139–145.

Block, J. *The challenge of response sets*. New York: Appleton-Century-Crofts, 1965.

Block, J. *Lives through time*. Berkeley, Calif.: Bancroft Books, 1971.

Block, J. Advancing the psychology of personality: Paradigmatic shift or improving the quality of research. In D. Magnusson & N. S. Endler (Eds.), *Personality at the crossroads: Current issues in interactional psychology*. Hillsdale, N.J.: Erlbaum, 1977.

Botwinick, J. Disinclination to venture response versus cautiousness in responding: Age differences. *Journal of Genetic Psychology*, 1969, *115*, 55–62.

Buss, A. H., & Plomin, R. *A temperament theory of personality development*. New York: Wiley, 1975.

Byrne, D. Repression–Sensitization as a dimension of personality. In B. A. Maher (Ed.), *Progress in experimental personality research* (Vol. 1). New York: Academic Press, 1964.

Cattell, R. B. *Personality and mood by questionnaire*. San Francisco: Jossey-Bass, 1973.

Cooper, M. W. *An empirical investigation of the male midlife period: A descriptive, cohort study*. Unpublished undergraduate honors thesis, University of Massachusetts at Boston, 1977.

Costa, P. T., Jr., & McCrae, R. R. Age differences in personality structure: A cluster analytic approach. *Journal of Gerontoloy*, 1976, *31*, 564–570.

Costa, P. T., Jr., & McCrae, R. R. Age differences in personality structure revisited: Studies in validity, stability, and change. *Aging and Human Development*, 1977, *8*, 261–275.

Costa, P. T., Jr., & McCrae, R. R. Letter to the editor. *Journal of Gerontology*, 1978, *33*, 4. (a)

Costa, P. T., Jr., & McCrae, R. R. Objective personality assessment. In M. Storandt, I. C. Siegler, & M. F. Elias (Eds.), *The clinical psychology of aging*. New York: Plenum, 1978. (b)

Costa, P. T., Jr., & McCrae, R. R. The influence of extraversion and neuroticism on subjective well-being. Happy and unhappy people. *Journal of Personality and Social Psychology*, 1980, *38*, 668–678. (a)

Costa, P. T., Jr., & McCrae, R. R. Somatic complaints in males as a function of age and neuroticism: A longitudinal analysis. *Journal of Behavioral Medicine*, 1980, *3*, 245–257. (b)

Costa, P. T., Jr., & McCrae, R. R. Still stable after all these years: Personality as a key to some issues in adulthood and old age. In P. B. Baltes & O. G. Brim (Eds.), *Life span development and behavior* (Vol. 3). New York: Academic Press, 1980. (c)

Costa, P. T., Jr., McCrae, R. R., Andres, R., & Tobin, J. D. Hypertension, somatic complaints and personality. In M. F. Elias & D. Streeten (Eds.), *Hypertension and cognitive processes.* Mt. Desert, Me.: Beech Hill Publishing, 1980.

Costa, P. T., Jr., McCrae, R. R., & Arenberg, D. Enduring dispositions in adult males. *Journal of Personality and Social Psychology,* 1980, *38,* 793-800.

Costa, P. T., Jr., McCrae, R. R., & Norris, A. Personal adjustment to aging: Longitudinal prediction from Neuroticism and Extraversion. *Journal of Gerontology,* 1981, *36,* 78-85.

Costa, P. T., Jr., Flegg, J., Lakata, E. & McCrae, R. R. *Longitudinal personality predictors of anginal complaints in males.* Paper presented at the 33rd Annual Meeting of the Gerontological Society, San Diego, Calif., November 1980.

Cunningham, W. R. Principles for identifying structural differences: Some methodological issues related to comparative factor analyses. *Journal of Gerontology,* 1978, *33,* 82-86.

Douglas, K., & Arenberg, D. Age changes, cohort differences, and cultural change on the Guilford-Zimmerman Temperament Survey. *Journal of Gerontology,* 1978, *33,* 737-747.

Eysenck, H. J. *The structure of human personality.* London: Methuen, 1960.

Eysenck, H. J., & Eysenck, S. B. G. *Manual of the Eysenck Personality Inventory.* San Diego, Calif.: Educational and Industrial Testing Service, 1975.

Floderus, B. Psycho-social factors in relation to coronary heart disease and associated risk factors. *Nordisk Hygienisk Tidskrift Supplementum 6,* Stockholm, Sweden, 1974.

Fozard, J. L., & Thomas, J. C. Psychology of aging: Basic findings and their psychiatric applications. In J. G. Howells (Ed.), *Modern perspectives in the psychiatry of old age.* New York: Brunner-Mazel, 1975.

Froelicher, V. F. Use of the exercise electrocardiogram to identify latent coronary atherosclerotic heart disease. In E. A. Amsterdam, J. H. Wilmore, & A. N. DeMaria (Eds.), *Exercise in cardiovascular health and disease.* New York: Yorke Medical Books, 1977.

Gorsuch, R. L. *Factor analysis.* Philadelphia: W. B. Saunders, 1974.

Gould, R. L. *Transformations.* New York: Simon & Schuster, 1978.

Grombach, H. Consistency and change of personality variables in late life. In H. Thomae (Ed.), *Patterns of aging: Findings from the Bonn Longitudinal Study of Aging.* Basel, Switzerland: S. Karger, 1976.

Guilford, J. P., & Zimmerman, W. S. *The Guilford-Zimmerman Temperament Survey: Manual of instructions and interpretations.* Beverly Hills, Calif.: Sheridan Supply Company, 1949.

Guilford, J. S., Zimmerman, W. S., & Guilford, J. P. *The Guilford-Zimmerman Temperament Survey handbook: Twenty-five years of research and application.* San Diego, Calif.: EdITS Publishers, 1976.

Gutmann, D. Alternatives to disengagement: The old men of the Highland Druze. In R. Levine (Ed.), *Culture and personality: Contemporary readings.* Chicago: Aldine, 1974.

Gynther, M. D. Aging and personality. In J. N. Butcher (Ed.), *New directions in MMPI research.* Minneapolis: University of Minnesota Press, 1980.

Heise, D. R. Separating reliability and stability in test-retest correlation. *American Sociological Review,* 1969, *34,* 93-101.

Hurst, J. W., Logue, R. B., Schlant, R. C., & Wenger, N. K. (Eds.). *The heart.* New York: McGraw-Hill, 1978.

Jung, C. G. *Psychological types.* New York: Harcourt, Brace & World, 1933.

Kenny, D. A. *Correlation and causality.* New York: Wiley, 1979.

Lawton, M. P., Whelihan, W. M., & Belsky, J. K. Personality tests and their uses with older adults. In J. Birren (Ed.), *Handbook of mental health and aging.* New York: Prentice-Hall, 1980.

Leon, G. R., Gillum, B., Gillum, R., & Gouze, M. Personality stability and change over a 30 year period—Middle age to old age. *Journal of Consulting and Clinical Psychology*, 1979, *23*, 245–259.

Levinson, D. J., Darrow, C. N., Klein, E. B., Levinson, M. H., & McKee, B. *The seasons of a man's life*. New York: Alfred A. Knopf, 1978.

McCrae, R. R. & Costa, P. T., Jr. Aging, the life course, and models of personality. In T. Field (Ed.), *Review of human development*. New York: Wiley, 1982.

McCrae, R. R., Costa, P. T., Jr., & Arenberg, D. Constancy of adult personality structure in males: Longitudinal, cross-sectional and times-of-measurement analyses. *Journal of Gerontology*, 1980, *35*, 877–883.

Nesselroade, J. R., & Baltes, P. B. Adolescent personality development and historical change: 1970–1972. *Monographs of the Society for Research in Child Development*, 1974, *39* (Serial No. 154).

Neugarten, B. L. *Personality in middle and late life*. New York: Atherton, 1964.

Rokeach, M. *The open and closed mind*. New York: Basic Books, 1960.

Schaie, K. W. The effect of age on a scale of social responsibility. *Journal of Social Psychology*, 1959, *50*, 221–224.

Schaie, K. W. A general model for the study of developmental problems. *Psychological Bulletin*, 1965, *64*, 92–107.

Schaie, K. W. Quasi-experimental research designs in the psychology of aging. In J. E. Birren & K. W. Schaie (Eds.), *Handbook of the psychology of aging*. New York: Van Nostrand Reinhold, 1977.

Schaie, K. W., & Parham, I. A. Stability of adult personality: Fact or fable. *Journal of Personality and Social Psychology*, 1976, *34*, 146–158.

Schaie, K. W., & Schaie, J. Clinical assessment and aging. In J. Birren & K. W. Schaie (Eds.), *Handbook of the psychology of aging*. New York: Van Nostrand Reinhold, 1977.

Sealy, A. P., & Cattell, R. B. *Standard trends in personality development in men and women of 16 to 70 years, determined by 16PF measurements*. Paper presented at the British Social Psychology Conference, London, April 1965.

Siegler, I. C., George, L. K., & Okun, M. A. Cross-sequential analysis of adult personality. *Developmental Psychology*, 1979, *15*, 350–351.

Spielberger, C. D. Anxiety as an emotional state. In C. D. Spielberger (Ed.), *Anxiety: Current trends in theory and research* (Vol. 1). New York: Academic Press, 1972.

Tellegen, A., & Atkinson, G. Openness to absorbing and self-altering experiences ("absorption"), a trait related to hypnotic susceptibility. *Journal of Abnormal Psychology*, 1974, *83*, 268–277.

Thomae, H. Personality and adjustment to aging. In J. E. Birren & R. B. Sloane (Eds.), *Handbook of mental health and aging*. Englewood Cliffs, N.J.: Prentice-Hall, 1980.

Wagner, E. E. Differences between old and young executives on objective psychological test variables. *Journal of Gerontology*, 1960, *15*, 296–299.

Wiggins, J. S. Substantive dimensions of self-report in the MMPI item pool. *Psychological Monographs*, 1966, *80* (22, Whole No. 630).

Wilson, W. Correlates of avowed happiness. *Psychological Bulletin*, 1967, *67*, 294–306.

Zemore, R., & Eames, N. Psychic and somatic symptoms of depression among young adults, institutionalized aged and noninstitutionalized aged. *Journal of Gerontology*, 1979, *34*, 716–722.

Zuckerman, M. *Sensation seeking: Beyond the optimal level of arousal*. Hillsdale, N.J.: Erlbaum, 1979.

8 The AT&T Longitudinal Studies of Managers

DOUGLAS W. BRAY AND ANN HOWARD

Introduction

Efforts to improve managerial performance and enhance managerial potential by training and development programs have long been a feature of corporate life. Cumulatively, mints of money and centuries of time have been devoted to such purposes. Yet basic knowledge of growth as a manager in the absence of deliberate interventions is sparse. Such concerns prompted the Bell System, employer of a vast number of managers, to initiate, in 1956, longitudinal research into managerial lives.

The desire to have a scientifically sound basis for the selection and development of managers was not the only motivation for starting the ambitious research project. During the 1950s, it was fashionable to lament the effects on the individual of life as a manager in a big corporation. Books like *The Organization Man* (Whyte, 1956) pictured the course of adulthood in such an environment as an ever greater uniformity in thinking and feeling among clones in white shirts and grey flannel suits. It was important to question, therefore, what effect a career in big business really had on those who undertook it.

The Management Progress Study (MPS), as the research was titled, has now passed the 20-year mark and appears likely to continue, following the participants into retirement. As these careers unfolded, and striking motivational and personality changes were observed, even more insistent questions arose. Are the changes in the now middle-aged managers really age- or experience-related or due to a change in the times? Are today's young managers like those of 20 years ago? Will they change in a similar fashion? To answer these and other questions, new longitudinal research, the Management Continuity Study (MCS), was launched in 1977.

DOUGLAS W. BRAY AND ANN HOWARD. American Telephone and Telegraph Company, Basking Ridge, New Jersey.

The materials amassed from this program of research are rich and voluminous enough to provide data for several books. This chapter allows only an overview. Included are the design of the studies, the methods of data collection, illustrative data analyses, and summaries of the major results thus far. Because of space limitations, these summaries do not always contain supporting data. In most instances, however, such data have been reported elsewhere.

Design of the Management Progress Study

Certain critical decisions made at the start of the study in 1956 laid the groundwork for the research design. As the years went by, additional decisions were made which completed the design for the first 20 years of the study, a point recently reached. One initial decision was that the study would not only be longitudinal, following a group of new managers through the early years of their careers, but also "in process"; that is, there would be frequent (annual) contact with the participants, primarily by interviews. It was not believed sufficient merely to let a number of years elapse and then check up on the participants' status, with perhaps some retrospective interviewing. On the contrary, it was thought important to record each participant's perceptions and feelings at the time, or close to the time, at which events were taking place. It was also thought essential to get additional information from someone in a position to report on the participant's performance on the job, the nature of his assignment and work group, and so on. This was done through annual interviews with someone in the participant's organization who could provide meaningful information. Methods more elaborate than an interview were considered for these purposes but were rejected because of limitations of staff.

A major early decision was to begin the study by putting the participants through an assessment center designed to provide as complete a picture as possible of their abilities and motivations. It was not believed that paper-and-pencil testing and interviews, by themselves, would capture the molar ability and motivational aspects of these young managers as they moved into their careers. Details of the assessment center method are described later.

A final early key decision was to make medical data part of the study. This aspect of the research was initiated because it was believed that relationships between work and health might later become of great interest. The initial medical examination, conducted at the time of original assessment by non-Bell System physicians, was more extensive than that normally given and was supplemented by an extensive questionnaire concerning the medical history and other matters. The examination was repeated at two later points in time. No medical results are presented in this chapter, however, since these data are still being collected and analyzed.

The 20-year design of the MPS, which emerged from the initial planning as well as from later decisions, is shown in Table 8.1. The study was launched by putting 422 new managers through a 3½-day assessment center. For staffing reasons, assessment center activities took place only in the summer. Thus the initial assessments at Year 0 ran from 1956 to 1960, and later data-collection points also spanned periods of 5 years.

Two populations of new managers from six Bell System operating telephone companies were tapped to participate in the study. One consisted of recent college graduates just hired as management trainees, and the other, individuals who had not graduated from college at the time of their employment, but who had risen from nonmanagement jobs into management before they were 32 years of age. These two sources were expected to represent nearly all the persons who would reach middle management or higher in the years to come. Since it was rare to find women or minorities in middle and upper management 20 years ago, all the participants in the MPS were white males.

In each of the years following assessment, the participants were interviewed at length about their perceptions of and reactions to the company, their jobs, supervisors, future career expectations, and so on. Although the heaviest emphasis was on their work lives, they were also asked about their families, avocations, community activities, religious involvement, health, and anything else that would serve to give a complete picture of their current lives. In conjunction with this interview, they filled out, each

TABLE 8.1. Design and Sample of MPS

		Sample size		
Year	Design	College	Noncollege	Total
0	Assessment	274	148	422
1–7	Annual interviews with participants, company representatives			
	Annual expectations and attitude questionnaires			
8	Reassessment	167	142	309
9–19	Triannual interviews with participants, bosses, and terminators			
	Triannual biographical questionnaires			
20	MPS:20 assessment[a] (midlife and midcareer)	137	129	266

[a]The 20-year reassessment.

year, the Expectations Inventory they had first taken at assessment and a management attitude questionnaire. Also annually, someone in the same organization was asked to provide information as complete as possible about each participant. To avoid focusing too much attention directly on the participants early in their careers, these company people were originally in the Personnel Department, rather than direct supervisors. Later on, past supervisors were interviewed until, finally, at Year 6, interviews with the current supervisor were instituted. To promote full and frank participation, confidentiality of all study data with respect to individual participants was guaranteed.

When the MPS was initiated, it was thought that the complete design of the research would be confined to what has been presented so far. The men would be assessed and then followed, for 8 years or so, by interviews conducted with them and with representatives in their companies. Data collection would stop, and the analysis could proceed. The annual interviews would provide information about changes in motivation and attitudes; the company information would provide advancement and performance criteria; and the original assessment center results could be combed for predictors of both career success and changes, if any, in personal characteristics.

As Year 8 approached, however, such a design was seen as far from fully adequate to answer the major question to which the study was addressed: What are the changes and stabilities in individuals as their lives as business managers proceed? It was decided, therefore, to bring back those participants still employed by the Bell System (about 75% of the total group) and to put them through another assessment center duplicating or paralleling the center they had undergone 8 years previously. This procedure was thought to afford a better opportunity to measure and evaluate specific changes and stabilities in the group and in each individual over the first 8 years of a management career. Even with this reassessment accomplished, it was not thought defensible to stop following the participants further. Interviewing the men and their bosses therefore continued, although on a 3-year, rather than an annual, basis.

As the 20th year of the study grew near, the idea of conducting a third assessment center arose. The participants had now spread out over six levels of management (in a seven-level hierarchy), and much had happened in their lives off the job. Nearly all of the participants were in their 40s, many careers had plateaued, and thoughts of early retirement had begun to appear. A change in the orientation of the assessment process seemed to be called for. And so, at Year 20, the participants confronted still another assessment center, but with a difference. Only about one-third of the assessment time was devoted to repeating tests and questionnaires given at the previous two centers. The remainder was spent in a series of new exercises focused on midcareer and midlife issues.

Although the final round of assessment has only recently been completed, attention has turned, once again, to follow-up activities. The frequency of interviews for both participants and their supervisors has now been stretched to 5 years. Although the time seems remote to participants and researchers alike, tentative plans have been made for another assessment at Year 35, when more than half of the participants would be expected to have retired.

For the sake of completeness, it should be noted that contact has been maintained with nearly all of the men who have left Bell System employment. The lives of some who left very early have been followed for a full 20 years. Perhaps surprisingly, these men have often consented to interviews, either face-to-face or by telephone, and much is known about their careers. These data, however, have not yet been analyzed.

The Assessment Center Method

The assessment center method first came to general attention in 1948 with the publication of *Assessment of Men* (OSS, 1948). This was the exciting and scholarly report on the use of the method by the Office of Strategic Services (OSS) in selecting intelligence agents during World War II. The book inspired the development and utilization of an assessment center in AT&T's longitudinal research.

The following description covers the Year 0 and Year 8 assessment centers of the MPS, which were nearly identical. Changes made for the 20th-year assessment or for the MCS assessment are described later.

Dimensions and Ratings

Assessment centers are organized around dimensions, those characteristics that the creators of the particular assessment center want to evaluate. There are no rules for the selection of dimensions, except that logic dictates that they be known, or at least hypothesized, to be relevant to the overall purpose for which the assessment center is being conducted. Dimensions can also range from such macro variables as face-to-face leadership ability to such presumed elements of personality as seclusiveness. Nor need the dimensions looked for in a particular assessment center be at the same level of generality.

The dimensions for the original MPS assessment centers were chosen to represent seven areas of managerial ability and motivation. These dimensions, with their definitions, are listed in Table 8.2, grouped under appropriate headings. Factor-analytic work with assessment center results (Bray & Grant, 1966) supported this *a priori* clustering of the dimensions quite well.

Most of the assessment staff members at the first two assessment centers (Year 0 and Year 8) were psychologists, supplemented by one or two Bell System executives. Their responsibility in a staff integration session, which occupied the final 2 days of each assessment week, was to rate each participant on each of the 26 dimensions. These ratings were made on a 5-point scale, with 5 being high and 3 representing the average standing on the dimension believed to be characteristic of an acceptable candidate for the lowest level of middle management (the third, or "district," level). These dimension ratings were made independently by each assessor after hearing all the evidence gathered at the assessment center on all dimensions. Where marked differences of opinion arose, discussion was required in order to arrive at consensus. One important product of each assessment center was, then, a modal assessor rating for each participant on each of the 26 dimensions. In addition, at the conclusion of the review of each participant, some overall ratings of managerial potential were made.

Assessment Exercises

The assessors considered a wealth of material gathered during the 3 days the participants were at the assessment center. Some came from conventional types of exercises: cognitive tests, personality/motivational inventories, and attitude surveys. In addition, two sentence-completion tests and six cards from the Thematic Apperception Test (TAT) were administered. There was a lengthy personal interview, conducted by an assessor and summarized in a narrative report.

Approximately half of the participants' time at the assessment center was occupied in behavioral simulations. Two of these were for six-person groups (the participants normally attended the assessment center in groups of 12). One was a simple business game, and the other a group discussion with competitive assigned roles and positions. The final simulation was a paperwork administrative exercise called the "In-Basket," which presented realistic management problems to the participant through the letters, memos, reports, and so on, that normally cross a manager's desk. Behavior

TABLE 8.2. Original MPS Assessment Dimensions

Administrative skills
  Organizing and Planning—How effectively can this person organize work, and how well does he or she plan ahead?
  Decision Making—How ready is this person to make decisions, and how good are the decisions made?
  Creativity—How likely is this person to solve a management problem in a novel way?
Interpersonal skills
  Leadership Skills—How effectively can this person lead a group to accomplish a task without arousing hostility?
  Oral Communication Skills—How well would this person present an oral report to a small conference group on a subject he or she knew well?
  Behavior Flexibility—How readily can this person, when motivated, modify his or her behavior to reach a goal? How able is this person to change roles or style of behavior to accomplish objectives?
  Personal Impact—How forceful and likable an early impression does this person make?
  Social Objectivity—How free is this person from prejudices against racial, ethnic, socioeconomic, educational, and other social groups?
  Perception of Threshold Social Cues—How readily does this person perceive minimal cues in the behavior of others?
Cognitive skills
  General Mental Ability—How able is this person in terms of the functions measured by tests of intelligence, scholastic aptitude, and/or learning ability?
  Range of Interests—To what extent is this person interested in a variety of fields of activity such as science, politics, sports, music, and art?
  Written Communication Skills—How well would this person compose a communicative and formally correct memorandum on a subject he or she knew well? How well written are memos and reports likely to be?
Stability of performance
  Tolerance of Uncertainty—To what extent will this person's work performance stand up under uncertain or unstructured conditions?
  Resistance to Stress—To what extent will this person's work performance stand up in the face of personal stress?
Work motivation
  Primacy of Work—To what extent does this person find satisfaction from work more important than satisfaction from other areas of life?
  Inner Work Standards—To what extent will this person want to do a good job even if a less good one is acceptable to the boss and others?
  Energy—How continuously can this person sustain a high level of work activity?
  Self-Objectivity—How realistic a view does this person have of his or her own assets and liabilities, and how much insight into his or her own motives?
Career orientation
  Need for Advancement—To what extent does this person need to be promoted significantly earlier than his or her peers? To what extent are further promotions needed for career satisfaction?
  Need for Security—How strongly does this person want a secure job?
  Ability to Delay Gratification—To what extent will this person be willing to wait patiently for advancement if confident advancement will come?
  Realism of Expectations—To what extent do this person's expectations about his or her

TABLE 8.2. (*Continued*)

work life with the company conform to what is likely to be true? Convention: If *underestimates*, rate 5.

Bell System Value Orientation—To what extent has this person incorporated Bell System values such as service, friendliness, and justice of company position on earnings, rates, and wages?

Dependency

Need for Superior Approval—To what extent does this person need warmth and nurturant support from immediate supervisors?

Need for Peer Approval—To what extent does this person need warmth and acceptance from peers and subordinates?

Goal Flexibility—To what extent is this person likely to reorient his or her life toward a different goal?

in the three simulations was observed by subgroups of assessors, who prepared comprehensive narrative reports of each participant's performance.

The materials presented at the staff integration session included the reports on each participant's behavior in the three behavioral simulations, a projective test report, and a report of the personal interview. In addition, scores converted into Bell System norms were presented from the various tests and scales.

To further complicate matters, there were at least three levels of exercise data. One was the scores on the tests and inventories, and a second possibility was the individual items in each of these scales. For example, on the Expectations Inventory, one item read, "I feel an increasing amount of conflict between obligations of my job and my family." Responses to such an item might change with advancement, or, alternatively, a positive response to this item might predict future unhappiness. The third level of data was not available in quantitative form at the time of assessment. It consisted of ratings made from the narrative reports on the interview, projective tests, and behavioral simulations. After assessment, it was possible to go back and develop coding schemes for each of the behavioral reports and to use the behavior ratings in specific exercises as additional variables. Two reports based on such ratings are in the literature (Grant & Bray, 1969; Grant, Katkovsky, & Bray, 1967).

In summary, then, the following kinds of data were available from each assessment center: overall ratings of potential, ratings of dimensions, test and inventory scores, test and inventory item responses, and postassessment codings of narrative assessment reports. An important characteristic of these data was that each type could be considered as either a dependent or an independent variable. As dependent variables, they might be respondent or resistant to influences in the environment or to the passage of time. Yet they might also be examined as independent predictors of future events or changes and stabilities in personal characteristics and thus portend the later course of life, occupational or otherwise.

Initial Characteristics of Young Managers

What the college graduates in the study were like at the time of their first assessment has been detailed in *Formative Years in Business* (Bray, Campbell, & Grant, 1974). With a mean age of 24.6 years at assessment ($SD = 2.4$), they were a better-than-average sample of America's college graduates. Sixty-one percent had ranked above the median of their college graduating classes, and an equal proportion had attended better than average schools. They looked to the future with highly favorable expectations: The company would be a fine place to work, and they would succeed in it. Motivationally, the average participant desired rapid advancement, yet was interested also in doing a good job for its own sake. He was, however, perhaps too interested in job security and overly dependent, seeking approval from his bosses and his peers.

The remainder of the sample was made up of men who were not hired as college graduates, but who had started with the Bell System in nonmanagement jobs. These men were mostly in the Plant Department, the part of the business responsible for installing and maintaining communications equipment. The men in this group had been seen as performing well in their nonmanagement jobs and had been moved up into management while still young. One-quarter of the group were already above the first level of management; all but one of them were at the second level, with the remaining person already at district level. When these men attended their first assessment center, they averaged 10 years of telephone company employment, of which 2 years were in management. They had a mean age of 29.6 years ($SD = 1.6$), 5 years older than the college recruits.

The noncollege men were similar to the college graduates in some ways. For example, their expectations about their future lives as Bell System managers were almost as highy favorable. One of the questionnaires filled out by both groups was the Expectations Inventory. This inventory consisted of 56 statements, half of them positive and half negative, about their future situations in the Bell System and about outside circumstances related to telephone company employment, such as the desirability of the community in which they would live. Each item was responded to on a 4-point scale, running from +2 (fairly certain to be true) to −2 (fairly certain to be false), with no zero point. Scores were computed for the 28 favorable items by adding these responses algebraically. Thus the total score could run from -56 to $+56$. The expectations of both groups were highly favorable: $+26.6$ for the college graduates and $+24.0$ for the noncollege men.

The two groups of participants were also similar in several aspects of work motivation. There was no appreciable difference between them, for example, in Primacy of Work, and both groups had the same strong interest in job security. Where they did differ significantly was in drive for rapid advancement. The college graduates were more concerned with this and appeared significantly more likely to be impatient if early promotions did not materialize.

As far as dependency on others was concerned, the noncollege men appeared to be just as desirous as the college recruits of having a warm, supportive boss, but they were significantly less likely than the recruits to be dependent on their peers. (This last finding may well be an age effect. The noncollege men were, on the average, 5 years older, and, as is discussed later, affiliation motivation appears to decline with age.) Finally, the noncollege men were judged significantly less likely to experience any change in their life goals; they were already solidly planted in the Bell System.

There was a wide gap between the two groups in the cognitive skills area. On the School and College Ability Test (SCAT), 62% of the college graduates scored higher than the average college senior in a national sample, and only 9% were found in the lowest quartile of the college-senior distribution. By comparison, the noncollege managers fared poorly. Only 17% were above the national median, and 63% were in the lowest quartile.

The assessment test battery included the Contemporary Affairs Test, measuring knowledge of current national and international events, science, medicine, the arts, and hobbies. The norms for this test had been established by administering it to a random sample of 400 third-level Bell System managers. This population had been chosen because it was the presumed minimum target level for college recruits. When compared to this standard, both the college and noncollege new managers looked weak indeed. Only 6% of the college graduates and 3% of the noncollege men were in the top quartile, and many fell into the lowest quartile (49% of the college group and 71% of the noncollege group).

The college graduates had been employed with the expectation that they would reach the third level, the lowest rung of middle management, early in their careers. But in the majority of cases, the assessment staff disagreed with this evaluation of their potential. The staff's vote was in terms of "should be district," which was a shorthand way of saying that the participant had the abilities and motivation that they judged to be required in a person who would deservedly reach the third level in no more than 10 years. Only 37% of these young college graduates were seen in that light by the assessors. Most of the remainder did not meet this standard, although a few were people about whom a clear majority of the assessors could not agree.

Although the college graduates could not have been employed unless one or more Bell System managers had evaluated them as having third-level management potential, this was not true of the great majority of the noncollege managers. Although some had been appraised as having third-level potential *after* they had performed well in first- or second-level management jobs, they had originally been promoted into first-level management simply because it was thought that they could do well at that level. When the assessment staffs applied the "should-be-district" standard to these up-from-the-ranks participants, they agreed that 24% did have that degree of potential. Although this judgment might have dismayed some of these men, who might have interpreted it as just another sign of prejudice in favor of the college graduate, it really was not that negative an outcome when compared to the corresponding figure of 37% for the college men.

Early Managerial Lives

Those participants in the study who remained with the Bell System for another 8 years—and three-fourths of them did—returned to another assessment center. A comparison of the evaluations made at the two centers revealed changes and stabilities in many characteristics. Such results were, of course, of interest in themselves, but questions would inevitably arise about the relationship between the results and events in the intervening 8 years. Fortunately, the original plans for the study included an extensive annual interview with each participant. The reports of these interviews eventually filled many typewritten pages and contained a wealth of information about job assignments, supervisors, successes and failures, wives and families, and much else.

Life Themes

Although the 20,000 or so interview pages available at the 8-year mark could always be read to extract specific items of information, it was thought advisable to devise a system for evaluating the major orientations revealed in these reports. Nine life themes, listed in Table 8.3, were identified and defined by Joseph F. Rychlak.

The ego functional theme will be used to illustrate one use of these codings of the personal interviews. Two initial observations may be made about the course of this theme over the first 7 years of the study. (Eight interviews in all are involved per participant: the interview at the initial assessment center and the seven annual follow-up interviews.) First, there is a significant difference between the college and noncollege samples. The college men scored higher at initial assessment and in every one of the following 7 years. The gap between the two groups was larger at the time of the final interview than at the time of the first one. The second general observation is that both groups declined gradually on this theme over the 7-year period and were significantly lower at Year 7 than at Year 0. The noncollege men experienced a greater total decline than the college group.

Of perhaps more interest is the relationship between involvement on this life theme and occupational success in terms of having reached the third level of management within 8 years from the time of original assessment. Figure 8.1 shows the 7-year trends for the college and noncollege groups subdivided into those who had reached the third level by the time of reassessment. The relationship between being more successful

TABLE 8.3. Descriptions of Life Themes

Occupational—Statements made by the subject concerning his work life, including comments not only about job content, but also about supervisors, raises or the likelihood thereof, promotions, and attitude toward the company.

Ego functional—Concerns about the condition and development of the personal ego—mind and body—including self-development activities such as broadened reading, educational pursuits, and exercise to improve or maintain physical condition. Concern with disease or disability resulted in higher scores.

Financial-acquisitive—The accumulation of wealth or material possessions such as real estate (including desire to have an impressive home), stocks and bonds, and expensive automobiles. Concern with having enough money to make ends meet also resulted in higher scores.

Locale-residential—Comments on the type of location in which one lives and the kind of housing.

Marital-familial—Preoccupations and activities concerned with the subject's spouse, including in-law matters; also covered premarital relationships such as dating and engagement.

Parental-familial—References to parents, siblings, and relatives on the parents' sides, and involvement in activities with the parental family.

Recreational-social—Leisure-time pursuits, including hobbies, sports, partying, and socializing.

Religious-humanistic—Ethical and humanistic involvements, not necessarily part of an organized religion; concern with a philosophy of life that acts as an ethic.

Service—Community activities such as the Chamber of Commerce, Boy Scouts, and political parties, excluding church activities, which were scored under religious–humantistic.

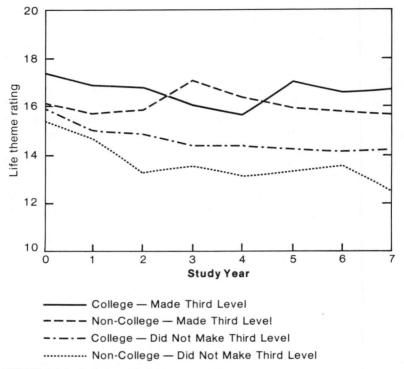

FIGURE 8.1. Relationship between ego functional life theme and achievement of third level by reassessment, by educational group.

and remaining highly involved on this theme is readily apparent. The more successful men in both the college and the noncollege groups, although showing variation from year to year, ended up only slightly, and not statistically significantly, lower than where they started. The less successful participants, on the other hand, dropped off on this theme and were significantly lower at Year 7 than they were at Year 0. It is apparent that the decline on this theme noted for the total group was mainly due to those who were less occupationally successful.

It would be tempting to conclude that the relationship between success and investment on the ego functional theme is a cause-and-effect relationship. It might be believed that people more concerned with self-development do, in fact, develop some abilities that improve their job performance and lead to promotion. The data at hand do not disprove that hypothesis, but an alternative is possible. It may be that certain individuals reach out for more stimulation and challenge on the job and also reach out energetically into other areas of life.

A study of the life themes led to the hypothesis in *Formative Years in Business* (Bray, Campbell, & Grant, 1974) of two antithetical types, "Enlarger" and "Enfolder." The Enlarger is drawn to the more challenging aspects of a work setting, reaching out to make learning more likely and extending his or her scope. Job-related activities such as night school or community involvement seem to be a natural extention of what the life period (young business manager) calls for. The Enfolder is not greatly concerned with extending himself or herself into new involvements and responsibilities. He or she is not preoccupied with the work environment and tends, rather, to deepen ties with family and religion. Enlargers, as might be expected, tend to move up more rapidly in the management hierarchy.

Predictions, Job Challenge, and Advancement

During these first 7 postassessment years, annual interviews were also conducted with knowledgeable persons in the participants' organizations concerning job assignments, work environment, job performance, career prospects, and so on. These interviews form a counterpoint to the participants' own perceptions of what was happening and have the potential of providing rich data concerning what went wrong, or right, with participants' careers. The interviews have been coded to provide a picture of the amount of job challenge each participant experienced early in his career. Research with these ratings has incorporated analyses of predictions of progress in management. It is necessary, therefore, to turn to this matter before considering the supervisors' interviews further.

At the conclusion of the discussion of each participant during the first series of assessment centers, the staff made a rating not only of "should be district" (discussed previously), but also of "will make district." This last rating was intended to be a straight prediction of advancement, which, it was thought, would not correlate perfectly with management ability. It was expected that some men might not impress their supervisors commensurate with their potential whereas others might gain more favorable appraisals than their ability warranted. Table 8.4 shows the relationship between this prediction and actual attainment of third-level management, the district level, 8 years later.

The table shows that, in both the college and noncollege groups, there was a highly significant relationship between assessment staff predictions and progress. In the case of the college graduates, the success rate was

TABLE 8.4. Assessment Predictions and Attainment of Middle Management 8 Years Later

	n^a	Number reaching middle management	Percentage reaching middle management
College			
Predicted to reach middle management	61	39	64%
Predicted not to reach middle management	62	20	32%
Total	123	59	48%
Noncollege			
Predicted to reach middle management	40	16	40%
Predicted not to reach middle management	103	9	9%
Total	143	25	17%

^{a}Predictions of advancement were not made in the initial stage of the college-sample assessment. Tables involving such predictions therefore include less than the total number of study participants.

twice as high among those who had done well at assessment ("will make district") as for the others (64% compared to 32%). Among the noncollege men, the success rates were even more markedly different (40% vs. 9%). It should be emphasized that assessment results for these men were never available to anyone outside of the research organization and played no part in the participants' advancement.

Table 8.4 also illustrates that a far higher percentage of the college recruits had reached the third level than the men who were not college graduates when employed (48% vs. 17%). The discrepancy between the progress of the two groups held true both for those men who had done well at assessment and for the remainder. Thus, even when ability was roughly equated, there was a tendency for the company to select college graduates for promotion.

The difference in the overall success rates for the college and noncollege samples reflects in part the fact that the college graduates were hired into a special program in which there was a presupposition that participants had the ability to reach the third level. The noncollege men were on no such program and had to stand out clearly from their fellows in order to advance. This is, however, not the sole explanation. There was a far greater range of abilities among the college sample than among the noncollege sample. More of the college men who were assessed as having third-level potential had fourth, fifth, or even higher level potential. These participants could be expected to move along briskly. At the other end of the scale, many of the noncollege group had no more than first-level ability.

To return to the major use made so far of the in-company interviews with personnel representatives and bosses, the impact of environmental stimulation upon achievement and advancement was deemed important to investigate. It is clear from the predictive data just presented that individual characteristics observable at the time of employment were a strong determinant of success in management. On the other hand, it is common knowledge that some people enter much richer job climates than others, and it seemed reasonable to believe that this might have important effects. The in-company interviews were therefore read along with the interviews conducted with the participants in order to arrive at ratings of the work situation.

For this illustration, the four relevant characteristics were achievement models provided by bosses, job stimulation and challenge, supervisory responsibilities, and unstructured assignments. Ratings of these four areas were combined into one overall set of ratings called "Job Challenge." The young managers were classified into three groups (high, moderate, and low), depending on the overall rating of their job situations for the 7 years. These groups were then cross-classified against the prediction of reaching middle management within 10 years. Table 8.5 shows the results.

The table shows a strong and statistically highly significant relationship between ratings of Job Challenge and advancement, although, once again, all the percentages are lower for the noncollege than for the college group.

TABLE 8.5. Relationship of Assessment Prediction, Job Challenge, and Management Level at Reassessment

	College		Noncollege	
	n	Percentage reaching middle management	*n*	Percentage reaching middle management
Predicted to reach middle management				
High job challenge	33	76%	23	52%
Moderate job challenge	22	55%	12	25%
Low job challenge	6	33%	5	20%
Total	61	64%	40	40%
Predicted not to reach middle management				
High job challenge	18	61%	18	28%
Moderate job challenge	24	33%	45	7%
Low job challenge	20	5%	40	3%
Total	62	32%	103	9%

Those whom the assessors had not predicted to reach middle management are of considerable interest. Here 61% of the college graduates who had not been so predicted, but who had experienced high Job Challenge, had arrived at middle management. The corresponding figure for the comparable noncollege group was 28%.

It must be noted that these data may be contaminated; that is, the ratings of Job Challenge would be expected to be correlated with the management level at which the person was working. By and large, higher level jobs are more challenging than lower level jobs. Nevertheless, it does not seem likely that all of the strong relationship is artifactual. Data presented later show the positive relationship between work motivation and advancement. Perhaps the most tenable hypothesis pending further analyses of the data is that the effect is circular. More job challenge supports strong motivation, which leads to better job performance, which leads to more challenging jobs.

Eight-Year Changes in Abilities

The reassessment of study participants 8 years after their first assessment provided a wealth of data on possible changes in their characteristics over that period. Of particular interest from the organization's point of view was what had happened to their management ability. One hypothesis was that 8 years' experience in management would produce an improvement in characteristics such as decision making and leadership skills. The alternative hypothesis was that such characteristics had already developed and stabilized by the time of the first assessment and were not likely to show improvement with experience.

The characteristics of greatest interest in the ability domain were in the areas of cognitive, administrative, and interpersonal skills. Mental ability was measured by the SCAT at original assessment and by a parallel form of the same test at reassessment. Both the college and the noncollege groups scored significantly higher at reassessment than 8 years previously, with the gains in raw-score points being approximately equal. Statistically significant gains were made on both the verbal and the quantitative parts of the test. Norms for the SCAT were provided in 1958 by administration of the test to a random sample of 585 college graduates newly hired into the Bell System. Against this standard, the change in total SCAT score for the MPS college graduates in 8 years was from the 49th to the 64th percentile. For the noncollege men, the gain was from the 13th to the 24th percentile.

Such gains in measured mental ability in the adult years would have been surprising a generation ago. Early studies had led to the conclusion that mental ability declined gradually from the early teen years on, but such research was based on cross-sectional data. Since then, longitudinal studies have shown, as here, increases well into middle age, if not beyond.

Both groups also gained significantly between assessments in their scores on the Contemporary Affairs Test. The college sample moved up from the 31st percentile on Bell System third-level management norms to the 46th percentile. In other words, the college men who had looked so weak at assessment compared to third-level managers had almost equaled them by the time 8 more years had passed. The noncollege men rose from the 19th to the 24th percentile on these same norms. Although this gain was statistically significant, it was a much smaller gain than that shown by the college graduates.

Table 8.6 shows the average ratings on selected assessment dimensions in the areas of administrative and interpersonal skills for the college and noncollege groups at assessment and reassessment. The results are surprising, to say the least. Not only is there no support for the hypothesis that management abilities grow as a result of experience in management, but there are many statistically significant declines. Although the decline for the college-graduate group in administrative skills (Organizing and Planning and Decision Making) is not statistically significant, the drop in interpersonal skills (Leadership Skills and Behavior Flexibility) is. The noncollege group declined significantly in all these dimensions.

It is also interesting that both groups were rated as less likable at the 8-year mark. This Personal Impact dimension, like Forcefulness, was based on each assessor's "love rating" of the individual. This rating did not have

TABLE 8.6. Average Ratings on Selected Ability Dimensions at Assessment and Reassessment for College and Noncollege Participants

Dimension	College		Noncollege		
	Assessment	Reassessment	Assessment		Reassessment
Organizing and Planning	2.9	2.9	2.9	**	2.2
Decision Making	2.8	2.6	2.9	**	1.9
Leadership Skills	2.7 **	2.4	2.8	**	2.0
Behavior Flexibility	3.1 **	2.5	2.9	**	2.2
Personal Impact (Forcefulness)	2.8	2.7***	2.7	**	2.4
Personal Impact (Likableness)	3.0 *	2.7***	3.2	**	2.6

*Difference significant, $p < .05$.
**Difference significant, $p < .01$.
***Interaction with advancement significant, $p < .05$.

to be defended with evidence, and consensus was not required in the assessor discussion. When this rating is considered along with the significant declines in Leadership Skills and Behavior Flexibility, it seems clear that these men were not as interpersonally pleasing as they were originally.

Granted that these changes in behavior from one assessment center to another 8 years later are real, in what sense can it be said that there is a decline in management abilities? Most likely, if a series of elementalistic ability tests had been given, such as those that might derive from the factor-analytic approach of Thurstone or Guilford, no such decline would have been seen. In fact, a gain was observed on the SCAT. The concept of "ability" is, however, different in the organismic approach of the assessment center. The assessment center concept of ability includes all individual determinants of behavior other than those subsumed under the category "motivation." These determinants include not only such cognitive factors as general mental ability and past accretions of knowledge, but also determinants usually conceptualized as part of "personality," such as flexibility–rigidity, dominance–submission, and friendliness–hostility. Thus a person might lack ability to be an effective member of a task force breaking ground in a new area because (1) the subject of task-force deliberations is beyond his or her cognitive grasp, (2) he or she cannot relinquish old concepts, (3) he or she is too submissive to be assertive in the group process, and/or (4) his or her interpersonal hostility causes other members of the group to reject the person's ideas. The difference in interpersonal behavior noted at the two assessment centers, then, may be due to personality changes that affected the way the average manager related to others.

Personality and motivation changes are discussed later in this chapter. Because of the different focuses of the assessment centers at Year 8 and Year 20, detailed later, the assessment at Year 8 has much more to say about management abilities than that at Year 20. Conversely, analyses of the 20-year material have proceeded far enough that a long-term look at personality and motivational changes is possible.

Since many of the findings of the study showed a relationship to advancement in management, or lack thereof, it is important to ask whether any of the changes in management ability reported were associated with progress. There is some minimal evidence of an association, with those who did not reach the third level of management 8 years later suffering the greater declines. In the college-graduate group, those who had not reached middle management by reassessment not only were rated lower on all the previously cited dimensions 8 years earlier, but also showed a greater decline over the 8 years than those who had achieved the third level or higher. In only one case, however, was the interaction effect statistically significant at the 5% level of confidence, as shown in Table 8.6. This was in the two facets of Personal Impact, Forcefulness and Likableness. In Likableness, those who had reached middle management went from an average rating of 3.0 to 2.9 over the 8-year period, while the less successful men dropped from 3.0 to 2.5. In Forcefulness, the more successful men managed a small gain from 2.9 to 3.0, while those less successful declined from 2.7 to 2.5.

A similar pattern was observed among the noncollege participants, with those who were not to reach middle management 8 years later scoring lower on all of the cited assessment dimensions at the start of the study and in nearly every case showing a greater drop on these dimensions over 8 years. The only interaction approaching statistical significance ($p < .10$), however, was with Behavior Flexibility. Here, the more succesful men had gone from 3.4 to 3.0, while the less successful dropped from 2.7 to 2.0.

Since ratings of assessment dimensions are judgmental, an ever-present question is whether the reassessment staffs had the same standards as those at assessment 8 years earlier. Although there is no unassailable evidence that the standards remained the same, there are several reasons for believing that they did. One is that all staffs were trained and directed by the same individual, the senior author of this chapter. Furthermore, the original assessment ratings proved predictive of advancement in management, and changes made in those ratings at reassessment enhanced the prediction of progress 11 years after that (19 years from the start of the study). It should be mentioned, finally, that not only was the director the same person at all centers, but several of the assessors served at both assessment centers.

As an additional check, two psychologists highly experienced in assessment were instructed to review, for assessment and reassessment separately, all the individual assessment reports and ratings on each participant and to assign an overall management ability rating for each assessment. The two reviewers were specifically instructed to be alert to any possible shifts of rating standards on the part of the assessment staffs. It was emphasized that the reviewers were free, for example, to give the same rating to a participant at both assessments, even though the staff had given a different one. Ratings were made on the usual 5-point scale, with 5 being high. Table 8.7 shows the average ratings given for assessment and reassessment performance. When the groups were subdivided according to the advancement criterion, the only significant assessment–reassessment difference was for the noncollege men who had not advanced to third level. Already the lowest rated group at original assessment, they dropped to a point well below that of any of the others.

TABLE 8.7. Average Management Ability Ratings of College and Noncollege Participants at Assessment and Reassessment, by Advancement Groups

	n	Assessment		Reassessment
College				
Achieved middle management	59	3.2		3.4
Did not achieve middle management	64	2.4		2.5
Total	123	2.8		2.9
Noncollege				
Achieved middle management	25	3.3		3.2
Did not achieve middle management	118	2.3	*	2.0
Total	143	2.5	*	2.2

*Difference significant, $p < .01$.

One conclusion that seems certain from all of the preceding data is that there was no average improvement in basic management skills over the first 8 years of the study. This conclusion, it must be emphasized, does not mean that 8 years of experience were of no consequence or that the recruits were not better managers. One aspect of management ability is the knowledge the manager has of the company, the department, and the work managed. The assessment center made no attempt to measure such knowledge, but it is almost certain that such an evaluation would have revealed great changes in the positive direction.

Some 20-Year Changes in Work Attitudes, Motivation, and Personality

Once it became obvious that the MPS was to be not just a longitudinal follow-up of managers, but a *long-term* longitudinal study of managers, the decision was made to bring the participants back together for one more assessment center at the 20-year point. The first plan was to repeat the first two assessments to see if managerial abilities and motivations had undergone significant changes in two decades of experiencing life as a Bell System manager. On reflection, there was doubt that enough new knowledge would be generated by such a repetition to justify the costs. A great deal was already known about the men's managerial characteristics from the two previous assessments and from the many interviews with bosses and others in the company over the years.

As the 20th year approached for the first MPS company, another consideration began to predominate. The time was the mid-1970s, and there was a newly developing interest in midlife as a phase of adult development (Gould, 1978; Levinson, 1978), including the somewhat sensational treatment, in the popular literature, of the midlife crisis (Sheehy, 1974). The MPS men, most of whom would be in their 40s at the 20th year of the study, offered a unique opportunity for studying some of the problems and pleasures of midlife as well as those of midcareer in a business organization. Thus the emphasis of the study was shifted toward personal adjustments and satisfactions during this critical phase of life, with a somewhat reduced emphasis on managerial abilities.

The 20-year reassessment, dubbed MPS:20, was developed with the following specific purposes in mind:

1. To evaluate the work motivation, company commitment, career satisfaction, and retirement proneness of midcareer managers.
2. To measure changes in their abilities, attitudes, and personality characteristics over a 20-year span and to explore the reasons for those changes.
3. To assess the effects on them of plateauing promotional and salary opportunities, Affirmative Action, and outside pressures on and challenges to the Bell System.
4. To appraise the quality of life in the middle years—its rewards and hazards, and possible crises and reorientations.
5. To develop an assessment center procedure for the study of middle life.

To achieve the second purpose, exploring reasons for changes in abilities, attitudes, and personality over the 20-year span, MPS:20 was conducted in two parts. In Phase I, participants were reunited in large groups for 1 day to retake a number of attitude and personality measures that had been administered in previous assessments. There were ten of these exercises: the Edwards Personal Preference Schedule (EPPS), the Guilford–Martin Survey of Factors GAMIN, the Survey of Attitudes toward Life, the Opinion Questionnaire (a version of the California F scale), the Expectations Inventory, the Management Questionnaire, a Q sort, six cards of the TAT, the Rotter Incomplete Sentences Blank, and the Business Incomplete Sentences Test.

Following the Phase I sessions, the questionnaires were scored, and a report was prepared summarizing responses to the three projective measures (TAT and incomplete sentences). A team of graduate students, hired each summer, worked with these data to prepare a case review binder for each participant. The case reviews contained graphs of trends in questionnaire scale scores over time, changes in item responses relative to significant scale scores, a selected contrast of incomplete-sentence responses over time, the highlights of performance at past assessment centers, summaries of the personal interviews conducted over the years, and the most recent projectives summary. The case reviews condensed five notebook binders of data per person into one and prepared psychologists for a feedback interview with each participant in Phase II of MPS:20. The feedback was a first in the history of the MPS, since all data had been confidential not only with respect to management, but also with respect to the participants themselves. After 20 years, it was decided that some individual feedback would be unlikely to change the men's careers or lives in any significant way and might also be a small reward to them for so many years of unrequited disclosure.

Each of the 15 scales of the EPPS, the five scales of the GAMIN, a General Management Attitude score (from the Management Questionnaire), the Expectations Inventory score, and the Survey of Attitudes toward Life score were fed back to the participants graphically, showing their position relative to Bell System norms at each time of testing. The men were asked to try to reconcile the scores with their self-perceptions, describing their typical behavior in the process. In addition, they were asked to speculate about the reasons for any changes observed in scores over time. This was an attempt to identify causal links in self-perceived changes in attitudes, motivations, and behavior over a span of 20 years.

Work Attitudes

A representative example of changes in work attitudes is provided by the Expectations Inventory. This questionnaire was first administered at the original assessment, when participants were asked to speculate on and predict what their lives would be like 5 years later. The items on the questionnaire concerned various aspects of managerial life, including advancement, salary progress, intellectual stimulation from peers, access to company information and resources, and geographical desirability of work location. The inventory was readministered with the interviews that followed the assessment in each of the next 7 years, initially asking for speculation to the same 5-year point and later asking for descriptions of current circumstances. After Year 7, the Expectations Inventory was not administered again until Year 20.

Average scores over each administration of the inventory revealed that, as young managers, the participants were very optimistic and enthusiastic about what their lives would be like as Bell System managers. Such youthful enthusiasm was no doubt appreciated by the corporation but was not very realistic, for many expected to rise far beyond their abilities and had a Pollyanna view of what life in the real world would be like. Thus, with each passing year and readministration of the inventory, participants got more and more realistic and less and less optimistic. Most of this happened early in their careers. In fact, by Year 5, the average college-graduate manager had a view of life that changed little over the next 15 years. A similar pattern was shown on the General Management Attitude scale, measuring organizational and job satisfaction, which was given annually for the first 7 years after the original assessment and again at MPS:20. These early declines in attitude measures were interpreted not as the development of true negativism toward the Bell System, since later scores were not really low, but as the evaporation of initial naiveté.

There was a second major finding from these attitude measures. Satisfaction with work, career, and company was strongly related to relative success achieved in the organization. By the time of MPS:20, the average college man was at the third level of management, although the range went from first to sixth (vice president); only a handful of the noncollege men had made it to the fourth level, and their modal level was second. As shown in Figure 8.2, those who achieved a moderate level of success (third level) maintained about the same average score on the Expectations

FIGURE 8.2. Relationship between Expectations Inventory scores and level of management at MPS:20.

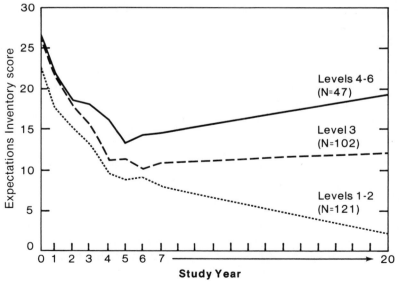

Inventory from Year 5 through Year 20. Those who were less successful declined consistently over the 20-year period, while those who went on to high levels of the organization reversed the early decline in the first 5 years and by MPS:20 had surpassed the average score they achieved in Year 2. Thus, once the initial disillusionment had gone and a more realistic level of expectations had set in (by Year 5), career success and career satisfaction seemed to go hand in hand.

Motivation

A full exploration of work motivation factors over the 20-year span awaits deeper analyses of MPS:20 data, which are just beginning as of this writing. There are, however, some initial indications of changes from the Phase I results alone. The Survey of Attitudes toward Life is a short questionnaire measure with items on the importance of advancement, financial rewards, and generally working toward future goals. At the initial assessment, the noncollege men were less motivated toward advancement than the college men, and their average questionnaire score was only at the 44th percentile of the college norms. Both groups dropped in average score by reassessment, and by MPS:20, both groups had declined still further, to the 16th (college) and 15th (noncollege) percentiles.

The decline in scores was partly due to the realization that careers had plateaued; for most, there would be no more promotions before retirement. In spite of horror tales of the tragedy of the plateau and its precipitation of a midlife crisis, most of the men in the study had adjusted to this state of affairs. When interviewed about their lower scores on the Survey of Attitudes toward Life in the Phase II feedback interview at MPS:20, many claimed to be no longer interested in further promotions. They did not want to move their homes and families for one thing, and some saw more aggravation in a higher level job than they cared to deal with. Moreover, many were pleased with the level they had achieved, and few complained about their standard of living, which was generally considered quite good.

A diminution of the pursuit of advancement did not appear to affect all work motivation, however. One scale of the EPPS measures Need Achievement, or motivation to perform a difficult job well. The items in this scale make no reference to desires for the extrinsic rewards of advancement or money, but address only successful task accomplishment. Between the assessment and reassessment periods, average scores on the EPPS scale of Need Achievement went up significantly, and the higher score was maintained at MPS:20 for both the college and the noncollege men. Thus the work itself, if challenging, still appeared to be a potent motivator for these men in midcareer, even though advancement was unlikely to result from their efforts.

Although the men confirmed that they liked challenging jobs, this did not necessarily mean that the job was the most important thing in their lives. One indicator of the primacy of work comes from the life themes coding of the personal interviews with the participants over the years. The pattern of work involvement expressed in the occupational life theme is shown in Figure 8.3 for the college and noncollege participants separately. The first 5 years showed opposite trends for the two educational groups. The noncollege men scored appreciably higher than the college men at initial assessment, but took a steep plunge downward in the early years; at the same time, the college men's scores moved steadily upward until they reached the initial noncollege high point.

One plausible explanation for this pattern is that the first few years of employment involve settling down and embracing work as a new and predominant life interest. Since the college men were often fresh from the campus at assessment, they spent the first few years acquiring the role of adult businessman, and the job and company absorbed much of their time and interest. The noncollege men, on the other hand, had been with the

FIGURE 8.3. Comparison of scores on occupational life theme between educational groups.

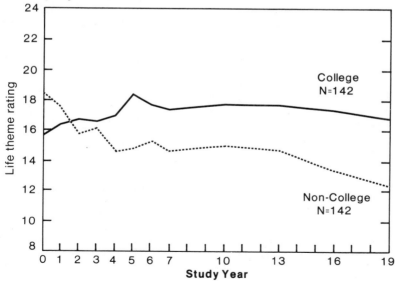

organization an average of 10 years. It is unfortunate that the MPS did not begin at the start of their careers, but a likely hypothesis is that they, too, may have shown an initial increase in work involvement when newly employed, with perhaps an additional boost in work interest with their promotions into management approximately 8 years later.

Scores on the occupational life theme showed a decline in the later years that was more precipitous for the noncollege than the college group. A more meaningful illustration of this later disengagement from work is shown in Figure 8.4, where the results are grouped by management level achieved. It is readily apparent that occupational involvement as a dominant theme in life was highly related to career success. Though the men were undifferentiated by future management level at the original assessment when the college and noncollege groups were combined, as early as the first year it was already becoming clear who was getting interested and moving ahead. The differences between the groups continued to spread as the years went by.

One critical aspect to observe in Figure 8.4 is the evidence for disengagement, or withdrawal, from job involvement (Schein, 1978). For those who ended up at the lowest levels, the first and the second, the

FIGURE 8.4. Relationship between scores on occupational life theme and management level achieved by Year 19.

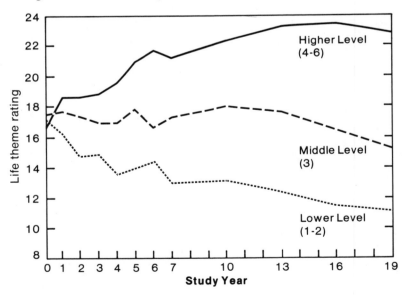

process of disengagement began almost immediately, when they were in their early 30s. For those reaching the third level, disengagement began at the 10th year for the noncollege men and at the 13th year for the college men, when both were in their late 30s. Those who reached the fourth level and beyond (primarily college graduates) still had not withdrawn by the mid-40s. Thus *when* individual managers disengage from occupational involvement seems to be a function of both age and relative career success. What the men turn to after they begin to disengage from work is a subject that needs to be explored in future analyses of the MPS:20 data.

Personality

Various measures of personality have been used in the MPS, including questionnaire measures, projective tests, and, to some extent, the interview. Although the management assessment center method was not designed to focus on personality *per se*, several dimensions point directly to personality variables, such as Need for Superior Approval as an indication of dependency.

One of the strongest effects surfacing from the study in terms of personality development was a continual increase over the years in tendencies toward independence from others. The assessment dimensions Need for Superior Approval and Need for Peer Approval, both reflecting emotional dependency, decreased between the assessment and reassessment periods and continued in that direction at MPS:20. Coding of assessment and reassessment interviews had shown this same type of decrease in Need for Superior Approval over the first 8 years.

The participants also revealed this increasing tendency toward independence and autonomy on a questionnaire, as shown in Figure 8.5. Of the 15 scales on the EPPS, that of Need Autonomy, or motivation to be free and independent of others, changed the most over the 20 years. From an original score near the average of the 1958 Bell System college recruit norms, the men rose significantly by reassessment, and even higher by MPS:20, when the average participant scored at the 86th percentile. This increase characterized both the college and the noncollege groups and was independent of relative success in the organization.

Several other test scores broadened the scope of this thrust toward independence that occurred over the years. The men showed a decline in motivation to make and enjoy friends, to understand others' motives or feelings, and to conform to authority and regulations, all suggesting movement away from others and toward establishment of individual identity. There were increased tendencies over the 20 years to want to lead

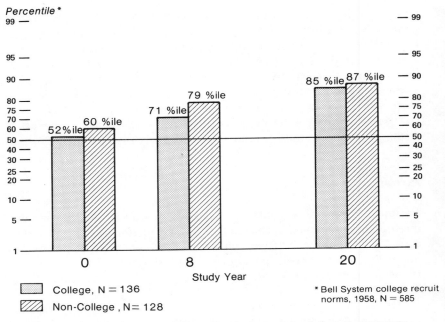

FIGURE 8.5. Average EPPS Need Autonomy scores at three assessments.

others, take charge, and, in some cases, even aggress against others. At the same time, the men decreased in the tendency to feel guilty for errors and wrongdoing, suggesting that they may aggress more with less shame!

The impact of these changes taken together is that the average man has become "harder" over time. Such a shift might, of course, be due either to aging or to environmental impact between times of measurement. In a single longitudinal study, there is no way to disentangle these two causes (Schaie, 1973). In addition, there were at least two broad domains of possible environmental impact: events in the Bell System and influences from society at large.

Although there were no systematic treatments of the MPS men over the years, such as participation in a particular training program, there may have been modifications in the Bell System environment that affected this group in a relatively uniform way. For example, there has been an increase in the number of controls on individual managers over the period from the late 1950s to the late 1970s, both from governmental intervention (e.g., Equal Employment, Occupational Safety and Health Act regulations) and from internal applications of quantitative measures to gauge service and production performance more precisely. Thus increased independence striving on the part of the MPS man could be a reaction to controls as well as a maturational event. Even confirmatory data from other organizations would not completely resolve this distinction, since the advent of increased government controls and internal centralization has not been unique to the Bell System over this period of time.

It is also possible that broad sociocultural changes were at work rather than those in individual organizations. The use of an additional cohort to help explore this possibility is described later in the discussion of the MCS.

Nevertheless, in the feedback interviews, the participants were most likely to point to developmental changes within themselves as they moved through managerial life. They cited such things as the experience of supervising, successful outcomes of assertive behavior, and the recognition of accomplishments as influences making them "tougher."

Managerial Success and Life Satisfaction

The second phase of MPS:20 contained much more than the feedback interview. The men were called together in groups of 6 or 12 for a 2-day session, which consisted mostly of new exercises to explore midcareer and midlife. Only one exercise was repeated, the SCAT. Another cognitive test, the General Information Test, supplanted the Contemporary Affairs Test used in earlier years as a measure of range of interests and knowledge.

Since the MPS:20 assessment was to point the study in a somewhat different direction, the original 26 dimensions on which the participants were rated at the first two assessments were insufficient for the task. It was decided to repeat the original dimensions at MPS:20 in order to reflect changes over time, but 21 new dimensions were added to focus on issues of midcareer and midlife. These new dimensions, listed in Table 8.8, concerned the areas of work satisfaction, financial concerns, family concerns, philosophical attitudes, and self concerns.

After rating the 47 dimensions and obtaining agreement on them, the assessment staff, now solely psychologists, made seven predictions about each man. At the first two assessments, forecasts had been made concerning potential for middle management and probability of staying with the Bell System, but by MPS:20 the future involved different concerns. In the career realm, the assessors predicted whether each man's job performance and commitment to the company would change between the present and his retirement, if he would retire early (before age 65), what his level of adjustment would be in retirement, and how satisfied he would feel

TABLE 8.8. New MPS:20 Assessment Dimensions

Work satisfaction
Job Satisfaction—To what extent does this person have positive feelings about the current assignment?

Career Satisfaction—To what extent does this person have positive feelings about his or her entire Bell System experience, including advancement?

Retirement Proneness—To what extent is this person motivated to retire early?

Financial concerns
Absence of Financial Worries—To what extent is this person free from concerns about finances, both now and in the future?

Financial Motivation—To what extent does this person want a significantly higher income than that currently provided from Bell System employment?

Family concerns
Stability of Marriage—How likely is it that this person will stay married to the same mate?

Marital Satisfaction—To what extent does this person have positive feelings about his or her present marriage? How content is this person with the spouse and the institution of marriage?

Absence of Familial Worries—To what extent is this person free from concern about his or her children, parents, or other family members (excluding spouse)?

Philosophical attitudes
Conservatism—To what extent does this person tend to oppose social change and refrain from challenging traditions?

Cynicism—To what extent does this person disbelieve in human goodness and refrain from idealizing human nature?

Involvement—To what extent does this person identify with, relate to, become concerned about, and/or take an active part in affairs of the world or the community?

Religiosity—To what extent does this person practice or abide by a system of religious or humanistic beliefs or ethical values?

Self-concerns
Avocational Interest—To what extent does this person find meaning and satisfaction in a hobby or hobbies? (Consider depth and intensity of interest, not breadth. Includes work if it is not Bell System work.)

Self-Development—To what extent does this person attempt to expand his or her skills, knowledge, or personality?

Escapism—To what extent does this person engage in activities to escape from the responsibilities and routine of real life (e.g., drinking, drugs, daily movies or TV, obsessive fantasizing)?

Adjustment—To what extent has this person changed or adapted to his or her life situation in an emotionally healthy way?

Happiness—To what extent does this person find pleasure in life at the present time?

Feelings of Crisis—To what extent does this person feel that he or she is at a turning point or crucial stage of life (i.e., a time of great danger or trouble)?

Concern with Health—To what extent is this person concerned with physical well-being (i.e., concerns about health problems, not generally keeping healthy)?

Concern with Aging—To what extent is this person negatively concerned about growing older?

Selfishness—To what extent is this person occupied with self-interest with little or no concern for others?

with his career when it was over. In the personal arena, forecasts were made as to how satisfied each participant would feel with his life as he reached old age and whether he would experience a critical disturbance in his personal adjustment or a significant value reorientation between the present and retirement.

The MPS:20 Phase II exercises, which explored the new dimensions and prediction questions, included two group exercises, administered on the afternoon of each day of the assessment center. Both were leaderless group discussions involving simulations, but the content of the two discussions was entirely different.

The first discussion was work related and entitled "The Being Who Fell to '195.'" The simulation posited that a creature from another universe had taken over as chairman of the board of AT&T at the world headquarters at 195 Broadway in New York City. The six participants supposedly had been appointed as a task force to report to the Being on what it was like to be a human manager in the Bell System. They were asked to address such issues as how promotions to top management were made, methods used for motivation and control, and the rewards and stresses of managerial life.

The second discussion put the participants in the role of senior advisers in a community "Counseling Center" and asked them to provide guidance to junior counselors seeing clients with problems of living. The participants had to deal with personal issues such as relocating one's residence in late middle age, care for an elderly in-law at home or in a nursing home, and marital infidelity. Both discussions were tape-recorded and transcribed so that they could be analyzed for content as well as leadership characteristics of the participants.

The remaining Phase II exercises were individual techniques interspersed between the two group discussions and the private feedback interviews during the 2-day sessions. One exercise, Time Lines, asked participants to note their primary pleasures and misfortunes during the last 20 years relative to job and career, home and family, or other aspects of the self. The Sunny/Stormy Exercise brought the time-line idea into the present and had the men elaborate on six "sunny" or "stormy" events in their current lives by six short essays.

Two new projective tests were also developed for MPS:20 Phase II. The Adult Development Incomplete Sentences Tests (ADIST) had 108 sentence stems to be completed, which were drawn from major areas of concern to middle-aged people, such as financial issues or relationships with children. The Middlescent Male Picture Test (MMPT) consisted of eight drawings of middle-aged people in typical, but ambiguous, life situations. As with the TAT in Phase I (which was not designed for people over 40), the participants wrote a story about each picture.

Success versus Satisfaction

A primary concern of the study has been to differentiate the men who were the most successful from those who did not achieve a very high level of success. "Success" for this purpose was defined as management level achieved. While not denying the relativity of this kind of success to aspirations, background, abilities, and past successes, the *sine qua non* for measuring success in this and many organizations is level in the management hierarchy. By MPS:20, the men differed considerably in this respect, as shown in Table 8.9.

Although none had reached the pinnacle of president of a telephone company (Level 7), three were at Level 6 (vice president). Many still were at Level 1, especially among the noncollege participants. Generally, the normative expectation for college graduates is that reaching the third level is a satisfactory career achievement and going above the third level is considered highly successful. By these standards three-fourths of the college men had achieved a satisfactory level after 20 years, and one-third could be considered highly successful. The noncollege men were one level lower on the average, and few had progressed beyond the third level.

Yet, in many respects, career success may be more important to the organization than to the employee. The individual may—perhaps should—care more about his satisfaction with life in general. The question for the employee then becomes whether or not career success contributes to overall life satisfaction.

A number of the new dimensions rated at the 20th-year assessment reflected various aspects of life satisfaction. The correlation of each of

TABLE 8.9. Management Levels at MPS:20

Level	College	Noncollege	Combined
6	3	0	3
5	13	0	13
4	27	4	31
3	64	37	101
2	26	61	87
1	4	27	31
Total	137	129	266

TABLE 8.10. Correlations of Life
Satisfaction Dimensions with Management Level at MPS:20

Dimension	r
Career Satisfaction	.40***
Job Satisfaction	.29***
Absence of Financial Worries	.19**
Marital Satisfaction	−.05
Stability of Marriage	−.05
Absence of Familial Worries	.02
Avocational Interest	−.04
Cynicism	−.07
Concern with Health	−.15*
Concern with Aging	−.06
Feelings of Crisis	.12*
Adjustment	.15*
Happiness	.10

Note. $n = 266$.
*$p < .05$.
**$p < .01$.
***$p < .001$.

these with management level is presented in Table 8.10. Most highly correlated with management level was Career Satisfaction; the more successful men felt better about their careers, as might be expected. Success was also related, though not quite as strongly, to satisfaction with the present job, again not surprising since one might assume that higher level jobs are more rewarding. The correlation between success and Absence of Financial Worries was also expected since the higher level men are compensated at a higher level, although this relationship was not a strong one.

Beyond these three work-related dimensions, the correlations between career success and life satisfaction were mostly negligible. The small negative relationship between success and Concern with Health probably has some basis in reality, since higher level managers report fewer health problems; this matter will be pursued further after the third round of medical data associated with MPS:20 is collected and analyzed. The lack of relationship between management level and marital and family concerns or depth of avocational interests disconfirms claims either that most or all of life's rewards go to the privileged few (Vaillant, 1977) or that success in business requires sacrificing home, family satisfactions, or recreational pursuits.

The last two dimensions, Adjustment and Happiness, are global measures of life satisfaction, the first related to coping, and the latter to feelings of pleasure or contentment. Since all significant aspects of the men's lives, including their work lives, were considered when making these judgments, it is somewhat surprising that the correlations of these dimensions with management level, which related strongly to career satisfaction, were not higher.

Since career success did not appear to be a major determinant of life satisfaction, the data were explored further to see what characterized and determined each.

Managerial Success

A number of characteristics were observable at MPS:20 that differentiated the more successful men from their age peers. Concurrent intercorrelations showed that nearly all of the original 26 assessment dimensions were significantly correlated with managerial success at MPS:20, a not unexpected finding since these dimensions were primarily concerned with managerial abilities and motivations. The more successful had greater intellectual ability, scored higher on the General Information Test, had a broader range of interests, and reported greater interest in current events. They expanded themselves in many areas of life, typifying the Enlarger described previously.

The more successful men were also notably more involved in their work. This was shown previously in the graph of the occupational life theme from the interviews (Figure 8.4). On a questionnaire administered with their 19th-year interviews, these men rated career as one of the most important things in their lives, and they indicated that they worked more hours at home than did less successful managers.

In terms of personality, the more successful men described themselves at MPS:20 as more achievement oriented and dominant than those lower in the management hierarchy. They were less deferential toward those in higher authority and less nurturant toward others. But in spite of their inclinations toward leadership and their relative disinterest in providing emotional support to others, they were more open minded and less authoritarian than the lower level men. Their energy level was higher, and their attitudes toward the company were more positive.

Given this description of the successful manager, a crucial question that a longitudinal study can best answer is, "How did he get that way?" One fact, expected by any personnel selection expert and well confirmed in the MPS, was that, to a great extent, measurable differences in managerial abilities and motivations that would foretell success were present when the men first came to the original assessment center. Without this fact, the assessment center method would not have been so widely adopted as a management selection tool in many organizations today. Most of the original 26 assessment dimensions had significant correlations with success after 8 years, and most of these relationships held even after 20 years.

Several exercise scores were also predictive of success over the 20-year period, as shown in Table 8.11. The greater cognitive achievements of the higher level men were well established at the original assessment by the SCAT and by the interview rating of Range of Interests. They more skillfully handled the In-Basket, demonstrating better Organizing and Planning and higher Inner work Standards. Their attraction toward leadership was already showing in such scales as Need Dominance and Ascendance. They expected more from their careers in the beginning, as shown by the Expectations Inventory score, and indicated greater motivation for advancement in the interview. To a large extent, then, the career fates of the MPS participants had already been determined by the time they arrived at the first assessment center.

However, not all was determined that first day. A certain amount of differential development took place over time in that the most successful appeared to develop in one way, while the less successful changed in a different way. These phenomena were revealed by significant interaction effects (group by time) in repeated-measures analyses of variance (ANOVAs). Although most of the assessment dimensions were originally predictive of success, most of them also showed a pattern of becoming even more so with time. Often it was a case of the rich getting richer and

TABLE 8.11. Some Assessment Exercises Predicting MPS:20 Level over 20 Years

Exercise	r
SCAT—Total	.40**
Range of Interests (Interview)	.30**
Organizing and Planning (In-Basket)	.19*
Inner Work Standards (In-Basket)	.24**
Need Dominance (EPPS)	.18*
Ascendance (GAMIN)	.20*
Expectations Inventory	.18*
Need for Advancement (Interview)	.44**

Note. n's = 199–266.
*$p < .005$.
**$p < .001$.

302 / AT&T STUDIES

the poor getting poorer; that is, the more successful men increased in their already better skills or motivations, while the less successful men lost ground. Leadership Skills and Inner Work Standards are examples of this phenomenon. In other cases, all the groups moved in the same direction, but one group moved more than the others. For example, all dropped on Behavior Flexibility, but the less successful rigidified to a considerably greater extent than did the more successful.

A final type of differential development occurred when the less and more successful groups were undifferentiated at the initial assessment, but became distinctly different as their careers developed. One example is Social Objectivity: Although both groups seemed rather prejudiced against minorities and authoritarian in attitudes in the late 1950s, the more successful men broadened their outlooks over the years, while the less successful men became more narrow minded.

Life Satisfaction

An investigation of concurrent correlations of exercises and dimensions with MPS:20 also casts some light on the nature of the well-adjusted and happy person. The Adjustment and Happiness dimensions were highly correlated ($r = .83$), so that many relationships established with one were also true for the other.

All of the life satisfaction dimensions listed in Table 8.10 correlated in the expected direction with Adjustment and Happiness, with the sole exception of Avocational Interest. Satisfaction with the two major areas of life, love and work (Freud, 1930), had equally high correlations with the overall life satisfaction dimensions (r's in the .50s). Test scores at MPS:20 showed that the best adjusted and happiest men had more self-confidence and greater emotional stability. A positive outlook characterized the best adjusted; their attitudes toward the organization were better, and they tended to think toward the future. They enjoyed leading others more and were less in need of emotional support from others.

None of the preceding relationships seemed inconsistent with the notion of an emotionally healthy and happy person, but two other scores were somewhat of a surprise. Those rated higher on Adjustment and Happiness scored lower on the EPPS scale of Heterosexuality, measuring motivation for erotic relationships with the opposite sex. The interpretation of this finding is that the less adjusted men often became overly dependent on their relationships with women as they searched for security outside of themselves. Another surprise was that the best adjusted and happiest men scored lower on the SCAT. Perhaps the brighter men found more things to worry about, and ignorance is bliss after all.

As with the exploration of the determinants of career success, it was expected that middle-aged happiness and adjustment might be at least partly determined by relatively enduring personality traits. If so, it should have been possible to predict later life satisfaction from assessment center data 20 years previously. This turned out to be the case. In particular, high scores on the Self-confidence and Emotional Stability scales of the GAMIN predicted both general life satisfaction dimensions 20 years later.

Other characteristics of the emotionally healthy middle-aged men developed over time in a way that distinguished them from those less healthy. For example, although most of the men in the study lowered their expectations, became less positive about the company, and reduced their drive to move ahead, the emotionally healthiest men changed less in this direction, as if less willing to give up their initial positive attitudes. The best adjusted also increased their motivation to lead and direct others, while the more poorly adjusted became less dominant over time.

The Bridge: Career Satisfaction

Bringing together the information about the determinants of career success and life satisfaction helps explain why they correlate so weakly with each other. A bridge between the two appears to be Career Satisfaction (Bray & Howard, 1980). Both the successful and the well-adjusted, happy men were more likely to be satisfied with their careers. They had positive attitudes toward the company and their work and considered work a primary source of satisfaction. Both enjoyed leading others and worried less about finances. Although the successful and happy had these qualities in common, the etiology of these characteristics often differed. For example, the most successful men had fewer financial concerns primarily because their incomes were greater; the best adjusted and happiest men worried less about finances because they worried less in general.

In other ways, the most successful and best adjusted were worlds apart. The most successful were cognitively astute; the best adjusted scored lower than others on cognitive tasks. The most successful were worldly Enlargers, had more general knowledge, and expanded themselves physically and intellectually; the best adjusted were less cynical, less oriented to heterosexual pleasures, and more religious than those rated lower on life satisfaction. The most successful were less nurturant and deferential and more aggressive than their age peers; the best adjusted had steadier temperaments and were less selfish. The constellation of scores indicated that the best adjusted and happiest people may not be particularly evaluative about life, but keep a positive outlook, whether directed toward themselves, their careers, others, or life in general.

The implication of these results with middle-aged managers is that career success may lead to career satisfaction, but that it does not necessarily lead to general happiness. On the other hand, there are no apparent detrimental effects of career success on life satisfaction. Although some would have us believe that success in one's vocation can be achieved only by sacrificing other aspects of one's personal life, data here do not support this contention.

A full exploration of the MPS men in middle age is still proceeding at present as the MPS:20 data are analyzed. Since MPS:20, three men have retired, and plans are being made to extend the research into the next stage of life for these managers—retirement.

The New Generation

Although much has been learned from the MPS about managerial characteristics and their development, with more expected as the study continues, in the mid-1970s, the question was raised as to whether the original findings were equally applicable to the new generation of young managers. Such questioning led to the initiation in 1977 of a new longitudinal study, similarly dedicated to studying managerial lives and careers. The study was named the Management Continuity Study, to symbolize the continuity in Bell System management from one generation to the next.

The MCS was designed with several specific questions in mind. An initial concern was whether today's new managers are significantly different from those of the last generation, and how they compare on abilities, motivations, values, attitudes, and personality characteristics. Second, since the MPS techniques are used widely in assessment centers, it was thought important to find out if the indicators of management progress are the same as they were 20 years ago. There was also the question of how today's new managers will change and develop over time, and whether current Bell System policies, practices, and climate will have different effects on individual behavior than did those of the past. Finally, the MCS provided the opportunity to test whether or not the changes over time observed in the MPS were attributable to developmental, or ontogenetic, changes or to changes in the general culture.

The MCS sample to date has included only college graduates, so they are compared here only with the college subsample of the MPS. In both cases, the recruits were hired within the previous year for general management jobs, not as specialists in fields such as engineering or computer science. Although managers were selected from only 6 telephone companies in the original study, the newer managers came from a broader range of operating companies—13 in the Bell System.

There was one major difference in the two management samples. In the 1950s, it was considered unrealistic to have any but white males in a sample expected to rise to middle management, but by the 1970s, things had changed. As Table 8.12 shows, one-half of the new college-recruit managers were women, and one-third were members of minority groups. The total sample size is still small but will be increased in the future.

The design of the MCS will be as parallel to that of the MPS as possible, time and funds permitting. The study began with an initial 3-day assessment center, and follow-up interviews are in progress. Because the precedent of confidentiality had been set with the MPS, the in-company interviews have involved immediate supervisors rather than the personnel department, as was the case in the early years of the MPS. We hope that there will be a reassessment at Year 8 for the MCS participants and perhaps an MCS:20 as well.

The original MCS assessment centers consisted of many of the same tests and exercises used in the MPS so that direct comparisons of results could be made. In some cases, such as the In-Basket, parallel forms were used, or revised versions of exercises were substituted. Two personality and values questionnaires were added to enrich the data. The business game was dropped in favor of a revised version of the MPS:20 Counseling Center leaderless group discussion, which provides the opportunity to compare values and social attitudes between the two generations as well as measuring leadership skills. A different assigned-role group discussion was the third simulation used, and there was a 2-hour personal interview. The three projective measures (TAT, Rotter, Business Incomplete Sentences Test) were administered again, but some female-oriented TAT pictures were substituted for male ones to help stimulate the women's fantasies.

TABLE 8.12. MCS Sample[a]

	White	Minority	Total
Male	65	39	104
Female	67	33	100
Total	132	72	

[a]Total participants = 204.

The original 26 assessment dimensions were repeated, with 10 appropriate additions from MPS: 20, for example, Happiness and Adjustment. Predictions about each recruit's future in the Bell System were repeated from the MPS assessment.

Comparisons of the Two Generations of College Recruits

There were several ways the two samples differed in background. Members of the MCS group were slightly older (mean age of 25.6 with SD 4.0) compared to those of the MPS group (mean of 24.6 with SD 2.4) and were more likely to have had a previous full-time job before joining the Bell System. Fewer MCS recruits had had military experience, however, not only because of the women in the MCS group, but also because of the elimination of the draft. Compared to the MPS participants, those in the MCS were more likely to be Catholic and to come from larger families. Their parents were somewhat better educated on the average than the parents of the MPS group, but the recruits themselves were better educated yet: 45% had some postgraduate education compared to only 11% of the MPS group. Other background differences between the two groups were a function of race or sex differences and are discussed later.

As mentioned previously, an advantage of the base data from the new longitudinal study was to help evaluate the meaning of changes occurring over time within the MPS, that is, whether they seem to be age-related changes or changes in the cultural environment over the 20-year span. For example, a number of scales on the EPPS showed significant score changes between the original MPS assessment and MPS:20. If the MCS group were to score at about the same level as the MPS group at the time of their original assessment, one might hypothesize that the MPS men had changed but the culture had not; young people now are like young people then. If the hypothesis of age-related change is correct, one would expect the MCS group's scores to change in a similar way over time. This can be checked at their reassessment. On the other hand, if the MCS group scored the same as the MPS group at MPS:20, one would hypothesize a possible cultural change, since two groups of different ages scored about the same when they took the questionnaire in approximately the same calendar year.

The increase in EPPS Need Autonomy scores observed in the MPS participants between all three assessments (see Figure 8.5) is a good example of the use of the two samples for delimiting hypotheses. If increase in Need Autonomy were an age-related change, related perhaps to greater maturity, self-confidence, wisdom, or acceptance of adult responsibility, it would be expected that the MCS group would score about the same as the MPS group had 20 years previously, when they were about the same age. But perhaps there has been a cultural change, for many current popular articles speak of "doing your own thing," or establishing one's own individuality. In this case, the MCS group should score about the same as the MPS group when they took the questionnaire in the mid- to late 1970s, at MPS:20. Results for Need Autonomy pointed to the first explanation rather than the second. The MCS group scored, on the average, at the 62nd percentile on the same Bell System norms used previously, which was not significantly different from the 57th-percentile score achieved by the MPS college participants at their original assessment. The MCS average score was significantly lower than the MPS:20 college men's score, which was at the 85th percentile ($p < .001$). The hypothesis that the increase in Need Autonomy is an age-related change will gather more support if the MCS participants significantly exceed their own scores when they retake the questionnaire at their reassessment.

The MCS results with the EPPS usually pointed to the age-related hypothesis as an explanation for the MPS changes described previously as a hardening of the personality. Race and sex differences had little to do with the MCS scores in these comparisons; contrasts between the white males of the MPS and MCS samples produced the same kind of results.

One EPPS scale did point to the possibility of a cultural change, that of Need Deference, or motivation to conform to authority and regulations. The MPS group had dropped from the 46th percentile of the norms to the 36th percentile at MPS:20; the MCS group scored the same as the MPS:20 average, at the 36th percentile. It may be that disrespect for rules and authority has crept into our culture and affected middle-aged and young alike. An alternative explanation is that experience led to less deference for the middle-aged men once assured of their positions, but changing values affected the young in a similar direction. Again, later retesting of the MCS group is needed for clarification.

The last explanation suggests a third type of hypothesis, that of a cultural change that has affected primarily the young people. If the older generation does not show a corresponding shift in behavior or values, it creates what might be called a "generation gap" (cohort difference). This pattern was shown with the EPPS scale of Need Dominance (motivation to lead and direct others), where the MCS group scored at only the 22nd percentile compared to the original MPS assessment score at the 49th percentile. The MCS result was not attributable solely to sex differences, although there was one; the average score for the MCS males was only at the 28th percentile. These scores in combination with others showing lower expectations for managerial careers and less motivation for advancement have led to some concerns as to whether these recruits will want to take up the mantle of leadership in the future (Howard & Bray, 1980).

Ratings of the assessment dimensions based on all the data reinforced some of the concerns about the motivations of the new generation of Bell System managers, although they appeared fully as capable as their predecessors in abilities such as administrative skills, interpersonal skills, and intellectual abilities. Fortunately, they seemed just as interested in job challenge as the MPS men were, but there may be some problems looming ahead when the organization begins to expect them to fill higher and higher leadership roles. In spite of these problems, about the same proportion of MCS recruits and MPS recruits were seen as having middle-management potential.

Race and Sex Differences

In the MCS sample, "minorities" stood for 72 managers, 92% of whom were black. Background differences between the white and minority group members were often quite pronounced. The minority participants came from larger families, and in 60% of the cases, their parents were either separated or divorced (compared to 12% of the whites). Most of the minority members had grown up in the city, and a greater proportion were Protestants. More than one-quarter of their fathers had unskilled jobs (compared to only 4% of whites), and nearly three-quarters of their mothers worked outside the home (compared to less than half of the whites).

At the assessment center, some of these background differences probably took their toll in the performance of the minority participants on the cognitive exercises. They scored at only the 22nd percentile of the Bell System norms on the SCAT Total, compared to the 57th percentile for the whites. They had more difficulty with the Quantitative scale than with the Verbal, although both showed highly significant race differences ($p < .001$). The whites also performed significantly better on the General Information Test and on the In-Basket. Primarily because of these ability differences, only 29% of the minority members were seen as having middle-management potential compared to 50% of the whites.

Though weaker on cognitive abilities and administrative skills, the minority group members generally performed just as well as whites on interpersonal skills. Their oral presentations and group participation in the Counseling Center discussion were just as effective as the whites', although a lack of flexibility and an unwillingness to compromise lowered their group performance in the competitive assigned-role group problem.

The various pencil-and-paper measures of personality, values, and motivations indicated that the whites saw themselves as more socially poised and spontaneous than did the minorities and that they more highly valued such things as social recognition, true friendship, and being loving and cheerful. The minorities, on the other hand, described themselves as more reflective and orderly, and they more highly valued self-control, being neat and clean, and equality. Motivationally, the minorities were more interested in making money, while the whites were somewhat more motivated by individual achievements. The minorities were more unrealistic about their futures and often expected more than their abilities were likely to bring them.

When males were compared to females in the MCS, differences in parental background tended to disappear, but personal histories indicated some other differences. The women were 2 years younger on the average, and 69% of them were single compared to 51% of the males. More of the men had degrees in business and engineering, but the women more often majored in mathematics. The greater number of women math majors was at least partly attributable to company recruiting methods; because of the dearth of female engineering majors, math majors were often selected as substitutes.

Sex differences on cognitive exercises were small compared to race differences, although the women did score significantly higher than the men on the Verbal scale of the SCAT, while the men scored higher on the General Information Test. The simulations also brought forth few sex differences of import; both made equally effective oral presentations, contributed as much to group functioning in the two discussions, and did equally well on the planning, organizing, and decision-making aspects of the In-Basket. The women were somewhat more creative on the In-Basket, however, and had better written communication skills. They also seemed to have a better grasp of the personal issues involved in the Counseling Center discussion and were seen as more sensitive and socially objective.

On personality questionnaires, the biggest sex differences occurred in scales designed to measure masculine versus feminine interests, in the expected direction. On a couple of measures, the women indicated greater valuations of independence and intellectual achievements, and they also were more interested in change. The men more highly valued being obedient and self-controlled, in spite of the fact that they described themselves as somewhat more aggressive.

The women were thought to have greater Goal Flexibility, but this was considered no asset from the organization's point of view. In many cases, it meant they were really not settled in their career choices yet and would consider other careers, going back to school, or giving both up at least temporarily to raise children. More females than males were expected to leave the organization voluntarily. There were no significant sex differences in overall potential for middle management.

One overriding characteristic of the MCS sample that the race and sex differences suggest is its great heterogeneity compared to the MPS sample. This greater variability was often true even for the white males. As a result, the overall differences outlined here are an oversimplification at best and only a suggestion of the true character of the new generation. One thing is clear: The MCS participants are different, both from the last generation and from each other. They will be a fascinating group to follow over the years.

Concluding Remarks

It would not serve much purpose to attempt a summary of what is already a summary of a vast amount of material. Yet it might be of value to point out some general findings that at this time seem to be of considerable importance. One of these is that certain changes over time appear to be age related. One example is the sharp and steady rise in Need Autonomy over the 20 years of the MPS. The data currently at hand do not allow for a definitive statement that this change is a general characteristic of at least white males in this culture, but later testing of the participants in the MCS may afford some confirmatory evidence. Even this, however, will still leave the question of whether persons in the Bell System are representative of their age groups generally. Here evidence from other populations will be needed, and initial plans for securing such data have been made.

Other changes in the MPS participants were related to success on the job as measured by advancement. A prime example is the occupational life theme. It also appears that even changes in more resistant characteristics such as management ability are related to the success that one experiences. Declines were exceptionally pronounced among those who had the least to offer in the first place and who did not experience much, if any, advancement. The extreme group in this respect is the noncollege men who never advanced to middle management. Already rated low at original assessment on many aspects of managerial ability and motivation, they showed the greatest loss of any group on these characteristics. It is as though they had reached their highest point in management potential at about the time they were elevated into management and then fell off as their involvement flagged and further promotions were not forthcoming.

Related to this differential development of abilities, motivations, attitudes, and personality is the general impression that the MPS men became less alike with time rather than more alike. Thus Whyte's (1956) fears that corporations squash individuality and produce clones were not borne out.

A very strong finding of the research with great practical importance was that advancement in management is predictable at considerably more than a chance level and, by the assessment center, considerably better than by preexisting methods. Concomitantly, since its introduction in 1956 as a research method in the MPS, the management assessment center has spread widely as an applied selection and development method in several thousand business, governmental, and educational organizations. This outcome, along with the continuing use of the assessment center in research, would no doubt please the authors of *Assessment of Men*, who declared over 30 years ago that "for researches into normal personality, the OSS system of assessment, or something comparable to it, is essential, since most other selection systems do not include investigations of the dynamic components of the total personality and without these, one cannot even hope to understand the character structure of human beings" (OSS, 1948, p. 467).

Shortly following this declaration, the OSS volume went on to lament that it is too seldom possible to verify one's conclusions by conducting follow-up studies of subsequent careers. This, of course, has been a wonderful opportunity afforded in the MPS. Since three out of four participants remained in the Bell System, it was possible to continue to study them at close range, and even that quarter who left the organization have been followed up to some extent. Another advantage of the participant population was that they all were striving occupationally in the same general environment, that of telephone company management. This meant, among other things, that a uniform success criterion was easily available, as contrasted to research like the Terman study and the Grant study at Harvard, where the participants fanned out into a wide variety of settings.

This advantage, of course, is a disadvantage when looked at in another light. It may be that Bell System managers are not representative even of other managers. An attempt is currently being made to shore up that weakness in research design. Under the title "Inter-Organizational Testing Study," the authors of this chapter are attempting to persuade other business, governmental, and educational organizations to administer some of the same tests to a sample of middle-aged middle managers and new college recruits. Such samples would be compared to those of the MPS and the MCS at the current time. If such comparative data can be produced, there will still be a more difficult path ahead. It is inevitable that questions will arise as to whether managers in organizations show the same characteristics as persons of comparable ages in completely different professions. Such data will not be easy to come by, but may not be out of reach. After all, no one in 1956 would have expected that the MPS would now be entering its 27th year.

References

Bray, D. W., Campbell, R. J., & Grant, D. L. *Formative years in business: A long-term AT&T study of managerial lives.* New York: Wiley, 1974. (Melbourne, Fla.: R. E. Krieger, 1979.)

Bray, D. W., & Grant, D. L. The assessment center in the measurement of potential for business management. *Psychological Monographs*, 1966, *80* (17, Whole No. 625).

Bray, D. W., & Howard, A. Career success and life satisfactions of middle-aged managers. In L. A. Bond & J. C. Rosen (Eds.), *Coping and competence during adulthood.* Hanover, N.H.: University Press of New England, 1980.

Freud, S. *Civilization and its discontents.* New York: Norton, 1930.

Gould, R. *Transformations: Growth and change in adult life.* New York: Simon & Schuster, 1978.

Grant, D. L., & Bray, D. W. Contributions of the interview to assessment of management potential. *Journal of Applied Psychology*, 1969, *53* (1), 24–34.

Grant, D. L., Katkovsky, W., & Bray, D. W. Contributions of projective techniques to assessment of management potential. *Journal of Applied Psychology*, 1967, *51*, 226–232.

Howard, A., & Bray, D. W. Continuities and discontinuities between two generations of Bell System managers. In D. W. Bray (Chair), *Today's college recruits: Managerial timber or deadwood?* Symposium presented at the meeting of the American Psychological Association, Montreal, 1980. (Published, slightly revised, as Today's young managers: They can do it, but will they? *The Wharton Magazine*, 1981, *5* (4), 23–28.)

Levinson, D. J., with D. N. Darrow, E. B. Klein, M. H. Levinson, & B. McKee. *The seasons of a man's life.* New York: Alfred A. Knopf, 1978.

Office of Strategic Services Assessment Staff. *Assessment of men.* New York: Rinehart, 1948.

Schaie, K. W. Methodological problems in descriptive developmental research on adulthood and aging. In J. R. Nesselroade & H. W. Reese (Eds.), *Life-Span developmental psychology: Methodological issues.* New York: Academic Press, 1973.

Schein, E. H. *Career dynamics: Matching individual and organizational needs.* Reading, Mass.: Addison-Wesley, 1978.

Sheehy, G. *Passages: Predictable crises in adult life.* New York: E. P. Dutton, 1974.

Vaillant, G. *Adaptation to life.* Boston: Little, Brown, 1977.

Whyte, W. H., Jr. *The organization man.* New York: Simon & Schuster, 1956.

Author Index

McFarlane, J.W., 192, 220*n*.
McGuire, V.M., 52, 61*n*.
McHugh, R.B., 20, 27–29, 38*n*.
McKee, B., 222, 265*n*.
McPartland, T.S., 174, 187*n*.
Meehl, P.E., 76, 131*n*.
Mehrotra, S.N., 42, 63*n*.
Miller, R., 52, 61*n*.
Mischel, W., 203, 220*n*.
Moralishvili, E., 52, 62*n*.
Morris, J.D., 174, 185*n*.
Morrison, D.F., 56, 60*n*., 191, 218*n*.
Munnichs, J.M., 195, 219*n*.
Munsinger, H., 50, 63*n*.
Murray, P., 144, 189*n*.
Mussen, P.H., 12*n*., 18*n*.

N

Nanda, H., 203, 218*n*.
Nardi, A.H., 71, 103, 130*n*.
Nehrke, F.M., 191, 220*n*.
Nesselroade, J.R., 2, 4, 6, 10, 19*n*., 23,
     38*n*., 57, 60*n*., 65, 71, 108*n*., 112,
     130*n*., 132*n*., 184, 187*n*., 241, 246,
     263*n*., 265*n*.
Neugarten, B., 195, 219*n*., 246, 265*n*.
Neurath, P., 52, 63*n*.
Nielsen, J., 52, 55, 63*n*.
Nordenson, I., 55, 63*n*.
Norris, A., 196, 220*n*., 257, 264*n*.
Nowlin, J.B., 161–165, 172, 175–177,
     187*n*.–190*n*..
Nowlis, V., 168, 188*n*.

O

Obrist, W.D., 157, 158, 188*n*., 189*n*.
Oden, M.H., 12*n*., 19*n*., 22, 38*n*., 70,
     130*n*.
Ohta, R.J., 45, 63*n*.
Okun, M.A., 171, 189*n*., 244, 265*n*.
Olbrich, E., 214, 220*n*.
O'Malley, P.M., 249, 263*n*.

Opton, E., 168, 189*n*.
Owens, W.A., Jr., 13, 19*n*., 20–39, 20,
     23, 25–33, 36, 37, 38*n*., 70, 132*n*.

P

Palmore, E., 16, 19*n*., 137, 139, 141,
     164–167, 172, 173, 182, 183, 188*n*.,
     191, 196, 220*n*.
Parham, I.A., 69, 71, 72, 76, 96, 106,
     116–119, 131*n*.–133*n*., 204, 220*n*.,
     244, 245, 265*n*.
Parr, J., 72, 134*n*.
Parsons, C.K., 124, 131*n*.
Patterson, R.D., 137, 187*n*.
Perlman, R.M., 69, 83, 84*n*., 85*n*., 134*n*.
Peterson, G., 218, 220*n*.
Pfeiffer, E., 164, 166, 188*n*.
Pfoetsch, C., 215, 220*n*.
Plomin, R., 224, 263*n*.
Poole, W.K., 8, 18*n*.
Pressey, S.L., 66, 132*n*.
Prinz, P.N., 158, 162, 188*n*.

Q

Quayhagen, M., 129, 133*n*.

R

Rahe, R.H., 169, 181, 187*n*.
Rajaratnam, N., 203, 218*n*.
Ramm, D., 140, 172, 177, 188*n*.
Raven, J.C., 21, 33, 38*n*.
Reese, H.W., 4, 18*n*., 23, 38*n*., 71,
     130*n*., 241, 263*n*.
Reichard, S., 218, 220*n*.
Renner, V.J., 209, 220*n*.
Riegel, K.F., 3, 19*n*., 48, 60*n*., 146,
     188*n*., 197, 202, 220*n*.
Riegel, R.M., 202, 220*n*.
Rimm, A.A., 52, 63*n*.
Robbin, M.A., 48, 60*n*.

Subject Index

A